Transnational Chinese Cinemas

Ju Dou (Gong Li) and Tianqing (Li Baotian) in *Ju Dou,* directed by Zhang Yimou, 1990. British Film Institute.

Transnational Chinese Cinemas

Identity, Nationhood, Gender

Edited by Sheldon Hsiao-peng Lu

University of Hawai'i Press
Honolulu

02   5 4 3

Library of Congress Cataloging-in-Publication Data

Transnational Chinese cinemas : identity, nationhood, gender / edited
  by Sheldon Hsiao-peng Lu.
    p.   cm.
  Includes bibliographical references and index.
  ISBN 0-8248-1845-8 (pbk. : alk. paper)
    1. Motion pictures—China.   2. Motion pictures—Taiwan.   3. Motion
pictures—Hong Kong.   I. Lu, Hsiao-peng.
PN1993.5.C4T65   1997
791.43'0951—dc21   97-11153
                                                                         CIP

University of Hawai'i Press books are printed
on acid-free paper and meet the guidelines for
permanence and durability of the Council
on Library Resources

Designed by Barbara Pope

For my brother, Lu Xiaolong,
and my sister, Lu Xiaoyan

Contents

List of Illustrations

Preface

The idea of a volume of critical essays on Chinese film originated from the conference "Rethinking Cross-Cultural Analysis and Chinese Cinema Studies" that I organized at the University of Pittsburgh in 1994. The participation of film scholars from all over the country as well as the presence of colleagues and students at the University of Pittsburgh made the conference an especially meaningful and productive event. For their attendance, support, and presentations, I thank Nick Browne, Diane Carson, Leo Chan-Jen Chen, Mao Chen, Xihe Chen, Anne T. Ciecko, Shuqin Cui, Wimal Dissanayake, Kristine Harris, E. Ann Kaplan, Jon Kowallis, Wendy Larson, Kang Liu, George S. Semsel, Paola Voci, Ban Wang, Min Wu, Zhiwei Xiao, Mingyu Yang, Xudong Zhang, Yingjin Zhang, and Yi Zheng. I am also indebted to my colleagues and the staff at the University of Pittsburgh for making inquiries, providing advice and wisdom, and helping me put things in order before, during, and after the conference. I extend my gratitude to Dianne F. Dakis, Lucy Fischer, Elizabeth K. Greene, Marcia Landy, Katheryn Linduff, Patrizia Lombardo (now at the University of Geneva), Colin MacCabe, Keiko McDonald, Cindy Neff, J. Thomas Rimer, Jonathan Wolff, and Joseph Zasloff.

As this book evolved, I received good advice, encouragement, and constructive criticism from a number of people. The anonymous readers of the University of Hawai'i Press, Gina Marchetti, Lucy Fischer, and Nick Browne went over the entire manuscript or portions of it and offered helpful comments for reconsideration and revision. All the contributors of the volume collaborated with me with patience and trust. I personally have learned a great deal from each one of their essays. Gina Marchetti, Steve Fore, June Yip, Wei Ming Dariotis, and Eileen Fung, who were not present at the conference, readily sent their essays to me at my request, and their contributions have enriched the content of the book. May M. Wang, who collaborated with me on the bibliography and Chinese glossary, also deserves a note of thanks.

For their support of both the conference and the book project by providing funds or making arrangements, I am thankful to the Asian Studies Program, the University Center for International Studies, the China Council, the Department of East Asian Languages and Literatures, Film Studies Program, Cultural Studies Program, and the Media Center at the University of Pittsburgh.

Since 1993, I have been supported by the University of Pittsburgh, mostly through the China Council, to travel and conduct research in China every summer. In the summer of 1994, I was awarded a grant by the Central Research Development Fund of the Office of Research, and another grant by the Faculty of Arts and Sciences to conduct research on New Chinese Cinema in China. While in China, I was able to meet and interview film artists and critics such as Li Yongxin, Xie Fei, the late Zhang Nuanxin, Huang Zongjiang, Li Baotian, Li Tuo, and Dai Jinhua. Li Yongxin and Chen Keli at the Beijing Film Academy have continuously assisted me in finding my way in the Chinese film world. My Junior Faculty Research Leave in fall 1996 released me from teaching duties and gave me time to finalize the manuscript. A combined research grant from the Office of the Dean of the Faculty of Arts and Sciences and the China Council made it possible for me to travel to the British Film Institute in London to obtain relevant research materials in October 1996. To the above individuals and institutions I owe a debt of gratitude.

It has been a pleasure to work with the editors of the University of Hawai'i Press. Sharon F. Yamamoto first expressed an interest in the project. Her intelligent, smooth, graceful, and pleasant manner of handling the project is unforgettable. Cheri Dunn's efficient work style kept the project moving in a timely manner in the later stage of preparation. Michael E. Macmillan's meticulous and masterful copyediting of the manuscript not only cleaned up errors and inconsistencies but also decisively enhanced its overall quality. I should also mention that when I was looking for a suitable publisher, Eugene Eoyang readily lent a helping hand.

Gina Marchetti's chapter first appeared in *Jump Cut* 34 (1989): 95–106, under the same title. Yingjin Zhang's chapter first appeared in *Cinema Journal* 36, no. 3 (1997): 73–90. An earlier version of Kristine Harris' chapter, under the title of "The New Woman: Image, Subject, and Dissent in 1930s Shanghai Film Culture," appeared in *Republican China* 20, no. 2 (1995): 55–79. I thank the editors of *Jump Cut* and *Republican China* and the University of Texas Press for permission to reprint these essays.

Keiko McDonald, whose office is next to mine, shares with me an intense professional interest in East Asian film studies. We have collaborated on several joint ventures such as a course on East Asian cinema, an East Asian film festival, and a workshop on teaching Asia through film. Katheryn Linduff and Tom Rimer are behind my professional development and all the projects I do at the University of Pittsburgh. Together with Kathy, I intend to explore a larger historical poetics of visuality throughout twentieth-century China. To Keiko, Kathy, and Tom, I must express my profound gratitude for their unfailing support of my career.

Anne T. Ciecko not only joins me as a fan of John Woo, Chow Yun-fat, and Jackie Chan but also has been a source of love and inspiration in many ways in the last two years. She patiently reads everything I write and offers wise suggestions. I have benefited a great deal from her knowledge of film and visual arts.

My brother Lu Xiaolong and my sister Lu Xiaoyan (Lo Siu-yin), one in Beijing and one in Hong Kong, are present in this book. Although situated far away on the other side of the Pacific Ocean, their love sustains me. When I was young, they took me to theaters to watch moving "electric images" (*kan dian-ying'er*). To them and my mother I dedicate this book.

· A Note on Transliteration from the Chinese

The transliteration system used in this book is *pinyin*. However, there are exceptions. It is more natural, respectful, and "politically correct" to keep certain names in their original Taiwanese, Hong Kongese, and Cantonese forms of romanization or as they appear in English subtitles in films. (John Woo, Ang Lee, Jia-chien, Wai-tung, Li T'en-luk, etc.) In many cases, two or multiple transliterations are provided for a name or term in its first appearance in order to familiarize readers and viewers of different backgrounds. (For instance, Fang Yuping/Allen Fong/Fong Yuk-ping, Guan Jinpeng/Stanley Kwan, Li Tianlu/Li T'ien-lu/Li T'en-luk, Wenqing/Wen-ch'ing/Bun-ch'ing, and so on). While *pinyin* helps create some sense of uniformity and order, for the purpose of, say, compiling a Chinese glossary, it is important for the reader to keep in mind the multilingual, multidialectal, polyglot, crosscultural, transnational, and diasporic condition of Chinese "proper names."

Sheldon Lu/Xiaopeng Lu/Hsiao-peng Lu

Historical Introduction
·
Chinese Cinemas (1896–1996) and Transnational Film Studies
·
Sheldon Hsiao-peng Lu

This volume of essays is a collective rethinking of the national/transnational interface in Chinese film history and in film studies and cultural studies at large. The contributors come from the various disciplines of Chinese history, Chinese literature, comparative literature, cultural studies, English, and film studies. We embark on an interdisciplinary, cross-cultural venture into a topic of shared interest. The occasion for such a project is the globalization of Chinese cinemas in the international film market and the rapid rise of Chinese cinema studies in Western academia. The entrance of Chinese cinemas in the international film community prompts us to closely examine the nature of Chinese "national cinema," the advent of "transnational cinema," the relation of film to the modern nation-state, the nexus between visual technology and gender formation, and film culture in the age of global capitalism after the end of the Cold War.

Chinese cinemas cover a broad geographic and historical terrain, including Mainland China, Taiwan, Hong Kong, and to some extent overseas Chinese communities. Asserting themselves boldly on the world stage since the mid-1980s, Chinese filmmakers have captured numerous major international film awards in recent years, and the international following for Chinese films grows annually. With this increasing popularity, the Chinese film industry has attracted a sizable amount of foreign capital and has been involved in frequent joint productions. With internationalization on this scale at both production and consumption levels, the issue of what actually constitutes Chinese cinema comes to the forefront—is it film produced by Chinese for Chinese? Assuming that some consensus on the nature of Chinese cinema can be reached, are there characteristics of this cinema that draw upon Chinese deep culture and set it apart from the Hollywood phenomenon? How reliably can these characteristics be perceived and interpreted by the international film community, and to what extent can these characteristics inform and influence the international dialogue on the meaning of film?

When I reflect on the development of a century of Chinese cinemas, a number of historical events of global significance come to mind. A little more than a hundred years ago, in 1895, film was invented in the West. The year was significant not only in world film history but was also the year when the Qing empire ceded Taiwan to Japan after a military defeat. Since then, developments in the technologies of visuality in the international arena and the domestic political events of China, a would-be modern nation-state, have become more and more connected. On August 11, 1896, "Western shadowplays" (*xiyang yingxi*) were exhibited in the Xu Garden in Shanghai. In the ensuing one hundred years, imported Western film technology has been put to indigenous use and has become an indispensable part of the social, political, and cultural life of the Chinese nation.

As this book goes to press, another monumental historical event is approaching. Hong Kong, which became a British colony in the aftermath of the Opium War in the mid-nineteenth century, will revert to its "mother-land" on July 1, 1997, and will be once again part of the Chinese nation. It is gratifying to know that the publication of this book will coincide with an international political occasion as rare and momentous as the return of Hong Kong to China. In fact, in May 1996, the veteran Chinese director Xie Jin began the production of the historical epic *The Opium War* to commemorate the event. In a few short years, a new century, and indeed a new millennium in the Christian calendar, will arrive, and history will turn another page.

The precise centennial scope (1896–1996) of the periodization of Chinese film history in this study is not accidental but was predetermined by the far-reaching global and national events mentioned above. We begin in 1896 because that was the year of the beginning of film consumption and distribution of an essentially transnational nature in China. (It is conceivable that an account of Chinese *national* cinema could start with the first Chinese film production in 1905 or with the first Chinese-made narrative film in 1913.) We end our discussion of the tripolar (Mainland, Taiwan, Hong Kong) Chinese cinemas in 1996, for from mid-1997 Hong Kong will no longer be a geopolitical entity separate from the Mainland. This entirely new chapter of Chinese history will undoubtedly have implications for the development of its cinemas, especially postcolonial Hong Kong cinema.

Although it is premature to predict the future configurations of Chinese national politics and Chinese film, we can at this critical juncture examine a century-long history of transnational Chinese cinemas as it comes to completion. We will track the successive modes of image production and consumption, from traditional "shadowplay" (*yingxi*), to "electric shadows" (*dianying,* the Chinese word for film) in the modern age of mechanical reproduction, and finally to electronic images in the postmodern era of simulacrum, throughout the course of exactly one hundred years of Chinese film history. It is my assumption that such a historical poetics of visuality is inextricably linked to the politics of the modern nation-state and deeply embedded in the economics of transnational capital. Since the film medium is fully integrated in both the economy and culture and mediates the two, it provides us with a privileged instance to scan and map the contours of Chinese cultural politics in relation to the capitalist world-system in the twentieth century.[1]

In what follows I will present a brief history and propose a theory of a century of what might be called "transnational Chinese cinemas." For reasons that will become apparent, it seems that Chinese *national* cinema can only be understood in its properly *transnational* context. One must speak of Chinese cinemas in the plural and as transnational in the ongoing process of image-making throughout the twentieth century. Transnationalism in the Chinese case can be observed at the following levels: first, the split of China into several geopolitical entities since the nineteenth century—the Mainland, Taiwan, and Hong Kong—and consequently the triangulation of competing national/local "Chinese cinemas," especially after 1949; second, the globalization of the production, marketing, and consumption of Chinese film in the age of transnational capitalism in the 1990s; third, the representation and questioning of "China" and "Chineseness" in filmic discourse itself, namely, the cross-examination of the national, cultural, political, ethnic, and gender identity of individuals and communities in the Mainland, Taiwan, Hong Kong, and the Chinese diaspora; and fourth, a re-viewing and revisiting of the history of Chinese "national cinemas," as if to read the "prehistory" of transnational filmic discourse backwards. Such an operation has the aim of uncovering the "political unconscious" of filmic discourse—the transnational roots and condition of cinema, which any project of national cinema is bound to suppress and surmount, for the sake of defending the country against real or perceived dangers of imperialism or in order to uphold national unity by silencing the voices of ethnic and national minorities.

I take the Chinese example as paradigmatic of the situation of world cinema at the present time. Transnational cinema in the Chinese case as well as in the rest of the world is the result of the globalization of the mechanisms of film production, distribution, and consumption. The transformations in the world film industry call into question the notion of "national cinema" and complicate the construction of "nationhood" in filmic discourse. Thus, my outline of Chinese film history may be read as an exemplary instance and a case study of the general tendencies in world film history. The study of a given national cinema then becomes the project of transnational film studies.

As a new technology and form of art originated in the West, film was first brought to Shanghai in 1896, one year after its invention. Short films were exhibited in a variety show in the Xu Garden, perhaps by a cameraman-showman of the Lumière brothers. The next showman to arrive in Shanghai was an American, James Ricalton, who brought Edison's films and screened them in teahouses and amusement parks in 1897.[2] In the years up to 1949, foreign films were regularly shown in China, first in teahouses and then in movie theaters, and dominated the Chinese film market, accounting for as much as 90 percent of the market. As one might expect, Hollywood films were the predominant presence.

In 1905, the first Chinese film, *Dingjun Mountain* (Dingjun shan), was made by Ren Jingfeng at his photography shop in Beijing. It was a filming of an act of Beijing opera performed by the famous actor Tan Xinpei. Zheng Zhengqiu's short family drama, *The Difficult Couple* (Nanfu nanqi), made in 1913, has been regarded as the first Chinese feature film. Yet this film was produced by the Asia Film Company, an American studio in China owned by Benjamin Polaski. In the same year, Li Minwei and Polaski produced the first Chinese film in Hong Kong, *Zhuangzi Tests His Wife* (Zhuangzi shiqi). Polaski later took the film back to the United States, and it became the first Chinese film screened abroad. We can conclude from this that Chinese film was an event of transnational capital from its beginning.

The emergence and consolidation of a Chinese "national cinema" (*minzu dianying*) in the ensuing years must be read against this background of the importation of film as a Western technology, ideology, and medium of art.[3] In the official narrative of Chinese film history, *The History of the Development of Chinese Film* (Zhongguo dianying fazhan shi), a monumental study written by Cheng Jihua and others in the early 1960s, the development of a leftist, progressive national cinema is to a great extent the story of an agonistic struggle against the cultural domination of foreign film, especially American film.[4] The life-and-death struggle of China's national film industry is isomorphic with the plight of China as a nation-state in the twentieth century. Modernity, nation-building, nationalism, anti-imperialism, antifeudalism, and new gender identities are among the central themes of such a national cinema. Chinese national cinema necessarily becomes part and parcel of the forging of a new national culture. Amidst the proliferation of "soft" entertainment films (romance, butterfly fiction, martial arts, ghosts, costume drama), the left-wing film workers seized upon the political and revolutionary potential of this new technology of visuality and attempted to make it into a mass art of conscious social criticism.[5] Like other national cinemas, Chinese cinema is the "mobiliser of the nation's myths and the myth of the nation."[6] Through the creation of a coherent set of images and meanings, the narration of a collective history, and the enactment of the dramas and lives of ordinary people, cinema gives a symbolic unity to what would otherwise appear to be a quite heterogeneous entity: "modern China."

Film production aside, film censorship, studio ownership, government intervention, and public opinion are all important terrains in the establishment of a new symbolic China. Zhiwei Xiao's essay in this volume, "Anti-Imperialism and Film Censorship During the Nanjing Decade, 1927–1937," amply documents the contours of a national policy of film censorship. Immediately after the unification of China by the Guomindang (Nationalist Party) in 1927, the central government established a film censorship board, which continued until the outbreak of the Sino-Japanese War in 1937, to check foreign films to be screened in China. Films perceived to portray the Chinese people in a degrading, offensive way could not be released in China.[7] A famous case, as Xiao describes, is the controversy surrounding the screening of Harold Lloyd's film *Welcome Danger* in Shanghai in 1930. Other banned Western films include *Death in Shanghai* (1933), *Shanghai Express* (1932), *The Bitter Tea of General Yen* (1933), *Wandering Through China* (1931), *Klondike Annie* (1936), *Cat's Paw* (1934), *Thief of Bagdad* (1924), and the German/Japanese coproduction *New Land* (1937). American films such as *The Ten Commandments, Frankenstein,* and *Top Hat* were also banned on the grounds of "superstition," as in the first two cases, or "sexual content," as in the last case.

In the same period, a conscious effort was also made to prevent foreign ownership of film studios. There was often a "united front" among intellectuals, the public, and the government to protect a vulnerable Chinese film industry and resist foreign "cultural invasion." Film censorship and the protection of the national film industry have been enduring legacies throughout the twentieth-century in China. During the period of Nationalist rule the government also stipulated that Mandarin be the standard dialect in films for the sake of cultural unity. (This policy had ramifications for any "local" Chinese cinema, such as that of Hong Kong, in which Cantonese rather than Mandarin has been the favorite dialect of filmgoers. Here is an instance of the resistance of the local to the national.)

Over the years, Chinese national cinema has grown to be a key apparatus in the nation-building process. It is an indispensable cultural link in the modern Chinese nation-state, an essential political component of Chinese nationalism. As Andrew Higson has written, national cinema has performed a dual function:

a hegemonising, mythologising process, involving both the production and assignation of a particular set of meanings, and the attempt to contain, or prevent the potential proliferation of other meanings. At the same time, the concept of a national cinema has almost invariably been mobilized as a strategy of cultural (economic) resistance; a means of asserting national autonomy in the face of (usually) Hollywood's international domination.[8]

The double process of hegemony and resistance in relation to the domestic audience and international film culture has defined the path and function of Chinese national cinema.

After the founding of the People's Republic of China in 1949, national cinema turned into a state-sponsored, state-owned enterprise. As Paul Clark has argued, it was the key to fostering a mass national culture in Maoist China.[9] The effort to build a unified and unifying picture of national identity through cinema has been intense and ferocious. This can be observed at both the level of the film industry and the level of the filmic text or film aesthetics.[10] Film studios are no longer privately owned. They are reorganized and merged into a new national film industry. The biggest studios to emerge from the reorganization and consolidation include Changchun Film Studio, Shanghai Film Studio, Beijing Film Studio, and August First Film Studio, all under the ultimate surveillance and leadership of the Ministry of Culture and the Ministry of Propaganda. The state has the absolute and exclusive right in film production and distribution. Cinema is often subject to being a vehicle of political propaganda and ideological indoctrination. There is strict censorship of both domestic and foreign films. The foreign films that the Chinese audience is allowed to see are selected predominantly from socialist-bloc countries. Hollywood films virtually disappeared from China.

The nationalization of cinema does not, however, imply a smooth and easy road, free from conflicts, contradictions, and collisions. The "Sinification" of a Western technology and the development of a native form of socialist art remain the paramount tasks for Chinese film artists. The enormity and complexity of such a process can only be hinted at here. Gina Marchetti's essay, *"Two Stage Sisters:* The Blossoming of a Revolutionary Aesthetic," examines the arduous search for a new aesthetic. Film artists such as Xie Jin must find a solution to the question of how can one create an art form that must be, paradoxically, at once Chinese and Western, Marxist and Maoist, revolutionary and socialist. What is "socialist" cinema with unique "national," "Chinese" characteristics like? As Douglas Wilkerson puts it, "Can Western modes of cinematography, linked to the very mechanism of the camera through the dominant postmedieval perspective system, be replaced by modes which are linked to traditional Chinese aesthetics?"[11] First, filmic texts must render Marxist, Maoist, and socialist interpretations of Chinese history. The subject matter of film is to depict the revolutionary struggle of the Chinese people to overthrow their imperialist, feudal, and capitalist oppressors and to reflect the socialist construction and nation-building in the postliberation (post-1949) period. Second, it is imperative that artists find ways to achieve a synthesis of film as an imported Western medium and indigenous, Chinese artistic conventions (traditional Chinese painting, literature, poetry, storytelling, local operas, folk art). The struggle to find a new film aesthetic in Maoist China was more often than not far from being a smooth process, but was instead full of intense debates and conflicts between different factions within the Communist Party apparatus and film circles, frequently resulting in criticism, self-criticism, and purge.

The myth-making and legitimizing function of film narrative in the formation of a homogeneous Chinese national identity was also accomplished by reducing internal ethnic and cultural differences. Questions of nationhood and ethnicity are important issues for the new regime. A major film genre that emerged in the late 1950s and 1960s is the "ethnic minorities film." Yingjin Zhang's essay, "From 'Minority Film' to 'Minority Discourse': The Questions of Nationhood and Ethnicity in Chinese Cinema," offers a refreshing, critical perspective on the matter. In exoticizing and eroticizing the ethnic minorities, this genre in fact consolidates the central position of the Han (Chinese) nationality. Be it the display of "ethnic harmony and solidarity" or the representation of the Han nationality as the liberator from slavery, feudalism, and ignorance, films of this genre are essential for the formation and legitimation of the Chinese nation-state. The other is needed for the confirmation of the self, and the peripheral is appropriated for the purpose of the central. Real internal differences and tensions in race, ethnicity, class, gender, and region are erased for the sake of the construction of an imaginary homogeneous national identity.

In the post-Mao era, a new wave of filmmaking emerged in the New Chinese Cinema, most noticeably "Fifth-Generation film"[12] (film by the class that graduated from the Beijing Film Academy in 1982) in the 1980s. The makers of these films are active participants and definitive fashioners of a broad, nationwide intellectual movement self-styled as "cultural reflection" (wenhua fansi) and "historical reflection" (lishi fansi). (At approximately the same time, Taiwanese New Cinema and the Hong Kong New Wave also arose.) Their task is to reflect deeply on the entrenched patterns of the history and society of the Chinese nation and civilization. This critical enterprise is sustained by an ambivalent attitude toward China's past: an iconoclastic attack on tradition in the fashion of the intellectuals of the May 4th

Movement (1919) and, at the same time, a return to, or a search for, the deep roots that gave life to Chinese civilization in the first place.

While engaging in relentless cultural critique, the Fifth Generation forged a distinctive style of its own, an "autoethnography."[13] Chinese national cinema is the self-reflexive gaze of the nation. The signature pieces from this period, such as *Old Well* (Lao jing),[14] *Yellow Earth* (Huang tudi), *Big Parade* (Da yuebing), *King of the Children* (Haizi wang), *Red Sorghum* (Hong gaoliang), and *Life on a String* (Bianzou bianchang), are profound national allegories of China in the sense defined by Fredric Jameson.[15] The stylistic mannerism of these films is significant in the imagining and imaging of China as a community, for as Benedict Anderson states, "Communities are to be distinguished, not by their falsity/genuineness, but by the style in which they are imagined."[16] The explorations in the art of cinematography and manner of narration in these films have contributed to the innovation of Chinese cinematic conventions and the creation of a new film language.

The self-reflexive ethnographic turn is again accomplished by way of a detour—a search for the *other*. In films such as Zhang Nuanxin's famous *Sacrificed Youth* (Qingchun ji), the ethnic other is still needed for a critique of the self. Even though the politics and culture of the Han nationality are subject to interrogation in view of the values of the ethnic minority, the cinematic gaze, the "point of view," the narrative voice, and the consciousness and memory of the storyteller are those of the Han/Chinese "ethnographer." Ultimately, difference and marginality are wooed and pursued for the self-same interest of the center.

In 1988, Zhang Yimou's first film, *Red Sorghum,* received the Golden Bear Award at the Berlin international film festival. It was the first Chinese film to receive a major award from a Western film festival; it was also the beginning of an end. As some film scholars contend, this entrance of Chinese cinema into the global film market marked the end of the short-lived classical phase of New Chinese Cinema, a phase characterized by intellectual elitism, disregard for the film market, idiosyncratic mannerism, and artistic experimentation.

One may say that New Chinese Cinema in the 1980s was primarily a national cinema, and the predominant trope was "cultural critique."[17] Film was a crucial constituent of the intellectual and critical currents that swept across China in that period. Chinese cinema in the 1990s has entered a new phase of development and thus demands a fresh theoretical description. It is undergoing an unprecedented process of internationalization and is on its way to becoming a transnational cinema in the conditions created by global capital/capitalism.[18] While formerly targeted primarily at the domestic film audience, Chinese cinema is an integral part of the international film market today. Some films that originated from centers of Chinese culture such as the Mainland, Taiwan, and Hong Kong have been viewed and accepted by a large overseas public. As part of the broader trends in the global film industry, Chinese cinema partakes of a process of transnational production, exhibition, distribution, and consumption in the world market. The number of coproductions with foreign companies has been increasing since the beginning of the 1990s, and in 1993 about a quarter of China's films were funded by foreign capital.[19] There were twenty-one coproductions in 1992, fifty-six in 1993, and thirty in 1994.[20] Most of these coproductions were funded by sources in Hong Kong and Taiwan. China's film industry is caught in the throes of a transition from a state-controlled system to a market mechanism. National cinema suffers from a decline in funding and audience and is in a deep crisis.

One may observe several categories of film production in terms of funding and audience in contemporary China. The state gives funds directly to major studios such as August First Studio to produce "mainstream" (zhu xuanlü) pictures. These films depict historic moments in the communist revolution, lives of important communist leaders, and stories of honest, model workers and cadres. A number of films from this category, for example, Zhou Enlai and Jiao Yulu, seem to be rather popular among audiences. Needless to say, the producers are not concerned with funds and the film market. Another category is that of "entertainment pictures" (yule pian, that is, kung-fu, detective, gangster, comedy) funded by a wide range of sources such as state-owned studios, Hong Kong and Taiwan producers, and nonstate Chinese producers with backing from businesses. Then there are "art films." They are mostly new productions, or more precisely, coproductions, of the former Fifth-Generation film artists. Some of them, such as Zhang Yimou and Chen Kaige, have been working with producers outside of the Mainland. Their "transnational" films are primarily targeted to non-Mainland audiences and international film festivals and are distributed outside of China. Finally, there are small-scale, experimental films by Sixth-Generation and post–Fifth-Generation film artists. These young filmmakers, such as Zhang Yuan, Hu Xueyang, and Wang Xiaoshuai, are in no position to compete with the Fifth Generation in attracting major funds at the moment. They operate with small budgets, sometimes a cash award won at an international film festival, to put through their conceptions of film art. There is little interest on the part of domestic producers and general audiences in the kind of off-beat films they produce.

In early 1995, the United States and China signed an agreement regarding intellectual property rights. Under the agreement, the People's Republic lifted the quota on the import of Hollywood films to China for the first time while retaining the right to exercise censorship. American feature films and Disney cartoons such as *Forrest Gump, The Fugitive, True Lies,* and *The Lion King* were soon imported to China and screened all over the country. "Hundreds of thousands of enthusiastic Chinese viewers filled once desolate theaters in order to see the films, producing hefty profits for an industry which had experienced lackluster business in recent years."[21] The arrival of American films is both an opportunity to regain the domestic film audience and a potential threat to China's own film industry. In an even more interesting development, the first Sundance Film Festival in China opened in Beijing in October 1995.[22] Quentin Tarantino's *Pulp Fiction,* along with some other American films, was premiered at the event. At the end of the twentieth century, Chinese national cinema is once again seriously challenged by the global cultural hegemony of Hollywood even as the state attempts to save it by censoring the foreign.

In the post-Tiananmen era (1989 to the present), or what Chinese intellectual historians call the "post-New Era" *(hou xin shiqi),* Chinese society is characterized by the expansion of consumerism, the spread of popular culture, the commercialization of cultural production, and the advent of postmodern formations.[23] Postmodern Chinese film is already in sight at the fin de siècle. The film *In the Heat of the Sun* (Yangguang canlan de rizi, 1995) by Jiang Wen, based on the stories of Wang Shuo, exhibits in its uncut version ostensively postmodern stylistic features. Fragmentary and random narration, pastiche, parody, irony, the blurring of the distinction between history and fiction and between film and reality, semiautobiographical narrative, the appearance of Jiang Wen and Wang Shuo themselves in the film, the deconstructive reconstitution of the history and memory of the Cultural Revolution, carnivalistic self-abandon—all these characteristics point to the possible beginning of another direction in filmmaking.[24]

In the historical transition to an era of transnational postmodern cultural production, film constitutes a crucial site. The entrance of Chinese cinema into the global market of film culture has provided the occasion for ongoing contemporary debates among critics of Chinese film. Several crucial issues emerge from this context. For native/nativist Chinese critics, what they witness seems to be the global homogenization of cultural production. They feel compelled to formulate a discursive resistance to what they see as commodification of Chinese film to an unprecedented degree. (Hence, resistance of the local to the global in China means resistance to encroaching neocolonialism, Orientalism, and other "hegemonic" discourses from the West.)

On the domestic front, many indigenous critics are also opposed to the commercialization of film in China's cultural market. In the conditions of the 1990s the production of avant-gardist, experimental film is no longer possible; artists, writers, and filmmakers have to operate according to the principles of a market economy and consumerism. There is little domestic audience for serious film. Art film suffers from the rapid commercialization of popular culture in China. Other forms of mass media and mass entertainment such as television programs have drastically reduced the size of the film audience. The question is whether there is still a place for art film in China and whether the internationalization of Chinese film is the solution.

Furthermore, the transnational production and distribution of Chinese film may turn out to be an oppositional discursive formation on another level. It is a viable strategy of survival and of resistance to a domestic hegemony; it is a means to evade film censorship. The filmmakers can still carry out, in a larger international arena, the project of "historical-cultural reflection," a project that is by all appearances hopelessly narcissistic and out of fashion in the consumer society of the 1990s. Internationalization as such is a way both to evade and to defy the internal domination of the regime. Here, indigenous cultural critique and global capital seem to merge in this transnational process.

Because of these new developments, the very idea of national cinema becomes problematic in Chinese film study and film studies in general. Films such as *Raise the Red Lantern* and *Farewell My Concubine,* directed respectively by Zhang Yimou and Chen Kaige, the two most renowned auteurs of China's New Cinema, are unmistakably "Mainland" films in terms of thematic concerns and stylistic characteristics. Yet, as soon as the question of their country of origin is brought up, they belong to the category of Hong Kong cinema. First of all, the political economy of these films is such that they were funded by foreign capital (Hong Kong, Taiwan, Japan, Europe), produced by Chinese labor, distributed in a global network, and consumed by an international audience. Second, and even more important for film scholars, the very process of reading, reception, and interpretation in these instances is always already of a transnational nature. Any critical understanding of what we call transnational Chinese cinema must go beyond national boundaries. National cinema founded upon the notion of the modern nation-state is now subject to interrogation in the postmodern and postindustrial condition of global cultural production and consumption.[25] The borderlines between nations are blurred by new telecommunications technologies, which can transmit electronic images and simulacra instantly across the globe.

To make films not for the domestic audience but for international consumption entails certain stylistic and thematic changes in the film art of distinguished Fifth-Generation directors such as Zhang Yimou and Chen Kaige. It seems that there is still the ambition and commitment to continually engage in a historical/cultural critique of the Chinese nation on the part of the film artists. At the same time, it is imperative for them to utilize popular cinematic conventions and cater to the tastes of international audiences for commercial success. My own essay in this collection, "National Cinema, Cultural Critique, Transnational Capital: The Films of Zhang Yimou," spells out both the continuities and discontinuities in New Chinese Cinema. It points to the significant changes and linkages between the earlier experimental, introspective "avant-garde" film (mid- and late 1980s) and contemporary "transnational Chinese cinema," between a desire for the artistic purity of "cultural critique" and the contingencies of film as an (inter)cultural commodity. The greatest irony of contemporary Chinese cinema seems to be that some films achieve a transnational status precisely because they are seen as possessing an authentically "national," "Chinese," "Oriental" flavor by Western audiences. In the meantime, the domestic Chinese audience dismisses the same films as "misrepresentations" and "mystifications" of China.[26] In an interesting development, Zhang was invited to produce a new film version of the opera *Turandot* in Italy in 1996. His gifted "Oriental" sensibility, as shown in his earlier films, was thought to be most suitable for making such a classic, romantic (Orientalist) work about the East. This anecdote sheds some light on a serious matter, namely, the nature of East-West, international cultural dynamics at the end of the century.

· Transnationalism in the Cinemas of Taiwan, Hong Kong, and the Chinese Diaspora

It is difficult to speak of Chinese national cinema after 1949 as a single entity. Rather, there are three cinemas: those of the Mainland, Taiwan, and Hong Kong. These three cinematic traditions have developed in separate directions and yet all attempt to signify a shared object: "China." China as a modern nation-state, a "location of culture," however, is subject to deconstruction, hybridization, multiplication, fragmentation, division, and erasure.[27] Modern China is a collective of communities, peoples, ethnicities, regions, dialects, languages, and temporalities. The history of the Inter-China area, or "Greater China" (Mainland, Taiwan, and Hong Kong), is one of migration, diaspora, colonialism, nationalism, political rivalry, military confrontation, and cultural interflow all at the same time. To reduce the history of Taiwan and Hong Kong to that of the Mainland is to suppress their cultural and political specificity.

Nearly simultaneously with the rise of the Mainland's New Cinema, Taiwan's New Cinema emerged in the 1980s. Like its Mainland counterpart, Taiwan's New Cinema aims at the innovation of worn-out film language as well as a deep reflection on the history, society, and culture of Taiwan. Hou Hsiao-hsien's films have become the most representative case of this movement. June Yip's ambitious, instructive essay, "Constructing a Nation: Taiwanese History and the Films of Hou Hsiao-hsien," analyzes the issue of the "national" identity in Hou's Taiwan Trilogy—*City of Sadness, The Puppetmaster,* and *Good Men, Good Women.* The Trilogy spans the history of one hundred years of Taiwan's colonial, postcolonial, and Nationalist rule (1895–1995). Taiwanese history has its unique memory of the past, a past shaped by the forces of the Mainland, ex-colonizer Japan, the Nationalist government, and the West. Taiwan's nationality or "transnationality" in relation to these forces is marked by deep political, geopolitical, cultural, and emotional ties as well as ruptures. Jon Kowallis' essay, "The Diaspora in Postmodern Taiwan and Hong Kong Film: Framing Stan Lai's *Peach Blossom Land* with Allen Fong's *Ah Ying,*" is another study of the representation of the "transnational identity" of Chinese in the cinemas of Taiwan and Hong Kong. It examines, among other provocative subjects, how Lai's film responds to the competing territorial, political, cultural, and emotional claims of Mainland China as homeland on the one hand and the Republic of China in Taiwan as land of residence on the other.

In another important juncture, all these films discussed by Yip and Kowallis enact for us what might be called the poetics and politics of successive modes of visuality in the span of a century and trace how modes of visuality are imbricated in the formation of history, memory, nationhood, and modernity. From photography *(City of Sadness),* puppet show/shadowplay *(The Puppetmaster),* and theater *(The Peach Blossom Land* and *Ah Ying)* to film itself *(Good Men, Good Women),* the stories within stories chronicle the history of visual technologies, exacerbate the possibility and modality of representation itself, and configure the convoluted relationship between illusion and reality, image and history, and stage and the world. It is no coincidence that such issues also constitute the narratives of several other historical films examined in this volume: *Two Stage Sisters* (more than twenty years of Shaoxing opera), *Farewell My Concubine* (half a century of Beijing opera), and *To Live* (several decades of Chinese puppet show).

While delving into the specific locality of the indigenous Taiwanese experience, Taiwan cinema also renders a dizzying representation of postmodern urban spatial dislocation. Taiwan, as a "newly industrializing First World tier of the Third World,"[28] is itself a map of the unevenness of the world system of global capitalism. As Fredric Jameson describes it, a film such as *Terrorizer* (Kongbu fenzi, 1986) by Edward Yang contains an overlap of various spaces in Taipei: *traditional* space (the barrack apartments of the policeman), *national* space (the hospital), *multinational* space (the publisher's office housed in a great glass high-rise), and *transnational* anonymity (the hotel corridor with its identical bedrooms).[29] The overdetermination of spatiality in Taiwanese urban cinema points in the direction of an expanding global postmodern culture that seems to transcend national boundaries.

The best-known Taiwanese director in America (or Chinese American director?) is undoubtedly Ang Lee, whose films are the subject of study by Wei Ming Dariotis and Eileen Fung in their collaborative essay, "Breaking the Soy Sauce Jar: Diaspora and Displacement in the Films of Ang Lee." In their essay, they bring up the crucial issues of subject position, identity politics, and multiculturalism in Lee's films. *The Wedding Banquet* and *Eat Drink Man Woman* were tremendously popular films in the United States and were nominated for an Oscar for best foreign film. *Pushing Hands* and *Eat Drink Man Woman* take place in cross-cultural, transnational settings and deal with the themes of the Chinese diaspora, migration, and cultural identity. *Sense and Sensibility,* based on Jane Austen's novel, scripted by Emma Thompson, and starring Thompson and Hugh Grant, was named the Best Motion Picture at the Golden Globe Awards and nominated for several Oscars. Lee said that as a Taiwanese/Chinese he was closer to the world of Jane Austen than many people in contemporary Britain could be. Lee's film art, as a paradigmatic case of transnationalism, not only crosses national boundaries but also consolidates national and local identities in uncanny ways. Although he does not reconstruct Taiwanese history in the way Hou Hsiao-hsien does, there is still an attempt to foreground a unique Taiwanese experience. The transnational, cross-cultural background in some of his films opens up new ways for the expression of Taiwanese, Chinese, national sentiments.

Hong Kong, a hybrid cosmopolitan space, a nexus in the flow of transnational capital, a colony and soon-to-be postcolony, is a particularly noteworthy case in the discussion of global film culture. What is Hong Kong like? Who owns it? In the epic film *Commissioner Lin* (Lin Zexu), produced in 1959, the Mainland offered its official filmic account of the loss of Hong Kong to Great Britain. In fact, it was suggested that the event signaled the beginning of a century of Chinese heroic resistance to Western imperialism, and the peasant uprising in Sanyuanli at the end of the film prefigured the Communist revolution. On May 8, 1996, Xie Jin, the seventy-three-year-old veteran Mainland director, began shooting his historical film *The Opium War* (Yapian zhanzheng) at the town of Tiger Gate (Humen), at whose fortress Lin Zexu burned Western opium shipped to China in 1839, causing the start of the Opium War. Production of the film (at 80 million *yuan*) is expected to be finished by July 1, 1997, the day of the return of Hong Kong to the Mainland, in order to commemorate the historic, monumental occasion.[30]

What is the self-image of Hong Kong in Hong Kong cinema then? Does Hong Kong have its own voice? Hong Kong cinema often reenacts the ambivalent relation of the city to the Mainland.[31] Hong Kong's cultural identity seen through its cinema is at once an identification with and distancing from the Mainland. In the "grand narratives" of Mainland cinema, the identity of Hong Kong is omitted, elided, and erased. Hong Kong does not fit in the world-historical scheme of China. Even in the recent epic film *Farewell My Concubine,* a properly Hong Kong production, Hong Kong itself has no place in the narrative. In the original novel, the main characters emigrated to Hong Kong in 1984, the time when the Sino-British Joint Declaration on returning Hong Kong was signed. Chen Kaige's film version altered the ending and utterly cut out the existence of Hong Kong.

Small as it is in size and population, Hong Kong as a city-state boasts the third largest film industry in the world, after the United States and India. To see Hong Kong cinema as local cinema is misleading. For decades Hong Kong cinema has been a regional and transnational cinema in a way that Mainland cinema could not be. Its viewers and fans stretch across East and Southeast Asia. Box-office sales from these regions contribute a significant portion of the revenue of the Hong Kong film industry. Even more broadly, Hong Kong films, in the varieties of action film and kung-fu film, have fans and dedicated followers in "Chinatowns" and overseas Chinese communities, on college campuses, and among the general public throughout North America, Latin America, Africa, Europe, and indeed all over the globe. Superstars such as Jackie Chan and Chow Yun-fat have cult status among their fans around the world. There is no lack of fanzines, websites, cyberspace, and Internet activity devoted to Hong Kong cinema and its stars. Thus, a *Village Voice* reporter wrote of Hong Kong cinema in cyberspace:

> For the moment, though, movie-related Web time still bears a close relationship to channel surfing. Some of these sites, like the elaborate Hong Kong Cinema you can find at University of Pittsburgh.edu, are obviously labors of love, maintained by fans for fans at what I'd imagine are significant financial [costs].[32]

To be able to log onto http://hkcinema not only allows entry into cyberspace but also poses a crucial question for us as to what constitutes the filmic text at the present time. With advances in computer technology and the appearances of CD-ROMs, the information highway, the Internet, and computer graphics, the media of cinema are going through a profound change. The global screening of China/Hong Kong/Taiwan, not in a theater or in front of a VCR, but through a computer, say, on a college campus or in one's private home in North America, adds a new dimension to the nature of transnational cinema. "Electric shadows" (dianying) on the screen in the public space of a theater are transforming themselves into electronic images in cyberspace.

Anne T. Ciecko's essay, "Transnational Action: John Woo, Hong Kong, Hollywood," dissects the operation of global capital and follows the transnational trans/action of Woo's film productions between Hong Kong and Hollywood. In his contribution, "Jackie Chan and the Cultural Dynamics of Global Entertainment," Steve Fore analyzes aspects of Hong Kong's film industry, its international presence, and another Hong Kong superstar-director-producer, Jackie Chan. Both Ciecko and Fore also guide us in navigating the intricate cultural politics of screening Asian masculinity in the present setting of global entertainment. Building on the international appeal of his earlier hits, *A Better Tomorrow* (1986) and *The Killer* (1989), and with the uncertain future of Hong Kong after July 1997, John Woo has left Hong Kong for Hollywood. That a high-profile Hong Kong auteur with a most distinct individual style, a style that amounts to a staple of Hong Kong cinema, now directs Hollywood productions further complicates the problem of national cinema. Traveling between Hong Kong and Hollywood, Woo's films such as *Hard Target* (1993, starring Jean-Claude Van Damme) and *Broken Arrow* (1996, starring John Travolta) cross and cross out national and geographic boundaries. It is worth noticing how a Hong Kong director transforms local film genres, with all their culture-specific symbols and meanings, into spectacles for cultural consumption on an international scale. While Woo readily acknowledges the influence of Western film artists on his career, American filmmakers such as Quentin Tarantino and Robert Rodriguez are eager to appropriate Woo-esque stylistic elements in their own films. Genres of Hong Kong action film are undergoing a process of globalization in the hands of filmmakers from various regions.[33]

With the release of *Rumble in the Bronx* in multiplexes all over the United States on February 23, 1996, Jackie Chan, hailed as "Asia's number one star," finally "made it" in America after his failed attempt to cross the Pacific in the 1980s. *Rumble* was one of the best-selling films of the year in the United States. As a result of the success of the film in the U.S. market, Chan's future films, as well as past films (*Supercop* and others), will be gradually released in U.S. theaters. With the arrival of Chan, one must redefine what global entertainment film is. It is no longer an exclusive, one-way Hollywood export to other parts of the world. A Hong Kong film, such as a Golden Harvest production in the case of Chan, offers an alternative route for the global circulation of cultural products.

The globalization of cinema brings with it an erosion of the fixed geographic boundaries of nation-states. Yet, it may not necessitate the disappearance and homogenization of cultural and ethnic identity. At times, transnationalism in fact strengthens and reasserts a sense of cultural selfhood. It is evident that in Jackie Chan's films there is often a subtle or not so subtle assertion of his *Chineseness*. There is never a mistake about his Chinese identity. Lovable, affable, funny, and heroic to a broad spectrum of viewers of all nationalities, Chan is positioned above all as a Chinese kung-fu hero who always wins in the end. While Hong Kong talents such as John Woo, Jackie Chan, Tsui Hark, Wong Kar-wai, and Ringo Lam are appearing in the United States one by one, Chow Yun-fat, another Hong Kong/Asian superstar, is contemplating his move to Hollywood. Yet he has been more cautious as an Asian *male* action film superstar. His Asian masculinity, visage, and physique will be under the scrutiny of broad segments of the American audience. (His case is different from both Woo and Chan. While Woo is a director, Chan is a kung-fu star, an admittedly Asian skill by Western reckoning.) When asked by a reporter about his plans to act in a Hollywood film, Chow expressed both anguish and responsibility as an Asian star:

> A good role is important. But more than that is the script. Because for me, an Asian, I have a lot of fans, people that support me. If I choose the wrong role in a movie, they will feel shame. For me and for them. If the first movie is not a big success in the United States, I don't give a damn. But for Asia. . . .[34]

With the proliferation of Chinese cinemas on the international scene, there have appeared a plethora of films that attempt to write and rewrite Chinese histories. Each of the Chinese cinemas creates its own authentic version of "Chinese" history. Each signifies a different China and preserves a national or local history of its own through the art of historiography/"historiophoty."[35] While discussions of the relation of Chinese film to the world tend to center on the binary opposition of China versus the West or the "Third World" versus the "First World," more attention should perhaps be given to the tensions and relations among distinct Chinese communities: the Mainland, Taiwan, Hong Kong, and overseas Chinese communities. Each has its own claim to China's past and present. Mainland Chinese critics seem to be less sensitive to the relations of center versus periphery and global versus local that exist explicitly or implicitly in the minds of the people in these locales of Chinese culture. Whereas a Mainland critic may only see the possibility of a Chinese film such as *Farewell My Concubine* becoming a victim of the "cultural hegemony" of the West (via the Orientalist route), a Taiwanese critic may think otherwise. He or she may feel particularly uneasy about the "grand narrative," the "epic style" of this film by Chen Kaige.[36] The film covers a long sweep of China's modern history: the warlord period,

Japanese occupation, Guomindang rule, the Communist victory, the Cultural Revolution, and the New Era. Its narration of Chinese history is Sinocentric, or more precisely, Mainland-centered, relative to the "local" histories of Taiwan and Hong Kong. It constructs a monolithic, monological modern China. For the people of Chen Kaige's generation, the momentous historical events of the Mainland such as the Cultural Revolution are the most important, most formative, and yet most disillusioning experiences in both their personal and collective lives. Chen's portrayal of Chinese history (i.e., Mainland history) is thus passionate and totalizing, lacking in irony and distance. The film constitutes nothing less than a hegemonic discourse of its own kind which marginalizes the claims and stories of people from Taiwan and Hong Kong. Any version of China-centered cultural imperialism is as dangerous as Western cultural imperialism. Thus, the writing and rewriting of forgotten, repressed national, regional, and local histories from a non-Mainland perspective remain equally important tasks for the filmmaker.

At this juncture, it is pertinent to mention nascent Chinese American film (or Chinese Canadian film, Chinese European film, for that matter) in a volume that purports to problematize the concept of "national cinema." I take Chinese American film as a telling instance of the formation of what might be called a new transnational Chinese culture. There have been several films directed and produced by Chinese Americans; most notably, Wayne Wang's 1993 film, *The Joy Luck Club,* achieved box-office success in the United States. The event signaled the beginning of the entrance of Chinese American film into mainstream American film culture.[37] Questions of the Chinese diaspora, cross-cultural/double identity, and generation gaps become central themes in such films. An instructive example is again Ang Lee. One may ask: Are Ang Lee and his films Taiwanese? Chinese? American? Taiwanese American? Chinese American? In the case of *The Wedding Banquet,* the film has been advertised under different rubrics for different audiences: a gay and lesbian film, a Chinese American film, a Taiwanese film, and so forth. The lack of a clear answer to such questions indicates the very nature of transnational Chinese cinema.

Chinese American film is a revealing manifestation of a resurgent transnational Chinese culture. This is what Tu Wei-ming refers to as "Cultural China" in a well-known essay.[38] Cultural China includes the Mainland, Taiwan, and Hong Kong in its first "symbolic universe," overseas Chinese communities in the second symbolic universe, and non-Chinese who have an interest in Chinese affairs in the third symbolic universe. The idea of Cultural China is closely tied to a revival of Confucianism. The identification with China is not a matter of legal or territorial consideration but a matter of cultural affiliation. "Greater China," "Greater China economic zone," "East Asian modernity," and "Cultural China" are notions that stake out a grand global role for China at the end of the twentieth century and in the next century. Whether perceived as a renewed Sinocentrism or a counterhegemonic discourse against Euro-American domination, the idea of Cultural China fully articulates the ambition and reality of a new transnational Chinese culture in the making. Along with Chinese "national" cinemas, Chinese American film is to become an active participant in this trans-Pacific, global film discourse.

It is instructive to return to the films of Wayne Wang at this point for a look into the shaping of trans-Pacific ethnic communities. One of his earlier films, *Eat a Bowl of Tea* (1989), reenacts the horrors and effects of the infamous Chinese Exclusion Act upon two generations of Chinese immigrants in the New York Chinatown, albeit in a gentle and humorous tone.[39] The act separated Chinese families and deprived Chinese men of women. Its systematic extinction of Chinese families created a severe psychic trauma among Chinese communities that cannot but remind us of what T. W. Adorno said about the Holocaust (one cannot write poetry after Auschwitz). In the opening sequence, a long line of Chinese men wait in turn to see a prostitute. Chinatown is reduced to a withering bachelors' town. The dysfunctional sexuality of the old generation caused by racial discrimination did have lingering effects on the children. Yet, the ending of the film tells a story of recuperation as Mei Oi gives Ben Loy, her husband, a special tea "all the way from China" to restore his potency. The final shots betoken ethnic continuity, the birth of grandchildren, and the reestablishment of a new family in a new land.

Likewise, *The Joy Luck Club* narrates the tale of another Chinese community, this time on the West Coast—San Francisco. It is a story of two generations of Chinese women—four mothers from the Old China and their four daughters born and reared in America. Despite the lack of communication between moms and daughters, June embarks on a soul-searching journey to China to meet her long-lost twin sisters and find her roots. The question for herself and her generation is: What does it mean to be a Chinese? Or an American, for that matter?[40] There is a suggestion of the possible forging of a new "Chinese-American" ethnic identity by reconciling the forces of past and present, China and the West. The envisioning of Chinese communities by émigré Chinese film artists in America not only adds a new voice to the discourse of ethnicity and nationhood in American film culture but also contributes to the formation of a trans-Pacific, transnational Chinese film culture.[41]

• Gender, Modernity, Nationhood in Chinese Film History

The construction of nationhood has been intimately bound to gender formation in Chinese film from the beginning. Gender issues come to the forefront in Chinese film whether dealing with "women's problems" or offering star images to its spectators. To re-view Chinese cinemas not from a male-centered perspective but from a consciously gendered and feminist standpoint is part of our undertaking. The question of perspective becomes doubly important and difficult at this point for it must be at the same time a "cross-cultural" one. In fact, any investigation involving more than one culture or seeing one culture from the eye of another must be conscious of its own risks, potentials, and challenges. Does an effort to engage a non-Western text by a Western scholar or Western-trained scholar always result in some form of cultural imperialism or neocolonialism?

As E. Ann Kaplan suggests in "Reading Formations and Chen Kaige's *Farewell My Concubine,*" the first thing that a U.S. feminist critic might do in dealing with a non-Western text is to be at least self-conscious of the emotional impact of a film on her and of her subjectivity. It is fruitful to examine the mechanism of subject-formation of a white, Western woman trained in Western academia who uses feminist theories, psychoanalysis, and cultural studies in specific ways. While being fully aware of its limitations, a white feminist reading of Chinese film texts might uncover strands of multiple meanings that escape the notice of critics of the originating culture by bringing in different perspectives and frameworks. To test her assumptions, Kaplan reads a Chinese film text, *Farewell My Concubine,* from her gendered, white feminist perspective. The alternative to not paying attention to cross-cultural analysis is to turn back to an essentialist position, to "cultivate one's own garden."

Engendering Chinese history and nationhood through a gendered discourse is a strategy frequently used since early Chinese cinema. In the progressive, left-wing film tradition before 1949, many films were produced to represent the plight of Chinese women. In fact, the theme of "modern women" in cinema has been tied to a series of weighty questions such as modernity, the spiritual health of the nation, and anti-imperialism.[42] Over the years, film studios that were infiltrated or influenced by left-wing filmmakers, such as Mingxing (1920s–1930s), Lianhua (1930s), and Kunlun (late 1940s), produced a series of provocatively titled films dealing with women's issues. These films include *Three Modern Women* (San'ge modeng nüxing, 1933), *The Goddess* (Shennü, 1934), *A Modern Woman* (Xiandai yi nüxing, 1933), *The New Woman* (Xin nüxing, 1934), and *Three Beautiful Women* (Li renxing, 1949). Womanhood is often a trope for the nation, a national allegory. As in modern Chinese literature since the May 4th Movement, women have been portrayed as victims of feudal oppression. Their bodies have been the bearers of suffering and cruelty in a dehumanizing society. Kristine Harris' essay, "*The New Woman* Incident: Cinema, Scandal, and Spectacle in 1935 Shanghai," examines the representation of women in a silent film of the 1930s. In a feminist approach different from Kaplan's psychoanalytic, Lacanian orientation, Harris focuses on the social history of women, stars, and spectatorship in Chinese cinema of the period. The story of Ruan Lingyu, nicknamed the "Chinese Garbo," the lead actress in the film, who committed suicide at the age of twenty-five after its completion, has become a legend. The film roles she played and her own life have all become symbols of the modern Chinese woman. (A testimonial to the perpetual allure of her story is the 1991 Hong Kong film *Ruan Lingyu/Centre Stage,* directed by Guan Jinpeng [Stanley Kwan].) It appears that in films of this sort there is an ambiguity and uneasy tension between the goals of what might seem to be a Chinese feminist discourse as such and the language of some overarching, sublime, national, collective struggle that transcends gender specificity.

After 1949, gender politics was no less visible and crucial for the sake of socialist nation-building. What should be emphasized here is that gender discourse is usually reduced to and subsumed in the grand discourse of class struggle and national liberation. While the female symbolizes the victim of oppression (in the forms of child bride, concubinage, slavery, and the like), the male represents the agency of revolutionary change (through a series of familiar symbols and characters: male commissar, armed struggle, the gun, the Party, and the sun). Class consciousness overshadows gender identity. Women's newly found freedom from feudal, capitalist, and imperialist bondage is followed by integration into a new social order, a "socialist patriarchy."[43] In many cases, the liberation of women is concomitant with a process of gender erasure (for instance, the familiar sight of Chinese women wearing unisex Maoist uniforms). While revolutionary heroes and heroines are depicted to be in full possession of newly empowered masculinity and femininity, sexuality itself is minimized and elided.

These new revolutionary gender formations are most vividly staged and choreographed in two revolutionary film classics and their subsequent ballet versions: *The White-Haired Girl* (Baimao nü, 1950) and *The Red Detachment of Women* (Hongse niangzijun, 1961). Both films were turned into "revolutionary modern ballets" during the Cultural Revolution. (Needless to say, the ballets owed their life and popularity to their film versions, which were shown all over China for revolutionary education.) While the female lead characters, Xi'er and Wu Qinghua, are victims of cruel feudal oppression, the lead male characters, Dachun and Hong Changqing, represent the Party, the

Red Army, and the agent of revolutionary change. It is men who liberate women from slavery and lead them to revolution.[44] In fact, Xie Jin, director of the film *The Red Detachment of Women,* also rehearsed the by-then popular legend of the "White-Haired Girl" within the narrative of another famed film, *Two Stage Sisters* (Wutai jiemei, 1964/65, the subject of Gina Marchetti's essay). Chunhua, the heroine of the film, a formerly abused and oppressed actress of Shaoxing opera in the "old society," had transformed, liberated, and empowered herself by performing progressive programs (Lu Xun's story, *The New Year's Sacrifice* [Zhufu]) and revolutionary subjects ("The White-Haired Girl"). Toward the end of the film, her performance of the role of Xi'er (the White-Haired Girl) on the new, reformed stage of the Shaoxing opera brought tears and identification from the female audience (a characteristically non-Brechtian moment in Chinese opera). In the final shot of the film, Chunhua tells her stage sister, Yuehong, to "sing a lifetime of revolutonary opera" together. The (melo)drama of the "stage within a stage" has been over a long stretch of time an apt metaphor for new gender formation and social change in many Chinese films in the Mao era as well as the post-Mao era. (Consider, for instance, *Woman Demon Human* [Ren gui qing, 1988] by the woman director Huang Shuqin and the tale of "two stage brothers" in *Farewell My Concubine* by Chen Kaige).

In New Chinese Cinema, the rediscovery of gender differences is also the process of rediscovering individuality. Regendering history and nationhood involves a multiple critique of masculinity, femininity, sexuality, and their lack. The remaining essays in this section, "Gendered Perspective: The Construction and Representation of Subjectivity and Sexuality in *Ju Dou*" by Shuqin Cui, "The Concubine and the Figure of History: Chen Kaige's *Farewell My Concubine*" by Wendy Larson, and "Narrative Images of the Historical Passion: Those *Other* Women—On the Alterity in the New Wave of Chinese Cinema" by Yi Zheng, address gender politics in this period of Chinese cinema. Through a meticulous examination of the cinematic conventions of the film *Ju Dou* (offstage sound, point of view, narrative structure), Cui traces some characteristics of gender construction in Zhang Yimou's films. We witness a situation where an unconscious male desire searches for and reasserts a lost subjectivity and an emasculated sexuality. The woman character Ju Dou embodies a visible female sexuality, a signifier of male desire, a recipient of punishment. No matter how powerfully she is framed in the foreground, Ju Dou is not a subject, nor an agent of change, but remains a confirmation of the psychical wound suffered by Chinese men under a repressive social system. It seems that these observations are generally true of much of Chinese cinema in the post-Mao era. In Larson's analysis, Chen Kaige's films are usually grand, male, narcissistic narratives where women play marginal roles. In the historical epic film *Farewell My Concubine,* half a century of modern Chinese history is configured through personal stories of males despite the presence of Juxian, played by Gong Li. The central roles of history are played by men, not by women. Zheng's essay takes on the theme of gendering China as the "feminine" and the "other" in the imagination of both the West and New Chinese Cinema. The obsessive self-recasting of women in film is the century old "obsession with China." Woman in Chinese cinematic expression is the trope for the modern Chinese nation. In their feminist critiques, Cui, Larson, and Zheng all perceptively demonstrate that the male filmmakers of the New Cinema have displaced the burden of Chinese history and modernity and have re-placed them upon the shoulders of Chinese women.

Broadly speaking, gender formation in filmic discourse in the Mao era (1949–1976) was manifested as the empowerment of both masculinity and femininity through revolutionary struggle and socialist construction. In the post-Mao era (late 1970s and 1980s), New Cinema's cultural and social critique was necessarily couched in gender terms as well. Dysfunctional sexuality and "abnormal" gender relations, for example, impotency, emasculation, and concubinage, are veiled allegories of the nation. Again, Zhang Yimou's film art is an exemplary case in portraying Chinese masculinity in trouble and crisis. He offers the viewer spectacles of impotence and incest *(Ju Dou),* concubinage and polygamy *(Raise the Red Lantern),* injured phallus and testicles *(The Story of Qiu Ju),* the inability of men to save their spouses and children *(To Live),* and adultery *(Shanghai Triad).* Impotence, idiocy, and handicap on the part of the father and the son are the causes of the lack of emotional and libidinal fulfillment of a family in rural China in yet another highly publicized film, *Women from the Lake of Scented Souls* (Xianghun nü) by Xie Fei, which was the co-winner of the Golden Lion Award at the 1993 Berlin Film Festival with Ang Lee's *The Wedding Banquet.*[45]

In the 1990s, there is a resurgent recuperation of Chinese masculinity in the condition of transnational capitalism. The accelerated transformation of Hong Kong action and martial arts film into a global cinema foregrounds the heroics of Asian masculinity. After a hiatus of several decades, Bruce Lee's position is finally to be filled by a new Asian star, Jackie Chan. These Asian heroes must now compare and compete with "indigenous" American male mythologies established by actors such as Sylvester Stallone, Arnold Schwarzenegger, and Jean-Claude Van Damme in the American and international film markets. Hence, Chow Yun-fat's anguished, uneasy crossing to Hollywood, as mentioned earlier. (In regard to Asian kung-fu heroines in Hong Kong action films, their physical prowess, to the contrary, is not a sign of the assertion of an independent Asian female subjectivity. Their femininity, like the scantily covered female bodies in the woman-warrior genre of American cult film, seems to be fabricated for the visual pleasure of the masculine gaze.)

In January 1997, Jackie Chan's film *First Strike (Police Story 4)* was released in theaters across the United States at the same time that two other sexually charged American films—*The People vs. Larry Flynt* and *Evita* (starring Madonna)—were being screened. Chan, in the role of a Hong Kong cop/detective, embarks on a heroic transnational adventure and sets out to break a smuggling ring that steals nuclear weapons from Ukraine. The spectator watches him perform his characteristically extraordinary, breathtaking stunts first in the snowcapped landscape of Ukraine in the cold of winter and then in blue water in the warm climate of Australia on the other side of the globe. We witness Chan's triumphant tracking of the world for a righteous cause one more time, as he did the same in Yugoslavia (*Armor of God*, 1987) and New York City/Vancouver (*Rumble in the Bronx*, 1995). In this film, Chan's "spectacular body," acting, and performance may outdo his American counterparts, such as John Travolta and Christian Slater in John Woo's film *Broken Arrow*, on the same subject of stopping the theft of nuclear weapons. Yet, Chan's sexuality is as ambivalent and troubled as ever. At times he is stripped naked, and his tanned, muscular, nude body is exhibited to and scrutinized by passing women. One of the most self-reflexive moments within the diegesis of the film is when Chan says that his adventurous career is very much like that of James Bond but without the company of pretty girls. He casts himself in the role of something resembling an asexual, Chinese/Hong Kong James Bond. His role has been invariably a comic, lovable, optimistic, dutiful person dedicated solely to the completion of the task assigned to him, disinterested in and dodging the pursuit of libidinal fulfillment, although such opportunities are always present.

In Mainland China in the 1990s, unabashed recuperation and aggrandizement of Chinese masculinity have occurred in the domestic film and TV industries, which have taken on a transnational gender character. Films and TV serials such as *Beijing'ers in New York* (Beijingren zai Niuyue), starring Jiang Wen; *Russian Girls in Harbin* (Eluosi guniang zai Harbin), starring Jiang Wu, Jiang Wen's brother; *A Wild Kiss to Russia* (Kuangwen Eluosi); *Chinese Girls in Foreign Companies* (Yanghang li de Zhongguo xiaojie); and *Foreign Babes in Beijing* (Yangniu'er zai Beijing) describe the trafficking between Chinese and foreign men and women. Most noticeably, these texts depict how Chinese men have won the love of "foreign babes" through their entrepreneurial ability in the creation and accumulation of capital and wealth. The libidinal economy of Chinese nationals is linked to the political economy of the nation. The recuperation of the Chinese nation via Chinese masculinity is now achieved through transnational libidinal dynamics. The projection of such a transnational male imaginary is a disguised attempt to resurrect the Chinese nation/patriarchy.

As we come to the end of this brief overview, the contours of the evolution of Chinese cinemas become clear to us. Film first came to China as a foreign, Western technology at the end of the nineteenth century. In the early decades of the twentieth century, the struggle for the formation of a distinct Chinese national cinema, as part of the construction of the modern Chinese nation-state, was first and foremost a reaction to the international domination of its *other,* namely, Western film. Hence, film in China has always been of a transnational character. Since the founding of the People's Republic in 1949, Chinese cinemas have consisted of those of the Mainland, Taiwan, Hong Kong, and to a certain extent a diverse overseas community. They cross national borders and traverse vast geographic territories. In the case of the Mainland and Taiwan (Republic of China), we may speak of two competing Chinese "national" cinemas as a function of the Chinese nation-state; in the case of Hong Kong and Taiwan again (as a Chinese "province"), what we see is the flourishing of local Chinese cinemas, often spoken in dialects (Cantonese, Fukienese); the popularity of Chinese films, especially Hong Kong action films, in Southeast Asia and East Asia also creates a regional Chinese cinema; finally, the spread of Chinese films across the entire world makes Chinese cinema a global cinema. In the late 1980s and the 1990s, at the end of the twentieth century, new patterns of international coproduction and global distribution render the idea of Chinese national cinema rather problematic. The study of *national* cinemas must then transform into *transnational* film studies.

Therefore, it seems impossible to justify the notion of a single Chinese cinema—thus the plural in the title of this book. The emergence of China as a modern nation has in part been molded by the concurrent emergence of a national cinematic style. The development of nationhood is multifaceted; it is based to some extent on defining itself by identifying what it is *not*—by rejecting and reacting against foreign influences or by validating its own values through the depiction of exoticized national minorities, for example. Yet, as we know, a pure, clean, distinct national cinema can never exist but remains an imaginary construct. Some degree of hybridity is built into the very fabric of the medium of film. Film has always been a transnational entity. Before long, nationhood evolved into transnationalism in the age of global capitalism, with all its attendant peculiarities. To this point, there are already several versions of Chinese cinema: the official mainstream tradition, popular entertainment film, the avant-garde in its formative stage, and the emergent transnational cinema. Taiwan cinema and Hong Kong cinema, thriving but largely unrecognized on the periphery of mainstream Chinese (People's Republic) cinema, chronicle the effects of marginalization in some way and contribute to an alternative discourse of nationhood. Yet another voice from the margin emerges when we reinterpret the film corpus through a feminist perspective. A careful examination of gender formation in filmic discourse reveals to us the strategies of nation-building in a century of Chinese cinemas.

To query the transformation of Chinese national cinema, to inscribe the emergence of a transnational Chinese film culture, and to engender, to give rebirth to Chinese film discourse through regendering it, have been our collective desire in this study. To accomplish such a task requires an alertness to the changing historical conditions in the formations of national and transnational cinemas throughout twentieth-century China. The unprecedented globalization of film culture in the "new world order" at the end of this century provides cultural workers a unique opportunity for critical intervention. It is in such a spirit of critical, interdisciplinary, and cross-cultural intervention that we intend to revisit and reenvision cinema studies.

· Notes

Lucy Fischer, Anne T. Ciecko, and the readers of the University of Hawai'i Press read earlier drafts of this essay and kindly offered insightful comments for revision. I have incorporated many of their suggestions and have also benefitted from queries at the society for Cinema Studies conference held in Ottowa in 1997.

1. For an explanation of a Marxist approach to film, see Colin MacCabe's preface to Fredric Jameson's book, *The Geopolitical Aesthetic: Cinema and Space in the World System* (Bloomington: Indiana University Press, 1992), ix–xvi.

2. For accounts of the early history of film in China, see Cheng Jihua et al., *Zhongguo dianying fazhan shi* [History of the development of Chinese film], 2 vols. (Beijing: Zhongguo dianying chubanshe, 1963); Jay Leyda, *Dianying: An Account of Films and the Film Audience in China* (Cambridge, Mass.: MIT Press, 1972).

3. "National cinema" and *minzu dianying* are similar but not synonymous terms. The Chinese term *minzu* has the connotation of "race," "ethnicity," and "people," and *minzu dianying* signifies a Chinese effort to develop an indigenous film distinct from the Western model. For relevant discussions, see Chris Berry, "Race: Chinese Film and the Politics of Nationalism," *Cinema Journal* 31, no. 2 (1992): 45–58; Chris Berry, "A Nation T(w/o)o: Chinese Cinema(s) and Nationhood(s)," *East-West Film Journal* 7, no. 1 (1993): 24–51. For a critique of Berry's position, see Yingjin Zhang's essay in this volume. For a study of the relation between nationalism and early Chinese cinema, see Ma Junxiang, "Minzu zhuyi suo suzao de xiandai Zhongguo dianying"

[Modern Chinese cinema as shaped by nationalism], *Ershi yi shiji* [Twenty-first century] (February 1993): 112–119.

4. Cheng et al., *Zhongguo dianying fazhan shi.*

5. As a European contemporary of left-wing, underground communist Chinese film workers in the 1930s, Walter Benjamin also reflected upon the revolutionary utility of film as a new mass art. See his often-quoted 1935 essay, "The Work of Art in the Age of Mechanical Reproduction," in *Film and Criticism,* ed. Gerald Mast and Marshall Cohen (New York: Oxford University Press, 1992), 665–681.

6. Susan Hayward, *French National Cinema* (London: Routledge, 1993), 14. For recent parallel studies of other national and regional cinemas, see Andrew Higson, *Waving the Flag: Constructing a National Cinema in Britain* (Oxford: Clarendon Press, 1995); Sumita Chakravarty, *National Identity in Indian Popular Cinema* (Austin: University of Texas Press, 1993); Manthia Diawara, *African Cinema* (Bloomington: Indiana University Press, 1992); Nwachukwu Frank Ukadike, *Black African Cinema* (Berkeley: University of California Press, 1994); Pierre Sorlin, *Italian National Cinema, 1896–1996* (London: Routledge, 1996); Pierre Sorlin, *European Cinemas, European Societies, 1939–1990* (London: Routledge, 1991); Tom O'Regan, *Australian National Cinema* (London: Routledge, 1996); Ella Shohat and Robert Stam, *Unthinking Eurocentrism: Multiculturalism and the Media* (London: Routledge, 1994).

7. For an informative historical study of the obverse side of the issue, namely, Hollywood's strategies of representing Asians in relation to race and sex, see Gina Marchetti, *Romance and the "Yellow Peril": Race, Sex and Discursive Strategies in Hollywood Fiction* (Berkeley: University of California Press, 1993).

8. Andrew Higson, "The Concept of National Cinema," *Screen* 30, no. 4 (1989): 37.

9. See Paul Clark, *Chinese Cinema: Culture and Politics Since 1949* (New York: Cambridge University Press, 1987).

10. Wimal Dissanayake suggests that national cinema in Asia "can be analyzed very broadly at two levels: the textual and the industrial. At the textual level we can examine the uniqueness of a given cinema in terms of content, style, and indigenous aesthetics while at the industrial level we can examine the relationship between cinema and industry in terms of production, distribution, and exhibition." See Wimal Dissanayake, ed., *Colonialism and Nationalism in Asian Cinema* (Bloomington: Indiana University Press, 1994), xiii–xiv.

11. Douglas Wilkerson, "Film and the Visual Arts in China: An Introduction," in *Cinematic Landscapes: Observations on the Visual Arts and Cinema of China and Japan,* ed. Linda Ehrlich and David Desser (Austin: University of Texas Press, 1994), 40.

12. For a classification of the five generations of Chinese film artists, see George S. Semsel, ed., *Chinese Film: The State of the Art in the People's Republic* (New York: Praeger, 1987), 11–14.

13. For a study of contemporary Chinese cinema as "autoethnography," see Rey

Chow, *Primitive Passions: Visuality, Sexuality, Ethnography, and Contemporary Chinese Cinema* (New York: Columbia University Press, 1995).

14. *Old Well* was directed by Wu Tianming, a "Fourth-Generation" director, then head of the Xi'an Studio. He was regarded as the father of the Fifth Generation in helping the new directors start their careers at his studio. Zhang Yimou played the lead role in this film.

15. See Fredric Jameson, "Third-World Literature in the Era of Multinational Capitalism," *Social Text* 15 (fall 1986): 65–88.

16. Benedict Anderson, *Imagined Communities: Reflections on the Origin and Spread of Nationalism* (London: Verso, 1991), 6. As Fredric Jameson comments on the style of New Chinese Cinema, there might be a connection between the privileging of "an epic midshot" of landscape, a "midpanoramic perspective," an epic narrativity, and the desire to recuperate the Chinese nation. See Fredric Jameson, "Remapping Taipei," in *New Chinese Cinemas: Forms, Identities, Politics,* ed. Nick Browne, Paul G. Pickowicz, Vivian Sobchack, and Esther Yau (Cambridge: Cambridge University Press, 1994), 120–121.

17. See Nick Browne's introduction in *New Chinese Cinemas,* 1–11.

18. See Masao Miyoshi's seminal essay, "A Borderless World? From Colonialism to Transnationalism and the Decline of the Nation-State," *Critical Inquiry* 19, no. 4 (1993): 726–751. For informative discussions of "global capitalism" as it relates to China, see Arif Dirlik, *After the Revolution: Waking to Global Capitalism* (Hanover, N.H.: Wesleyan University Press, 1994), and Arif Dirlik, "The Postcolonial Aura: Third-World Criticism in the Age of Global Capitalism," *Critical Inquiry* 20, no. 2 (1994): 328–356.

19. See William Brent, "Lights! Cameras! Action!" *The China Business Review* (September-October 1994): 36–39. Also see George S. Semsel, "Report on the Current Situation in the Chinese Film Industry," paper presented at the Chinese cinema studies conference, University of Pittsburgh, September 1994.

20. See Lin Lisheng, "Jiushi niandai Zhongguo dianying de jingji biangeng he yishu fenye" [The economic changes and artistic patterns of Chinese cinema in the nineties], *Dianying yishu* [Film art] (May 1996): 37–41, 83.

21. Cui Lili, "Facing the Challenge From Hollywood," *Beijing Review* (February 5–11, 1996): 13.

22. Rex Weiner, "China Opens Its Doors to Sundance Fest," *Variety,* October 9–15, 1995, 13, 16; Rex Weiner, "Sundance Festival Takes Show on the Silk Road: Chinese Independents," *Variety,* October 16–22, 1995, 24.

23. For attempts to arrive at an inventory of constitutive features of postmodern culture in China in the late twentieth century, see my "Postmodernity, Popular Culture, and the Intellectual: A Report on Post-Tiananmen China," *boundary* 2 23, no. 2 (1996): 139–169; "Art, Culture, and Cultural Criticism in Post-New China," *New Literary History* 28, no. 1 (1997): 111–133; "Global POSTmodernIZATION: The Intel-

lectual, the Artist, and China's Condition," forthcoming in *boundary 2* 24, no. 3 (1997).

24. See Wang Ning, "Lüelun Zhongguo dangdai dianying de liangnan ji chulu" [On the dilemma and solution of contemporary Chinese film], *Dianying yishu* [Film art] 6 (1996): 4–7.

25. For recent discussions of the problems of national/international film, the nation-state, and transnationalism, see the special issue "Mediating the National," *Quarterly Review of Film and Video* 14, no. 3 (1993); Katherine Verdery, "Beyond the Nation in Eastern Europe," *Social Text* 38 (spring 1994): 1–19.

26. The manufacture of images and spectacles of China for the Western gaze is in part fulfilled through the strategy of self-exoticization and self-eroticization in Fifth-Generation films. Such a procedure has achieved some measure of success, for example, in the case of *Farewell My Concubine*. Yet, there is a sign of exhaustion. Consider the disappointing reception of Chen Kaige's *Temptress Moon* (Feng yue) at the 1996 Cannes Film Festival. Its producer, Xu Feng, invested much more heavily in this film than in *Farewell*. Despite the appearance of stars such as Gong Li and Leslie Cheung (Zhang Guorong), the film was badly received. A story about Oriental sexuality (incest, this time) eluded the gaze of Western spectators in Cannes. The complete, thorough transformation from narcissistic, elitist experimentation in the early period to the relentless, blind pursuit of commercial success and sensationalism is the tragedy of Chen. See Yuan Shengjun and Wang Jun, "Chen Kaige de beiju gaosu le women shenmo?" [What does Chen Kaige's tragedy tell us?], *Zhongguo yinmu* [China screen] (July/August 1996): 30–34.

27. See Homi K. Bhabha, *The Location of Culture* (London: Routledge, 1994).

28. Jameson, "Remapping Taipei," 148.

29. Jameson, "Remapping Taipei," 148.

30. See "Humen yiri: *Yapian zhanzheng* shezhizu paishe jishi" [One day in Humen: A report of the shooting of the production team of *Yapian zhanzheng*], *Zhongguo yinmu* [China screen] (July-August 1996): 20; Patrick E. Tyler, "In China, Letting a Hundred Films Wither," *New York Times*, December 1, 1996, H1, H26.

31. For a discussion of this aspect, see Ping-kwan Leung, "Minzu dianying yu Xianggang wenhua shenfen: Cong *Bawang bieji*, *Qiwang*, *Ruan Lingyu* kan wenhua dingwei" [National cinema and the cultural identity of Hong Kong: Looking at cultural orientation in *Farewell My Concubine*, *Chess King*, and *Ruan Lingyu*], *Jintian* [Today] no. 26 (autumn 1994): 193–204.

32. Gary Dauphin, "Cyber: Ready for My Website, Mr. DeMille," *Village Voice*, January 2, 1996, 15.

33. For an informative introduction to the world of Hong Kong action films, see Bey Logan, *Hong Kong Action Cinema* (London: Titan Books, 1995).

34. Quoted from R. J. Smith, "The Coolest Actor in the World," *Los Angeles Times*, March 12, 1995.

35. See Hayden White, "Historiography and Historiophoty," *American Historical Review* 93, no. 5 (1988): 1193–1199.

36. Liao Ping-hui, "Shikong yu xingbie de cuoluan: Lun *Bawang bieji*" [Temporal, spatial, and gender disorder: On *Farewell My Concubine*], *Chung-wai Literary Monthly* 22, no. 1 (1993): 6–18.

37. Indeed, the narrative strategy of telling about two generations of Chinese women in an ethnic community in the film has had a discernible influence on other new films. See, for example, *How to Make an American Quilt* (1995), which tropes on the structure and theme of *The Joy Luck Club* and narrates the tale of two generations of women in several Caucasian American and African American families.

38. Tu Wei-ming. "Cultural China: The Periphery as the Center," *Daedalus* 120, no. 2 (1991): 1–32. For a critique of Tu's notion in relation to Chinese film culture, see W. A. Callahan, "Gender, Ideology, Nation: *Ju Dou* in the Cultural Politics of China," *East-West Film Journal* 7, no. 1 (1993): 52–80.

39. For a discussion of other Wayne Wang films, see Peter Feng, "Being Chinese American, Becoming Asian American: *Chan is Missing*," *Cinema Journal* 35, no. 4 (1996): 88–118.

40. June's heightened sense of self-awareness is also vividly described in Amy Tan's original novel of the same title, on which the film is based. The passage needs to be quoted at length:

> The minute our train leaves the Hong Kong border and enters Shen-zhen, China, I feel different. I can feel the skin on my forehead tingling, my blood rushing through a new course, my bones aching with a famil-iar old pain. And I think, my mother was right. I am becoming Chinese.
>
> "Cannot be helped," my mother said when I was fifteen and had vigorously denied that I had any Chinese whatsoever below my skin. I was a sophomore at Galileo High in San Francisco, and all my Cauca-sian friends agreed: I was about as Chinese as they were. . . .
>
> But today I realize I've never really known what it means to be Chi-nese. I am thirty-six years old. Mother is dead and I am on a train, carrying with me her dreams of coming home. I am going to China. (Amy Tan, *The Joy Luck Club* [New York: Ivy Books, 1989], 306–307.)

41. Ming-na Wen, the lead actress in *Joy Luck Club,* performing the role of June, is a Pittsburgh native and now resides in Los Angeles. Her family restaurant, China-town Inn, is the only surviving Chinese restaurant in Pittsburgh's old Chinatown, which has long disappeared in the cityscape and memory of Pittsburgh. Her family has opened a new karaoke bar, appropriately named Club Joy, to serve as a meeting place for students and new immigrants from Taiwan, Hong Kong, and Mainland China on weekend evenings. The entrance of the restaurant is filled with posters of scenes from the film. What I may call "ethnic film" as such has its origins in the life

story of immigrants and does seem to have a real "after-life" and an effect on the given ethnic community.

42. See, for instance, Paul G. Pickowicz' essay, "The Theme of Spiritual Pollution in Chinese Films of the 1930s," *Modern China* 17, no. 1 (1991): 38–75. See also Yingjin Zhang, "Engendering Chinese Filmic Discourse of the 1930's: Configurations of Modern Women in Shanghai in Three Silent Films," *positions: east asia cultures critique* 2, no. 3 (1994): 603–628.

43. See Judith Stacey, *Patriarchy and Socialist Revolution* (Berkeley: University of California Press, 1983).

44. In August 1996, I saw a new performance of the *White-Haired Girl* by the Shanghai Ballet Troupe at the Theater of Beijing Exhibition Hall in Beijing, an example of Soviet-style architecture that, like ballet itself in China, dates back to the 1950s. There have been some changes in choreography from the old Cultural Revolution version. The new choreography of the duet between Xi'er (White-haired girl) and Dachun in their reunion scene makes their relationship more intimate. The romantic dimension of the original story was basically eliminated in the old ballet version in order to minimize private libidinal dynamics and highlight revolutionary devotion.

The life story of ballerinas in Red China, the Soviet influence on Chinese ballet, and the emergence of a "revolutionary" Chinese ballet have been the subject of several new films. See, for instance, the 1996 production *Red Swan* (Hong tian'e).

45. The whole idea of turning impotence into a critique and allegory of the Chinese nation can be traced back to the literature of the mid-1980s, most notably to Zhang Xianliang's stories. See my "When Mimosa Blossoms: The Ideology of the Self in Modern Chinese Literature," *Journal of Chinese Language Teachers Association* 28, no. 3 (1993): 1–16.

Part I

————— • —————

Nation-Building, National Cinema, Transnational Cinema

Chapter 1
·
Anti-Imperialism and Film Censorship During the Nanjing Decade, 1927–1937
·
Zhiwei Xiao

Beginning in the late nineteenth century, Chinese revolutionaries faced two tasks simultaneously: externally, they wanted to free China from the grips of the imperialist powers; internally, they sought to fundamentally reform Chinese society so that China could embark on the path to modernity. The anti-imperialism and antifeudalism slogans of the Nationalist revolution of 1924–1927 well captured these central themes of modern Chinese history. The Nationalist government during the Nanjing decade sought to recover China's sovereignty and rights from the Western and Japanese imperialist powers. Meanwhile, the state tried to foster a new national consciousness among the people. In both endeavors, film censorship played an important role. In this study I will focus on the Nationalists' efforts to control foreign film distribution and studio activities inside China, placing these issues in the context of the overall struggle to gain national sovereignty from the imperialist powers and promote nationalist consciousness.[1]

The Nationalist Party clearly demonstrated its nationalist stand during the Northern Expedition when its troops reclaimed the British concession in Hankou in 1926.[2] After the Nanjing government was founded in 1927, the minister of foreign affairs, Wu Chaoshu, informed the foreign consuls in China that his government would not recognize the unequal treaties signed by previous governments. On December 28, 1929, the Nanjing government issued an edict stating that all foreigners residing in China would be subject to Chinese laws and regulations beginning January 1, 1930. By February 1930, more than a dozen foreign concessions in China had been taken back, and negotiations were under way with the major Western powers about returning all the concessions, including the British and French concessions in Shanghai.[3] In accord with this nationalist spirit, the Nanjing government began to censor foreign films, curbed foreign studios' activities in China, and in 1937 condoned and eventually spearheaded a popular campaign to abolish foreign censorship on Chinese soil.

Confrontations with Western and Japanese imperialism on issues related to film censorship during this period were an important part of China's struggle for equality, freedom, and sovereignty in the international community. I will discuss three cases in the following pages. The first case demonstrates that the censoring of foreign films in China originated from the nationalistic resentment of their negative portrayal of China and the Chinese people. The initiative for censorship came from the Chinese public and the film industry, then was taken up by the government. The second case is an examination of the Film Censorship Committee's endeavors over the years to deal with foreign films and foreign film studios' activities in China. It was mainly through the censorial efforts of the National Film Censorship Committee (NFCC) and later the Central Film Censorship Committee (CFCC) that the showing of offensive foreign films in China was brought to an end.[4] Equally important was the fact that the NFCC/CFCC provided the Chinese film industry some protection from foreign competition by curbing the expansionist maneuvers of foreign studios, particularly Hollywood's plan to transplant an "Oriental Hollywood" to China. Finally I describe the Chinese cultural workers' campaign to abolish film censorship by foreign powers within the concessions, a movement that enjoyed the Nanjing government's tacit approval. Although the endeavor was aborted due to the outbreak of war with Japan, it demonstrated some interesting aspects of nationalism in China.

• Nationalist Protests and the Beginning of Film Censorship in China

Although Chinese began to try their own hand at filmmaking as early as 1905,[5] their efforts remained sporadic and of little mass significance until the mid-1920s. The rapid growth of an indigenous film industry in the mid-1920s did not fundamentally alter the foreign domination of China's film market. Until the late 1920s most of the movie houses in Shanghai were owned by foreigners, and the majority of films shown in them were of foreign origin.

Most foreign films were Hollywood products and were generally very popular with Chinese audiences. Foreign movie stars such as Charlie Chaplin, Douglas Fairbanks, and Lillian Gish were familiar to many Chinese.[6] Many movies infuriated Chinese audiences, however, because of their negative portrayals of China and Chinese people. In such films, Chinese invariably appeared as opium smokers, gamblers, servants, and thieves. In the words of Paul K. Whang, a frequent contributor to *China Weekly Review,*

> In American films, wherever a Chinese character is introduced, he must be an ugly-looking creature with queue hanging behind his back and his

part is always a personage of the underworld; wherever any Chinese scenes are adopted, they are laid in the Chinatowns of American cities, and featured with rowdy scenes in the chop-suey houses, in the fan-tan joints, and in the opium dens.[7]

The Chinese were certainly aware that there were gamblers, prostitutes, and other ugly manifestations of social ills in reality, but they objected to their presentation in foreign films because those films "pretend to represent the whole nation of China" when in fact presenting "only the evil, and never the good side of the Chinese people."[8]

During the 1920s Chinese movie magazines and newspaper film columns were full of articles protesting offensive foreign films. For example, one critic charged some foreign films with showing "white people's racial superiority" and "presenting themselves as the rulers of the whole world."[9] Another writer pointed out that there were hardly any "good Chinese" in "imported films." A Chinese theater owner, responding to such complaints, replied: "What you have seen is nothing compared to what we did not show. The ones that you have seen are among the least offensive because we have made a careful selection. If we showed every one of the imported movies that had Chinese in them, there would have been another Boxer uprising."[10] Thanks perhaps to the theater owners' careful selection, no uprising occurred, but the popular protests against offensive foreign movies did lead some people to complain about the government's "no interference, no support" policy in this matter. Zhou Jianyun, one of the founders of Star Film Studio (Mingxing), published an article criticizing the government's indifferent attitude toward film in *Mingxing tekan,* a movie magazine sponsored by the studio, one of the most influential in China in the 1920s.[11] Another critic also voiced his frustration with government policy, or rather its lack, in regard to the inflow of foreign films and called for establishing government control over the showing of films.[12]

Although the initiative for film censorship came from the general public and people in the film industry,[13] no concerted action was ever taken by them. It was not until 1928, when the Nanjing government was established, that the state began to respond to the Chinese public as well as the film industry's call for film censorship. In 1928, the Ministry of Internal Affairs issued *Thirteen Regulations on Film,* which explicitly stated that no films offensive to China and Chinese people's dignity could be shown in China.[14] Six months later, the Ministry of Interior joined the Ministry of Education to issue another set of regulations with a similar clause on offensive foreign films.[15] Then, in 1930, the Executive Yuan of the Nanjing government published the first film censorship law in China which also prohibited the

Fig. 1. *Welcome Danger.* USA. Harold Lloyd Corporation, 1929. British Film Institute.

showing of films that were contemptuous of the dignity of the Chinese people.[16] In other words, the Chinese government's policy was clearly stated and consistent with regard to offensive foreign films. In 1930 Harold Lloyd's film, *Welcome Danger,* became the first test case.

This film was brought to China in February 1930 and was shown in two theaters in Shanghai. The Chinese characters in this film are all presented as stupid, ridiculous, and uncouth. The premiere of *Welcome Danger* in Shanghai immediately sparked protests from Chinese audiences. An article signed by thirty-six people appeared in *Minguo ribao* (National daily), calling the attention of citizens of Shanghai to this objectionable foreign film. The authors of the article accused Lloyd of "degrading Chinese people" and called for public action against the showing of this film. However, the two theaters where the film was playing were located in the foreign concessions and did not heed the public reaction. They continued to show the film as scheduled. A group of angry college students planned a public protest,[17] but before they did so, another individual stood up, pointedly disrupted the film's screening, and made headlines in newspapers throughout Shanghai. This individual was Hong Shen.[18]

Hong was a well-known playwright. He went to the United States on a scholarship in 1916 and studied drama at Harvard. He returned to China in 1922 and became a prominent figure in the still unfolding New Culture Movement. He was also one of the cofounders of the Mingxing studio in the mid-1920s. At the time that popular resentment over Harold Lloyd's film was mounting, he was a professor of drama at Fudan University. Hearing that some university students intended to protest the showing of the film, Hong feared their protests might be perceived as mob action and hence not taken seriously. He decided to step in himself. He thought that his stature as one of the leading intellectuals in China and his social prestige as a university professor would add gravity to the protest. So, on February 23, 1930, Hong staged a protest in the Grand Theater (Da Guangming) against the screening of *Welcome Danger*.[19] According to the account of a contemporary witness, this is what happened:

Shortly before *Welcome Danger*'s 5:30 P.M. screening at the Grand Theater in Shanghai, Hong Shen rose from his seat and spoke to the audience. He told them that he had seen the 3:00 show of this film and found it offensive to Chinese dignity. He told the audience that he had purchased a ticket to the 5:30 show only in order to warn them about the film. The 350-member audience was quite moved by his speech and began to exit the theater in protest. The theater manager called the police, and Hong was arrested but later released on bail.[20]

The next day, Hong submitted a request to the Shanghai branch of the Nationalist Party asking that the Grand Theater be penalized for showing a film that insulted the Chinese people. In his letter to the party branch, Hong referred to an event that had taken place in the United States in 1924. A group of black people seized D. W. Griffith's *The Birth of A Nation* in a Chicago theater and burned it because the film was offensive to their sense of dignity. Later, the director of the film apologized and added another thousand feet of film glorifying black people. Hong then remarked: "We and the black people are both oppressed people. How can we Chinese fall behind American black people in reacting to this kind of humiliation and racism?"[21]

Soon after Hong's arrest, nine theater groups in Shanghai published a joint manifesto in his support. The manifesto decried the "cultural invasion"

Fig. 2. *Welcome Danger.* USA. Harold Lloyd Corporation, 1929. British Film Institute.

from the West and blamed the Chinese government for allowing the film to play in China. It condemned Hong Shen's arrest as an insult not only to Hong himself but to all Chinese theater people.[22]

The Chinese government also responded quickly. The Shanghai Board of Film Censors, the Nationalist Party's Shanghai branch, and Nanjing's Central Department of Propaganda jointly issued an order banning *Welcome Danger* throughout China.[23] As for the two theaters, since they were located in the foreign concession area and thus beyond the jurisdiction of the Chinese authorities, Hong took the case to the Shanghai Mixed Court. After a year of legal struggle, Hong won the case. The court ruled that (1) the film should never be shown in China again, (2) the American ambassador should make a formal apology to China's Ministry of Foreign Affairs, (3) Harold Lloyd, the director and star of the film, should write a formal letter apologizing to the Chinese people, (4) Capitol Theater, which also showed the film, should make a public apology in the newspapers, (5) the Grand Theater should be banned from advertising in newspapers, (6) the Grand Theater should donate five thousand *yuan* to schools, and (7) films shown in the foreign concession areas should also be subject to Chinese film censorship.[24]

This incident marked the beginning of Chinese government censorship of foreign films.[25] Soon after, the Nationalist government's Department of Propaganda and Board of Film Censors in Shanghai banned all Harold Lloyd movies in China.[26] In response, Lloyd wrote a letter to the American consulate in China, explaining that "the comedy was not intended as a reflection against Chinese dignity, but was simply made in the spirit of fun."[27] But that did not allay the Chinese audience's indignation. Several years later when another of Lloyd's films was brought to China, someone threw tear gas into the theater where the film was being shown. A note was found that read: "We have not yet forgotten the *Welcome Danger* incident!"[28] It was not just audiences who harbored a hatred for Lloyd; the government censors, too, held an animosity toward him. In August 1936, two American films were banned for their negative portrayals of Chinese people. One of them, *Cat's Paw,* was by Lloyd. The American consulate protested to the Ministry of Foreign Affairs, which in turn sent a letter of inquiry to the CFCC. The CFCC answered quite explicitly that Lloyd's previous offense was a factor in the ban on *Cat's Paw.*[29]

As this case shows, the censorship of foreign films in China originated from nationalistic resentment toward negative portrayals of China and the Chinese people.[30] The initiative came from the film industry and the movie-going public. The newly established Nanjing government responded to this nationalistic sentiment by implementing a firm policy and control apparatus. Once the National Film Censorship Committee was established in March 1931, it became an important tool by which the Chinese government could exert control over offensive foreign films. These operations greatly contributed to China's efforts to assert itself in the international community.

• Control over Foreign Films and Foreign Film Studio Activities in China

From March 1931, when the National Film Censorship Committee was inaugurated, to 1938, when it was dissolved, the NFCC/CFCC adopted an unflinching stand toward both offensive foreign films and foreign film studio activities in China.

One incident occurred in spring 1933 when the Chinese Ministry of Education received a report from Chinese students studying in Germany regarding a film called *Death in Shanghai* (Tod über Shanghai). The report said that the film, produced by Germany's Ultra-Ton Film Gesellschaft, ridiculed China and Chinese people. In response, the Ministry of Education brought the issue to the attention of the Ministry of Foreign Affairs, which in turn requested that German authorities destroy the film. Meanwhile, the National Film Censorship Committee stopped reviewing all German films produced by the studio.[31]

In November of the same year, after viewing a Columbia Pictures production titled *The Bitter Tea of General Yen,* the NFCC sent a letter to the studio's headquarters in Los Angeles via the Chinese consulate there, requesting a number of cuts. Columbia ignored the request, so the NFCC intensified pressure by suspending the review of all Columbia movies. Since according to the Film Censorship Statute no films could be shown in China without the NFCC's seal of approval, the suspension amounted to banning all Columbia movies from the China market. Columbia Pictures gave in to NFCC pressure and agreed to make the demanded cuts. To further assure the NFCC, Columbia Pictures invited Chinese diplomats in Los Angeles to its Hollywood headquarters to supervise and endorse the reediting of the film.[32]

There were no clearly stated rules delineating what was considered offensive, but judging from the list of banned foreign films and segments of foreign films that Chinese censors penciled for deletion, one can infer what qualified as taboo representations. These seem to include scenes that showed China as a backward country and her people as an uncivilized race;[33] scenes in which the Chinese appeared as villains,[34] as morally corrupt (smoking opium and gambling),[35] or even as servants;[36] and dialogue that ridiculed the Chinese and the Chinese way of life[37] or referred to the Chinese in a less than respectable way.[38]

The Chinese censors' attitudes became ever more stringent. In the early 1930s, many problematic foreign films could pass the censors by making the required cuts. In the case of banned films, their proprietors were required to submit to the NFCC/CFCC the customs receipts indicating that the films in question had been sent back to their countries of origin. In contrast, by 1936, fewer and fewer foreign films were given the option of editing. In some cases, the proprietors of banned films begged the CFCC for instructions as to what cuts they should make in order to receive the censors' approval but were rejected.[39] In August 1936, the CFCC went further by notifying major foreign studios that in the future all offending films, regardless of their degree of offensiveness, would be confiscated.[40] These measures apparently were very effective in calling the attention of foreign film producers to the issue and reducing the number of films that portrayed China in a negative light. In 1937, Samuel Goldwyn, one of the most influential movie producers in the United States, cautioned his colleagues to be more sensitive in their portrayals of Chinese.[41] Some studios in Hollywood began to hire Chinese advisers when filming subjects that involved China. For instance, during the production of *The Good Earth,* the film crew invited Du Tingxiu, one of the censors on the CFCC, to supervise production.[42] Clearly, by the mid-1930s, foreign film people well recognized the power and authority of the Chinese government's censors.

The National Film Censorship Committee's control over foreign films was not limited to censoring the undesirable contents of films but also involved regulating foreign studio activities in China. In June 1931, only three months into its operation, the NFCC drafted the *Regulations Regarding Foreigners Shooting Films in China.* These regulations were aimed at preventing foreigners from filming scenes that could later be used to disgrace China and Chinese people.[43]

The genuine indignation that fueled such measures overlapped with certain practical motivations. During the 1920s and 1930s, foreign films, especially Hollywood movies, dominated China's film market. Ninety percent of the films being shown were of foreign origin. This situation lasted until 1949.[44] During the 1920s all of Shanghai's first-class theaters were foreign owned. In economic terms, this was a significant factor in draining China's financial resources. According to one estimate, during the decade from the mid-1910s to the mid-1920s, more than twenty million *yuan* of Chinese money went into the hands of foreigners on movies alone each year.[45] Chinese filmmakers had long complained about the government's lack of control over the tremendous influx of foreign films. In an article published in *Dianying yuebao* (Film monthly), a publication sponsored by several major Shanghai studios, an author lamented that "in Japan, where filmmaking is not yet as highly developed as in China, the number of foreign films being shown in the theaters is limited to under 30 percent so as to guarantee domestically made films no less than 70 percent of showing time. . . . In comparison, there is no such control over foreign films in China. . . ." The author went on to point out that even Chinese-owned theaters had a disproportionate number of foreign films on their programs. "To change the situation," he suggested, "Chinese authorities must limit the number of foreign films being imported."[46]

Such an appeal articulated a common desire among Chinese filmmakers. Early Chinese filmmaking faced many obstacles. The operation of the camera, the mechanics of lighting, the technology of film developing, and so forth were all new to the first generation of Chinese filmmakers—so much so that Zhou Jianyun even questioned the validity of the term

"Chinese film," because, according to Zhou, all the materials used to make films were imported from foreign countries. He suggested that a more appropriate term, "Chinese-made films," be used instead.[47] Under these circumstances, winning an audience away from highly sophisticated foreign films was crucial to the survival of the Chinese film industry. In the 1920s, it was not unusual for a Chinese film to be praised merely on the grounds that everything on the screen was "clear" and recognizable.[48] Obviously, Chinese filmmakers had yet to master techniques of lighting, focus, and film developing.

Shortage of funds was another problem limiting what Chinese filmmakers could accomplish.[49] They often had to shoot a picture with only a few thousand *yuan,* a tiny fraction of what their Western counterparts could spend on a project. In addition, equipment and film stock had to be imported, and the technicians, often foreigners, demanded extravagant salaries. All this carved into filmmakers' already shallow pockets. Indeed, the infant Chinese film industry was in a very vulnerable position. Even during the industry's heyday, Chinese films had never more than 15 percent of the market.[50]

Although the quality of Chinese-made films was not always impressive, they were extremely popular among the lower strata of the urban populace. The demand seemed insatiable. One Chinese film critic explained: "No matter how 'bad' domestically made films are, they have one merit that foreign films don't have, namely, Chinese films are more intelligible to most of audiences. That is why the Chinese film industry experienced a boom in its early days. It is really not about patriotism."[51] Most foreign-owned theaters refused to show Chinese-made films; they only played in smaller, Chinese-owned theaters. In 1923, the British American Tobacco Company found film an effective means for advertising its products and started making films about Chinese life. Meanwhile, it planned to buy out all the smaller, Chinese-owned movie houses so that it could monopolize film distribution in China.[52] Fortunately for the Chinese film industry, the plan was aborted because the company got into financial trouble.[53]

In 1931, lured by the potential market, Paramount Pictures planned to buy off all Chinese film studios with $15 million. Allured by the tremendous "China market," Paramount intended to hire Chinese actors and directors and make "Chinese films" (in Chinese and about Chinese lives) for distribution in China. This plan was aborted, however, because Paramount failed to recruit the support and cooperation of China's business sector while also stumbling up against obstruction from the government.[54]

Still, the existence of an enormous audience of Chinese film lovers was irresistibly appealing to foreign companies. In July 1932, some American capitalists, with the help of some Chinese partners, launched another ambitious program: they wanted to build an "Oriental Hollywood" in Shanghai. As one source revealed, American investors planned to spend $2.5 million building China's Number One Sound Film studio and another $5 million for a smaller film studio called United Pictures.[55] They announced this plan in one of the major newspapers in Shanghai, *Morning News* (Chen bao) and invited people to purchase stock. In addition to advertising in the newspapers, they also tried to reach investors through the mail. In the words of one contemporary observer, "the Shanghai investing public is being bombarded both by mail and by huge newspaper advertisements."[56]

On July 21 Hong Shen, who had led the charge against *Welcome Danger*, published an article in the "Everyday Film" column of the *Morning News*. Hong pointed out that by buying off China's smaller studios first and then building their own studios in China, foreign imperialists would eventually wipe out the Chinese film industry and have total dominance over filmmaking in China. He warned his countrymen to be alert against this "economic and cultural invasion."[57]

Hong's article caused an immediate stir in the film world. A series of discussions on the buy-out plan soon erupted in newspapers and movie magazines. Most writers expressed concern about the plan's implications, echoing Hong's assertion that it amounted to cultural and economic invasion.[58] In an attempt to ease the Chinese public's anxiety, a representative of one of the two planned film studios refuted Hong, describing the slated companies as genuine joint ventures and not fully American owned. He further argued that art knew no borders and that China would have a better opportunity to learn and benefit from having American film studios producing films in China.[59]

People, however, were not convinced. Many film critics expressed their worries about the foreign invasion of China's film market and exhorted the government to take action to stop the trend.[60] One Chinese legal analyst questioned the legality of the two companies and possible implications for their investors. At this point, the NFCC intervened by requesting the Social Bureau of Shanghai to take action against the plan. The bureau then ordered the two companies to stop selling stock. As justification, the bureau asserted that the two companies had not registered with the local authorities before selling stock, thus their activities were illegal.[61] The two companies finally surrendered to the pressure from the Chinese authorities and film industry. The planning committee of the two companies dissolved upon receiving the Social Bureau's order.[62] A number of Chinese individuals working for the American planners made public announcements disassociating themselves from the companies.[63]

To a large extent, the defeat of these two companies could be attributed to the strong public opinion opposing them.[64] The government responded to the public protest and supported the effort to thwart the total buy-out plan. But the threat from foreign film companies continued to exist. For instance, in 1934, there was another attempt by some Americans to build a film studio in Shanghai.[65] In 1935, an American film studio was set up in Hong Kong with $1.5 million.[66]

To protect Chinese filmmakers from foreign competitors, the NFCC/CFCC adopted a series of measures to safeguard the best interests of China's film industry. Luo Gang, the chairman of the CFCC, stated quite explicitly in 1934, "Since we cannot control the quantity of foreign films being imported, we have to pick on their quality as a means of exerting our rights."[67] What Luo meant was that although China at this time did not have tariff autonomy and thus was unable to control the quantity of foreign goods being imported, including the quantity of foreign films, the CFCC did have the power to dictate what kinds of films could be imported, and this could be used as leverage against foreign film interests in China. One can even argue that the NFCC/CFCC willfully discriminated against foreign films. For instance, it charged foreign films reviewing fees while exempting Chinese films from such charges. Later when, out of necessity, it had to charge fees for Chinese films, they were significantly lighter than those charged foreign film companies.[68]

In November 1936, the Society for China's Cultural Reconstruction, a rather conservative group of intellectuals, sent a recommendation to the Ministry of Propaganda of the Nationalist Party suggesting that foreign films be shown with Chinese subtitles. The Ministry of Propaganda passed the recommendation on to the CFCC and asked the latter to decide the issue. In its reply, the CFCC stated:

> Despite the merits of the suggestion, we find it unwise to adopt it. We had a discussion about this issue among ourselves in the past, but decided it would not be a good idea to dub foreign films. . . . Chinese films fall behind Western countries in both technical sophistication and capital investment. In some ways, the revival of Chinese films in the last few years could be attributed to the fact that they don't pose a language problem for the audience. If we encourage foreign films to be projected with Chinese translations, we are going to entice more audience to foreign films. . . . This must not be forgotten.[69]

The need to protect the Chinese film industry affected the way in which film censorship was carried out by the NFCC/CFCC, which was often rather lenient with domestic productions while seemingly relentless with foreign ones. As the lists of censored films suggest, very few Chinese films were totally banned. In most cases, "problematic" Chinese films could pass the censors by making some cuts. Foreign films were rarely given that option. On more than one occasion a film was banned just because of one or two offensive scenes or lines of dialogue. According to one incomplete survey, about thirty American films were banned in 1936 and 1937,[70] whereas on average only two or three Chinese films were banned each year.[71]

It is difficult to measure in quantitative terms how the government's policy regarding foreign films affected the Chinese film industry. Nevertheless, these cases clearly demonstrate the NFCC/CFCC's nationalist position and the concrete steps it took to protect China's native film industry. Those who view the institution as nothing more than a suppressive force in the Chinese film world during the 1930s have failed to take the NFCC/CFCC's operations on the international front into account.

· The *New Land* Incident and the Campaign to Abolish Censorship by Foreign Powers

Although numerous foreign concessions returned to Chinese governance after 1927, the International Settlement (ruled by the British) and the French concession in Shanghai remained untouched, and foreign authorities continued to exert their power there. The French and English also enforced their own brand of film censorship in the concessions. As early as 1927, they set up a film censorship committee to control the films being shown in their jurisdiction.[72] The English dominated the committee, but following the model of the Mixed Court, it included two Chinese representatives, Zhu Boquan and Chen Liting. Power of censorial enforcement rested in the hands of the police in the concession areas. The function of the committee was to assist the police in film-related matters.[73]

The film censorship regulations in the foreign concessions were similar to those that existed in Great Britain and France. The major difference was that British and French censors in China were more sensitive to materials that were deemed detrimental to the best interests of their two nations. For instance, the British authorities in Shanghai prohibited any films showing criminals in British uniforms,[74] a rule that did not exist in censorship regulations enforced in Great Britain.

Foreign officials in the concessions never recognized the NFCC's authority, and they often allowed films banned by the NFCC to be shown in the concessions, while banning others approved by the Chinese censors. There was a long history of animosity between the two. In the summer of 1931, the NFCC requested the education and interior ministries to grant it full authority to deal with films in the foreign concessions, an obvious step to take on the foreign film censors. The Nationalist central government did not want to take a confrontational approach to the Western powers, however, so the two ministries turned down this request and ordered the NFCC to leave the matter to the officials in the provincial and municipal governments.[75] Thus rebuked, the NFCC insistently voiced its resentment toward the film censorship policy practiced in the concessions. For instance, in February 1933, it protested to the censors in the concession for allowing an anti-Chinese Japanese film to be shown in the theaters under their jurisdiction.[76]

Although the Chinese censors could not directly interfere in concession officials' film policy, the NFCC/CFCC had de facto control over the concession areas in matters related to film. Because the film producers and theater owners relied on newspapers to advertise their films, and the distribution of the newspapers in the Chinese district was under the Chinese government's control, the NFCC/CFCC could exert its authority in foreign concessions by controlling newspapers. One of the NFCC's rules was that no film without its seal of approval could be advertised in the newspapers; violation of this rule would result in penalties for both the film proprietor and the newspaper. For practical reasons, the film producers and theater owners in the concession willingly accepted the NFCC/CFCC's authority and submitted their films to Chinese censors for review.

The Chinese film censors in Nanjing and their counterparts in Shanghai's foreign concessions usually had similar standards with regard to amoral content in films and shared an aversion to graphic depictions of obscenity, cruelty, sexual activity, and so forth. Conflicts arose, however, over nationalistic Chinese films. The Chinese censors encouraged such films,[77] but those in the concessions frowned on them.

In September 1931, Japanese troops invaded Manchuria and a few months later attacked Shanghai. Nationalist sentiments in China were boiling. Chinese film audiences demanded that China's film studios produce patriotic films.[78] At one point, *Yingxi shenghuo* (Movie life), a popular film magazine, received more than six hundred letters from its readers, all asking film studios to produce anti-Japanese films. In response to the high tide of popular nationalism, film studios in Shanghai churned out a number of films that had clear anti-Japanese messages, including documentaries, cartoons, and feature films.[79] The veteran film director, Sun Yu, recalled this situation in 1932: "With the increased imperialist onslaught, we were convinced that the most needed films had to be the ones that inspired nationalist spirit."[80]

Most of these patriotic Chinese films were approved by the Chinese censors in Nanjing, because they accorded with the government's policy to indoctrinate the masses with nationalism. But the English and the French did not want to offend the Japanese and adopted a restrictive policy toward nationalist Chinese movies. They forbade any references in Chinese films to September 18 (the date Japanese troops moved into Manchuria) or January 28 (the date the Japanese attacked Shanghai). Even the image of China's map was proscribed because that would remind people of Manchuria's being part of China's territory.[81] Moreover, censorship in the foreign concession was not limited to movies; music, theater performances, and radio programs were all subject to the control of the foreign censors. Understandably, Chinese "cultural workers" (filmmakers, musicians, writers, and stage performers), the general public, and government censors were all infuriated by the restrictive policies of the foreign censors. They saw this as an infringement on China's sovereignty and an insult to China's national pride.[82] For years, however, the situation was tolerated except for occasional short-lived protests.[83]

The smoldering fuse of tolerance burned to a nub in the summer of 1937. The foreign censors in the concessions allowed the screening of a film titled *The New Land* (Xin tu), leading to an explosion of Chinese protests.

The New Land was a joint production of Japanese and German film studios.[84] As it turned out, "new land" in this film referred to Manchuria. The film's theme was to encourage Japanese to migrate to Manchuria. To drive that point home, the theme song of the film chorused: "Across the ocean is a vast land, awaiting you to tread on it. It is a new land!" The film ignored the fact that Manchuria was a part of Chinese territory and championed Japan's claim to it. The film also glorified Japan and Japanese culture and presented the Japanese as the bearers of a hopeful future for all Asian peoples. The mise-en-scène at the end of the film depicts a Japanese soldier's silhouette against a brilliant rising sun.[85]

Right after the premiere of the movie in Shanghai, more than one hundred citizen groups protested against its exhibition. Their anger was first directed at a Chinese newspaper that advertised this film and the Chinese owner of the theater that premiered the film. They appealed to the Chinese authorities to punish the newspaper and the theater. Meanwhile, more than one hundred forty celebrities from the entertainment industry publicly denounced the film. They, too, asked the Chinese government to take action and demanded that copies of the film be destroyed. According to China's Film Censorship Statute no film could be shown without the CFCC's approval, and *The New Land* did not have such approval. Some began to question why the censors in the foreign concessions treated the Japanese film as an exception.[86]

It is noteworthy that, unlike their counterparts in the West, the Chinese cultural elite never rejected government film censorship.[87] The majority of this group even welcomed government control over the film industry.[88] The issue here was rather which governmental authorities should exercise censorship. The campaign to abolish censorship in the foreign concessions certainly reflected Chinese indignation over the policy practiced by the concession authorities, and it was also in accord with the Nanjing government's stand with regard to this issue. Although not sponsored by the Chinese government, the campaign had the support of government officials and played a role in the larger movement to take back China's sovereignty over the foreign concessions.

Despite the sound and fury over this film, *The New Land* continued to be shown in the foreign concession areas. While being restrictive toward nationalistic Chinese film, the censors in the concessions took a very different stand toward this Japanese-German production. Anticipating possible Chinese protests, the concession authorities sent extra police to the theater where the film was scheduled for screening to "maintain order." This discriminatory act further angered the Chinese. The pent-up frustrations with censorship practices in the concessions finally exploded. As one Chinese writer charged, *The New Land* violated China's Film Censorship Statute because "it insulted our nation's sovereignty. It also violated the standard procedure as stipulated in the *Procedures for Implementing the Film Censorship Statute* because it was not sent to the CFCC for review. Yet, the censors in the foreign concessions not only allowed its screening, but also sent police to safeguard the premiere. Such discriminatory treatment is outrageous!"[89]

The turning point of the movement came when the Association of Educational Film held its sixth conference. At the conference, the association passed a resolution to appeal to the Nationalist Party's central authorities to negotiate with authorities in the foreign concessions to abolish their film censorship.[90] The protests against the showing of *The New Land* had now turned into a campaign to abolish film censorship by foreigners in China altogether. It should be noted that the Association of Educational Film was a semigovernmental institution. It was partially funded by the CFCC, and its top officials included people like Pan Gongzhan (secretary of the Central Propaganda Department), Zhang Daofan (a high-ranking party official), Shao Lizi (a member of the party central committee), Chen Lifu (an ideologue of the party), and Luo Gang (director of the CFCC). With this organization joining the cause, the campaign to abolish film censorship in the concessions became officially sanctioned.

Soon, the Executive Committee of the newly founded Shanghai Film Studio Association called on its members to join the cause.[91] Two days later, the association held another meeting and invited representatives from the Nationalist Party, the government, and sixteen other civic organizations to discuss the situation.[92] The participants of this meeting decided to expand the scope of the campaign. They wanted not only to abolish film censorship in the concessions but also music and theater censorship as well.[93]

The commotion reached its peak on July 11, when the representatives of all arts and literary organizations in Shanghai gathered in the conference room of the Shanghai Chamber of Commerce and celebrated the formation of the campaign committee. In addition to submitting a request to the Nationalist central government in Nanjing, in which they asked the government to settle this matter through diplomatic channels, the committee also sent appeals to the lower house of Great Britain's Parliament, U.S. President Franklin D. Roosevelt, and the Association for International Cultural Cooperation in France, asking for their sympathies and cooperation.

The campaign committee also published a manifesto that enumerated several cases that involved abuses of power by the authorities in the foreign concessions. The manifesto charged the censors in the foreign concessions with "exercising discriminatory treatment toward Chinese filmmakers, song writers and theater people. . . . While being restrictive with the Chinese, the concession authorities allowed the Japanese aggressor's propaganda to invade China." In the end, it announced that the cultural workers of Shanghai would firmly stand behind the government in this confrontation with the British and French imperialists.[94]

On July 15, a few days after the campaign committee's inauguration, the Guomindang's *Zhongyang ribao* (Central daily) reported the event and published a part of the campaign's manifesto.[95] The Nationalist Party's Central Propaganda Committee also sent a request to the Executive Yuan, asking its permission to allow the Ministry of Foreign Affairs to settle the issue with the concession authorities.[96] But before any result came out of this campaign to abolish censorship in the concessions, the war with Japan broke out full-scale. All nationalist organizing shifted attention to the new crisis. New organizations were formed, new programs declared. China now needed cooperation from, not confrontation with, the British and the French.

In all these cases, whether they involved censoring of offensive foreign films, control of foreign film studio activities, or the campaign to abolish foreign censorship, anti-imperialism was a driving force. The Chinese government banned foreign film that contained negative depictions of China and Chinese people, in part, because those portrayals deviated from the image that the Nanjing government was trying to project to the world, namely, a China that was progressive, civilized, and modern. In this sense, the effort was more than trivial. It was a way to reassert China's position in the international community.

The confrontation with foreign forces often brought the Chinese government, the film industry, and the general public, who otherwise had very different interests, into a coalition. In contrast to its operations on the domestic front, the NFCC/CFCC's censorial efforts worked very effectively on the foreign front, largely because of the popular support and cooperation from the Chinese film industry as well as the general public. The NFCC/CFCC and the Chinese film industry had a common interest in fighting foreign films and therefore were supportive of each other. Instead of being a suppressive force, the NFCC/CFCC protected the Chinese film industry from foreign competitors. Although there were tensions between Chinese filmmakers and government censors, by and large, the Chinese filmmakers welcomed the government's control over the films because that control served their interests. The NFCC/CFCC understood this and exploited the film industry's support and cooperation for its own ends. In picking on foreign films and foreign film studios' activities in China, the NFCC/CFCC gained popularity and legitimacy for itself and became a power to be reckoned with.

Both the film industry and the government censors exploited the rhetoric of nationalism in their public claims. The industry exploited this rhetoric so that it could enlist the government's help and public sympathy in its competition with foreign rivals. The government made political gains by playing the protective role. In so doing, it won the film industry's cooperation and rallied popular support. But when it came to issues involving domestic films, the cooperation between the NFCC/CFCC and the Chinese film industry became much more elusive and problematic.

· Notes

1. Wu Songgao, "Shi nian lai de Zhongguo waijiao" [China's diplomatic achievements in the last ten years], *Shi nian lai zhi Zhongguo* [China in the last ten years], ed. Zhongguo Wenhua Jianshe Xiehui (1937; reprint, Hong Kong: Longmen shudian, 1965), 27–52.

2. Martin Wilbur, "The Nationalist Revolution: From Canton to Nanjing, 1923–1928," in *Cambridge History of China,* ed. John K. Fairbank, vol. 12 (Cambridge: Cambridge University Press, 1983), 599–603.

3. "Zhongguo Guomindang di san ci quanguo daibiao dahui waijiao baogao" [The work report on foreign relations at the party's third plenum], in *Geming wenxian di qishier ji: Kangzhan qian guojia jianshe shiliao-wai jiao fangmian* [Revolutionary documents, vol. 72: The decade of reconstruction before the war: Foreign relations], ed. Zhongguo Guomindang zhongyang weiyuanhui dangshi weiyuanhui (Taibei, 1977), 280–320.

4. By the late 1930s most film studios in the West had begun to prohibit unfavorable presentation of other peoples in their movie productions. See John E. Harley, *World-wide Influences of the Cinema: A Study of Official Censorship and the International Cultural Aspects of Motion Pictures* (Los Angeles: University of Southern California Press, 1940).

5. Cheng Jihua, *Zhongguo dianying fazhan shi* [The history of the development of Chinese cinema] (Beijing: Zhongguo dianying chuban she, 1981), 13–15.

6. Richard C. Patterson, Jr., "The Cinema in China," *China Weekly Review,* March 12, 1927, 48.

7. Paul K. Whang, "Boycotting of Harold Lloyd's *Welcome Danger,*" *China Weekly Review,* March 8, 1930, 51.

8. K.K.K., "Ping *Yi kuai qian* yu *Shen seng*" [A review of *Yi kuai qian* and *Shen seng*], *Yingxi chunqiu* 9 (1925).

9. Yin Min, "Yingpian shang zhi you se renzhong" [Colored people on the screen], *Dianying zhoukan* 9 (May 1924).

10. Chen Dabei, "Zhongguo yingpian qiye jia de san ge e meng" [The three nightmares of Chinese filmmakers], *Dongfang zazhi* 21, no. 16 (1924).

11. Zhou Jianyun, "Wu sa can an hou zhi Zhongguo ying xi jie" [The situation of Chinese cinema and theater in the post-May Thirtieth era], *Mingxing tekan* 3 (1925).

12. Zheng Chaoren, "Ge guo dianying qudi ji shencha tiaoli" [An introduction to film censorship in other countries], *Dianying yuebao* 8 (1928).

13. Zhou Jianyun, "Dianying shencha wenti" [The question of film censorship], *Dianying yuebao* 1, no. 5 (1928).

14. "Neizheng bu gongbu dianying pian jiancha guize" [The Ministry of Interior announced regulations regarding film censorship], *Shen bao,* September 6, 1928.

15. "Jiao nei liang bu gongbu dianying pian jiancha guize" [The Ministries of Education and the Interior announce regulations on film censorship], *Shen bao,* April 19, 1929.

16. For details of the Film Censorship Statute, see Zhiwei Xiao, "Film Censorship in China, 1927–1937," Ph.D. diss., University of California, San Diego, 1994.

17. Huang Su, "Women duiyu *Bu pa si* shijian de pinglun zhi pinglun" [Our views regarding the views on *Welcome Danger*], *Dianying* 1 (1930).

18. Zhi Song, "Zhuishu *Bu pa si* shijian de jiaoshe jingguo" [A recollection of the *Welcome Danger* incident], *Dian sheng* 5, no. 47 (November 1936): 1247. In this account, the author traced the incident to March 22, 1930, which is a mistake. The event took place on February 23, 1930.

19. Whang, "Boycotting," *China Weekly Review,* March 8, 1930, 51.

20. Zhi, "Zhuishu *Bu pa si* shijian de jiaoshe jingguo."

21. Huang, "Women duiyu *Bu pa si* shijian de pinglun zhi pinglun."

22. "Yingpian shang de guochi" [The national disgrace on the screen], *Minguo ribao*, February 26, 1930.

23. Ru Ling, "Duiyu Meiguo ruhua yingpian de yi ci zhuangyan de shenpan" [A righteous protest against an offensive American film], *Dazhong dianying* 5-6, 1961.

24. Zhi, "Zhuishu *Bu pa si* shijian de jiaoshe jingguo."

25. "Harold Lloyd Apologizes Over Showing of *Welcome Danger*," *China Weekly Review*, June 7, 1930.

26. "Harold Lloyd Films All Banned," *China Weekly Review*, May 10, 1930, 430; Ru Ling, "Duiyu Meiguo ruhua yingpian de yi ci zhuangyan de shenpan."

27. "Harold Lloyd Apologizes Over Showing of *Welcome Danger*," 38.

28. "Kai ying Luoke yingpian, Daguangming xiyuan bei ren tou liu lei wasi dan" [Grand Theater was bombed with tear gas for showing a Lloyd's film], *Dian sheng* 5, no. 13 (1936): 304.

29. *Zhongyang dianying jiancha weiyuanhui gongbao* [The bulletin of the Central Film Censorship Committee] 3, no. 8 (August 1936): 2 (hereafter, ZYGB).

30. It should be noted here, however, that there were a few people who opposed banning offensive foreign films. They argued that Chinese audiences ought to be given an opportunity to see those films so that they would become more patriotic. Besides, even if those films were banned in China they were being shown in other parts of the world, so the ban would not make much sense. See Xiao Luo, "Women xuyao wuru" [Do we need to be insulted?], *Dianying shibao*, August 18, 1932. Lu Xun also expressed a similar opinion. See Li Houji, "Lu Xun xiansheng zai dianying zhanxian shang" [Mr. Lu Xun on cinema], *Dianying wenxue* 9 (1961): 2-5.

31. *Dianying jiancha weiyuanhui gongzuo baogao* [Work report of the Film Censorship Committee], Nanjing, 1934, 100-102 (hereafter, GZBG).

32. GZGB, 91-92.

33. For example, *Wandering Through China* was banned because it showed China as a backward country. See *Jiao nei liang bu dianying shencha weiyuanhui gongbao* [The bulletin of the National Film Censorship Committee) 1, no. 1 (1932): 73 (hereafter, JNGB).

34. *The Bitter Tea of General Yen* (Columbia, 1933) was banned because it portrays Chinese soldiers as cruel and vicious. See GZBG, 90-94.

35. In *Klondike Annie* (Paramount, 1936), there is a scene of Chinese smoking opium and gambling. The film was banned throughout China. See *China Weekly Review*, November 14, 1936, 398.

36. Many foreign films were banned for this reason. One of the earlier examples was *Thief of Bagdad* (Fox, 1924). JNGB 1, no. 1 (January 1932): 77.

37. For example, *Shanghai Express* (Paramount, 1932) was banned because of remarks such as "Time and life have no value in China" by one of the characters in the movie. See JNGB 1, no. 7 (July 1932): 4-5.

38. GZBG, 92-93.

39. ZYGB 3, no. 9 (September 1936): 7.

40. ZYGB 8 (August 1936): 11.

41. Harley, *World-wide Influences,* 23.

42. "Pailameng yingpian jinhou bu de zai woguo kaiying" [Paramount films banned in China], *Dian sheng* 5, no. 46 (1936): 1224–1226. See also Dorothy B. Jones, *The Portrayal of China and India on the American Screen, 1896–1955: The Evolution of Chinese and Indian Themes, Locales, and Characters as Portrayed on the American Screen* (Cambridge, Mass.: Center for International Studies, MIT, 1955), 43–47.

43. GZBG, 21; *Dian sheng* 5, no. 35 (September 6, 1936): 888.

44. *Haolaiwu de qinlüe* [The invasion from Hollywood] (Beijing: Shiyue chuban she, 1951).

45. Wang Jingtao, "Dianying jie muqian de xuyao" [What Chinese film industry needs?], *Yingxi chunqiu* 9 (1925).

46. Ji An, "Fa kan ci" [The opening remarks], *Dianying yuebao* 1, no. 1 (April 1, 1928).

47. Zhou Jianyun, "Zhongguo yingpian zhi qiantu [2]" [The future of Chinese cinema, part II], *Dianying yuebao* 1, no. 2 (1928).

48. The phrase "sufficient lighting" was used frequently by film critics to praise a film. For example, see the review articles on *Gujing chongbo ji* [The ancient well, 1923], *Shen bao,* May 3, 1923, and April 28, 1924. See also Qing Shi, "Zi zhi yingpian de quedian" [The shortcomings of Chinese-made movies], *Dianying zazhi* 18 (July 4, 1924): 8–10.

49. Zhou Jianyun, "Zhongguo yingpian zhi qiantu" [The future of Chinese cinema, part III], *Dianying yuebao* 1, no. 3 (1928).

50. Luo Gang, "Zhongguo xiandai dianying shiye zhi niaokan" [An overview of China's film industry], *Jiao yu xue yuekan* 1, no. 8 (1936).

51. Chen Dabei, "Zhongguo dianying zhi jianglai" [The future of Chinese film], *Dianying yuebao* 7 (1928).

52. He Weixin, "Zhongguo dianying jie ji da de weiji" [The biggest crisis of the Chinese film industry], *Yingxi chunqiu* 6 (April 5, 1925).

53. Cheng, *Zhongguo dianying fazhan shi,* 121–127.

54. Wan Cheng, "Chu mu jing xin de xiaoxi" [Shocking news], *Yingxi shenghuo* 1, no. 6 (1931).

55. Xi, "Jin yi bu de jiantao" [A further examination], *Chen bao,* August 1, 1932.

56. "Talking Picture Prospectuses Which Do Not 'Say' Enough," *China Weekly Review,* July 23, 1932, 266.

57. Hong Shen, "Meiguo ren wei shenmo yao dao Zhongguo lai ban yingpian gongsi she Zhongguo pian" [Why are Americans coming to China to set up movie studios and make 'Chinese' films?), *Chen bao,* July 21, 1932.

58. See articles appearing in *Chen bao* between July and September 1932 and *Dianying yishu* 1 (1932).

59. Dao Yan, "Yu Hong Shen xiansheng tan Zhongguo diyi you sheng yingpian gongsi" [A reply to Mr. Hong regarding China's Number One sound film studio], *Chen bao,* July 27, 1932.

60. Bu Shaotian, "Dianying de moluo" [The degradation of the movies], *Chen bao,* August 3, 1932.

61. Mao Zhenchu, "Zhongguo diyi ji lianhe liang gongsi zhi zuzhi feifa" [The illegality of China's Number One and United Pictures], *Chen bao,* August 1, 1932.

62. Qing Niao, "Jin yi bu de baolu" [Further exposure], *Chen bao,* August 10, 1932.

63. Zhen Chu, "Zhongguo diyi gongsi yi cheng wajie" [The collapse of China's Number One Company], *Chen bao,* August 9, 1932.

64. Tong Zhen, "Yi jiu san er nian women de yintan" [Our film industry in 1932], *Chen bao,* January 10, 1933.

65. See "Mei yue ying tan" [The monthly movie news], *Dianying huabao* 18 (1935): 3.

66. See Shui Jiang, "Meiren zai Gang chuang dongfang gongsi" [Americans set up Oriental Studio in Hong Kong], *Dianying xinwen* I, no. 6 (August 11, 1935): 3.

67. Luo Gang, "Zhongguo xiandai dianying shiye zhi niaokan."

68. Typically, a foreign film was charged 20 *yuan* per 500 meters whereas Chinese film was only charged 15 *yuan* for the whole film. See *Yingxi zazhi* 2, no. 2 (October 1931). See also *China Weekly Review,* April 6, 1936, 204.

69. ZYGB 3, no. II (November 1936): 2.

70. Harley, *World-wide Influences,* 112–113.

71. These data are based on JNGB and ZYGB, 1932–1937.

72. Some Americans residing in China at the time believed that the whole purpose of this initiative was to protect the English and French films from Hollywood's competition in China. See the editorial article, "American Movie Interests Should Watch This," *China Weekly Review,* March 30, 1927, 210.

73. "Zujie ying jian hui zuzhi" [Film censorship in foreign concessions], *Dian sheng* 3, no. 49 (December 21, 1934).

74. "Nanyang jin ying yingpian zhi biaozhun" [The prohibited subjects in Southeast Asia], *Dian sheng* 3, no. 44 (November 1934).

75. JNGB I, no. I (1932): 6.

76. GZBG, 27.

77. GZBG, 5.

78. Kui, "Guanyu aiguo junshi pian" [On patriotic war films], *Chen bao,* October 4, 1932.

79. Cheng, *Zhongguo dianying fazhan shi,* 180.

80. Sun's article was published in *Dianying* 13 (1932).

81. See the editorial article in *Dian sheng* 6, no. 26 (July 1937).

82. "Guanyu gongbuju jiancha dianying shi" [About the film censorship in the foreign concessions], *Chen bao,* October 26, 1932.

83. For instance, in 1936, two Chinese theater groups, the Shiyan Xiao Juchang (Experimental theater) and the Mayi Jutuan (Ant theater), were banned by the censors in the International Settlement because of their alleged nationalistic orientations. This led the theater people to join the cause. See *Mingxing ban yuekan* 6, no. 1 (1936).

84. Americans tended to view this film as an effort to counter the Sino-U.S. coproduction, *The Good Earth,* but that was not how the Chinese saw it. See *China Weekly Review,* April 17, 1937.

85. Tie Bi, "*Xin tu* yingpian shi ying hou ji" [Reflections on *The New Land*], *Dian sheng* 6, no. 23 (1937): 996.

86. Tie, "*Xin tu* yingpian shi ying hou ji," 997, 1117, 1005.

87. In fact, the Chinese response to Mrs. Roosevelt's call to abolish censorship was a negative one. Chinese filmmakers and members of the cultural elite believed in the necessity of government control over cultural expressions. See the editorial article in *Dian sheng* 3, no. 13 (1934).

88. See the editorial article in *Dianying huabao* 8 (1934): 4.

89. See the editorial article in *Dian sheng* 6, no. 26 (1937).

90. *Zhongyang ribao,* May 28, 1937.

91. *Dianying shibao,* June 15, 1937.

92. *Dianying shibao,* June 18, 1937.

93. *Dian sheng* 6, no. 27 (July 1937): 1158.

94. *Dian sheng* 6, no. 27 (July 1937): 1196–1204.

95. "Wenhua jie kangyi zujie jiancha xiju dianying" [Protests from Chinese artists against censorship in foreign settlement], *Zhongyang ribao,* July 15, 1937.

96. *Dian sheng* 6, no. 28 (July 16, 1937): 1193.

Chapter 2

•

Two Stage Sisters

The Blossoming of a Revolutionary Aesthetic

•

Gina Marchetti

On the eve of the Great Proletarian Cultural Revolution in 1964, Xie Jin brought to the screen a story about the changing lives of women in twentieth-century China set against the backdrop of the Shaoxing opera world. Although rooted in the intimate story of two actresses and the vicissitudes of their relationship, Xie gave the film, *Two Stage Sisters* (Wutai jiemei), an epic scope by showing these women's lives buffeted by tremendous social and political upheavals.[1] The film covers the years from 1935 to 1950, the expanses of the Zhejiang countryside as well as Shanghai under Japanese, Guomindang, and Communist rule.

Chunhua (Xie Fang), a young widow about to be sold by her in-laws, escapes and becomes an apprentice in a traveling Shaoxing folk opera troupe. Yuehong (Cao Yindi), who plays the male roles in the all-female opera company, befriends Chunhua. After the death of Yuehong's father, Chunhua and Yuehong find themselves sold to a Shanghai opera theater to replace the fading star, Shang Shuihua (Shangguan Yunzhu). Eventually, Yuehong falls in love with their manipulative stage manager, Tang (Li Wei), and the sisters quarrel and separate.

Inspired by the radical woman journalist, Jiang Bo (Gao Yuansheng), Chunhua continues her career, giving a political flavor to her performances. After an attempt to blind and ruin Chunhua by using Yuehong's testimony to trick her in court, Tang goes off to Taiwan to escape the revolution. Although unable to harm her stage sister in court, Yuehong has been publicly humiliated. Abandoned by Tang, she disappears into the countryside. After Shanghai's liberation by the Communists, however, Chunhua manages to track down Yuehong, and the two reconcile.

Two Stage Sisters uses the theatrical world of Shaoxing as a metaphor for political and social change. The film also represents a search for a Chinese cinema aesthetic based on these traditions as well as on Hollywood and socialist realist forms. This analysis will explore the intermingling of these aesthetic currents and the ways in which art and politics intertwine in *Two Stage Sisters*. By placing the film within the context of the political and cultural movements that spawned it, the drama of the development of Chinese cinema aesthetics since 1949 can be understood more clearly.

• The Place of *Two Stage Sisters* in Xie Jin's Career

Xie Jin's own background made him particularly well-qualified to direct this tale of Shaoxing opera and Shanghai's theatrical world. Xie was born in Shaoxing (Zhejiang province) in 1923. At the age of eight, he and his family moved to Shanghai. From an early age, Xie was fascinated by the theater and cinema. While growing up in the 1930s, he had the opportunity to see the work of directors like Cai Chusheng, Sun Yu, and Yuan Muzhi, the cream of Shanghai film's "golden era." Also, he began a life-long enthusiasm for the Shaoxing opera of the region.

During the Japanese occupation, Xie moved to Sichuan province in the interior and studied theater at the Jiangen Drama Academy. There, he worked with noted theatrical personalities like Huang Zuolin and Zhang Junxiang. In Shanghai and Sichuan, Xie encountered both Chinese folk traditions and Western dramatic and cinematographic forms. This blending of these two traditions came to characterize his mature work.

When Zhang Junxiang accepted work at the Datong film studio in Shanghai in 1948, Xie went along as his assistant director. After 1949, Xie continued on in Shanghai, codirecting *A Wave of Unrest* (Yichang fengbo; also translated as *An Incident*) with Lin Nong in 1954. His first solo effort was *Spring Days in Water Village* (Shuixiang de chuntian; also translated as *Spring Over the Irrigated Land*) in 1955. From the mid-1950s to the mid-1960s, Xie's style matured in an aesthetic crucible that ground together Hollywood classicism, Soviet socialist realism, Shanghai dramatic traditions, and indigenous Chinese folk opera forms.

Many of Xie's films focus on the lives of women, workers, artists, or students. *Woman Basketball Player No. 5* (Nülan wuhao, 1957) explores the problems that a young female athlete faces in coming to grips with her ambitions in the field of sports. *The Red Detachment of Women* (Hongse niangzijun, 1961) deals with the heroism of women who go from peasant life to guerrilla warfare in the 1930s. *Two Stage Sisters* explores the lives of women working on the Chinese stage. In all these films, women's lives represent both hardship and oppression as well as the potential for revolutionary change. In fact, throughout most of his career, Xie Jin has been at the forefront of the exploration of different representations of women within socialist cinema.

With the condemnation of Xie's comedy, *Big Li, Little Li, and Old Li* (Da

Li, Xiao Li, he Lao Li, 1962), and *Two Stage Sisters* (1964) soon after, followed by the complete shutdown of the Shanghai studios, Xie's output dwindled to next to nothing during the Cultural Revolution. During that period, however, Xie did work on two films based on model operas—*The Port* (Haigang, 1972; also translated as *On the Docks*) and *Panshiwan* (1975).[2] Since 1976, Xie has made several films, including *Youth* (Qingchun, 1977), *Ah, Cradle* (A! Yaolan, 1979), *The Legend of Tianyun Mountain* (Tianyunshan chuanqi, 1980), *The Herdsman* (Muma ren, 1982), *Qiu Jin* (1983), *Garlands at the Foot of the Mountain* (Gaoshan xia de huahuan, 1984), *Hibiscus Town* (Furong zhen, 1986), and *The Last Aristocrats* (Zuihou de guizu, 1989).

These films made after the Cultural Revolution show a marked change in Xie's oeuvre. Diverging from his earlier films that deal with and ostensibly support socialist revolution, the later works seem to be more nationalistic than revolutionary in character. Several explicitly criticize past party policies.[3]

· The Theatrical World of *Two Stage Sisters*

Two Stage Sisters is one of the few films made at that time in the People's Republic of China (PRC) to be based on an original screenplay rather than a script adapted from a well-known and accepted literary or dramatic work. However, the film still remains deeply indebted to the literary and theatrical world of modern China. In fact, the entire film revolves around the theater and uses the stage to underscore the changes in its protagonists' lives as well as the dramatic political changes that occurred between 1935 and 1950.

The first third of *Two Stage Sisters* deals with the itinerant opera theater of Zhejiang province. Shaoxing opera differs considerably from the Beijing-style opera better known outside of China. Although Beijing opera has set a certain standard of performance that has influenced regional styles considerably, other non-Mandarin-language opera styles have existed and continue to flourish in most regions of China. According to Colin Mackerras' account of Chinese opera, Shaoxing opera originated in the later days of the Qing dynasty and is, therefore, a rather recent addition to the history of Chinese regional theater.[4] Arising out of folk music traditions in the countryside, Shaoxing eventually became popular in urban areas, where it began to be performed in permanent theaters as well as tea houses and open-air market pavilions.

The prevalence of all-female troupes makes Shaoxing stand out among other Chinese regional opera forms. Records show that in 1923 an all-female company performed in Shanghai. Eventually, schools were started in the countryside for actresses, and many troupes either added women to their companies or performed with exclusively female casts.

Because of its elegant costumes, complex gestures, and often intricate plot lines, many may be under the mistaken impression that Chinese opera is an art form exclusively for aristocrats, intellectuals, and the wealthy. Although performed at court and patronized by powerful landlords and businessmen, Chinese opera has always remained a folk form enjoyed by a broad range of people in Chinese society. In fact, the opening sequence of *Two Stage Sisters* delineates the differences between the glittering fantasy of the stage performance and the poverty of both the players and their audience. Performed in marketplaces and financed by the passing of a hat, opera could be listened to and enjoyed by everyone regardless of social station or gender. The volume and exaggerated articulation of the singing, the use of stylized gestures in pantomimes, and the elaborate costumes attracted the attention of passersby, who may have had no intention of watching the opera but who were drawn in by the commotion.

If nothing else, Chinese opera is loud, and its extensive use of percussion instruments like the *ban* (clapper) not only emphasizes important actions for dramatic effect but also reminds an audience preoccupied with gambling, bartering, snoozing, or chitchat that something important is happening on stage. Thus, as Chunhua's escape from her in-laws causes a tremendous ruckus in an already cacophonous marketplace, Yuehong, playing the young gentleman, and Xiao Xing, another actress playing a comic servant, as indicated by the white band of makeup across her nose, barely bat an eye and continue singing.

Although many urban intellectuals were attracted to and wrote for the opera stage and although a select few opera performers such as the noted female impersonator of Beijing opera, Mei Lanfang, achieved super-stardom, most opera singers and musicians were of peasant stock and as poor as their audiences. Most of these itinerant performers, much like the theater artists of the Elizabethan stage, were treated like thieves and prostitutes and considered the lowest rung of society. Despite this stigma, however, desperate women, trying to escape the harshness of the feudal peasant family in an overpopulated countryside bled dry by greedy landlords, continuously fueled the Shaoxing opera ranks.

In many ways, the life story of the Shaoxing actress Fan Ruijuan parallels that of the fictitious Chunhua in *Two Stage Sisters*. Fan's account of her life on the Shaoxing stage reflects the same sense of desperation and determination evident in the film. As Fan Ruijuan states in her memoir, hers was not an uncommon life:

I was only II when I joined a Shaoxing opera theater in 1935. At that time, more than 20,000 of the 400,000 people living in Chengxian County, my native place in Zhejiang Province and the birthplace of Shaoxing Opera, had left their homes to become opera singers. Life was hard. My family was living on bran cakes, sweet potatoes and clover, which were all we could afford on father's meager income as an odd job man. To me, opera singing seemed to be the only alternative to the miserable life of a childbride.[5]

Ironically, for Fan as well as for Chunhua in *Two Stage Sisters,* joining the Shaoxing opera meant jumping from the frying pan into the fire. Early opera training for these young girls consisted of beatings, starvation, humiliation, and long hours of hard labor. Virtually enslaved to the troupe's manager, opera performers often worked for room and board alone in order to pay for their training. Underfed and often lice-ridden or tubercular, they were forced to travel miles on foot through winter storms and still perform flawlessly the moment the troupe arrived at its destination.

Aside from being indentured to a theatrical manager, opera performers were also looked upon as sexually available to customers. Throughout the history of Chinese opera, stories abound about young boys taken into opera companies to play female roles and act as homosexual prostitutes. Traveling female performers also were known to serve as prostitutes. When the opera troupe in *Two Stage Sisters* performs an all-night engagement, expectations extend beyond the singing of opera tunes. Lord Ni, a wealthy land owner, hopes to enjoy more than an evening of opera from Yuehong and Chunhua as an unspoken part of his agreement.

This incident not only underscores opera performers' lack of power over their lives, but it also brings out the ironic contrast between the fantasies performed on stage and the actual lives of the Shaoxing actresses. Yuehong as the young gentleman scholar and Chunhua as the innocent ingénue sing operas about romantic love. Yet, this type of romance was completely beyond the expectations of young women born into a brutally patriarchal society of arranged marriages, child brides, concubines, prostitution, and child slavery.

Many operas feature dynamic female generals, swordswomen, and female fairy spirits with martial talents supported by a will to exercise them. In contrast, the lives of the actresses in Shaoxing opera only testify to the powerlessness of women in the Chinese countryside. In one scene, for example, the local policeman sent by Lord Ni, after Yuehong refused the lord's advances, drags off and pillories a defiant Chunhua, still wearing the opera costume associated with a female warrior role. Chunhua resists, but to no avail. Romance and martial victory for women on stage contrast sharply with oppression, humiliation, and total impotence off stage.

The theatrical world Yuehong and Chunhua enter in the Shanghai of 1941 is, in many ways, as harsh and demanding as the one left behind in the countryside. However, they also enter an urban environment very different from rural life. Shanghai was a thriving port filled with Western concessions not allowed in other parts of China during the late Qing and early Republican periods. It had a reputation as a wide-open port and city of intrigue, which continued through the Japanese occupation and civil war periods depicted in *Two Stage Sisters.* Shanghai was a center of progressive ideas and innovative theatrical forms, as well as a haven for those drawn to its seamier side of money, power, and corruption. Notorious for harboring revolutionists, the Shanghai theater district was home to many actors-turned-activists from the turn of the century.

When a demonstration in Beijing on May 4, 1919, led to China's refusal to sign the Treaty of Versailles because it favored Japanese interests in Asia, the Shanghai intellectual community also helped to usher in a new movement begun with the demonstration and called the May 4th or New Culture Movement. Trying to bring China into the modern world, artists, politicians, literary and theatrical figures, young scholars, and students in all disciplines looked to both Western culture and a new sense of Chinese nationalism for inspiration.

Although many artists involved with the May 4th Movement tried to survive in Shanghai under the Japanese occupation, most involved in radical politics fled either to the Communist Party strongholds around Yan'an or the Guomindang-controlled areas in the south. Traditional opera and the world of light entertainment, however, managed business as usual under the Japanese.

After World War II, Shanghai once again fell under the control of the Guomindang. In *Two Stage Sisters,* the bitter political struggles that ensued between the Communists and the Nationalists are metaphorically represented by the turmoil within the theatrical world. Jiang Bo, who represents the spirit of May 4th and its hope for the emancipation of women, and Chunhua go to battle with the Guomindang-backed theatrical producer Tang over their right to produce socially conscious operas and compete with Tang's more commercial productions.

In 1946, Jiang Bo takes Chunhua to an exhibition commemorating the tenth anniversary of the death of Lu Xun. A principal motive force behind the May 4th Movement, Lu Xun stands as a symbol of the interconnection between revolutionary politics and the arts. Born in Shaoxing, Lu Xun was associated throughout his life with the literary and theatrical world of Shanghai and Zhejiang province. Always a champion of the rights of women, Lu Xun wrote essays on Ibsen's *A Doll's House* and against enforced chastity for women and the sexual double standard, as well as several essays commemorating the deaths of young female student activists.

Lu Xun also dealt with poverty and women's issues in his fiction. His terse prose and use of keenly observed detail became the model for a type of critical realism still favored by many writers today. His novella, *The New Year's Sacrifice* (Zhufu), for example, deals with the plight of a poor widow in China known simply as "Xiang Lin's Wife." When Chunhua sees an etching of this character, a superimposition of her face with the print shows Chunhua's identification with Lu Xun's creation.

On stage, in an opera based on the novella, Chunhua appears as the doomed peasant widow, singing an aria in torn rags with whitened hair. This brief excerpt from the opera acts as a shorthand reference to the quantum changes going on within the Chinese theater at that time and, by extension, Chinese society. Western influences have been absorbed and come full circle, so that the plight of a downtrodden peasant widow can become fit subject matter for an art form that had entertained the imperial courts and the landed gentry. The opera world had changed significantly.

At this point, the onstage world of *Two Stage Sisters* parallels rather than contrasts with the backstage drama of the film. Instead of a world of light comedy and romance, *The New Year's Sacrifice* points to the possibility of a socially and politically committed theater. This theater takes the plight of the average woman in China as a metaphor for the oppressive aspect of the society generally.

After the revolution, Chunhua resumes her life as an itinerant opera performer—with a difference. Now, she performs revolutionary opera and travels from village to village as a theatrical cadre to educate the peasantry about revolution. She performs a type of opera stylistically closer to traditional Shaoxing than the socially committed *New Year's Sacrifice,* but with a clear political message.

In Hangzhou, where Chunhua had been pilloried, the troupe stages an opera version of *The White-Haired Girl* (Baimao nü). Written in Yan'an in 1943, this play became the standard for all sorts of revolutionary drama to follow after 1949. Originally a play, *The White-Haired Girl* has been produced as an opera, filmed, danced as a ballet, and has inspired revolutionary graphic art.

The White-Haired Girl tells the story of Xi'er, a young peasant woman brutalized by feudal landlords and their minions. After all sorts of violations and humiliations, she takes refuge in a cave, living like a wild animal.

Because of this adversity, her hair turns completely white, and she acquires a reputation for fierceness. The local population considers her mad. When the Red Army liberates the area, she is reunited with her fiancé and joins the revolution. As Raphael Bassan has pointed out, *The White-Haired Girl* (here referring to the earliest film version of the play) contains all the elements necessary to insure it a lasting place of influence on all revolutionary film and theater to follow in the PRC:

> It serves as a model, particularly at the level of the presentation of the conflicts of the people in opposition to the landlords, for all revolutionary realism to come. All is, in fact, judiciously coded: the unfailing will of the heroine, the courage and abnegation of the disinherited, the always 100% negative profile of the oppressors, and, finally, the idealistic portrait of the Communist soldiers (who are also party cadres), new guides of the Chinese nation.[6]

The spirit of Yan'an drama as well as the theater that followed the revolution can be traced to Mao's personal interest in art and cultural affairs. In his famous "Talks at the Yenan Forum on Literature and Art," Mao took time out from the arduous tasks of fighting the war against the Japanese and dealing with the daily difficulties of running the Yan'an soviet to discuss the importance of China's "cultural army" in the country's battle against both foreign enemies and domestic oppressors. He calls for committed artists to draw on a variety of forms, including traditional ones, to both appeal to and educate the Chinese masses:

> We should take over the rich legacy and the good traditions in literature and art that have been handed down from past ages in China and foreign countries, but the aim must still be serve the masses of the people. Nor do we refuse to utilize the literary and artistic forms of the past, but in our hands these old forms, remolded and infused with new content, also become something revolutionary in the service of the people.[7]

Not surprisingly, Mao's talks at Yan'an led to the type of revolutionary drama exemplified by *The White-Haired Girl*. Firmly rooted in traditional theater and folklore, the play presents a clear moral universe with peasants replacing noble lords and generals as heroes and heroines. Its mythic elements, magical transformations, and stock character types place it squarely within folk theater traditions. Later, Yan'an theater became the basis for Mao's "revolutionary romanticism" as well as the Cultural Revolution's model operas.

In *Two Stage Sisters,* Chunhua's performance of *The White-Haired Girl* bears as much resemblance to *The New Year's Sacrifice* as it does to traditional

Fig. 3.   Chunhua (back) and Yuehong (front) in *Two Stage Sisters* (Wutai jiemei), directed by Xie Jin, PRC, 1965. British Film Institute.

Shaoxing opera. Within the film, *The White-Haired Girl* functions as a synthesis of the old and the new, China and the West, spoken and opera forms, and as the culmination of all the other, often contradictory, aesthetic currents to which the film refers. Although it relies on the stylization of traditional opera for its effect, it also deals with contemporary life, with actual change, and with current political and social concerns. Performing in the public square of Hangzhou, Chunhua comes full circle. Her performance melds a May 4th, urban critical realism with the fantastical nature of folk opera.

Taken as a whole, *Two Stage Sisters* transcends the insular world of Shaoxing opera to make some far-reaching statements about the nature of oppression and the power of change in twentieth-century China. Shaoxing

The Blossoming of a Revolutionary Aesthetic   *67*

serves as a metaphor. Events of historical, social, political, and cultural import (from the feudal countryside through Shanghai enterprise to revolutionary promise) occur in the theater that functions as a microcosm of Chinese society at large. Chunhua, Yuehong, and Jiang Bo stand in as "every woman," extraordinary because of their notoriety, but only a step away from the peasantry. The structural parallels are obvious but effective. The personal dramas of the stage sisters parallel the fictional worlds of the plays they perform, which, in turn, parallel the political changes occurring in Chinese society.

Perhaps the most important parallel to consider, however, is the connection between the aesthetic of the film itself and the aesthetic development of the fictional theatrical world it chronicles. *Two Stage Sisters* is itself very much like Chinese opera. Its episodic narrative structure, for example, relies on often disjointed, autonomous sequences to give it a sweeping scope and an ability to deal with all aspects of society.

Moreover, like opera, the film relies on music to both frame and underscore important dramatic moments and to place these moments within a broader social and narrative context. For example, the film opens with a sweeping crane shot that takes in the expanses of the Zhejiang countryside before settling on the opera being performed in the marketplace. A female chorus accompanies the crane shot. The same chorus also accompanies similar crane shots later in the film as well as several montage sequences that interrupt and comment on the narrative flow. Similarly, traditional opera narrative may be interrupted by arias or by physical-action sequences choreographed to instrumental music.

As in traditional opera, an orchestra punctuates moments of intense drama with percussion or full orchestral musical phrases. For example, the music swells when Chunhua and Yuehong face each other after Chunhua's acceptance into the opera troupe and at other similarly dramatic moments. In addition, the gestures, speech, and movement of the characters in *Two Stage Sisters* often take on the highly stylized air of traditional opera.

Opera training, for example, involves hours of exercises devoted to making eye movements more expressive by following a candle flame in a darkened room. Many of the eye movements within the film draw on this aspect of opera tradition (e.g., Chunhua's passionate glances at Yuehong when the latter begins to drift away from her in Shanghai and Yuehong's startled and terrified glance at Tang after he slaps her across the face before their appearance in court).

The similarity of the characters in *Two Stage Sisters* to some traditional opera heroines must also be noted. In many ways, Chunhua appears as a modern recreation of the *wudan* or *daomadan,* martial heroines like Mu Guiying, the famous female general.[8] Like the female warrior characters she performs on stage, Chunhua is aggressive, physically powerful, morally upright, and inevitably victorious. In fact, the representation of the revolutionary heroine in the preponderance of films made in the PRC owes a great debt to traditional opera characterizations. Similarly, the villains take on characteristics of wicked generals, evil-spirited demons, or monks from their stage counterparts.

However, although *Two Stage Sisters'* aesthetics may be rooted in traditional opera in many important respects, the film also gathers stylistic momentum from the other developments in theater to which the film's plot alludes. In many ways, *Two Stage Sisters* owes a great deal to the same May 4th impulses that gave rise to Lu Xun's mature style, represented in the film by *The New Year's Sacrifice*. Like Lu Xun's novella, *Two Stage Sisters* uses central female characters to concretize all sorts of social ills. In addition, *Two Stage Sisters* makes full use of the naturalistic detail characteristic of May 4th literature. Seemingly insignificant images take on dramatic weight (e.g., laundry washed in the river after sunset, drops of blood in a bowl of water or on a white sleeve, the straw hats an abandoned woman must make to survive in the countryside).

Although epic in scope like traditional opera, *Two Stage Sisters* also has the chamber quality of a literature influenced by Ibsen and Western critical realism. Jiang Bo cooks rice that boils over as she discusses sexism, class differences, and the theater with Chunhua. A montage sequence shows the daily routine of the traveling troupe from calisthenics for martial roles to memorizing lines while walking from town to town. This attention to what may appear to be nearly irrelevant detail creates a sense of the particularity of the social fabric, a concrete feeling for the historical period, as it does in the best of critical realism globally.

Just as the narrative of *Two Stage Sisters* culminates with the performance of *The White-Haired Girl* and the reunion of Chunhua and Yuehong, the aesthetic strivings of the film itself find their culmination in the performance of this play. Mao's vision of a "revolutionary romanticism" is wedded to critical realism. Indeed, it is tempting to look at *Two Stage Sisters* as an example of revolutionary romanticism. The film's plot, for example, follows the trials of a young peasant woman, who, instead of ending her life as an obscure beggar like the peasant widow in *The New Year's Sacrifice,* almost magically transforms herself into a revolutionary heroine. With a few exceptions, *Two Stage Sisters* deals with crystal-clear conflicts, between masters and servants, lords and peasants, powerful men and helpless women, in which traditional power relations are overturned. As in all revolutionary romanticism, the revolution becomes the most important motive force for change. Its coming resolves virtually all of the narrative conflicts. Just as Xi'er joins up with her lover and the Red Army in *The White-Haired Girl*, Yuehong, transformed by her suffering at the hands of Tang, joins up with Chunhua and the revolutionary opera troupe at the end of *Two Stage Sisters*. Individual concerns find public resolution in the political arena.

Two Stage Sisters seems to conveniently contain the seeds of its own aesthetic unraveling within its plot. On closer examination, however, it becomes clear that this discussion does not do justice to the aesthetic complexity of the film. Although profoundly indebted to traditional opera, the May 4th Movement, and Mao's revolutionary romanticism, *Two Stage Sisters* takes up aesthetic concerns that transcend Chinese drama. Like most Chinese films of its era, *Two Stage Sisters* walks a tightrope between indigenous dramatic forms and foreign influences, between revolutionary romanticism and what Godard has called "Hollywood Mosfilm."

During his sojourn in China, Jay Leyda found himself quite taken aback by the Chinese film industry's indebtedness to Hollywood:

> The influence of Hollywood, and in one of its worse aspects, was a shock. First, it contradicted everything that I heard and read here about the poisons and falsehoods of Hollywood being discarded by a revolutionary, bold, new Chinese cinema. The Soviet cinema had been occasionally tempted in the same way, but never so unblushingly as here. And I was shocked to find here a part of the past revived that was long since judged as a sham and embarrassment, while a new important Chinese film [*Song of Youth* (Qingchun zhige; dir. Cui Wei and Chen Huaikai, 1959)] turned away deliberately from the progress being made in world cinema, even so near as Moscow and Warsaw.[9]

The influence of Hollywood on *Two Stage Sisters* cannot be denied. In fact, if the character of Jiang Bo and the revolution were erased from the script, the film could quite easily be mistaken for a Hollywood backstage melodrama. It has all the classic elements of that genre, for example, the hard struggle to the top of the theatrical profession, the bitterness of the aging actress' lot, the inevitability of decline, sour romances, misguided ambitions, competition, romantic needs vying with the dream of theatrical success, the hardships of exploitation by unsympathetic bosses.

In addition to this indebtedness to Hollywood and despite Leyda's comment that Chinese film tends to ignore Soviet cinema, *Two Stage Sisters* also owes much to Soviet socialist realism. In fact, a careful examination of the film underscores the similarities as well as the fundamental differences between classical Hollywood realism and Soviet socialist realism.

With some exceptions, for example, *Two Stage Sisters* strives for that transparency and clarity so prized by both Hollywood and socialist realism. The film creates a self-contained world. It is lit, photographed, composed, edited, and scripted in a self-effacing, Hollywood style. Characters are not as psychologically complex as their Hollywood counterparts, but they are more than one-dimensional. The narrative is linear, if episodic. The familiar codes of narrative and aesthetic form allow disbelief willingly to be suspended.

Despite their similarities, Hollywood classical realism and socialist realism differ fundamentally. Like other films of its era, *Two Stage Sisters* perhaps owes a greater debt to Moscow than Leyda would be willing to admit. Characterization in *Two Stage Sisters,* for example, follows many of the conventions traditionally associated with socialist realism. Each character represents a certain class position and the contradictions associated with a specific historical period. Lord Ni and Tang, for example, represent a position of power through ownership, and they exploit the women peasants and workers in the film. Although individually quite distinct, these characters function as "types," exemplary of the ruling order in both rural and urban prerevolutionary China.

Typification by gender and class does not rubber stamp a character. It does, however, allow for possible points of identification. Each character embodies a particular idea and has a certain abstract potential. Chunhua, for example, functions as an icon beyond the narrative, an abstraction of a "typical" woman's awakening into class and social consciousness. She represents both a psychologically credible Hollywood-styled character and an abstract idea, that is, a type in the socialist realist mold.

With history foregrounded as a narrative force in socialist realism, other classical realist narrative techniques also change. In the socialist realist text, a tension surfaces between polemics and plot; plot structure becomes subordinated to the rhetorical necessity of making a political point. Narrative structure seems to be transformed by this injection of history and the necessity for generalization and abstraction operative in socialist realism.

For example, although *Two Stage Sisters'* narrative is, for the most part, linear, it certainly does not follow the Aristotelian dramatic unity so dear to most types of classical realist fictions. In order to broaden the geographic, temporal, and social scope of the issues dealt with in the film, the episodic narrative presents incidents often only tangentially related to the development of the principal plot line. The device of the itinerant theatrical troupe provides an excellent vehicle for this. Both before and after the revolution, the troupe drifts along the river in the countryside, encountering peasants and wealthy landowners. Characters appear, are used to make a point, disappear, occasionally reappear to make another point, or simply vanish.

In addition, the film structures events into a series of dialectical relationships. Chunhua's and Yuehong's lives not only parallel one another, for example, but have a profound effect on one another. They each represent distinct choices and attributes that contradict one another at an abstract level. By seeing their lives juxtaposed, the viewer can synthesize certain ideas about the treatment of women, the limitations on their lives, and their struggles.

In the cases of Chunhua and Yuehong, two approaches are explored. Thus, Chunhua's choice to work against the system is understandable only in relation to Yuehong's decision to live within it. When the two clash in the courtroom, the whole system explodes, and the revolution arrives in the streets of Shanghai in the following scene, a direct result of the dialectical conflict within the narrative.

• The Brecht Connection: Chinese Opera and Epic Theater

After looking at *Two Stage Sisters'* roots in Chinese theater, Hollywood melodrama, and socialist realism, the aesthetic sum of all this seems to be something rather different from the aggregate of its parts. Xie Jin has taken from a genre at the edges of Hollywood classicism—the melodrama. The place of the melodrama within the tradition of classical Hollywood realism must be taken into account in order to better understand the textual operation of *Two Stage Sisters*.

Recent criticism has pointed out that melodramas often strain the formal foundations of classical Hollywood realism to their limits.[10] If *Two Stage Sisters* resembles classical Hollywood cinema or Soviet socialist realism, it remains at the edge of those forms. It must be placed at the boundary between classical realist conventions and something quite different.

There seems to be something within the formal structure of *Two Stage Sisters*, coupled with the film's revolutionary politics, that places it very close to Brecht's notion of epic theater. Although Xie Jin would be the first to deny any conscious similarity between his work and Brecht's, a closer look at both the film and Brecht's writings reveals some interesting aesthetic parallels.[11]

Despite the notoriety of his debates with Lukács on the applicability/ inappropriateness of taking up the nineteenth-century realist novel as a model for socialist art, Brecht, while arguing against that form of realism, never placed his own aesthetic ideas outside of a broader realist tradition. Anti-illusionist and anti-Aristotelian rather than antirealist, Brecht sought to break down the illusion of transparency created by bourgeois theater as well as the emotional identification and catharsis invited by Aristotelian drama.

Instead, Brecht tried to distance the spectator from the drama by breaking the illusion of an invisible fourth wall. This was done by distancing the spectator from the actors on stage by making the audience constantly aware of the fact that the players were simply presenting a role constructed for them. In this way, Brecht hoped to create a critical distance between the play and the spectator, so that the playgoer would be inspired to think about the social and political issues under discussion rather than become overly involved with the characters as "real people" with individual problems.

Similar principles of distanciation can be seen at work in *Two Stage Sisters*. For example, the film revolves around the performance of other fictions, that is, operas, that constantly alert the viewer to the fact that the film, too, is a constructed fiction. Moreover, *Two Stage Sisters'* structure resembles opera; for example, it has disjointed episodes, major leaps in time and place, choral interludes, and many other elements that foreground its structuring principles and place it far outside Aristotelian traditions. Both the orchestra and the camera intrude self-consciously on the drama, acting as storytellers, commenting and reflecting on the characters' placements within the historical moment.

Also, just as Sirk and Fassbinder create compositions that frame characters within doorways and windows to place them figuratively outside the drama, Xie uses the same techniques for political analysis. This distance allows the viewer room for reflection on issues outside of any emotional involvement with the characters as individuals.

For example, after a scene that features a political discussion in Jiang Bo's apartment, a storm develops outside. Chunhua and Jiang Bo go to the rooftop apartment's doorway. The camera frames them inside and dollies back. With this shot, the camera figuratively places the characters' lives in perspective. The narrative comes to a temporary halt, allowing the viewer to reflect on the position of these characters within history, within the developing political struggle. Political changes break like a storm, and the implicit metaphor takes the viewer away from the drama for a moment. As Brecht hopes "the spectator stands outside, studies" in epic theater, Xie Jin's camera allows the viewer this same critical distance in *Two Stage Sisters*.[12]

The similarity between *Two Stage Sisters* and Brecht's notion of epic theater goes beyond mere coincidence. However, although *Two Stage Sisters* postdated epic theater and achieves several of its hoped-for effects, it would be taking the argument too far to say that Brechtian aesthetics directly influenced Xie Jin. Rather, the common roots and purposes of Brecht and Xie must be kept in mind.

Brecht and Xie both owe a considerable aesthetic debt to traditional Chinese opera. Although originally a folk form, Chinese opera developed a high degree of stylistic sophistication within its long history. Outside of traditions of Western realism, Chinese opera formed its own aesthetic standards, with its own perspective on the relationship between art and actuality. Brecht particularly admired Chinese opera's aesthetic self-consciousness and delight in conventionality.

In an essay titled "Mei Lanfang, Stanislavsky, Brecht—A Study in Contrasts," Huang Zuolin notes that Brecht was particularly taken with the famous opera star Mei Lanfang's acting technique and with the Chinese opera's attitude toward performance in general. In fact, Huang traces Brecht's notion of "quotation" acting to traditional Chinese storytelling techniques:

> In the course of his work, Brecht actually adopted a number of techniques from the traditional Chinese theater. One of these is his method of 'quotation.' He makes an actor 'quote' the character played, like a traditional Chinese storyteller who steps in and out of the role at will, sometimes into the part, sometimes making comments in the first person. This shifting of position facilitates the unfolding of the story, the delineation of character, and the elucidation of the author's intention.[13]

In his essay, "Alienation Effects in Chinese Acting," Brecht states:

> Above all, the Chinese artist never acts as if there were a fourth wall besides the three surrounding him. He expresses his awareness of being watched. This immediately removes one of the European stage's characteristic illusions. The audience can no longer have the illusion of being the unseen spectator at an event which is really taking place. A whole elaborate European stage technique, which helps to conceal the fact that the scenes are so arranged that the audience can view them in the easiest way, is thereby made unnecessary. The actors openly choose those positions which will best show them off to the audience, just as if they were acrobats. . . . The artist's object is to appear strange and even surprising to the audience. He achieves this by looking strangely at himself and his work.[14]

Similarly, in *Two Stage Sisters,* as the narrative bandies back and forth between onstage and offstage life, characterization takes on a quality of quotation.

In addition, the visual presentation of the self to be looked at by others operates as an "alienation effect." To cite one example, when Chunhua and Yuehong first arrive in Shanghai, they see Shuihua for the first time backstage as she puts on her makeup. The camera's position allows the viewer to see Shuihua looking at her reflection in the mirror as well as the dumbfounded faces of Chunhua and Yuehong. Whether the two young actresses are open-mouthed because of the older actress' age or because they are simply star struck is never elucidated.

In this shot, however, the film viewer confronts a character, aware of being watched within the narrative, preparing to be watched within another fictional drama, that is, the opera to be performed on stage. Chunhua and Yuehong seem aware of their own similar positions as actresses aging within the theater. Perhaps the viewer becomes aware, at this dramatically charged moment, of yet another element, that is, the fact that all three are portrayed by screen actresses who may face similar career problems. (Since this film was not released to the general public until after the Cultural Revolution, this effect may have been further heightened by the fact that the actress who portrays Shuihua, Shangguan Yunzhu, had died during that period. Her death was subsequently blamed on the stress she underwent during the Cultural Revolution.) This moment allows the viewer to think critically about women's lives, class struggle, and the nature of oppression. The spectator can reflect on the drama as Shuihua reflects on her aging image in the mirror.

Two Stage Sisters' allusions to other dramatic works, its narrative ellipses, its stylistic self-consciousness must be regarded as very sophisticated aesthetically by Western standards. The film has certain affinities with Western modernism and international developments in Marxist aesthetics. Beneath this complexity, however, there is also an innocence, a moral directness, an ingenuous hope for a brighter future.

Coming from traditional theater and its folk aesthetic, *Two Stage Sisters* has a "naive" quality, and this quality finally brings the film close to Brecht's dream of a drama that is both didactic and popular, critical and supportive of revolutionary change. Alan Lovell has astutely observed: "Increasingly, Brecht described the quality he was searching for in his art as 'Naïveté.'"[15]

Perhaps *Two Stage Sisters* comes close to Brecht's longing for "naïveté," since it draws on the folk art roots of Chinese opera to shape a modern aesthetic, to reform a relationship between art and the people obscured within modern, industrialized, commercial culture.

• *Two Stage Sisters* and the Cultural Revolution

After tracing the aesthetic roots of *Two Stage Sisters* from folk opera through Lu Xun to Brecht and Mao himself, it seems unlikely that anyone could come up with another Chinese film indebted to as many strains of Marxist aesthetics so vividly described through narrative devices and cinematographic techniques. However, *Two Stage Sisters* was not released to the public until after the Cultural Revolution had ended, and the film was viciously attacked politically while it was still in production. In order to understand the reasons for the suppression of *Two Stage Sisters,* the film must be placed within the context of the political events going on at the time of its production.

In 1958, Mao Zedong launched China on an exceedingly ambitious project of reform called The Great Leap Forward. Designed to quicken the transformation of China into a model socialist society by increasing the size and power of both rural and urban communes, the program rather quickly collapsed the following year. In 1959, Mao stepped down as chairman of the People's Republic in favor of Liu Shaoqi, although Mao remained head of the Communist Party.[16]

Paul G. Pickowicz has noted that the end of the Great Leap Forward and Mao's temporary loss of power had some significant effects on the Chinese film industry.[17] Even though there was a decrease in production, greater emphasis was placed on quality filmmaking and carefully crafted stories.

As Pickowicz points out, the publication in 1961 of an essay by Xia Yan titled "Raise Our Country's Film Art to a New Level" ushered in the new era for the Chinese cinema. One of the best known of the "left-wing" film-makers during the golden age of the Shanghai studios in the 1930s, Xia Yan had risen in the party ranks after 1949 to become vice-minister of culture. In this 1961 essay, implicitly critical of the Great Leap Forward, Xia calls for greater autonomy for artists and for more diversity within the cinema.

Xia's directives had a definite impact. The period between the Great Leap Forward and the Cultural Revolution was characterized by a tremendous diversity in both form and subject matter within the cinema. Production ranged from domestic comedies like *Li Shuangshuang* (dir. Lu Ren, 1962) to dramas about life in prerevolutionary China like *The Lin Family Shop* (Linjia puzi; dir. Shui Hua, 1959). Stories about intellectuals and their romantic as well as political exploits like Xie Tieli's *Early Spring* (Zaochun eryue; a.k.a. *Second Lunar Month, Threshold of Spring,* 1964) were produced alongside films about revolutionary activities like Xie Jin's *The Red Detachment of Women* (1961).

This period came to a rather abrupt end, however, with the reassertion of Mao's power in the mid-1960s. The Cultural Revolution saw the mobil- ization of youth in the guise of the Red Guard, further radicalization of peasants and workers, dismantling of huge chunks of the bureaucratic superstructure, and purge of many party cadres.

Interestingly, many of the Cultural Revolution's most heated battles were fought in the aesthetic realm, and the Shanghai film industry became one of the prime targets. In fact, during much of the Cultural Revolution, feature-film production ceased. Because of his calls for reform after the Great

Leap Forward, Xia Yan stood out for censure. As Xie Jin has pointed out, *Two Stage Sisters* fared particularly badly because of Xia Yan's association with the project:

> "Wutai jiemei" [*Two Stage Sisters*] and "Zaochun eryue" [Xie Tieli's *Early Spring*] were attacked above all because of Xia Yan who had made corrections and suggestions on the screenplay. By attacking the films, they wanted to attack him. For "Wutai jiemei," Xia Yan not only helped me a lot in writing the screenplay, but it was he himself who encouraged me to make the film. And that was one of the 'crimes' of which he was accused during the Cultural Revolution.[18]

Jiang Qing, Mao's wife and head of the "Gang of Four" in power during the Cultural Revolution, had a particular dislike for Xia Yan that extended back to her days as an actress in Shanghai. Beyond the personality clashes, Jiang Qing also had very clear and firm ideas about what a Chinese revolutionary drama should look like. The controversy became divided along geographic lines, which paralleled political camps. Revolutionary art outside the boundaries of the aesthetics developed in the Yan'an soviet during World War II lost all validity and was thought of as somehow "impure."

If *Two Stage Sisters* is looked at not as a harmonious mixture of Yan'an and Shanghai influences but as a battleground between two notions of what a politically progressive art should look like, then perhaps the bitterness of the film's condemnation can be better understood. Although indebted to Yan'an's *The White-Haired Girl* and Mao's "revolutionary romanticism," *Two Stage Sisters'* aesthetic heart remains in Shanghai, and this aesthetic debt assured its condemnation.

Even in works like *Two Stage Sisters* that so fervently support the party and the revolution, the Cultural Revolution's proponents could unearth a bourgeois, Western sensibility. In literary and dramatic works, characterization became a politically charged issue. A notion of the "middle" character developed. In *Two Stage Sisters,* for example, Yuehong stands out. Neither heroic nor villainous, she aids her own oppressor because of avarice and sheer stupidity. She is, however, sympathetic. She is a victim and a "sinner" who is eventually "redeemed" by the love of her stage sister. The morally ambivalent nature of this character places her somewhere outside the realm of heroics or infamy. In the "middle," her moral ambivalence leads to textual ambiguity and, in turn, the possibility of counterrevolutionary readings. Likewise, the illusion of psychological complexity that characterizes the "middle character" places Yuehong squarely within a Western tradition of naturalism. Descriptive detail outweighs didactic precision, and, once again, the possibility of a subversive reading appears.

In retrospect, this reasoning seems strained, to say the least. More importantly, however, no degree of censure should rob *Two Stage Sisters* of its right to be taken seriously within the history of Marxist aesthetics. In its attempt to locate a peculiarly Chinese socialist aesthetic that can do justice to the representation of women, *Two Stage Sisters* merits attention. Beyond this, *Two Stage Sisters* remains at the cusp of aesthetic currents that still rage not only within Chinese cinema but within cinemas committed to social change worldwide.

· Notes

1. Most of the research for this essay was done in Paris, France, in the fall of 1982 and spring of 1983 under the auspices of a French Government Grant. I would like to thank Janet Yang of World Entertainment, Inc., for arranging for me to interview Xie Jin while he was in the United States and for translating for us. A shorter version of this paper was presented at the 1985 Society for Cinema Studies conference at New York University. I am grateful to Sheldon Lu, the editor of this volume, for giving me the opportunity to have this essay reprinted with corrections and some minor changes. I would also like to thank Chuck Kleinhans, Julia Lesage, John Hess, and the other members of the editorial board of *Jump Cut*, where this essay originally appeared.

Two Stage Sisters' Chinese title, Wutai jiemei, is also translated as *Stage Sisters, Two Actresses, Sisters of the Stage.* For an overview of film in the People's Republic of China, see Jay Leyda, *Dianying–Electric Shadows: An Account of Films and Film Audience in China* (Cambridge, Mass.: MIT Press, 1972), or Régis Bergeron, *Le cinéma chinois: 1949–1983* (Paris: L'Harmattan, 1984). Kwok and M.-C. Quiquemelle, "Le cinéma chinois et le réalisme," *Ombres électriques: panorama du cinéma chinois—1925-1983* (Paris: Centre de Documentation sur le Cinéma Chinois, 1982) is also informative.

At the time *Jump Cut* decided to devote two special sections to cinema from the People's Republic of China in 1986 and 1989, little existed in English on Chinese-language film. Since this essay was first published, however, there has been a welcome blossoming of scholarly works on Chinese cinema. Thankfully, Xie Jin and his oeuvre have not been ignored. Chris Berry, ed., *Perspectives on Chinese Cinema* (London: British Film Institute, 1991), includes a biography and other critical material on Xie Jin. Nick Browne, "Society and Subjectivity: On the Political Economy of Chinese Melodrama," in *New Chinese Cinemas: Forms, Identities, Politics,* ed. Nick Browne, Paul G. Pickowicz, Vivian Sobchack, and Esther Yau (Cambridge: Cambridge University Press, 1994), 40–56, contains extensive discussion of Xie's *Hibiscus Town.*

Other useful works include Paul Clark, *Chinese Cinema: Culture and Politics Since 1949* (New York: Cambridge University Press, 1987); Da Huo'er, "An Interview with Xie Jin," *Jump Cut* 34 (March 1989): 107-109; John A. Lent, *The Asian Film In-*

dustry (Austin: University of Texas Press, 1990); Ma Ning, "Spatiality and Subjectivity in Xie Jin's Film Melodrama of the New Period," in *New Chinese Cinemas: Forms, Identities, Politics,* ed. Nick Browne, Paul G. Pickowicz, Vivian Sobchack, and Esther Yau (New York: Cambridge University Press, 1994), 15–39; George S. Semsel, ed., *Chinese Film: The State of the Art in the People's Republic* (New York: Praeger, 1987); and Timothy Tung, "The Work of Xie Jin: A Personal Letter To the Editor," in *Film and Politics in the Third World,* ed. John D. H. Downing (New York: Praeger, 1987). The latter volume also contains a translation of the Kwok and Quiquemelle article mentioned above.

2. For information on film during the Cultural Revolution, see Paul Clark, "Filmmaking in China: From the Cultural Revolution to 1981," *China Quarterly* 94 (June 1983): 304–322.

3. For more biographical information on Xie Jin, see Marco Muller, "Les tribulations d'un cineaste chinois en Chine," *Cahiers du cinéma* 344 (February 1983): 16–21. Same interview in Italian: Marco Muller, "Intervista con Xie Jin," in *Ombre Electriche: Saggi e Richerche sul Cinema Cinese* (Milan: Gruppo Editoriale Electra, 1982). Charles Tesson, "Xie Jin: Celui par qui le mélo arrive," *Cahiers du cinéma* no. 344 (February 1983): 12–15.

4. Colin Mackerras, *The Chinese Theater in Modern Times: From 1840 to the Present Day* (London: Thames and Hudson, 1975).

5. Fan Ruijuan, "An Actress' Life in Old China," in *When They Were Young,* ed. Women of China and New World Press (Beijing: New World Press, 1983), 158.

6. Raphael Bassan, "Ombre électrique sur la cite interdite: La longue marche du cinéma chinois," *La revue du cinéma* 380 (February 1983): 77. My translation.

7. Mao Zedong, "Talks at the Yenan Forum on Literature and Art," in *Selected Readings from the Works of Mao Zedong* (Beijing: Foreign Languages Press, 1971), 259.

8. Opera terms are in Mandarin, taken from Dong Chensheng, *Paintings of Beijing Opera Characters* (Beijing: Zhaohua Publishing House, 1981). For more information on the relationship between Chinese opera and film, see Geremie Barmé, "Persistance de la tradition au 'royaume des ombres'. Quelques notes visant à contributer à une approche nouvelle du cinéma chinois," in *Le cinéma chinois,* ed. Marie-Claire Quiquemelle and Jean-Loup Passek (Paris: Centre Georges Pompidou, 1985).

9. Leyda, *Dianying,* 247.

10. For example, see Griselda Pollock, Geoffrey Nowell-Smith, and Stephen Heath, "Dossier on Melodrama," *Screen* 18, no. 2 (1977): 105–119.

11. Interview with Xie Jin, translation by Janet Yang, San Francisco, April 1985.

12. Bertolt Brecht, *Brecht on Theatre: The Development of an Aesthetic,* ed. and trans. John Willett (New York: Hill and Wang, 1964), 37.

13. Huang Zuolin, "Mei Lanfang, Stanislavsky, Brecht—A Study in Contrasts," in *Peking Opera and Mei Lanfang: A Guide to China's Traditional Theater and the Art of Its Great Master* (Beijing: New World Press, 1981), 16.

14. Brecht, "Alienation Effects in Chinese Acting," in *Brecht on Theatre*, 91–92.

15. Alan Lovell, "Epic Theater and Counter Cinema's Principles," *Jump Cut* 27 (July 1982): 66.

16. For more information on the relationship between revolutionary politics and aesthetics in twentieth-century China, see Jonathan D. Spence, *The Gate of Heavenly Peace: The Chinese and Their Revolution*—1895–1980 (Middlesex, England: Penguin Books, 1981). Chapter 12 includes extensive background information on the period under discussion here.

17. Paul G. Pickowicz, "The Limits of Cultural Thaw: Chinese Cinema in the Early 1960s," in *Perspectives on Chinese Cinema*, ed. Chris Berry (Ithaca, N.Y.: China-Japan Program, Cornell University, 1985), 97–148.

18. Muller, "Les tribulations," 19.

Chapter 3

From "Minority Film" to "Minority Discourse"
Questions of Nationhood and Ethnicity in Chinese Cinema
•
Yingjin Zhang

In recent years, cultural critics have returned to the relationship between nationhood and ethnicity with a renewed sense of urgency if not anxiety. This has been, in part, to criticize the established paradigms and *epistemes* (such as "center-periphery" and "majority-minority") and, in part, to reconfigure the geopolitical space in the contemporary world. This study seeks to investigate the functioning of a set of critical categories—ethnicity, race, nation-state—as well as other related terms, such as nation-people, nationalism, state discourse, cultural hegemony, and subjectivity, in the field of Chinese cinema. Proceeding from "minority film" (*shaoshu minzu dianying*) as a special genre in Mainland China to "minority discourse" as a critical practice in New Chinese Cinema,[1] I will demonstrate that the categories of the nation and ethnicity have been put to use through a complex process of negotiation in Chinese cinema from the early 1920s to the present. Two levels of such negotiation can be differentiated at this point: the level of filmic discourse (i.e., film narrative and narration) and the level of critical discourse (i.e., film theory and criticism). I shall start with the second level so as to identify issues of crucial importance and then return to the first level by way of reading a number of films that illuminate these issues.

• Theoretical Excursions: Race or Ethnicity?

Chris Berry published an article in which he equates *minzu*, an ambiguous Chinese term, with "race," an extremely loaded English term. By insisting on equivalents such as "race characteristics" for *minzu tedian*, "race form" for *minzu xingshi*, "race-ization" for *minzuhua*, "race color" for *minzu fengge*, and "racial minority" for *shaoshu minzu*, he attempts a deconstructive reading of *minzu* that has resulted in, unfortunately, not so much a clarification as a conflation of several distinct categories in Chinese film studies.[2] While Berry is certainly correct in identifying "sinocentrism," which he would rather term "race-centrism," in post-1949 Chinese film, what he sees as "race-ization" (or "sinification" as used elsewhere by Paul Clark)[3] is, I would contend, a politically motivated and manipulated process of cultural production. This cultural production brings out not just a unified discourse of solidarity among fifty-five "ethnic minorities" (*shaoshu minzu*) in China but also an *ambivalent* filmic discourse on which the dialectic of Self and Other is inevitably predicated. From this perspective, Berry's formulation becomes problematic. His indiscriminate use of "race" as an overriding term on the one hand obscures the difference between "race" and "ethnicity" and, on the other, conflates the "state discourse," which champions the Han Chinese cultural hegemony over ethnic minorities, and the "politics of nationalism" in Chinese film, which has strategically drawn on minority cultures in the formation of the "Chinese characteristics" (*minzu tedian*) as opposed to Western discourses and technologies. As a consequence of this conflation, Berry readily locates in recent Chinese films a fundamental challenge to the discourse of race and "race-ization," while altogether neglecting the possibility that some of these same films might have unknowingly reinforced the Han cultural hegemony in their individual efforts to challenge the state discourse.

Before discussing specific representations of ethnic minorities in Chinese cinema, I will read through a set of definitions of ethnicity, race, and nation-state in the social sciences and literary studies. In *China and Its National Minorities,* Thomas Herberer asserts that "China is a multinational state formed from the territorial expansion of the largest nationality (Han) and from a fusion between the Han and different peoples over the course of history."[4] According to Herberer, the term "minority" in China embraces a group of non-Han people who share their distinctive specific characteristics derived from race, language, religion, customs, morals, traditions, dress, social organization, and so forth.[5] While Herberer notices that the Chinese language never distinguishes among peoples, nation, nationality, and ethnos—all of them being lumped together under a single term, *minzu*—he refuses to collapse them into the English term, "race."

My objection to the equation of *minzu* with "race" should not be taken to mean that racial discourse does not exist in modern China. As a matter of fact, the discourse of race has been studied by Frank Dikötter, who argues, among other things, that there were no pervasive differences between the Han Chinese and the Manchus with respect to racial perceptions of outgroups (like the Europeans and the Africans). Dikötter's belief in the fundamental similarity among Chinese nationalities in their attitudes toward other races leads him to this conclusion: "The phenotype of most minorities was not significantly at variance with that of the Han Chinese: there was a physical continuity that precluded the elaboration of racial theories."[6] Based on this conviction, he does not treat interethnic issues in his study.

The preference of "ethnicity" over "race" as an equivalent of *minzu* in historical and social-scientific literatures in the field of Chinese studies, however, does not amount to a denial of the usefulness of "race" as a critical category in Chinese film studies. The point I am making here is that we would do much better if we recognize rather than erase differences in critical categories as they evolved *historically* in literary and cultural studies.

In the entry on "race" in *Critical Terms for Literary Study*, Kwame Anthony Appiah draws attention to a shocking discovery: "that there is a fairly widespread consensus in the sciences of biology and anthropology that the word 'race,' at least as it is used in most unscientific discussions, refers to nothing that science should recognize as real."[7] This discovery is shocking in that references to "race" as a conception of biological heredity—borne in visible characteristics ranging from skin color and hair to intelligence and honesty —were made over past centuries in the West with such frequency and consistency that "race" as a category seems to have been taken for granted, most noticeably in everyday stereotypes of other peoples, but increasingly in literary scholarship as well. One famous example is Hippolyte-Adolphe Taine's introduction to his *History of English Literature*, which posits "race," "epoch" (or "moment"), and "surroundings" (or "milieu") as three determining factors in the constitution of a national literature.[8] To be sure, Taine's positivist theory was enthusiastically embraced by Chinese literary critics in the 1920s in their efforts to build a national literature in modern China, and for that reason it must have exerted a considerable if indirect impact on the subsequent conceptualization of Chinese "national cinema" *(guopian)* in the 1930s.[9] If in the concept of race one can locate a modern understanding of what it is to be a people, then this understanding is intertwined with further understandings of a people as a nation and of the role of culture in the life of nations. In Appiah's words, "the nation is the key middle term in understanding the relations between the concept of race and the idea of literature."[10]

As early as 1882, Ernest Renan pointed out a grave mistake whereby "race is confused with nation."[11] By way of rejecting one by one a list of "scientific" or "naturalist" categories—race, language, material interest, religious affinities, geography, and military necessity—as inadequate for the creation of a nation, Renan envisioned the nation instead as "a soul, a spiritual principle," constituted as it were in a rich legacy of memories of a shared past and a present-day consent or will to perpetuate the value of the heritage.[12] "A nation is therefore a large-scale solidarity," Renan claimed, a solidarity that transcends the boundaries of race, language, and territory.[13]

Yet, how does the will to nationhood articulate itself? To this question Homi Bhabha responded recently by formulating a theory of "nation as narration"—nation as inscribed in and disseminated through a variety of narratives and discourses. The category of people (or nation-people), for instance, is found constructed by means of double-writing: people as a "pedagogical object" in the state discourse (i.e., the nation's self-generation in and through its people) and people as the "performative subject," which splits Nation into It/Self and represents it as "a space that is *internally* marked by cultural difference and the heterogeneous histories of contending peoples, antagonistic authorities, and tense cultural locations."[14] In terms of such cultural difference, Renan's vision of the nation as a large-scale solidarity is ultimately untenable. On the contrary, as Bhabha contends, "The 'locality' of national culture is neither unified nor unitary in relation to itself, nor must it be seen simply as 'other' in relation to what is outside or beyond it."[15]

Bhabha's speculation on the heterogeneity of national culture dovetails with Prasenjit Duara's deconstructive reading of the Chinese nation. Rather than entertaining an accepted view of "the nation as a whole imagining itself to be the unified subject of history," Duara proposes "instead that we view national identity as founded upon fluid relationships."[16] This more flexible position enables Duara to redefine nationalism as "more appropriately a relationship between a constantly changing Self and Other."[17] By way of analyzing what he calls "discursive meaning" and "symbolic meaning" of the nation, Duara concludes with a picture of the Chinese nation as consisting of hard and soft boundaries identifiable on multiple levels—not just the boundaries between ethnic groups, but boundaries between dialects, regions, religions, means of subsistence, and so on.

Homi Bhabha's and Prasenjit Duara's emphasis on *fluid* relations and boundaries in conceptualizing the nation brings us to a similar emphasis in Werner Sollors' definition of "ethnicity"—namely, that ethnicity "refers not to a thing-in-itself but to a relationship."[18] Derived in part from the Greek word *ethnos,* which contains an ambivalence between the inclusive meaning, "people in general," and the dissociative sense, "other people" (e.g., "non-Jews" or "non-Christians"), ethnicity rests on a "contrast" or a "boundary" in its conceptualization.[19] Representations of ethnicity, therefore, usually involve an impressive array of boundary-constructing devices that tend to stereotype other people, evoking images of the Other only to distance or differentiate it.

Similar to the Greek *ethnos, min* in the Chinese term *minzu* refers to "the common people, people at large," while *zu* refers to something as small as a group of people with an acquired sense of kinship or as large as an established, historical people (especially of the Northeast). Coined around 1895 as a Chinese equivalent of the Japanese neologism *minzoku*, *minzu* quickly became a powerful term, frequently used to indicate majority peoples (i.e., the Han Chinese) rather than minority peoples (i.e., *shaoshu minzu*, a derivative term in subsequent usage). As Pamela Kyle Crossley explains, the Chinese *minzu* is closest to the Russian *narod* (people, nation), with an emphasis upon "popular" *(narodni)* and "nationality" *(narodnost)*.[20] Nationhood and ethnicity are thus deeply ingrained and intertwined in the Chinese term *minzu*.

It must be evident by now that in the field of Chinese studies "ethnicity" is by and large a less problematic term than "race" in dealing with majority (Han)/minority relationships. I will follow the same practice in the rest of this essay and leave the question of "race" in Chinese cinema for further study. More specifically, I will proceed from the "nation"—what Appiah sees as the key middle term—and investigate the historical manifestations of the intricate relationship between nationhood and ethnicity in Chinese cinema. Given the recent "slow contradictory movement from 'nationalism' to 'ethnicity' as a source of identities,"[21] we might find ethnicity to be as equally valid a concept as nationalism for a study of contemporary Chinese cinema, once ethnicity is conceived of as a relational (i.e., fluid) rather than essentialized (i.e., fixed) term.

• Thematic Variations: Nationhood and Ethnicity in Chinese Cinema

It is noteworthy that two historical events coincided in the year of 1895: the invention of cinema in France and the defeat of China in the first Sino-Japanese War. Ever since 1895, the year in which the first appearance of *minzu* was spotted,[22] "nationalism" (or *minzu zhuyi* in Chinese, literally "ideology of the nation") has become one of the central issues in the cultural and intellectual history of modern China. Even at the level of the political unconscious, the question of nationhood never failed to engage the Chinese film circle. This is first of all evident in the name "Western shadowplay" *(xiyang yingxi)*, given to movies shown as early as August 1896 in Shanghai's Xu Garden. Arguably, the "shadowplay" as a traditional Chinese form of entertainment might promise—at least to the Chinese scholars initially—some kind of "Chinese" contribution to film as an international art form.[23] When the first Chinese film, *Dingjun Mountain* (Dingjun shan, 1905), was produced by Ren Jingfeng in a Beijing photography shop, it was significantly a filming of Beijing opera performed by the famous actor Tan Xinpei.[24] One may suspect that at the beginning stage of Chinese cinema, an effort was already being made to impose certain "Chineseness" on film, which is after all an imported Western technology, despite the phantom "shadows" attached to its Chinese names—first *yingxi* (shadowplay) and then *dianying* (electric shadows).[25]

The assertion of "Chineseness" as a marker of national identity in the subsequent development of Chinese cinema was made in many different ways, ranging from the subtle cinematic treatment of ethical problems in family dramas to the radical political protest against the colonialist and imperialist presence in China. For instance, not only can one locate in Zheng Zhengqiu's films of the 1920s an allegorical structure whereby family dramas were eventually made to play out the overarching theme of "national salvation" *(minzu zijiu)*, but one can also discern in Zhang Shichuan's "escapist" films of romance (i.e., mandarin ducks and butterflies) and swordsmanship (i.e., *gongfu* or knight-errantry) in the same period a fundamental concern with the fate of the nation as a whole.[26] In the political arena, the "progressive" *(jinbu,* or "liberal-minded") Chinese film people worked together in the summer of 1932 and defeated the U.S. initiative to build a "Chinese Hollywood"; in June 1936 they protested against the public screening in Shanghai's International Settlement of *The New Land* (Xin tu, coproduced by Japan and Nazi Germany), a colonialist or "fascist" film calling for Japanese nationals to emigrate to Manchuria, their newly conquered territory.[27]

Generally speaking, nationalism was articulated more explicitly in "leftist film" *(zuoyi dianying)* of the 1930s,[28] which prospered upon growing urban patriotism in the wake of the Japanese invasion of Manchuria in September 1931 and the Japanese attack on Shanghai in January 1932. Films such as *Three Modern Women* (San'ge modeng nüxing, directed by Bu Wancang, 1933), *Little Playthings* (Xiao wanyi, directed by Sun Yu, 1933), *Big Road* (Dalu, directed by Sun Yu, 1934), and *Children of Troubled Times* (Fengyun ernü, directed by Xu Xingzhi, 1935) reenact in graphic details the traumas of the Japanese invasions. Needless to say, this type of nationalism has very little to do with a "discourse of race," but rather depends a great deal on a conceptualization of nationhood that transcends economic, ideological, and political differences. Historically, nationalism in leftist film marks the juncture where Chinese cinema gradually turned from earlier popular genres of romance, swordsmanship, and immortals/ghosts *(shengui)* to the existential crises in modern China (e.g., drought, flood, famine, war, and so on), although "soft-core" entertainment films continued to claim their share in the market.[29] When the slogan "cinema of national defense" *(guofang dianying)* was issued in 1936, a year before the full-scale second Sino-Japanese War broke out, there seemed to be no holding back of the ever-growing patriotic spirit.[30]

During the war (1937–1945), even the Nationalist government sponsored the production of patriotic films. For instance, *Defending Our Land* (Baowei women de tudi, directed by Shi Dongshan, 1938) and *Eight Hundred Heroic Soldiers* (Babai zhuangshi, directed by Ying Yunwei, 1938) were completed in ten months in Wuhan before the city was lost to the Japanese. In the immediate postwar period, it was the inscription of war memories that made two epic films achieve spectacular box-office success: *Spring River Flows East* (Yijiang chunshui xiang dong liu, directed by Cai Chusheng and Zheng Junli, 1947) and *Eight Thousand Li of Clouds and Moon* (Baqianli lu yun he yue, directed by Shi Dongshan, 1947).[31] Nationhood as projected in these films testifies to Renan's observation: "indeed, suffering in common unifies more than joy does. Where national memories are concerned, griefs are of more value than triumphs, for they impose duties, and require a common effort."[32]

It must be pointed out that the Nationalist government did have its own versions of nationhood to promote, especially in its Nanjing decade (1927–1937), although this fact has been largely ignored by the Mainland official history of Chinese cinema and is just being slowly recognized by the historians of modern China. Through its own organizations, such as the National Film Censorship Committee, established in 1931, the Nationalist government sought to incorporate filmmaking in its nation-building project. Specifically, it promoted the following as crucial elements of a modern nation: Mandarin (*guoyu*) as a unified national language (in this case, it tried to curtail if not terminate the production of Cantonese-dialect films in southern China), a rational mind (in this case, it banned films with explicit superstitious and religious themes), a healthy body (in this case, it promoted the athletic looks in a new generation of film stars), and Confucian ethics (in this case, it frequently ordered pornographic and sexy sequences to be cut before the films could be released). What is historically interesting—and perhaps ironic as well—is that some of the Nationalist agendas on film censorship were enthusiastically endorsed by "progressive" film people, some of them later classified as "leftist."[33] However, this example of common agendas among the pro-Nationalist and the "progressive" film people illustrates that nationalism, if understood in a broader sense, might become a unifying force in itself, especially at a time when the national existence is in jeopardy. This is particularly clear in *Storm on the Border* (Saishang fengyun, directed by Ying Yunwei, 1940), a feature film produced by Nationalist-controlled China Film Studio in Chongqing. A story of an intricate love-triangle among Mongolian and Han youths and their eventual overcoming of ethnic differences in their common fight against Japanese spies, *Storm on the Border* actually foreshadows some of the recurrent themes (e.g., solidarity) in minority films for decades to come.[34]

At this point, the "nation" in the discourse of nationalism in Chinese cinema may be decoded more accurately. Insofar as film is concerned, it was the "nationhood" as constituted by the "nation-people" (minzu) that was the major concern from the 1920s to the 1940s. As envisioned by film productions and film criticism of this period, a modern nation must depend on a strong people who could resist not only foreign military forces but also the cultural infiltration of the West.[35] In the post-1949 Communist era, nevertheless, the conception of "nationhood" had more and more to do with the "nation-state" (guojia), which, through its ideological state apparatuses, brought in "ethnicity" as one of the key categories in its state-building project.[36] One may postulate that a nation as envisioned by Renan had finally emerged in socialist China—a nation as "a large-scale solidarity, constituted by the feeling of the sacrifices that one has made in the past and of those that one is prepared to make in the future."[37] It is precisely in view of such solidarity achieved through shared experiences that minority film was gradually instituted as a genre in the late 1950s.[38]

· Minority Film: Homage to the Nation-State

One of the most popular minority films in the post-1949 era is *Third Sister Liu* (Liu sanjie, directed by Su Li, 1960), a musical about a legendary singer of Zhuang minority origin. Set on the Li River in Guilin, a famous scenic place in southern China, the film invites the audience to view the spectacular beauty of an exotic location. Even at the beginning of the film, however, a noticeable discrepancy between the beautiful visual images (the river, the cliffs, the fishing boat, and the pretty woman singer) and the sad story narrated in her lyrics slowly emerges. Sister Liu has been driven out of her native place by a landlord and forbidden to sing by her brother, but she manages to escape and arrives at a riverside village. She is soon recognized and welcomed by the poor villagers there, and through her songs she unites them in a struggle against the local landlord. After escaping from the landlord's house at night, she leaves with the young man who has been pursuing her for some time.[39]

With its picturesque scenery and its melodious folk songs, *Third Sister Liu* was praised as exemplifying the achievements of "national style" (minzu fengge) or "national form" (minzu xingshi) in post-1949 Chinese cinema.[40] In his commentary on the film, Paul Clark finds it paradoxical that "one of the most effective ways to make films with 'Chinese' style was to go to the most 'foreign' cultural areas in the nation."[41] To be sure, going to the "alien" and "exotic" minority regions did not entail an equal distribution of power in the symbolic structure. On the contrary, the outcome of locating "national style" in ethnic cultural practices was never a restoration of "minority" cultures to a "majority" status, but always a legitimation of minority peoples as part of the "solidarity" of the Chinese nation. Given the increasingly politicized climate of the 1950s and 1960s, which was translated into less artistic freedom for Chinese filmmakers, minority films functioned not so much as much-coveted "exotica" to satisfy the film audience's desire for the "foreign"[42] as an effective means by which the nation-state objectifies minority peoples through stereotypes and co-opts them in the construction of a socialist China.

The project of objectification and co-optation is better illustrated in *Five Golden Flowers* (Wuduo jinhua, directed by Wang Jiayi, 1959). In this film about an ethnic young man's search for his beloved among five ethnic girls named "Golden Flower," minority people are again stereotypically presented as fond of songs and dances, dressed in gorgeous colors, decorated with flashy ornaments, and engaged—among other things—in romantic affairs. As an indispensable ingredient, folk songs in minority films often became national hits instantly. Nonetheless, it must be borne in mind that minority films celebrate ethnic cultural diversity only at a superficial level, for all displays of "solidarity" and "ethnic harmony" in these films are actually *staged* as a spectacle mostly for the Han viewers, and there is an unmistakably Han-centered viewing position, visually as well as conceptually. Hence, in *Third Sister Liu*, the Zhuang people are represented as being "identical" with the Han in that both were oppressed by landlords and both must be united in order to overcome their class enemy. Hence, in *Five Golden Flowers*, minority people are figured as "model workers," enthusiastically participating in the socialist reconstruction. This kind of ideological identification of ethnic minorities with the Han people readily confirms both the necessity and the legitimacy of the state discourse in maintaining the Han cultural hegemony in the nation.

A further example of how ethnic minorities are configured in terms of their alleged ideological identification with the Han people is found in *Serfs* (Nongnu, directed by Li Jun, 1963). At the end of this film about the suppression of the Tibetan uprising by the People's Liberation Army in the late 1950s, Jampa, a Tibetan serf whose life was saved by a Han soldier, finally directs his gaze toward a portrait of Mao Zedong on the wall. In the care of his childhood girlfriend, Jampa utters with reverence the first words in many years—"Chairman Mao!"—an utterance coming as if spontaneously from his heart, but actually from a script imposed by the Han filmmakers if not the censors.[43]

In minority films such as *Serfs*, cinematic representation serves to contain the alien and potentially subversive elements in the frontier regions.[44] The Han cultural hegemony that ensues from the state discourse thus reinforces the existing structure of power and knowledge: secured in the Han-centered position, minority films worked symbolically as the celestial eye (i.e., "I" the Han subject) placing remote alien territories and exotic cultural practices under constant surveillance. The bottom line in such cinematic representation is that the object (in this case ethnic minorities) would never become a full-fledged subject of knowledge. In other words, minority people hardly if ever occupy the subject position in minority films. Instead of acting as agents of change in their own right, minority people are always directed to pay their homage to the nation-state.

My observations here dovetail with Dru Gladney's recent study, which contends that "the objectified portrayal of minorities as exoticized, and even eroticized, is essential to the construction of the Han Chinese majority, the very formulation of the Chinese 'nation' itself."[45] Following Gladney, one may even speculate that the by now mandatory staging of romanticized songs and eroticized dances in minority films for consumption mostly by the Han majority bears a "striking resemblance to the 'tribute' offerings of the ancient Chinese empires" and that, fixed in the state cultural machinery, minority films have in effect participated in some kind of "internal colonialism" and "internal orientalism," both proved to be effective discursive means to the establishment of the Han cultural hegemony.[46]

• Minority Discourse: Rethinking "New Chinese Cinema"

Insofar as majority/minority relations are concerned, the basic structure of power and knowledge remained unchanged in the mid-1980s, a period when "New Chinese Cinema" gradually took shape.[47] Even though *Horse Thief* (Daoma zei, directed by Tian Zhuangzhuang, 1985), a documentary-like film purportedly reporting the Tibetan religious life, differs radically from the previous minority films in its deliberate avoidance of a clearly defined ideological message, there is yet no denying that the viewing position is still fundamentally Han-centered. In the primitive landscape of Tibet, enigmatic religious rituals (such as the sky burial and the ghost dance) are repeatedly displayed, while the Tibetan protagonist, a horse thief ostracized by his tribe and exiled in the wild mountains, is engaged in a fatal struggle for survival. When questioned in an interview regarding the "incomprehensibility" of the film, Tian Zhuangzhuang unabashedly declared that *Horse Thief* was made for "audiences of the next century to watch."[48] Needless to say, the next generation Tian has in mind consists of Han rather than Tibetan viewers. Indeed, Tian even admits that *Horse Thief* reflects his "own view of life" in Han society and therefore has very little to do with what religion means to the Tibetan people.[49]

Fig. 4. Li Chun in *Sacrificed Youth* (Qingchun ji), directed by Zhang Nuanxin, PRC, 1985. British Film Institute.

In *Sacrificed Youth* (Qingchun ji, directed by Zhang Nuanxin, 1985), one encounters a similar concern with Han society more than with minority culture. During the Cultural Revolution, an urban Han girl is sent to a remote mountain village in the Dai (Thai) area, where she eventually regains her subjectivity through partial adaptation to the culture of the "Other," visually symbolized by the Dai costumes. In a "poetic" scene, a group of lovely Dai girls chase each other to a river after work, throwing off their sarongs and swimming naked in the water. Viewing from a distance such an "erotic" Dai practice whereby a "skin-close" contact with nature is renewed every day, the Han girl is stunned and stupefied, for she has been brought up in the Han community to be ashamed of her own body, not to mention her sexuality. Over time, however, she transforms herself, dressing in Dai costumes and swimming naked like the Dai girls.

Taken as a whole, *Sacrificed Youth* is less a film about the Dai people than a narrative of how a Han girl recovers her lost or repressed self. Throughout the film the Dai are evoked as the exoticized and eroticized Other, against whom the Han girl redefines her subject position. The nostalgic evocation of Dai culture comes to an end when, years later, returning from a college in the city, the Han girl finds that the entire Dai village had been wiped out in a massive landslide. The final barren landscape symbolically captures the politics of interethnic representation, for the Han girl remains the only survivor (and hence the only legitimated subject of knowledge), whereas Dai culture as the Other—despite its idyllic scenery and its exotic customs—has to be wiped out entirely from the surface of the earth, left forever for the Han subject to recall and reconstruct from her fragmented memories.[50]

While criticizing *Sacrificed Youth* as displaying "a rare bit of soft porn" in the mid-1980s, Dru Gladney finds it noteworthy that the woman director altered the original story, in which the Han girl was sent to a *nonminority* rural area.[51] Does this alteration automatically implicate the Han woman director in a "complicitous" relationship with the state discourse, which champions the Han cultural hegemony? If so, does the gender of the woman director, Zhang Nuanxin, contradict, complicate, or confirm Gladney's set-up of the following discursive parallels: "Minority is to the majority as female is to male, as 'Third' World to 'First,' and as subjectivized is to objectivized identity"?[52] The problem with Gladney's rather sweeping statement in this case actually has already been anticipated by James Clifford's critique of Edward Said's *Orientalism* (which no doubt influenced Gladney's choice of terms): "Said's work frequently relapses into the essentializing modes it attacks and is ambivalently enmeshed in the totalizing habits of Western humanism."[53] In other words, what is absent in Said's work—and by extension in Gladney's study—is a "developed theory of culture as a differentiating and expressive ensemble rather than as simply hegemonic and disciplinary."[54] Seen in this light, what is of *equal* importance to a study of nationhood and ethnicity—apart from discerning the political hierarchies in majority/minority representation—is a conceptualization of the hegemonic culture *not* as a self-stabilizing structure but rather as negotiated, present processes whereby the geopolitical boundaries of centers and margins are periodically redrawn and the localized differences tactfully articulated.

To locate various articulations of differences within the "hegemonic" culture of the nation, I find the concept "minority discourse" more useful than either "minority film" or "ethnography film" in dealing with New Chinese Cinema.[55] To be sure, films such as *Horse Thief* and *Sacrificed Youth* may conform to the "ethnographic" paradigm in that they usually end up legitimat-

Fig. 5. The late Zhang Nuanxin, director of *Sacrificed Youth,* in the summer of 1994.

ing the power and knowledge of the ethnographer (always a figure of the Han majority) rather than the alien (minority) culture investigated in the remote "jungle fields."⁵⁶ Nevertheless, what eventually distinguishes New Chinese Cinema of the past decade is its tactful building-up of a profound complexity and ambivalence, by means of which it not only interrogates— at a national level—the "grand myths" perpetuated in the previous films (e.g., the glorified revolutionary wars, the celebrated ethnic solidarity, and

the exaggerated achievements of the socialist construction) but also prob-
lematizes—at a local or localized level—its own position as a knowing subject, an oftentimes individualized subject burdened with the task of reassess-
ing the culture of the nation and of rewriting its history.[57]

Understood in this way, New Chinese Cinema may function like what
Homi Bhabha calls "minority discourse," which emerges "from the liminal
movement of the culture of the nation—at once opened up and held together," and which "acknowledges the status of national culture—and the
people—as a contentious, performative space of the perplexity of the living
in the midst of the pedagogical representations of the fullness of life."[58] It is
of crucial importance that a minority discourse take a strategic position of
"marginality"—a reconstructed marginality that questions and challenges the
"centrality" of the state discourse. To quote Bhabha again: "The marginal
or 'minority' is not the space of a celebratory, or utopian, self-marginaliza-
tion. It is a much more substantial intervention into those justifications of
modernity—progress, homogeneity, cultural organicism, the deep nation, the
long past—that rationalize the authoritarian, 'normalizing' tendencies within cultures in the name of the national interest or the ethnic prerogative."[59]

The Big Parade (Da yuebing, directed by Chen Kaige, 1985) emerges as a
ready example of the working of a "minority discourse" in contemporary
China. A film centered on the military training in preparation for a parade
in Beijing on the occasion of the thirty-fifth anniversary of the People's
Republic of China, *The Big Parade* tactfully challenges while explicitly celebrating the concept of the nation in the state discourse. In this connection,
Renan's commentary on the nation-state is worth quoting: "To have common glories in the past and to have a common will in the present; to have
performed great deeds together, to wish to perform still more—these are the
essential conditions for being a people."[60] What is remarkable in *The Big
Parade,* however, is its structuring of a subtext underneath the glorified surface of a national celebration, a subtext that comes to the fore if one disre-
gards the rhetoric of the state discourse and follows instead the individual
participants in the military training. By shifting voice-over from one individual to another, Chen Kaige in effect constructs the people as the "performative subject," whose very act of performing in the state-sponsored events
inevitably splits the unified subjectivity (people as "pedagogic object"—
nation-people) into various fragmented pieces. The film demonstrates that
the spectacular display of unity and discipline in the military parade in front
of the Tiananmen is nothing but a staged event, and that it is the individual
soldiers—whose sufferings are bracketed off or erased in the state discourse—
that ultimately deserve attention.

• Unresolved Questions: Cultural Nationalism in a "Hyphenated" World?

To return to Chris Berry's theory of "race," one realizes that he has made an overstatement in treating recent Chinese films as a radical challenge not only to "sinocentrism" but perhaps also "the very assumption of a fundamental duality separating the Han Chinese and the foreign."[61] As demonstrated above, *Horse Thief* and *Sacrificed Youth*—both cited as examples in Berry's essay—are still deeply anchored in a Han-centered position. Indeed, Berry's insistence on a "rupture" between recent Chinese films and what he calls "classical mainland Chinese cinema" of the 1950s and 1960s (represented, for example, by Xie Jin) tends to overlook an important fact, namely, that New Chinese Cinema may constitute a new alternative to—or even a new development of—*cultural nationalism* in contemporary China. In this regard, Dru Gladney's observation is more critical because it reveals a fundamental connection (rather than rupture) in the two periods of the ethnic minority genre: "Just as the singing and dancing, squeaky-clean minorities of an earlier genre failed to convince audiences that these people really were 'liberated' by the party, . . . so Tian's minorities films disappointed audiences: they both break with earlier representations of minorities and simultaneously reconstitute them."[62]

Cultural nationalism, as Harumi Befu writes, "focuses on the creation, crystallization, and expression of the cultural identity of the nation."[63] In the process of defining a national identity, cultural nationalism, to quote David Buck, "asserts the claim of certain cultural characteristics and traditions, almost always containing a strong primordialist element."[64] The fact that New Chinese Cinema has in varying degrees participated in reshaping cultural nationalism in contemporary China is evident in its characteristic, or even obsessive, fascination with an entire repertoire of recognizable cultural symbols and traditions in the nation: the Loess Plateau and the Yellow River (as in *Yellow Earth* [Huang tudi, directed by Chen Kaige, 1984] and *Life on a String* [Bianzou bianchang, directed by Chen Kaige, 1991]), traditional operas (as in *Woman, Demon, Human* [Ren gui qing, directed by Huang Shuqin, 1987] and *Farewell My Concubine* [Bawang bieji, directed by Chen Kaige, 1993]), folk music (as in *Swan Song* [Juexiang, directed by Zhang Zeming, 1985] and *Drum Singers* [Gushu yiren, directed by Tian Zhuang-zhuang, 1987]), marriage customs (as in *Bloody Morning* [Xuese qingchen, directed by Li Shaohong, 1990] and *Raise the Red Lantern* [Dahong denglong gaogao gua, directed by Zhang Yimou, 1991]), and funeral proceedings (as in *Ju Dou* [Ju Dou, directed by Zhang Yimou, 1990] and *The Big Mill* [Da mofang, directed by Wu Ziniu, 1990]). From watching these fascinating images, one gets the impression that it is its consistent exploration of the unfathomable depths of national culture—or the culture of the "Chinese nation" broadly defined, including its customs, legends, myths, and rituals—that has eventually secured an international reputation for New Chinese Cinema. Indeed, it might be speculated that one of the greatest successes of New Chinese Cinema lies in its "cultural exhibitionism," its repackaging—with remarkably sophisticated cinematic techniques, recently made available through overseas capital—of what is generally believed to be Chinese national culture (which is always already mystified and Orientalized in the West) and its redistributing to the international film market.[65]

For many Chinese viewers, it is precisely what the Western audiences might mistake for authentically "Chinese" in these recently successful Chinese films that has provoked indignation and criticism. The noted dissident journalist Dai Qing, for one, was not at all impressed by Zhang Yimou's *Raise the Red Lantern,* despite "its international cachet seemingly enhanced by the involvement of producers and financing from Hong Kong, Taiwan, Japan, and other countries." She sees clearly that "this kind of film is really shot for the casual pleasures of foreigners . . . [who] can go on and muddle-headedly satisfy their oriental fetishisms."[66] As a native Chinese, Dai Qing is not to be cheated "by half-baked new fashions and trends"; to prove her case, she compiles a long list of "false notes" (i.e., inauthenticities) in Zhang Yimou's filmic representation of Chinese culture (e.g., his invented rituals of foot-massage and raising the red lantern). To mitigate her indignation, Dai Qing thus persuades herself: "there is something worth our sympathy in the plight of a serious filmmaker being forced to make a living outside his own country."[67] What is interesting in Dai Qing's case is that, ironically, she sees the trendy practice of cultural nationalism in New Chinese Cinema as being complicitous with the Orientalist discourse in the West.

In spite of individual grievances or protests like Dai Qing's, many recent Chinese films, especially those by Chen Kaige and Zhang Yimou, are generously financed by foreign capital and continue to attract Western attention. To conclude my investigation of the relationship between nationhood and ethnicity, I would point out that we are now facing a critical moment of redefining our geopolitical world. That the products of cultural nationalism in New Chinese Cinema have not only met with "international" approval but have also attracted a "transnational" capital flow is itself an accentuated comment on the currently hard-to-define geopolitical world: whether labeled as "post-modern," "post-colonial," "post-Orientalist," "post-socialist," "post-contemporary," or even "post-future," the present-day world seems to have but a *hyphenated* existence.[68] In spite of all these hyphenated terms, however, one must not overlook a significant fact that our fin-de-siècle world is rarely imagined as ever "postnational." Does this conspicuous lack in critical language reveal any penchant for essentialism in our conceptualization of nationhood (i.e., a nation is so "fundamental" that it can never be "post" itself), even though the "nation" (in both senses of "nation-people" and "nation-state") has been repeatedly broken down into multiple ethnicities and regions, and the "nation as narration" been subject to interrogation by various instances of minority discourse?[69]

· Notes

1. This essay first appeared in *Cinema Journal* 36, no. 3 (1997) and is reprinted by permission of the University of Texas Press. Earlier versions were presented at Indiana University and the University of Pittsburgh in 1993–1994. My thanks to Sheldon Hsiao-peng Lu, David Nordloh, Sue Tuohy, and George M. Wilson for invitations and to the anonymous readers for *Cinema Journal* and the University of Hawai'i Press for their questions and suggestions.

In the system of classification used in Mainland China, "minority film" is a special genre of feature films. Other genres under feature films include comedy, film adaptation, historical drama, and revolutionary war; parallel to the features are listed cartoons, films of stage performances, newsreels, films of science and education, and sometimes children's features. See Chen Huangmei, ed., *Dangdai Zhongguo dianying* [Contemporary Chinese cinema], 2 vols. (Beijing: Zhongguo shehui kexue chubanshe, 1989). For New Chinese Cinema, see note 47 below.

2. Chris Berry, "Race: Chinese Film and the Politics of Nationalism," *Cinema Journal* 31, no. 2 (1992): 45–58.

3. Berry, "Race," 47. Cf. Paul Clark, *Chinese Cinema: Culture and Politics Since 1949* (New York: Cambridge University Press, 1987), 69. "Sinification" in Clark's somewhat ambiguous usage (as both *minzuhua* and *guoyouhua*) differs considerably from "sinicization" (*hanhua*) in anthropological and historical literatures, a term describing "acculturation to Chinese culture or assimilation by it." See Pamela Kyle Crossley, "Thinking About Ethnicity in Early Modern China," *Late Imperial China* 11, no. 1 (1990): 2–5.

4. Thomas Herberer, *China and Its Minorities: Autonomy or Assimilation?* (Armonk, N.Y.: M. E. Sharpe, 1989), 10.

5. Herberer, *China and Its Minorities*, 7. For further discussion, see Colin Mackerras, *China's Minorities: Integration and Modernization in the Twentieth Century* (New York: Oxford University Press, 1994), especially 3–45.

6. Frank Dikötter, *The Discourse of Race in Modern China* (Stanford: Stanford University Press, 1992), x. As Dikötter later points out, however, the concept of "race" (as in *zhongzu* or *renzhong*) was instrumental to the discursive formation of nationalism and national identity in modern China, although he does not want to see "a variabil-

ity of racial narratives . . . be reduced to a single model called 'Chinese racism.' " See Frank Dikötter, "Racial Identities in China: Context and Meaning," *China Quarterly* 138 (June 1994): 411.

7. See Frank Lentricchia and Thomas McLaughlin, ed., *Critical Terms for Literary Study* (Chicago: University of Chicago Press, 1990), 277.

8. For a brief discussion of Taine's concept of "race," see Henry Louis Gates, Jr., ed., *"Race," Writing, and Difference* (Chicago: University of Chicago Press, 1986), 3.

9. For instance, see Mao Dun's 1922 speech, "Wenxue yu rensheng" [Literature and life], in *Wenxue yundong shiliao xuan* [Selected readings in literary movements], Beijing Daxue et al., vol. 1 (Shanghai: Shanghai Jiaoyu chubanshe, 1979), 187. For the slogan "reviving national films," endorsed by Luo Mingyou in December 1929, see Cheng Jihua et al., ed., *Zhongguo dianying fazhan shi* [History of the development of Chinese cinema], vol. 1 (Beijing: Zhongguo dianying chubanshe, 1963), 148.

10. Lentricchia and McLaughlin, *Critical Terms,* 282.

11. Ernest Renan, "What Is a Nation?" in *Nation and Narration,* ed. Homi Bhabha (London: Routledge, 1990), 8.

12. Renan, "What Is a Nation?" 19.

13. Renan, "What Is a Nation?" 19.

14. Homi K. Bhabha, "DissemiNation: Time, Narrative, and the Margins of the Modern Nation," in *Nation and Narration,* ed. Homi K. Bhabha (New York: Routledge, 1990), 299; emphasis in the original.

15. Homi K. Bhabha, "Introduction: Narrating the Nation," in *Nation and Narration,* ed. Homi K. Bhabha (New York: Routledge, 1990), 4.

16. Prasenjit Duara, "De-constructing the Chinese Nation," *Australian Journal of Chinese Affairs* 30 (July 1993): 8, 1.

17. Duara, "De-constructing," 9.

18. Lentricchia and McLaughlin, *Critical Terms,* 288. In an earlier study, Werner Sollors considers race to be "merely one aspect of ethnicity"; see his *Beyond Ethnicity: Consent and Descent in American Culture* (New York: Oxford University Press, 1986), 36.

19. Lentricchia and McLaughlin, *Critical Terms,* 288, 299.

20. Crossley, "Thinking About Ethnicity," 19–20. For more discussion, see Peng Yingming, "Guanyu woguo minzu gainian lishi de chubu kaocha" [A preliminary investigation of the history of the concepts of *minzu* in China], *Minzu yanjiu* 2 (1985): 5–11.

21. Stuart Hall, "Minimal Selves," in ICA Document 6: *Identity* (1987), 46.

22. See Crossley, "Thinking About Ethnicity," 19.

23. See Cheng, *Zhongguo dianying,* vol. 1, 8. Even today, the "shadowplay" is still regarded as a viable Chinese film theory, distinct from any Western film theories. For instance, see Chen Xihe, "Shadowplay: Chinese Film Aesthetics and Their Philosophical and Cultural Fundamentals," in *Chinese Film Theory: A Guide to the New Era,*

ed. George S. Semsel, Xia Hong, and Hou Jianping (New York: Praeger, 1990), 192–204, and Zhong Dafeng, "An Historical Survey of Yingxi Theory," in *Film in Contemporary China: Critical Debates, 1979-1989,* ed. George S. Semsel, Chen Xihe, and Xia Hong (New York: Praeger, 1993), 65-73.

24. See Bao Yuheng, "The Mirror of Chinese Society," *Chinese Literature* 4 (1985): 191.

25. The term "electric shadows" was used as a book title: Jay Leyda, *Dianying—Electric Shadows: An Account of Films and the Film Audience in China* (Cambridge, Mass.: MIT Press, 1972).

26. See Ma Junxiang, "Minzu zhuyi suo suzao de xiandai Zhongguo dianying" [Modern Chinese film as shaped by nationalism], *Ershiyi shiji* no. 15 (February 1993): 112-119. Ma's view here corroborates Fredric Jameson's theory of Third World allegory; see Jameson, "Third-World Literature in the Era of Multinational Capitalism," *Social Text* 15 (fall 1986): 65-88.

27. See Cheng, *Zhongguo dianying,* vol. 1, 187-190, 507-509.

28. For lack of a better designation, I retain "leftist film" here as a widely circulated term in Chinese film studies, a term referring to a body of films of the 1930s and 1940s directed mostly by the "progressive" film workers at the time but based on scripts by underground Communist activists, such as Xia Yan and Tian Han. The slippage of the term is evident in these two films Wu Yonggang directed in the mid-1930s: whereas *Goddess* (Shennü, 1934) was later hailed as a classic example of leftist film, *The Little Angel* (Xiao tianshi, 1935) was an immediate product of the New Life Movement *(Xin shenghuo yundong)* launched by the Nationalist government in 1934, because it was based on a prize-winning script endorsed by the Ministry of Education for that movement.

29. One particular type of entertainment film in the early 1930s was the so-called soft film *(ruanxing dianying),* promoted by people like Liu Na'ou, who was assassinated in 1940 because of his involvement with the pro-Japanese government. For more information regarding the debate on "soft film," see Chen Bo, ed., *Zhongguo zuoyi dianying yundong* [The leftist film movement in China] (Beijing: Zhongguo dianying chubanshe, 1993), 142-174.

30. For the "cinema of national defense," see Sun Xun's and Meng Gongwei's *Da Wanbao* [Evening post] articles in May 1936, reprinted in *"Liangge kouhao" lunzheng ziliao xuanbian* [Selected materials on the debate over "two slogans"] (Beijing: Renmin wenxue chubanshe, 1982), vol. 1, 188-190, 197-201.

31. According to one source, *Spring River Flows East* was shown for more than three months and 712,874 tickets were sold; see Cheng, *Zhongguo dianying,* vol. 2, 222.

32. Renan, "What Is a Nation?" 19.

33. The films banned by the Nationalist censors during the period also included Hollywood productions such as *The Ten Commandments, Frankenstein* (both allegedly "superstitious"), and *Top Hat* (for being "sexy"). See Zhiwei Xiao, "Constructing a

New National Culture: The Problems of Cantonese Autonomy, Superstition and Sex," paper presented to the Association for Asian Studies annual meeting in Washington, D.C., April 6–9, 1995.

34. For a brief discussion of the film, see Cheng, *Zhongguo dianying*, vol. 2, 53–55.

35. For a study of film productions in the 1930s, see Paul G. Pickowicz, "The Theme of Spiritual Pollution in Chinese Films of the 1930s," *Modern China* 17, no. 1 (1991): 38–75.

36. For a distinction between the state apparatuses and the ideological state apparatuses, see Louis Althusser, *Lenin and Philosophy and Other Essays,* trans. Ben Brewster (New York: Monthly Review Press, 1971), 127–186.

37. Renan, "What Is a Nation?" 19.

38. About twenty minority films were produced in the 1950s, among which *Hasen and Jiamila* (Hasen yu Jiamila, directed by Wu Yonggang) was made in 1955. The early 1960s saw the rapid growth of this new genre; for instance, about twenty more minority films were made in a four-year period. See Chen, *Dangdai Zhongguo dianying*, vol. 1, 154–155, 263–269.

39. For a study of the legend of Third Sister Liu and its film adaptation, see Wai-fong Loh, "From Romantic Love to Class Struggle: Reflections on the Film *Liu Sanjie*," in *Popular Chinese Literature and Performing Arts in the People's Republic of China, 1949–1979,* ed. Bonnie McDougall (Berkeley: University of California Press, 1984), 165–176.

40. For a discussion along this line, see Lin Niantong, "A Study of the Theories of Chinese Cinema in Their Relationship to Classical Aesthetics," *Modern Chinese Literature* 1, no. 2 (1985): 186–189. For a more recent debate on the "nationalization of film" *(minzuhua),* see the articles collected in Semsel, Xia, and Hou, *Chinese Film Theory,* 97–140.

41. Paul Clark, "Ethnic Minorities in Chinese Films: Cinema and the Exotic," *East-West Film Journal* 1, no. 2 (1987): 25.

42. Some of Paul Clark's claims with regard to minority films need more evidence to sustain them. First, his thesis that "the tendency to regard films as a source of exotic, usually foreign, images has remained strong" from the first screening of Lumière brothers reel in 1896 down to the 1980s overlooks the entire legacy of "mainstream" Chinese cinema (namely, leftist film of the 1930s–1940s and socialist realism of the 1950s–1960s), whose aim was not only to "reflect" but also to "intervene" in sociopolitical realities. Second, Clark's remark that "After 1949, with fewer, mostly Soviet, foreign films on Chinese screens, the search for the exotic led Chinese filmmakers and filmgoers to the most non-Chinese parts" also fails to account for the complicity of minority films in the state's project of cultural hegemony. See Clark, "Ethnic Minorities," 15–16.

43. For a discussion of *Serfs,* see Clark, *Chinese Cinema,* 96–99.

44. Another film of this type is *Visitor on Ice Mountain* (Bingshan shang de laike, directed by Zhao Xingshui, 1963).

45. Dru C. Gladney, "Representing Nationality in China: Refiguring Majority/ Minority Identities," *Journal of Asian Studies* 53, no. 1 (1994): 94.

46. Gladney, "Representing Nationality," 96, 98, 114.

47. I prefer the term New Chinese Cinema to Fifth-Generation film for a number of reasons. First, the Fifth Generation (which oftentimes refers to Chen Kaige, Tian Zhuangzhuang, Wu Ziniu, Xia Gang, Zhang Junzhao, and Zhang Yimou, and sometimes also to Huang Jianxin, Sun Zhou, Zhang Zeming, and Zhou Xiaowen, as well as to women directors Hu Mei, Li Shaohong, and Peng Xiaolian) is a much narrower term than New Chinese Cinema, for the latter may also include films made more or less contemporaneously by both the pre-Fifth-Generation directors (such as Huang Shuqin, Wu Tianming, Wu Yigong, Xie Fei, and Zhang Nuanxin, all belonging to the "Fourth Generation") and the post-Fifth-Generation directors (such as He Ping, Jiang Wen, and Ning Ying, as well as the emerging "Sixth-Generation" directors like Wang Xiaoshuai and Zhang Yuan). Second, the term Fifth Generation gives an impression that their films are somehow homogeneous, which is obviously incorrect; for instance, both Tian Zhuangzhuang and Zhang Yimou were pressured to make "entertainment films" *(yule pian)*, such as Tian's *Rock 'n' Roll Kids* (Yaogun qingnian, 1988) and Zhang's *Code Name Puma* (Daihao Meizhoubao, 1988). Third, the incorrect association of the Fifth Generation almost exclusively with Chen Kaige and Zhang Yimou tends to obscure rather than illuminate the achievements of New Chinese Cinema, thereby creating an imbalance of critical attention devoted to them and to other equally gifted directors (Wu Ziniu, for one, is hardly discussed in Western film criticism). For sample discussions of New Chinese Cinema, see Paul Clark, "Reinventing China: The Fifth-Generation Filmmakers," *Modern Chinese Literature* 5 (1989): 121–136; Ma Ning, "Notes on the New Filmmakers," in Semsel, Xia, and Hou, *Chinese Film*, 63–93; and Chen Kaige and Tony Rayns, *King of the Children and New Chinese Cinema* (London: Faber and Faber, 1989), 1–58. For a "hit parade" of five generations of Chinese directors, see Huang Shixian, "Zhongguo dianying daoyan 'xingzuo' jiqi yishu puxi" [The 'galaxy' of Chinese film directors and their artistic genealogy], *Dangdai dianying* 6 (1992): 77–85.

48. See Yang Ping, "A Director Who is Trying to Change the Audience: A Chat with Young Director Tian Zhuangzhuang," in *Perspectives on Chinese Cinema,* enlarged and rev. ed., ed. Chris Berry (London: British Film Institute, 1991), 127.

49. See Semsel, *Chinese Film,* 132.

50. Esther Yau offers an incisive analysis of *Sacrificed Youth* in which she criticizes Zhang Nuanxin's ethnocentric practice in the film: "Such inability to perceive or act outside one's ideological inscription despite having gained insights from the Others underscores ethnocentrism as a stubborn blind spot of the mind that may generate

colonizing moves in cross-cultural encounters." See Esther Yau, "Is China the End of Hermeneutics?; or, Political and Cultural Usage of Non-Han Women in Mainland Chinese Films," in *Multiple Voices in Feminist Film Criticism,* ed. Diane Carson, Linda Dittmar, and Janice R. Welsch (Minneapolis: University of Minnesota Press, 1994), 290.

51. Gladney, "Representing Nationality," 105.

52. Gladney, "Representing Nationality," 93. One may, of course, follow Gladney by arguing in general terms that *Sacrificed Youth* participates in the state discourse of "internal Orientalism," but this argument alone does not account for the construction of a distinctively female voice in Zhang Nuanxin's film, which is a rare achievement in the post–Cultural Revolution era.

53. James Clifford, *The Predicament of Culture* (Cambridge, Mass: Harvard University Press, 1988), 271. See also Edward Said, *Orientalism* (New York: Vintage Books, 1979).

54. Clifford, *Predicament,* 263. However, Gladney seems to realize the problem at one point when he suggests that "Han-ness" in China be scrutinized in the same critical way as "whiteness" has been recently interrogated in the West; see Gladney, "Representing Nationality," 103.

55. I follow Homi Bhabha's formulation of "minority discourse," which is to be distinguished from JanMohamed and Lloyd's more general use of "minority discourse," defined as "a theoretical articulation of the political and cultural structures that connect different minority cultures in their subjugation and opposition to the dominant culture." See Abdul R. JanMohamed and David Lloyd, ed., *The Nature and Context of Minority Discourse* (New York: Oxford University Press, 1990), ix. JanMohamed and Lloyd's aim is to construct a "theoretical" discourse through which to articulate the relations between various minority discourses already in circulation (p. 1). Proceeding from this general formulation, Rey Chow redefines modern Chinese literature as a "minority discourse" linked to other postcolonial national literatures, all of them being "victimized" and "suppressed" by "the hegemonic discourse of the West"; see Rey Chow, "Against the Lures of Diaspora: Minority Discourse, Chinese Women, and Intellectual Hegemony," in her *Writing Diaspora: Tactics of Intervention in Contemporary Cultural Studies* (Bloomington: Indiana University Press, 1993), 100–101. My problem with this more general use of "minority discourse" is that it does not advance our knowledge any further than a mere rephrasing of the existing terms (e.g., the West versus the rest, colonialism/imperialism versus native resistance). To venture on a topic more relevant to this study, one may question whether a designation of Chinese leftist film of the 1930s as a "minority discourse"—in Rey Chow's sense—which was doubly victimized and suppressed by the hegemonic discourses of the West and of the Chinese regimes (both the Nationalist and the Communist) would help explain anything specific to the sociopolitical realities of modern China. Bhabha's notion of "minority discourse" as a localized tactic within the hege-

monic culture, on the other hand, may explain how New Chinese Cinema could achieve so much in the past decade by skillfully negotiating its way through the fissures and cracks split open by the discourse of the nation-state itself.

56. For instance, Esther Yau mentions "the ethnographic mode" in *Sacrificed Youth* and "Zhang Nuanxin's observation-participation techniques." See Yau, "Is China the End," 285, 288. Cf. also Rey Chow, *Primitive Passions: Visuality, Sexuality, Ethnography, and Contemporary Chinese Cinema* (New York: Columbia University Press, 1995).

57. For a discussion of some related questions, see Yingjin Zhang, "Ideology of the Body in *Red Sorghum*: National Allegory, National Roots, and Third Cinema," *East-West Film Journal* 4, no. 2 (1990): 38–53.

58. Bhabha, "DissemiNation," 305, 307.

59. Bhabha, "Introduction," 4.

60. Renan, "What Is a Nation?" 19.

61. Berry, "Race," 51.

62. Dru C. Gladney, "Tian Zhuangzhuang, the Fifth Generation, and Minorities Film in China," *Public Culture* 8, no. 1 (1995): 169.

63. Harumi Befu, ed., *Cultural Nationalism in East Asia: Representation and Identity* (Berkeley: Institute of East Asian Studies, University of California, 1993), 2.

64. David D. Buck, "Introduction to Dimensions of Ethnic and Cultural Nationalism in Asia—A Symposium," *Journal of Asian Studies* 53, no. 1 (1994): 6.

65. As Esther Yau puts it, "In the Western critics' fascinated and approving gaze, then, the young Chinese directors saw themselves as 'worthy of love,' and pride in 'national' cultural products grew as verified by international exchange"; see her "International Fantasy and the 'New Chinese Cinema,' " *Quarterly Review of Film and Video* 14, no. 3 (1993): 96. For more discussion of "exhibitionism" in recent Chinese films, see Chow, *Primitive Passions*, 152–154, 166–172.

66. Dai Qing, "Raised Eyebrows for *Raise the Red Lantern*," *Public Culture* 5, no. 2 (1993): 333–336.

67. Dai, "Raised Eyebrows," 337.

68. Critical literatures on postmodernity and postcoloniality have become too extensive and too diverse to be adequately sampled here. For a recent critique of postcolonial discourse, see Arif Dirlik, "The Postcolonial Aura: Third World Criticism in the Age of Global Capitalism," *Critical Inquiry* 20, no. 2 (1994): 328–356. For post-Orientalism, see John D. Rogers, "Post-Orientalism and the Interpretation of Premodern and Modern Political Identities: The Case of Sri Lanka," *Journal of Asian Studies* 53, no. 1 (1994): 10–23. For postsocialism, see Paul G. Pickowicz, "Huang Jianxin and the Notion of Postsocialism," in *New Chinese Cinemas: Forms, Identities, Politics*, ed. Nick Browne, Paul G. Pickowicz, Vivian Sobchack, and Esther Yau (Cambridge: Cambridge University Press, 1994), 57–87. The term "post-contemporary" is used in a critical series, "Post-Contemporary Interventions," coedited by Stanley Fish and Fredric Jameson and published by Duke University Press. "Post-

future" is used in the title of a special issue, "Views from the Post-Future/Soviet & Eastern European Cinema," edited by Jane Gaines and Thomas Lahusen, *Discourse* 17, no. 3 (1995): 3–125.

69. For instance, see Chris Berry, "A Nation T(w/o)o: Chinese Cinema(s) and Nationhood(s)," *East-West Film Journal* 7, no. 1 (1993): 24–51. Berry's article contains the only reference to the "postnational" in the Chinese context I have come across so far. In reading an epic film from Taiwan, *City of Sadness* (Beiqing chengshi, directed by Hou Hsiao-hsien, 1989), Berry locates "a collective self that is hybridized and riven with difference, a subject that cannot speak, and at least the shadow of a postnational imagined community founded on hybrid space" (p. 45). Nonetheless, even if a "postnational" space is conceivable in critical thinking, as is pursued in Martin J. Matustik's *Postnational Identity: Critical Theory and Existential Philosophy in Habermas, Kierkegaard, and Havel* (New York: Guilford Press, 1993), could we ever imagine something like a "postethnic" world system?

Chapter 4
•
National Cinema, Cultural Critique, Transnational Capital
The Films of Zhang Yimou
•
Sheldon Hsiao-peng Lu

In the burgeoning field of cultural studies in China in the 1990s, Zhang Yimou's film art has been the focal point of much critical discussion.[1] The international popularity of Zhang's films conveniently thematizes a set of interrelated main concerns of current cultural debates in China: the fate of Chinese national cinema in the condition of transnational capital, "cultural critique" and "cultural exhibitionism" in Fifth-Generation cinema, Third World cinema and Third World criticism, Orientalism, and postcolonialism in Chinese style.

Zhang's film art poses a central question, a paradox indeed, not only for Chinese critics themselves but for all interested cultural workers, in regard to Third World art in general: How does one re-create the Third World *national* allegory, through the cinematic apparatus, in the new *transnational* setting? What are the conditions and strategies for doing so? In the now classic essay, "Third-World Literature in the Era of Multinational Capitalism," Fredric Jameson theorized the linkage between Third World literature and national allegory. Yet the phenomena he investigated occurred well before the disintegration of the Soviet bloc and the advent of global capitalism in the 1990s. A new mapping of Third World allegory in the changed circumstances of the postnational and transnational era remains to be done.[2] To me, New Chinese Cinema, especially Zhang's film art, is paradigmatic of the fate and predicament of Third World culture in our present time.

It seems to me that the reinvention of Chinese national cinema through an indigenous cultural critique of the Chinese nation and the creation of what we may call "transnational Chinese cinema" with the support of transnational capital are the twin main aspects that underlie Zhang's film art. His films have attracted a large international audience precisely because they are regarded as authentically "national," "Chinese," and "Oriental." Thus, an indigenous cultural critique through the medium of national cinema becomes at the same time a cultural sellout of the Chinese nation in the international film market.

Fig. 6. Director Zhang Yimou. British Film Institute.

In the present study, I will first read and situate Zhang's films in relation to the intellectual background of "cultural reflection" that swept across China in the 1980s, a movement that ultimately reached back to some of the enduring themes of the May 4th Movement of the early twentieth century. My point is that Zhang's films can best be understood as an articulation and variation of certain perennial issues in modern Chinese intellectual, cultural, and literary history.

I will also look at the corpus of his major films as a complete artistic cycle and paradigm, with unique characteristics in terms of theme and style. They have won him auteur status in the pantheon of world film artists.

From his first film, *Red Sorghum* (Hong gaoliang), through *Ju Dou* (Judou), *Raise the Red Lantern* (Da hong denglong gaogao gua), *The Story of Qiu Ju* (Qiu Ju da guansi), *To Live* (Huozhe), and *Shanghai Triad* (Yao a yao, yao dao waipo-qiao), Gong Li was his lead actress on screen and lover off screen. Their passionate, intense collaboration brought them immense prestige and stardom in international film circles. With the breakup of their legendary relationship after *Shanghai Triad,* the future of Zhang's film art remains uncertain and the subject of much speculation. What will his films look like without Gong Li?[3] Given the lukewarm reception of his last collaborative work with Gong Li, *Shanghai Triad,* both in China and overseas, there are already signs of artistic exhaustion. This cycle of films traces for us a trajectory of creativity, inventiveness, innovation, and perhaps finally decline and exhaustion.

In the final part of this essay, I examine the consequences of the "success," for lack of a better term, of Zhang's films in the global market. In the eyes of many critics, especially native Chinese critics, Zhang's international popularity is dubious. He has been taken as an exemplary instance of the willful surrender of Third World cinema to the Orientalist gaze, as a classic case of the subjugation of Third World culture to Western hegemony. While I partially agree with these assessments, it is important that film critics be more aware of the dynamics of a new global film culture that unfolds around the world. Under the conditions of global capitalism, Zhang has been able to pursue and sustain a critical project that has become impossible in his home country. Transnational capital is therefore at once a constrictive and a liberating force for Chinese cinema. Furthermore, the entrance of Third World cinema such as Zhang's into mainstream Western film culture may indeed begin to make a "difference." These films offer alternative histories, stories, and images of nations and peoples that are unseen and unavailable in ordinary Hollywood films. Consequently, Zhang's film art has the potential to become an oppositional practice on the domestic front and an alternative discourse in the international arena.

• Cultural Critique and the Genealogy of Chinese Modernity

In the mid- and late 1980s, Fifth-Generation cinema was part of a broad, nationwide intellectual movement. Writers, artists, filmmakers, and intellectuals embarked on a "cultural critique" of the "deep structure" of the Chinese nation. Yet, there was an underlying, unresolved dilemma in the Fifth Generation's involvement in this critical project.[4] On the one hand, the Fifth Generation was to inherit the critical legacy of the May 4th Movement, to launch a thorough, iconoclastic attack on tradition, to clear away the obstacles on the path to modernity. This is the continuation of the May 4th legacy of "enlightenment" in the circumstances of the 1980s. On the other hand, "historical/cultural reflection" (lishi fansi, wenhua fansi) also implies a "search for the roots" (xungen), a return to the source of Chinese culture, and recovery of a national history obscured and distorted by authoritarian discourse. This double movement of "enlightenment" and "searching for the roots" shaped the discourse of this group of filmmakers. Fifth-Generation films were variations on these two themes. Chen Kaige's films such as *Yellow Earth* (Huang tudi), *King of the Children* (Haizi wang), and *Life on a String* (Bianzou bianchang), with their frequent deployment of long takes, long shots, and deep focus, are anguished, self-reflexive, slow-paced, scathing critiques of entrenched patterns of traditional Chinese culture. Although not the first film produced by the Fifth Generation, the release of *Yellow Earth* at the Hong Kong film festival in 1984 was an inaugural event for Fifth-Generation cinema. Yet, none of Chen's films had popular appeal and commercial success until *Farewell My Concubine* (Bawang bieji).

Unlike Chen's early films, Zhang's *Red Sorghum* proceeds in the other direction of historical reflection. Narrating a legendary, action-packed tale of a heroic past, the film reaches deep into the roots of China and attempts to rehabilitate and establish a new subjectivity of the Chinese nation. The story is a cinematic reenactment of libidinal and psychic liberation. Zhang weaves an allegory of an empowered masculinity freed from age-old repression. On the surface, the film appears to be a depoliticized film. Political overtones are reduced to a minimum in the narration of the story. Yet, behind the seeming depoliticization is a politics of sexuality, an "ideology of the body," an "aesthetics of masculinity." "Red Sorghum is a cinematic milestone that proposes a powerful Chinese version of masculinity as a means of cultural critique."[5] The film aspires to be free from the straitjacket of political indoctrination and "aspires to a liberation of the human body, a liberation that will return the Chinese people from their now uniform lifestyle and sterile way of thinking to their nurturing, regenerating origins (roots)."[6] The film was rightfully a product of the heyday of the "cultural fever" (wenhua re) in intellectual circles. It was a time when the regime still promised both economic and political reform for the Chinese people. By couching cultural reflection in the guise of visual grandeur, entertainment, and action, the film gained immense popularity upon release in China. As a crowning piece of Chinese national cinema, the film narrates the story of the rebirth and recovery of the Chinese nation.

Cultural critique in the style of the 1980s was effectively brought to an end by the tragic events of June 4, 1989, in Tiananmen Square. The "New Era" (xin shiqi) (late 1970s to 1989) in Chinese intellectual and cultural history was over; the "post-New Era" *(hou xin shiqi)* began. The social, economic, and cultural trends of the 1990s are unfavorable to elitist cultural reflection, high art, and avant-garde film. China is caught in a transition from a planned economy to a "socialist market economy." The Chinese economy has increasingly become part of a global post-Fordist, capitalist economy. The cultural scene is dominated by the flourishing of popular culture (in the forms of TV series, MTV, popular music, bestsellers, tabloid journalism, and karaoke). China's film audience is shrinking, and the film industry is in a state of crisis.

However, Zhang's film career did not end after Tiananmen. In fact, in the 1990s his films entered North America and achieved worldwide recognition. They were all nominees and winners of awards in rapid succession at major international film festivals such as Cannes and Venice. *Ju Dou* and *Raise the Red Lantern* were each nominated for the Best Foreign Picture at the Academy Awards. His targeted audience is no longer domestic but overseas. He has broken out of China's film industry by obtaining financial backing from outside of Mainland China. His films are periodically banned in his home country, but they have been regularly screened in movie theaters around the world. The videotapes of his films are readily available in commercial video stores all over America. By funding his production through transnational capital, and by distributing his films in the international film market, Zhang has created what might be called "transnational Chinese cinema." He has brought about a permanent change in the pattern of Chinese national cinema. After Zhang Yimou, the mechanisms of funding, production, marketing, distribution, and consumption of Chinese cinema were forever changed.

Despite his complicity in transnational capital/capitalism, Zhang situates his films as part of an indigenous critical enterprise. He himself places Fifth-Generation film and his own film art within the broad movement of cultural reflection. Speaking of the unique quality of New Chinese Cinema in comparison to filmmaking in Taiwan and Hong Kong, he says:

> "Using literature to transmit the Tao" *(wenyi zaidao)* is a habit of thought in literary and artistic creation that has been sedimented *(jidian)* in Mainland China for thousands of years. Therefore, the works from the Mainland have a heavily literary quality, and their main objective is to embody a humanistic content. The famous works of the Fifth-Generation directors are basically the awakenings of cultural reflection and cultural awareness in this broad humanistic background. From this standpoint, the artistic methods usually carry a necessarily rebellious spirit. Such a pursuit of ours is not only aimed at the innovation of

cinematic language and methods, but also to meet the strong demands of social change.[7]

On the one hand, it is the collective mission of his generation of filmmakers to launch a total attack on the very basis of Chinese tradition, which is perceived as inhuman and repressive to its people. On the other hand, this self-reflexive, humanistic, and critical impulse is in itself a legacy of China's past. Not unlike the Confucian literati, artists assume the role of speaking for the moral standards of the nation and the conscience of its people. Art is used as an instrument for enlightenment and cultural critique. Despite the vehemently antitraditional tendency, this form of critical thinking traces back to, as Zhang admits, a fundamentally traditional Chinese view of the function of art. Such an irony also lies at the heart of the May 4th generation of Chinese writers and thinkers.[8]

While directly commenting on his films *Ju Dou* and *Raise the Red Lantern* in an interview with the Chinese-American anthropologist Mayfair Yang, Zhang hinted at the political and critical thrust of his films:

> What I want to express is the Chinese people's oppression and confinement, which has been going on for thousands of years. Women express this more clearly on their bodies . . . because they bear a heavier burden than men. . . .
>
> I was so excited when I discovered the walled gentry mansion [where *Red Lantern* was filmed], which is hundreds of years old in Shanxi Province. Its high walls formed a rigid square grid pattern that perfectly expresses the age-old obsession with strict order. The Chinese people have for a long time confined themselves within a restricted walled space. Democracy is still very far off, and it will be slow in forming here. We have a historical legacy of extinguishing human desire *(miejue renyu).*[9]

According to Zhang, the liberation of the self from the oppressive tradition is still the unfulfilled task, the incomplete project of Chinese modernity. The emancipation of the individual was also the goal of the May 4th generation of Chinese intellectuals more than half a century ago, a goal that is yet to be realized today for Zhang.

Zhang's cultural critique of the Chinese nation harks back to the foundation of modern Chinese literature. There is a basic thematic continuity between Zhang's film, or Fifth-Generation film in general, and the legacy of modern Chinese literature since the May 4th Movement (1919). Similar to celebrated literary works such as the short stories of Lu Xun, Zhang's films represent the oppressed, the downtrodden, the dispossessed, peasants, women—the "subalterns" in the genealogy of Chinese (pre)modernity. Most evident is the repeated appearance of the figure of the child in his films. In such a manner, his filmic texts enter and reactivate a preexisting intertextual network of themes, archetypes, and symbols. For modern Chinese writers and filmmakers, the figure of the child is a favorite trope for China's future, for their "obsession with China" in C. T. Hsia's words. A study of the representation of children and the ending of the films will reveal much about the nature of Zhang's critical project. In the futurology of Zhang and his generation, the future is at times envisioned as a return to the past, as repetition, cyclicity, circularity, and even total destruction; at other times, there seems to be a glimmer of hope, renewal, and rebirth out of the ashes of the past.

In the renowned "foundational" text of the Fifth Generation, *Yellow Earth* by Chen Kaige, China's fate is intimately tied to the fate of her children, Cuiqiao and Hanhan. In a futile endeavor to escape from an arranged marriage and to join the Eighth Route Army, Cuiqiao drowns, significantly, in the Yellow River, the cradle of Chinese civilization, as she attempts to cross it. At the end of the film, the boy, Hanhan, runs toward the Eighth Route Army soldier Gu Qing in the midst of a rain prayer, only to be engulfed by the crowd of peasants praying for rain. The figure of the child is no less meaningful in Chen's other films. *King of the Children* is properly a story about China's children, a meditation on the transmission of knowledge to posterity. The ending of the film portrays the burning of mountains in the spring, an agricultural renewal, a total break from the past. *Life on a String* is a timeless allegory of a master musician and his disciple Shitou. The mystery posed at the end is whether Shitou and other children in the film will repeat the fate of their ancestors. In *Farewell My Concubine,* a film that is a dramatic departure from Chen's earlier works, a crucial aspect of the narrative hinges upon the relationship between Master Guan and his disciples, Duan Xiaolou and Cheng Dieyi, and the relationship between Xiaolou and Dieyi as teachers and their own student, Xiaosi'er. The ending of the film turns into a nightmare as Xiaosi'er betrays and struggles against his teachers during the Cultural Revolution. The Cultural Revolution, undoubtedly a supreme, frenzied "cultural critique" in its own fashion, was a radical rupture with the past and constituted an act of betrayal of tradition.

Similarly, Zhang's renderings of the figure of the child, who stands between China's past and future, are attempts to reinvent the myths of origins in the genealogy of Chinese modernity. These fabled beginnings and pasts, portrayed through children, foreshadow the history and fate of the nation. Zhang's strategy has been persistent from his first film, *Red*

Sorghum, all the way to *Shanghai Triad.* While *Red Sorghum* is narrated and framed by the memory of the narrator/grandchild, the events of *Shanghai Triad* are seen completely through the eyes of the fourteen-year-old boy Shuisheng. These tales of "fathers," "mothers," and "sons" reveal a perpetual fascination with origins, beginnings, rebirths, and endings.

The oedipal complex in the triangulation of the relationships between fathers, mothers, and sons is not only a fundamental element of the melodrama of most of Zhang's films but also the basic condition of the historic appearance of the Fifth Generation in relation to its predecessors. In the narrative of the films, one witnesses a number of gruesome instances of parricide: "my grandpa" killed Big Head Li in order to take my "grandma" in *Red Sorghum;* nephew Tianqing contemplated killing Uncle Yang Jingshan, but in the end Tianbai killed both of his "fathers," Yang Jinshan and Tianqing, in *Ju Dou;* the village head Wang Shantang, or the "Name of the Father," kicked his villager Qinglai, Qiu Ju's husband, in the groin, for the latter insulted him for his inability to father sons in *The Story of Qiu Ju;* Second Brother, Song, schemed to kill his boss, Mr. Tang, in order to possess Xiao Jinbao, but he was murdered by Mr. Tang in the end in *Shanghai Triad.*

The oedipal rivalry between fathers and sons does not remain solely on the level of the filmic text itself. As Dai Jinhua argues, it articulates, on another level, the difficult relationship of the Fifth Generation to the past.[10] Members of this generation spent their youth during the Cultural Revolution and grew up in the symbolic and linguistic order of the Father. With the demise and demystification of the Father in the post-Mao era, they became a generation of lost children without a "father." After growing up in a heroic past, they are now condemned to live in a state of cultural rupture and historical discontinuity. Hence, their art is characterized by a search for origins, beginnings, foundations, in other words, fathers. At the same time, it is necessary to slay the fathers and ancestors in order to stage their own appearance. The simultaneous search for and killing of fathers defines their ambivalent yet violent relationship to tradition, culture, and the nation, as well as previous generations of film artists, writers, and thinkers.

In *Red Sorghum,* the narrator tells a story about his "grandpa" and "grandma." He is outside of the diegesis of the film and is only heard in voice-over. The fact that he can tell a story today about the past already indicates that he has survived the trials and tribulations of modern Chinese history. His father, the child who appears in the film, was conceived in a passionate encounter between grandpa and grandma in the wild, fertile, green sorghum field. At the end of the film, grandma is shot to death by Japanese soldiers, but grandpa's heroic battle defeats the invaders. There is an eclipse in the sky, and the film ends with the singing of the child—the narrator's father. The child in this film becomes the figure of the revival and continuity of the Chinese nation.

The theme of children in filmic representations is a significant reworking of a major concern of modern Chinese literature since the May 4th Movement. Children haunt the ending of many of the most memorable stories of Lu Xun, the "father" of modern Chinese fiction. "Save the children" is the battle cry of the Madman against the "cannibalism" of Chinese society in the "Madman's Diary" (Kuangren riji). At the end of the story "My Old Home" (Guxiang), the narrator entertains the possibility of renewal, the existence of a road of "hope" for his childhood friend Runtu, and Runtu's children in turn. In the story "Medicine" (Yao), Little Shuan's illness is supposed to be cured by eating the bread stained in the blood of the revolutionary who died for the future of China. Little Shuan dies anyway, and the masses remain unenlightened as ever. In another example, the narrator/boy/bartender in the story "Kong Yiji" is as callous and indifferent to the fate of Kong Yiji as the jeering crowd in the tavern. He is incapable of consciousness independent from that of the crowd. The short story "Sinking" (Chenlun) by Yu Dafu, another major writer of May 4th literature, ends with the protagonist's cry: "China, your children are still suffering."

Viewers may have noticed that *Ju Dou* and *Raise the Red Lantern,* two films made after the tragic events in Tiananmen Square on June 4, 1989, strike a different note from Zhang's first film, *Red Sorghum.* The mood of *Red Sorghum* is festive and exuberant. The film is a rehearsal of the recuperation of masculinity and sexuality, and by extension of the underlying sexual politics, the regeneration of the Chinese nation. In stark contrast to *Red Sorghum,* the mood of *Ju Dou* and *Raise the Red Lantern* is somber and tragic. The endings of the films verge on insanity and total destruction. Except for glimpses of a few jovial and vital moments, the general atmosphere is as repressive as ever. The politics of sexuality is directed in another way this time. The aestheticization of sexuality and sexual repression in these two films is far from being innocuous. Beyond the visual grandeur and aesthetic appeal, there is an implicit, displaced political allegory. Although there is not a single commentary on the contemporary political scene, the films set out to take on the cultural infrastructure embedded in both contemporary China and thousands of years of Chinese history. They also reach toward the roots and origins of Chinese culture. The difference between these films and *Red Sorghum* becomes obvious. They do not return to the "nurturing, regenerating origins" of the Chinese people; on the contrary, they expose and criticize the stifling and degenerating origins of Chinese institutions and habits.

National Cinema, Cultural Critique, Transnational Capital   *113*

• *Ju Dou*

Ju Dou unfolds a story of "China" in the 1920s. In a closed filmic text where every shot and every detail seem impregnated with meaning, the film narrates events that happen in a family dye mill. The enclosed structure of the family mansion, the traditional Chinese dye mill, and the colorful strips of dyed cloth convey an aura of mystique and exoticism. In the first half of *Ju Dou*, it is apparent that the conflict of the story is between the couple of young lovers, Ju Dou and Tianqing, and the old owner of the dye mill, Yang Jinshan, who is the lawful husband of Ju Dou and the uncle of Tianqing. The illicit, "incestuous" affair between Ju Dou and Tianqing is a transgression of the laws of the patriarchal system, which is represented by Yang Jinshan and the whole Yang clan. The impotent old man becomes a living symbol of the oppressive social order which sets out to extinguish the desires of young people. Social relations are kept intact at the expense of libidinal drives. The fabric of the story is nothing less than the neo-Confucian motto: "preserve heavenly laws and extinguish human desire" (*cun tianli, mie renyu*), which had gained currency since the Song dynasty. Seen from a traditional Chinese moral perspective, the love affair is an unpardonable violation of ethical codes and human relationships. The excessive sexual desire on the part of the woman and the lack of filial piety on the part of the man are both to be condemned in the eyes of the apologists for traditional values.[11]

Toward the middle of the film, the love between Ju Dou and Tianqing culminates in the birth of an illegitimate son, Tianbai. Yet, within the social hierarchy, Tianbai is recognized as the legitimate son of Ju Dou and Yang Jinshan. Tianbai himself would never call Tianqing his father. The first time he speaks is the moment when he calls Yang Jinshan "dad" (*die*). By coincidence, perhaps, this makes a classic example of Lacanian psychoanalysis. The recognition of the Father marks his entrance into the Symbolic order. The child Tianqing transforms from a biological being to a social being, a "subject." He is thus "interpellated" as the son of Yang Jinshan, the legitimate heir to the old master. He is so recognized by the whole community, the entire Yang clan.

Interestingly enough, neither has Tianqing the courage to claim Tianbai as his son. Without exception, Tianqing is also necessarily "interpellated" by the patriarchal order as a "subject" who occupies a specific social position. He is rightfully the "brother" of Tianbai, the "nephew" of Ju Dou and Yang Jinshan. He is perpetually in a subordinate position even after the death of Master Yang. While Master Yang is physically impotent, Tianqing is psychically and socially emasculated. Neither has he the strength to stand up to oppose the Yang clan, nor can he summon the courage to run away with Ju Dou.[12] In discussing Chinese cinema, E. Ann Kaplan acutely points out the severe effect of emasculation that Chinese males suffer in a patriarchal society, be it modern or ancient:

> Given the prior phallic order, and given the classical Oedipal rivalry with the Father, they may be harmed even more than women. State communism, in demanding male submission to the Law of the Father with little possibility for obtaining at least some parity with the Father position (as in free-enterprise capitalism), may produce men psychically damaged in deeper ways even than women.[13]

The generational conflict between the impotent old man and the young lovers in the first half of the film turns into a new round of generation conflict in the second half. The "oedipal conflict" becomes more destructive, involving two incidents of parricide this time. Tianbai fights for his social position, his legitimacy by refusing to recognize Tianqing as his father. Earlier on, the child Tianbai had accidentally killed his "legitimate" father, Master Yang, who fell and drowned in a pool of red dye water. At the end of film, Tianbai kills Tianqing, his biological father, dumping him into the same pool of blood-red water after catching Tianqing and his mother, Ju Dou, sleeping together.

The film presents an unending, inescapable cycle of conflicts between generations. The social structure, which is the cause of it all, seems to have a momentum of its own independent of the wishes and actions of people. Individuals all fall victim to the social structure in turn.

The site of the story is the inner space of the dye mill. Stripes of red, orange, and blue cloth, which have been such a symbol of life and vitality against the gray, drab, stifling background, are all burned in a huge fire along with everything else in the dye mill. The patterns of repetition lead to nothing but total destruction. In the final shot, the cinematographer masterfully stops the film, leaving the sound of burning to be heard. Then a chorus of a children's song bursts out.

> Bell, bell, ding dong,
> We walk to the Wang village.
> The Wang village has a crowd of dogs.
> They bite us and we have nowhere to run.
> Nowhere to run, we go back home,
> Go back home to blow our little trumpets.

The song appeared a few times earlier in the film, serving as a structuring motif throughout the story. The juxtaposition of children's singing and the annihilation of the environment is as intriguing as it is ambivalent. To read the ending negatively, the words of the song may also reinforce the impression that the children are inescapably haunted by the dogs in an impending doom. Thus, the burning of the mill and the children's song may be read as an indication of hopeless destruction. Or, as one may also willfully read in the opposite way, the ending is an intimation of the myth of a new beginning, an allegory of the rebirth of a nation out of the ashes of the old. As one may recall, the poet Guo Moruo wrote the song of the "Rebirth (Nirvana) of Phoenixes" (Fenghuang niepan) at the height of the May 4th literary movement. The poem has since achieved canonical status.

• Raise the Red Lantern

Most of the events in *Raise the Red Lantern* occur within the claustrophobic, walled space of the mansion of Master Chen. The only exception is a brief moment at the beginning of the film when Songlian walks toward the home of Master Chen, her future home, while wearing the uniform of a college student. The open, green space soon disappears, and the rest of the film unfolds in enclosed space. The minute Songlian steps into the Chen house, her body is squarely framed against the backdrop of a black tablet inscribed with ancient Chinese characters. This is symbolic of her entrance and confinement in a semiotic, patriarchal system. Occasionally, Songlian and Meishan, the more adventurous and defiant of the wives, go to the rooftop, a semiopen space, to explore the physical environment. On the rooftop, there is a brief encounter between Songlian and Feipu, son of the first wife, a man of her own age. There is no eventual sexual intimacy between them, and they are kept apart. In contrast, Meishan's sexual transgression of having an affair with Doctor Gao is punished by death. The rooftop is also the place where Songlian discovers the death chamber where women who "committed sin" were hanged in the past and Meishan is hanged in the present.

In the house, ancestral rules reign supreme. The rituals and laws governing daily life such as visiting each other, eating, and sleeping were handed down from the past and are strictly observed by the inhabitants. Everyone is expected to learn and abide by the rules. At one moment, Meishan's small son, the figure of the child in the film, is examined by his father, Master Chen, and his old tutor for his school work. This is the familiar sight of a child reciting and memorizing classical poetry, the living image of the mechanical perpetuation and internalization of tradition. It is for the

Fig. 7. Gong Li as Songlian in *Raise the Red Lantern* (Da hong denglong gaogao gua), directed by Zhang Yimou, PRC/Hong Kong, 1991. British Film Institute.

sake of producing a male heir to the family and consolidating her place that Songlian goes so far as pretending to be pregnant. After her false pregnancy is discovered, she is duly punished by Master Chen.

Through various contrivances such as foot-massage and lantern-raising, Master Chen skillfully manipulates and regulates the libidinal drives of his four wives to his pleasure and satisfaction. The spectator is never offered a frontal view of him. He appears sideways, or with his back to the viewer, in long and medium shots. He is not individuated, but is rather part of an impersonal system. While the supremacy of his position is warranted by the social system and remains unchallenged by members of his household, deadly infighting arises among the jealous wives for the sexual favor of the master. Songlian, Meishan, Chuoyun, and the maidservant Yan'er inflict fatal blows on each other. As a result of the control of their desire and sexuality, their psyches are wounded and deformed even more severely.

Temporality is configured in a cyclical sequence in the film. The film begins in summer and ends the next summer. Summer, autumn, and winter arrive, but the season of spring is skipped. Exactly one year later, Songlian loses her position as the Fourth Mistress. With all the appropriate rituals, a new concubine, the Fifth Mistress, enters the house. The close-up of her expressionless face amid the festive sound of firecrackers at the end of the film is an echo and repetition of the close-up of Songlian's tearful face in the beginning sequence of the film when she sadly confronts the fate of being a concubine. Death and tragedy in the house all brushed aside, life returns to its former "normal" rhythm. The cycle of life repeats itself. The final shot is an extreme long shot of an orderly, symmetrically composed Chen compound with brightly lit red lanterns. Perhaps the most appropriate term to describe the Chen compound is what Lu Xun called, as early as the May 4th era, an "iron house which is absolutely indestructible." The film reenacts a living testimony to the imprisoned condition of the inhabitants. Noticeably, Songlian, who goes insane in the final scene, wears a student uniform again. Except for a brief moment at the beginning, she had been wearing colorful clothes as befitting the status of Fourth Mistress. The white and blue student uniform becomes a sign of her ostracism from "normal," "sane" society. As we are told by the old lady who once served her, she is now "mad." Beginning with the "Madman's Diary" by Lu Xun, the enlightened few had suffered the fate of being condemned as "mad" by the crowd. Typical of Lu Xun's irony, the reader is informed that the Madman was cured and returned to normality at the end of the story. In a similar fashion, neither the defiant Songlian before marriage nor the "insane" Songlian at the end fits into the social standards that were perceived as normal and sane by the "crowd," that is, the majority of inhabitants in the Chen household.

In both *Ju Dou* and *Raise the Red Lantern,* temporality is spatialized. An eternal space triumphs over time. Time does not move, or it moves in circular and cyclical patterns. Although the film is set in the past, time appears to be an eternal present, without differentiation and progression between the past, the present, the future. Spatial representation creates the overarching, overpowering spectacle. Be it the dye mill or the Chen mansion, the allegorization of a timeless space, an ancient "museum," as it were, annihilates the possibility of change, of real temporal or historical progression.

• The Story of Qiu Ju

By his own statement, Zhang Yimou was making a new kind of experiment with *The Story of Qiu Ju.*[14] The film represents a departure from previous films. While the previous films were grand attempts at "historico-cultural reflection," the focus of this film is the individual character and the contemporary setting. Zhang said that he neglected the problems of characterization and narration in his earlier films and wished to make up for the lapse. Now he was more interested in the life and fate of individual people. Liu Heng, the scriptwriter of the film, indicated that the film could be understood at three levels:

1. At the most external, most superficial, and yet most socially specific level, it is a story about a citizen accusing officials, in other words, a story about the struggle of a common person against local bureaucracy.

2. At the level of the character's fate and personality, it is a story about an injured, weak woman protecting her own dignity.

3. At the existential level, one's own dignity can be protected at the expense of others. This becomes the problem of the self-torture of humanity.[15]

Elsewhere, Zhang also stated that "in Qiu Ju, it's about a woman who comes to recognize her own self-worth (ziwo jiazhi), a woman who realizes that she controls her own fate."[16] To achieve these ends, Zhang experimented with a new film aesthetic—"documentary realism." His crew carried hidden cameras to capture realistic, authentic scenes. All the characters spoke the Shaanxi dialect. The purpose was to create an impression of a real-life situation, a reality effect, in a contemporary context.

What can be said, however, is that the film is in large measure still a continuation of certain concerns in his previous works. The setting of the film is the village and town of Zhang's birthplace, Shaanxi province. The place is China's backward interior, remote from the modern cities of the coastline. Yet, it is also the root of China, the earth that gave birth to Chinese civilization. Once again, Zhang confronts and critically engages Chinese culture from the ground up. The weight of tradition is apparent on all the characters, especially Qiu Ju. The difference is that he looks at contemporary China this time rather than rendering visions of the past.

Cultural critique through sexual politics is also at work here. The angry village head kicks the husband of Qiu Ju in the groin after a quarrel between the two. Qiu Ju "is hurt mainly in the pride."[17] Subsequently, she wrestles with different levels of the government in order to get satisfaction for the wrong done to her husband. The story becomes one of an indomitable woman in a predominantly phallocentric society. It is up to a woman to defend the dignity and reproductive capacity of her husband. The problem revolving around the honor of the "phallus" of her husband turns into a story about the strength of an ordinary peasant woman. Nonetheless, she is still in the service of men. In sharp contrast to the spatial confinement in *Ju Dou* and *Raise the Red Lantern, The Story of Qiu Ju* reveals a vast expanse of open country in northern China: family courtyard, village, town, and cityscape. Qiu Ju's trips to various levels of courts is structured through the road motif. The road introduces an open space, a space of free movement for women in contemporary rural China.

Qiu Ju carries the burden of tradition as well as harbors "feminist" consciousness. While seeking to defend the "face" of her husband, she ventures beyond the traditional role allotted to Chinese women to take on a task that is normally done by men. Against overwhelming pressure from all sides—various levels of the government and even her husband at one point—Qiu Ju, pregnant as she is, does not refrain from traveling the solitary road toward justice time and again on cold wintry days. Some Western critics place emphasis on the establishment of a new type of female subjectivity in the film, one that has the courage to liberate itself from the constraints of a male-dominated, traditional society. "She fights what should be her husband's battle. At the film's end, the camera frozen on her unadorned face, she seems to be preparing for another round of attacks on an elephantine system."[18] The film thus ends by "celebrating the strength of Chinese women"[19] and the coming into being of a new femininity.

The last sequence of the film is in fact more nuanced and subtle. The film closes with the sound of the siren of the police car that comes to apprehend the village head. Justice would seem to finally prevail. By this time, however, the conflict between the village head and Qiu Ju has been reconciled because he has just saved Qiu Ju's life. With his help, she safely gives birth to a healthy *son,* a significant *male heir,* to the immense happiness of herself, her whole family, and the entire village.

The film has an open ending that invites interpretation from the viewer. Qiu Ju reaches the road, her road to justice throughout the film, at the sound of the siren. The last shot is a close-up of her face, which is somewhat off the center of the picture frame. (Compare this to the square, symmetrical, centered close-ups in *Raise the Red Lantern.*) The viewer sees the frozen, perplexed expression on Qiu Ju's face. There is a sense of uncertainty and confusion. In Dai Jinhua's words, the film is Zhang Yimou's "conditional reconciliation with history and tradition."[20] What can be added is that it is also Zhang's reconciliation with the Chinese state. The government highly praised the film. And because of *The Story of Qiu Ju,* the ban on *Ju Dou* and *Raise the Red Lantern* was also lifted.

• *To Live*

Zhang Yimou sent his next film, *To Live,* to compete at the Cannes Film Festival in 1994 without obtaining prior permission from the Chinese government. The film won the Jury Prize, and Ge You won the Best Actor award for his performance. Zhang's domestic fortunes fell again because of the vagaries of the cultural politics of the regime. The film was officially banned film in China despite, or because of, its international success. Yet, when Zheng returned to his home city, Xi'an, he discovered that "everybody had seen it."[21] This fact reveals the inefficiency of the state censorship system and the public's indifference to it. It also testifies to the extent of private screenings and the widespread circulation of bootlegged videotapes in the underground market.

Zhang's cultural critique now takes the form of a critique of decades of modern Chinese history. The film differs from the earlier allegorical approach where a story of the past (say in the 1920s or 1930s) serves as an indirect critique of the present and Chinese history as such. Nor could it be said to be a predominantly "spatial film" where time is eternalized and spatialized. *To Live* covers a long span of modern Chinese history from the years before the "Liberation" (1949) all the way to the end of the Cultural Revolution. Political and social upheavals of the nation are all seen and enacted through the drama of one Chinese family. An ordinary, small Chinese family becomes the locus of historical change. Temporal sequence is important because it is constitutive of Chinese history and all the events and details of the story. It is through time that the Chinese nation is constituted and narrated. The blending of the intimate and the social, the lyrical and the epic, the familial and the historical in this film is also evident in two other Fifth-Generation films produced in the same year, if the term "Fifth Generation" is still appropriate: *Blue Kite* (Lan fengzheng) by Tian Zhuangzhuang and *Farewell My Concubine* by Chen Kaige. All three films share a similar fate: they have been circulated and screened in the international market but are either banned or have had limited release in China due to the hostility of the government.

To Live follows the family story of Fugui (played by Ge You) and Jiazhen (played by Gong Li) over decades of Chinese history. They and their children are victims of political events. Their son Youqing dies in the Great Leap Forward, and their daughter Fengxia dies in the hospital after giving birth to a son in the chaos of the Cultural Revolution. After all the tragedies, the grandson, "Little Bun," survives at the end. In the final scene, the survivors in the family, Fugui, Jiazhen, their son-in-law Wan Erxi, and their grandson sit together to enjoy dinner at home—eating steamed buns. (The overconsumption of steamed buns by the starving Doctor Wang nearly kills him and makes him unable to save Fengxia during the Cultural Revolution.) It is a rare scene of reunion, peace, and happiness in the family. Fugui's tale of the "little chickens" in a box is different this time from his previous version. The little chickens will grow to be ducks, the ducks will become geese, and the geese will become oxen, and tomorrow will be better. (In the early version, "tomorrow will be better" because of communism, as he told this story of transformation to his son, who was sleeping on his shoulder on the way to his school one day in the Great Leap Forward period.) The ending is one of survival and continuity, of faith in the future. After all the absurdities of history, time "means" in a higher perspective. *To Live* is rightfully a story about what it means "to live" in modern China. The faith in the future is not based on utopian longing or some grand redemptive ideology (communist ideology, etc.). The final scene serves as a compelling image of the will and ability of the Chinese people and nation to live and survive in the long run of history. The film is Zhang's unconditional, total rejection of modern Chinese political history but his reconciliation with Chinese History as such. By an ironic reversal, Zhang finally salvaged and vindicated temporality. Despite all the horrific personal losses and collective sufferings, the Chinese family perpetuates itself, and "Little Bun" and little chicks will *live*.

Within the sweeping historical narrative of the film is also a story of a traditional Chinese folk art, "puppet show," or in Chinese parlance, "shadowplay" (*yingxi*). The story of the fate of Chinese "shadowplay" is a film within a film, for as we recall, the Chinese name for film was "Western shadowplay" (*xiyang yingxi*) in the early days and has remained "electric shadow" (*dianying*) until today. (Treating the life story of a traditional artist as an index of national/local history is also the strategy adopted in Hou Hsiao-hsien's film, *Puppetmaster*, produced at about the same time.) Fugui had been an accomplished amateur "shadowplayer" since the beginning of the film. After losing his family fortune through gambling, he is forced to become a professional player to make a living. With his charming performance, he entertains the soldiers of the People's Liberation Army in the historic Huaihai campaign in the late 1940s. Indeed, it is through this traditional folk art that Fugui transforms from a "good-for-nothing" to an honest, useful member of the "New Society." He cheers the spirit of his fellow workers during the days and nights of intensive labor in the Great Leap Forward in the late 1950s. There is a positive, revolutionary appropriation of a traditional Chinese art form, an otherwise outdated technology of visuality, especially in comparison to the imported new technology of "electric shadows." When the Cultural Revolution comes in the 1960s, this art form is considered feudal and reactionary, for it only narrates old tales of "emperors, kings, generals, ministers, talented scholars, and beauties" (*di, wang, jiang, xiang, caizi jiaren*). The beautiful puppets are all burned in a flame as a gesture of a complete break with the past. The rise and fall of such a traditional visual/performance art in modern China is interwoven with the inner lives of the characters. Finally, at the end of the film, in the 1970s, there is an indication of a possible renewal of the old. As grandpa Fugui and grandson Little Bun are looking for a place to put Little Bun's chicks, they find the box that had stored the old puppets in the past. They decide that the box is a good place to put the chicks, the creatures of the future.

• *Shanghai Triad*

Zhang's sequence of films on the fate of China and its children takes on another variation with his 1995 film, *Shanghai Triad.* This is another period film, set in Shanghai in the 1930s, and thus avoids direct confrontation with contemporary Chinese society and politics. It belongs to the gangster film genre, a convention that one often associates with Hong Kong productions. Gong Li, in this final collaboration with Zhang, portrays Xiao Jinbao (Jewel, French *Bijou*), the mistress of Mr. Tang, the godfather of the gang. Xiao Jinbao depends on and lives off her rich and powerful man. She juggles and compromises herself with various forces of the mob world. As the film progresses, her loathing and boredom become unbearable beneath all the glamour and wealth, and her longing for freedom is desperate. At the end of the film, she meets a tragic death at the hands of her erstwhile lover, Mr. Tang. Her character is in some measure similar to Chen Pailu, the heroine in Cao Yu's classic play *Thunderstorm,* also set in Shanghai in the 1930s. She also "seems to take on the persona that critics have long imputed to her: Dietrich to Zhang's Josef von Sternberg."[22] The staging of her night-club musical sequences are overtly reminiscent of such Dietrich vehicles as *The Blue Angel (Der blaue Engel)* and perhaps even Madonna's video vixen appropriations of Dietrich's star persona and costume.[23]

What is perhaps most noteworthy in relation to his other film texts is the positioning of children. We watch the film through the eyes of a fourteen-year-old boy, Tang Shuisheng. He is taken to Shanghai from his village by his uncle, who had been waiting on Xiao Jinbao. Shanghai's underworld, with all its mystery and cruelty, revolves around the confused, muddled, and uncomprehending vision of the child. While Zhang's first film, *Red Sorghum,* is framed by the narrative voice of a child/grandchild, the story of this last production is encapsulated within the gaze of a small boy.

After a series of carnages and massacres, resulting in the death of many people, including Xiao Jinbao and Mr. Tang's chief aide, Second Brother, Mr. Tang's position in the mob remains secure and unchanged. (His unchallenged position parallels the role of the invisible yet all-powerful Master Chen in *Raise the Red Lantern.*) After a cycle of seven days, the film ends on the eighth day. Mr. Tang says to the little girl that well-groomed and well-

Fig. 8. Sheldon Hsiao-peng Lu with actor Li Baotian in the summer of 1994. Li is known for his roles in Zhang Yimou's films such as *Ju Dou* and *Shanghai Triad*.

trained, she would be another Xiao Jinbao in no time. Shuisheng is hung upside-down on a pole for his impulsive, rebellious behavior. This slight punishment is yet another necessary "rite of passage" for initiation into the gangster world. What he sees and what the viewers see is an upside-down world. The co-optation of the little boy and the little girl into the cruel, senseless underworld guarantees its continual existence. There seems to be no escape from the predetermined cycle of life. Thus, with *Shanghai Triad,* Zhang's cycle of films ends on an alarming note, however beautiful and soothing the theme song is throughout the sound track.

The dark vision of the film did not cause any problem for the director. (The production of the film was shut down for some time due to the government's distaste for his previous film, *To Live.*) The film was released in China. The trouble came when the film was chosen to open the 1995 New York Film Festival, and Zhang himself was expected to attend the event. He was forced to cancel his New York trip because the Chinese government decided to retaliate against the festival for the inclusion of another film about China, the American documentary *The Gate of Heavenly Peace,* which recounted the 1989 student movement in Tiananmen Square. In a highly ironic sense, this Third World production (or coproduction with France), a film about China's past, must nevertheless be viewed and read as an *allegory* of contemporary Chinese politics due to the circumstances of transnational film reception.

· Conclusion: Orientalism, Postcolonialism, and Cinematic Defamiliarization

Zhang's film career is synonymous with the globalization of Chinese cinema. His films have been big winners at major international film festivals. In receiving the Golden Bear Award at the Berlin Film Festival in 1988, *Red Sorghum* marked the beginning of the integration of Chinese national cinema in global film culture. In contrast to Zhang's victory, *King of the Children* (Haizi wang) by Chen Kaige, another founding figure of Fifth-Generation cinema, was a colossal failure at the Cannes film festival in the same year. It was given the unofficial title of the "most boring film" of the year at Cannes. These lessons of "success" and "failure" were significant, for good or bad, for the future orientation of Chinese national cinema in the coming years.

Technically speaking, Zhang Yimou's films made in the 1990s are not strictly "Chinese" or "Mainland" films. As I have stated, they were funded and produced by transnational capital funneled through foreign film companies (Hong Kongese, Taiwanese via Hong Kong, Japanese, French). Sometimes they are even nominated in the category of "Hong Kong cinema" at international film festivals (*Raise the Red Lantern* is one example). The target audience is not Mainland Chinese but the international community. In 1991, *Ju Dou* became the first Mainland Chinese film to be nominated for Best Foreign Picture in the Academy Awards in the United States. One year later, *Raise the Red Lantern* was also nominated for the same award. Large numbers of ordinary American moviegoers, not just China specialists, went to art-house movie theaters to watch this film. Ever since, Chinese "national cinema" has had a share of the international film market.

The end result of Zhang's film art may seem to be his ability to tell the Western audience enchanting, exotic stories about the other country "China" through stunning visual images. He has offered the Western viewer a "museum" of precious Chinese objects, costumes, and artifacts. He has presented a dazzling array of icons and symbols of his "China": green sorghum field, red sorghum wine, colorful strips of cloth, dye mill, red lanterns, red pepper, and puppet show. He has told lurid stories of murder, incest, polygamy, and concubinage. He has rendered on screen masquerades of terrifying political events such as the Great Leap Forward and the Cultural Revolution. All these spectacles have been masterfully manufactured for the pleasure and gaze of the Western viewer.

For many indigenous Chinese critics, the issue at stake is the cinematic construction and representation of the Chinese nation for the gaze of the West, or the question of "nation and narration," as it were, in his films. Unlike previous Fifth-Generation films such as the early works of Chen Kaige, Zhang's films are not made for the self-reflexive gaze of the Chinese but for the spectatorship of the other, the West. In the same process, the position of Chinese viewers is decentered, and the field of vision of the West takes the central seat. What is initially indigenous cultural critique transforms into "cultural sellout," or in Rey Chow's words, cultural "exhibitionism," "the Oriental's Orientalism," or "international fantasy," as Esther Yau puts it.[24]

Speaking of the popularity of Gong Li as a "Chinese actress" among Western viewers, Berenice Reynaud writes, "For what is remarkable about Gong is not so much her poise or versatility, but her ability to signify Chineseness, femininity and mystery outside her own culture."[25] It is precisely these perceived "Oriental" qualities of "Chineseness," "femininity," and "mystery" that separate Chinese and Western audience preferences for Zhang's films and Gong Li's images. Most Chinese viewers love *The Story of Qiu Ju* and *To Live*. The stories of the ordinary characters in these films reenact for Chinese spectators a shared, collective past and present, a life and history with which they are shockingly familiar and they can easily iden-

Fig. 9. Gong Li as Songlian in *Raise the Red Lantern* (Da hong denglong gaogao gua), directed by Zhang Yimou, PRC/Hong Kong, 1991. British Film Institute.

tify. They recognize a Chinese sentimentality, a "Chineseness," in the lives of the characters, especially in the plain (unglamorous) role of Jiazhen, portrayed by Gong Li. In contrast, the Chinese audience is not as enamored of the self-exoticization in *Ju Dou* and *Raise the Red Lantern,* the two films that catapulted Zhang and Gong to the center stage in the West. The glamour and mystery of Gong Li's star image as a Chinese woman have captured the attention of the Western spectator.

The entrance of Mainland Chinese cinema into the global film market, led by Zhang Yimou, has provided the occasion for recent debates in Chinese cultural criticism. The political economy of Chinese national cinema à la Zhang, if the word *national* could still be used, is such that it is funded by foreign capital, produced by Chinese labor, and sold to overseas consumers. The acceptance of cultural products such as film from China, the "East," a "Third-World" country, by the "West," the "First World," may not be a reason for celebration but rather a source of profound anxiety

National Cinema, Cultural Critique, Transnational Capital   *127* for many native Chinese critics. The resistance of local intellectuals to the global homogenization of cultural production is particularly strong in the China scene.[26]

While being hailed as "China's ambassador to sophisticated filmgoers" in the West,[27] Zhang is not so enthusiastically received in his home country. Some believe that his films misrepresent the "real" China in their desire to cater to the West's taste for an exotic other.[28] The popularity of these films in the West only reveals the fact that Third-World cinema is compelled to be part of a hegemonic, Orientalist discourse in order to be accepted by the West, which dominates the global cultural market.

For Chinese critics as well, Orientalism is understood as a strategy used by the dominant Western powers to domesticate, represent, and delimit the "Oriental." Orientalism is necessary for the West in the attempt to define its "self" in relation to the "other." It is in itself a hegemonic discourse and a system of representation.[29] These critics argue that the problem with Chinese films such as Zhang's is that they do not attempt to resist the Orientalist discourse but rather participate in it. They lend themselves to Western appropriation. Their popularity abroad is the result of the filmmakers' efforts to satisfy the tastes of the Western audience, and more damagingly, the result of their willful surrender to the dominant discourse of First-World culture. The real history of a Third-World country is repressed and marginalized. It can only come to expression in the language, images, ideology, and discourse of the First World. The value and aesthetic appeal of these films are also determined by the judges of the West. Previously, it was the role of China specialists to translate and introduce artistic works from China to the Western audience. Now, in a remarkable reversal of fortune, it is the West that points out what is outstanding and characteristically Chinese in artworks from China. The viewers and critics of the home country can do nothing but be astounded by and follow the judgment of the authority of the Western world. Chinese intellectuals are in a stupor, remain aphasic, and are unable to speak and pass judgment on the works of their own country.

In his provocatively titled essay, "Zhang Yimou in the Global Postcolonial Context," the Chinese critic Zhang Yiwu states that the director himself has become part of the cultural and ideological apparatuses of the discourse of Western postcolonialism in the 1990s.[30] Zhang's filmic representations, the creation of "pseudo-folklore" (the raising of red lanterns, foot-massage, concubinage, etc.) do nothing more than offer the Western viewer a "gaze" at "China," an Oriental world that is presented as a mysterious Other, an exotic showcase. In *Raise the Red Lantern,* Zhang created the theme of lantern-raising ex nihilo. It is neither an episode in Su Tong's original novel nor a real practice in Chinese culture. The spectacle is created purely for cinematic effects. The narration of the experience of a Third-World country turns into a spectacle for the satisfaction of the curiosity of the First-World audience. The most devastating part of this kind of criticism is the statement that by exhibiting the ugly, dark, backward sides of China's past on screen, such films provide a visual pleasure and confirm a sense of political superiority for the Western viewer.[31] As a consequence, "real Chinese history" is forgotten and becomes the repressed unconscious. Liao Ping-hui, a Taiwanese scholar, makes a similar point. For him, Zhang's films, along with Chen Kaige's *Farewell My Concubine,* which reaped a huge success in the West (winner of the Palme d'Or at the Cannes Film Festival in 1993 and nominee for Best Foreign Picture at the Academy Awards in 1994), reinforce the static images and worn stereotypes of Orientalism rather than deconstruct them.[32] In the words of another young Chinese critic:

> The films of Zhang Yimou often ask for an "explanation" *(shuofa)* from the West. Perhaps this should be examined in the context of postcolonialism. They rely on the allegorization of images of China, spatialization, synchronization, separation from China's historical continuity, exoticism, and so forth. These satisfy the requirement of Western authority. In contrast, the films of the fourth-generation are preoccupied with the historical salvation of China, temporal order, sequentiality, the anxiety of real-life existence, and so forth. There is no lack of outstanding works, and they are well liked by the domestic audience, but not well received in the West. The reason is simple: the Westerners have their own taste, and Zhang Yimou satisfies their taste.[33]

For a Third-World Chinese critic, the search for an authentic indigenous language, the reassertion of a non-Western self, and the establishment of a Third-World discourse are the paramount tasks. The nightmare of the Third-World critic and the native artist is that there is no other way to express themselves than by resorting to Western theoretical discourse and Western artistic means. There seems to be no escape from the iron cage of the cultural hegemony of the West. In order to find a language to speak, they have to draw on the cultural and symbolic capital of the postcolonialist West.

Evidently, indigenous Chinese critics tend to perceive the internationalization of Chinese cinema as an instance of the global homogenization of local differences in the interest of Western cultural imperialism. They are strongly opposed to the commodification of cultural production in the 1990s in both domestic and international markets. Their attempt to formulate a theoretical language of their own is a strategy of resistance and self-empowerment.

The case of Zhang Yimou is important in that it has been the point of departure for the discussion of a host of pressing issues facing China's national cinema. Behind the discussion are real crises and far-reaching changes in China's film industry, film audience, film market, and ultimately developments in China's cultural spheres. The "Orientalist" path is not a choice for many Chinese filmmakers, but a step they have to take in order to deal with the reality of their home country in the 1990s.

The 1980s were the golden times of Chinese cinema. Certain crucial factors allowed the production of artistic, exploratory, and avant-gardist films in that period. The filmmakers attempted to break away from China's past cinematic convention of socialist realism and the influence of Hollywood film and learn from European "author films." This could only be done in the 1980s. Abstract, obscure, artistic films simply would not sell at the box office under present conditions. Nor would film studios be willing to make films that have no commercial value. In this sense, the Chinese New Wave, characterized by its uncompromising experimental, avant-gardist quality, has now ended.

The flourishing of the New Wave in the 1980s was largely conditioned by China's state-run film industry at the time. In the old system, it was no one's concern if a film did not make a profit for the studio. Film production was subsidized by the state. Such was the necessary condition for the appearance of Fifth-Generation art film. A film such as *Horse Thief* (Daoma zei), directed by Tian Zhuangzhuang, which sold only a few prints and had virtually no audience, could only be made in this type of system. In today's market economy, film studios can no longer afford to lose money.[34]

In the late 1970s and early 1980s, film was perhaps the most popular form of entertainment, enjoyed by hundreds of millions of people. (To be sure, it is also an institutionalized form of ideological indoctrination, an important vehicle of party propaganda.) In the 1990s, the emergence of other forms of popular culture has drastically reduced the film market. The space formerly occupied by Chinese national cinema has been taken over by TV serials, home VCRS, and bootleg videotapes of Taiwanese, Hong Kongese, and Western films.

Given the shift toward an open-market economy as dictated by the reform policy of the state, film censorship is still in place and makes it impossible for the film industry to operate fully according to market-economy principles. The decision to release or withhold a film is as arbitrary as it has always been. There does not yet exist something like the American rating system for various kinds of films.

On the political side, after the defeat of the 1989 Democracy Movement, and under the combined forces of a capitalist economy and political intolerance, many citizens have become disinterested in ideological issues. There is apathy and confusion. Broad segments of the populace are not as enthusiastic about serious, exploratory films as before. The film market is flooded by cheaply produced films of sex and violence and second-rate and third-rate films imported from Taiwan, Hong Kong, and the West that offer the Chinese audience an exotic flavor, an imaginary wish-fulfillment. To the detriment of China's national cinema, the general public seems to have a predilection for foreign films. In view of these developments, the state of art film is seriously jeopardized. Those qualities that marked New Chinese Cinema in the 1980s would now run against the principles of the market economy. The Chinese film industry faces an unprecedented crisis.

Under the dual pressure of censorship and the rapid shrinking of the domestic market, entering the international market seems to be the inevitable solution. Even well before the shooting of a film, a director may have already decided to abandon the domestic market. He is prepared for his film's being banned in China. Chinese filmmakers are active in seeking external, foreign funding. Joint film production is the rule, not the exception today. The filmmakers invest an interest in their films' commercial value.

I am sympathetic with the concerns of Chinese critics and partially agree with their assessment of the situation. Yet, the internationalization of Chinese film in the 1990s as a new phenomenon in itself should be grasped dialectically. Given the dangers and pitfalls of "cultural exhibitionism," the new condition of transnational film culture also opens up prospects of critical intervention that were not available before.

At one level, one question in the debate on Orientalism is what constitutes cinematic verisimilitude for the Chinese audience. It seems that Chinese critics' conception of cinematic verisimilitude has been largely conditioned by the cinematic traditions (social realism, socialist realism, etc.) that dominated the Chinese screen for decades. They find the representation of China in new films to be "unreal," a "distortion" of the China they know. They are accustomed to the familiar images of China as constructed in earlier films by such well-known directors as Xie Jin. To me, this "unfamiliarity" seems to be the aesthetic effect of "defamiliarization" wrought by the new films. As is well known, one of the goals of the Fifth-Generation directors is to break away from past cinematic conventions in order to forge a language of their own. Some of the stylistic qualities of Zhang Yimou's films, as enumerated earlier by one Chinese critic, account for the differences between his film art and that of his predecessors. China "signifies" different realities with different filmmakers.[35] Zhang Yimou's allegorical, spatial, seemingly ahistorical approach in *Ju Dou* and *Raise the Red Lantern* and his departure from the classical realism of previous generations present an unfamiliar manner of filmmaking. These films provide alternative aesthetic conventions of filmmaking and new ways of viewing to the domestic audience. (This would account for their "unfamiliarity," or perhaps more appropriately, the quality of "defamiliarization.") They challenge codified official *mainstream* discourse about film in China and constitute an oppositional practice to the ruling ideology of the state.

As many indigenous Chinese critics may insist, Chinese filmmakers are obliged to operate in accordance with the logic of global commodification and to subjugate themselves to the scrutiny of the critical discourse and system of representation of the West. It also goes without saying that the process necessitates artistic and intellectual compromises. Yet, given the shrinking domestic film market, the system of film censorship, and the changes in China's film industry, what is termed "Orientalism," or the exit to the global cultural market, is also a strategy of survival and renewal for Chinese filmmakers.

I would also like to emphasize that under the new conditions, the transnational production of Chinese film could become an oppositional formation to national, domestic repression. It may well be argued that recent films of Chen Kaige (*Farewell My Concubine*), Zhang Yimou (*To Live*), and Tian Zhuangzhuang (*Blue Kite*) still largely fall within the paradigm of "cultural critique" but are repackaged for an international audience. While intellectualist, elitist "cultural reflection" was hushed in post-Tiananmen China, filmmakers are able to carry out their critical project with the support of transnational capital and the global market.

An important factor that native Chinese critics seem to have ignored is the dynamics of the international film market. Admittedly, Chinese national cinema is endangered in the global commodification process, as native Chinese critics caution. One should also be aware that Chinese films produce alternative images, narratives, and histories for the Western audience. These stories and histories of the "other" as constructed in the Chinese films are equally new and unfamiliar, or more precisely, "defamiliarizing," for the Western viewer. Although Chinese films may not be able to compete for audience with dominant Hollywood films yet, they have taken a firm foothold in art-house theaters. For the first time, Chinese-made films are screened on a large scale in Western theaters and become readily available in ordinary video stores across America. Previously, the "real China" and Chinese people's "collective memory," as it were, were rarely represented in Western film and TV except in the varieties of cheaply made kung-fu movies. In fact, the chance given to the "DissemiNation" of the Chinese "nation" through cinematic "narration," paraphrasing Homi Bhabha's terms, deconstructs the monolithic, ethnocentric vision of history and its "postcoloniality."[36] As one Western critic puts it, a Chinese film such as *Farewell My Concubine* "will bewitch audiences everywhere, people who have never before spent two consecutive moments thinking about the nature of the world's least-known major power."[37] In the international market, these Chinese films may give representations of other ethnic groups and countries that are not ordinarily seen in *mainstream* Hollywood film.[38] Their arrival breaks the closed circuit of First-World cinema in the political economy of global film culture.

· Notes

1. I thank Lucy Fischer, Gina Marchetti, and Anne T. Ciecko for reading earlier drafts of this essay and offering helpful comments for revision. All remaining shortcomings are entirely my responsibility.

2. For an attempt to resurrect the use of allegory in the postmodern era in relation to the "political unconscious," or more precisely, the "geopolitical unconscious," see Fredric Jameson's "Introduction: Beyond Landscape" in his *The Geopolitical Aesthetic: Cinema and Space in the World System* (Bloomington: Indiana University Press, 1992), 1–5. Jameson writes: "Allegory thereby fatally stages its historic reappearance in the postmodern era (after the long domination of the symbol from romanticism to late modernism), and seems to offer the most satisfactory (if varied and heterogeneous) solutions to these form-problems" (p. 4).

3. As I write this essay, Zhang Yimou is shooting his new film, *Please Make Peace* (Youhua haohao shuo) in Fengtai, a suburb of Beijing. It is mainly a story of two men, played by superstars Li Baotian and Jiang Wen. The new lead actress in the film is Qu Ying. Her role is expected to be small in comparison to the strong, dominant female roles portrayed by Gong Li in Zhang's past films.

4. See Dai Jinhua, *Dianying lilun yu piping shouce* [Handbook of film theory and criticism] (Beijing: Kexue jishu wenxian chubanshe, 1993), 16.

5. Wang Yuejin, *"Red Sorghum:* Mixing Memory and Desire," in *Perspectives on Chinese Cinema,* ed. Chris Berry (London: British Film Institute, 1991), 85.

6. Zhang Yingjin, "Ideology of the Body in *Red Sorghum:* National Allegory, National Roots, and Third Cinema," *East-West Film Journal* 4, no. 2 (1990): 49.

7. Zhang Yimou quoted in Luo Xueying, "Xieren, xushi, neihan" [Characterization, narration, meaning: A symposium on *The Story of Qiu Ju*] *Dangdai dianying* [Contemporary Cinema] 51 (November 1992): 12.

8. See Lin Yü-sheng, *The Crisis of Chinese Consciousness: Radical Antitraditionalism in the May Fourth Era* (Madison: University of Wisconsin Press, 1979).

9. Mayfair Yang, "Of Gender, State Censorship, and Overseas Capital: An Interview with Director Zhang Yimou," *Public Culture* 5, no. 2 (1993): 300–302.

10. Dai, *Dianying lilun,* 15–44.

II. For discussions of the film as a critique of Confucianism and Chinese patriarchy, see Jenny Kwok Wah Lau, "*Judou*—A Hermeneutical Reading of Cross-cultural Cinema," *Film Quarterly* 45, no. 2 (1991): 2–10; W. A. Callahan, "Gender, Ideology, Nation: *Ju Dou* in the Cultural Politics of China," *East-West Film Journal* 7, no. 1 (1993): 52–80. For an informative study of the cinematic convention and the libidinal economy of the film, see the essay by Shuqin Cui in this volume.

12. As a critique of masculinity, the lack of courage to elope with his lover in fear of punishment from society is a common theme in modern Chinese literature. For instance, Huagou (Motley) in Shen Congwen's story "Xiaoxiao" and Xia Dabao in Ding Ling's story "In the Xia Village" (Wo zai xiacun de shihou) both decline to run away from home as suggested by their lovers, Xiao and Chen. The consequence of their passivity is to bring more suffering to their female lovers.

13. E. Ann. Kaplan, "Problematising Cross-cultural Analysis: The Case of Women in the Recent Chinese Cinema," in *Perspectives on Chinese Cinema*, ed. Chris Berry (London: British Film Institute, 1991), 153.

14. See Luo, "Xieren, xushi, neihan," 12–24.

15. Luo, "Xieren, xushi, neihan," 16.

16. Yang, "Of Gender," 304.

17. Richard Corliss, "The Fire in Her Eyes" (review of *The Story of Qiu Ju*), *Time*, April 26, 1993, 69.

18. Howard Feinstein, "A Chinese Actress Blossoms on the Screen," *New York Times,* April 11, 1993.

19. Feinstein, "A Chinese Actress."

20. See Dai, *Dianying lilun,* 52–56.

21. Stuart Klawans, "Zhang Yimou: Local Hero," *Film Comment* 31, no. 5 (1995): 18.

22. Klawans, "Zhang Yimou," 11–12.

23. This aspect of the film was brought to my attention by Anne T. Ciecko. For a further discussion of the Von Sternberg–Dietrich dynamic, see Gaylyn Studlar's book, *In the Realm of Pleasure: Von Sternberg, Dietrich, and the Masochistic Aesthetic* (Urbana: University of Illinois Press, 1988). The masochistic pleasure is especially relevant for a reading of Gong Li's characterization in *Shanghai Triad* and the film's purported status as a final collaboration between director and star. It is noteworthy that Western film critics have made something of a fetish of Gong Li as a star. See, for instance, Berenice Reynaud, "Gong Li and the Glamour of the Chinese Star," *Sight and Sound* 3, no. 8 (1993): 12–15.

24. See Rey Chow, *Primitive Passions: Visuality, Sexuality, Ethnography, and Contemporary Chinese Cinema* (New York: Columbia University Press, 1995), 166–172, and Esther C. M. Yau, "International Fantasy and the 'New Chinese Cinema,' " *Quarterly Review of Film and Video* 14, no. 3 (1993): 95–108.

25. Reynaud, "Gong Li," 15.

26. For a series of interventions on the global/local nexus under transnational capitalism, see Rob Wilson and Wimal Dissanayake, ed., *Global/Local: Cultural Production and the Transnational Imaginary* (Durham: Duke University Press, 1996). For discussions of transnational cinema and spectatorship in the volume, see the essay by Hamid Naficy and the joint essay by Ella Shohat and Robert Stam.

If "transnationalization will define the twenty-first century," as John Hess and Patricia R. Zimmermann assert in their programmatic essay, "Transnational Documentaries: A Manifesto" (p. 10), cultural workers, global or local, Chinese or otherwise, will have a huge stake in their ability to chart out a new kind of radical media politics that cuts across national boundaries. See John Hess and Patricia R. Zimmermann, "Transnational Documentaries: A Manifesto," *Afterimage* 24, no. 4 (1997): 10–14.

27. Corliss, "The Fire," 68.

28. See Dai Qing, "Raised Eyebrows for *Raise the Red Lantern*," *Public Culture* 5, no. 2 (1993): 333–338; Jane Ying Zha, "Excerpts from 'Lore Segal, *Red Lantern,* and Exoticism,' " *Public Culture* 5, no. 2 (1993): 329–332.

29. See Qian Jun, "Tan Sayide tan wenhua" [Said on Culture], *Dushu* [Reading], September 1993, 10–17; Zhang Kuan, "Oumei ren yanzhong de 'feiwo zulei': Cong dongfang zhuyi dao xifang zhuyi" ["Other people" in the eyes of Europeans and Americans: From "Orientalism" to "Occidentalism"], *Dushu* [Reading], September 1993, 3–9.

30. See Zhang Yiwu, "Quanqiuxing houzhimin yujing zhong de Zhang Yimou" [Zhang Yimou in the global postcolonial context], *Dangdai dianying* [Contemporary film] 54, no. 3 (1993): 18-25; Zhang Yiwu, "Disan shijie wenhua, yige xin de qidian" [Third-World culture: A new point of departure], *Dushu* [Reading], June 1990, 28–34. For other positions in the debate, see Liao Shiqi, "'Disan' de hanyi: Jiemingxun de gushi he women de chujing" [The meaning of "third": Jameson's story and our condition], *Dianying yishu* [Film art], no. 1 (1991): 39–45; Zhang Jingyuan, "Disan shiji piping: Minzu, zhongzu, xingbie" [Third-World criticism: Ethnicity, race, gender), *Dianying yishu* [Film art], no. 1 (1991): 33–38.

31. The same thing is said about *The Joy Luck Club* by the Asian-American director Wayne Wang. The film renders a contrast between the four mothers' memory of a painful past lived in Mainland China and life in contemporary America, the land of opportunity, as enjoyed by their four daughters. Native Chinese critics take this as Wang's attempt to fortify a sense of political superiority on the part of the American audience. When I asked the students in my film classes what they thought about this, they responded, "America looks pretty bad in a lot of American films too."

32. See Liao Ping-hui, "Shikong yu xingbie de cuoluan: Lun *Bawang bieji*" [Temporal, spatial, and gender disorder: On *Farewell My Concubine*], *Chung-wai Literary Monthly* 22, no. 1 (1993): 6–18.

33. Wang Yichuan et al. "Bianyuan, zhongxin, dongfang, xifang" [Periphery, center, Orient, Occident], *Dushu* [Reading], January 1994, 149.

34. For a group of informative essays on China's film industry, the film audience, and prospects of reform, see "Dianying xianzhuang yu dianying gaige" [Forum on the current situation and reform of Chinese cinema], *Beijing dianying xueyuan xuebao* [Journal of the Beijing Film Academy] 18, no. 1 (1993): 1–102.

35. See Ru-shou Chen (Robert Chen), "Fuhao 'Zhongguo' zai dianying zhong de yiyi" [The significance of the sign 'China' in film), *Dangdai* [Contemporary] (Taiwan) 87, no. 7 (1993): 122–143.

36. See Homi K. Bhabha, "DissemiNation, Time, Narrative, and the Margins of the Modern Nation," in *Nation and Narration,* ed. Homi K. Bhabha (New York: Routledge, 1990), 291–322.

37. Vincent Canby, "Action, History, and Love Above All" (review of *Farewell My Concubine*), *New York Times,* October 8, 1993, B8.

38. In fact, there has been a pitiful decline of interest in foreign-language films on the part of film audiences in the United States in comparison to earlier periods, such as the 1960s. Thus, the entrance of Chinese-language films into American movie theaters is all the more significant. For a report on this situation, see Richard Corliss, "Fellini Go Home!" *Time,* January 13, 1997, 68–70.

Part II

———————————— • ————————————

The Politics of Cultural and National Identity in the Cinemas of Taiwan and Hong Kong

Chapter 5

Constructing a Nation
Taiwanese History and the Films of Hou Hsiao-hsien
·
June Yip

One of the most crucial factors that binds a group of people into a "nation" is "the possession in common of a rich legacy of memories,"[1] a shared heritage which, through repetition, creates and reinforces a sense of historical continuity and sense of community. Since its retreat from the Chinese mainland and assumption of control of Taiwan after World War II, therefore, the ruling Guomindang (Kuomintang) government has skillfully deployed the rhetoric of nation to integrate Taiwan into a larger "Chinese" cultural identity and to weave a seamless narrative of Chinese nationhood that ignores differences that could in any way separate the island from the Mainland. Chiang Kai-shek understood well the critical importance of constructing spatial and temporal continuity between Taiwan and the continent and insisted from the outset that "the promotion of civic education must pay special attention to the teaching of 'Chinese History' and 'Chinese Geography.' "[2] Through what Benedict Anderson has called the "political museumization"[3] of the Chinese heritage of the Mainland—historical, sociological, aesthetic, and archeological—the Guomindang government has sought to consecrate Taiwan as the rightful heir to China's five-thousand-year imperial tradition. Conveniently elided from their accounts of the historical tradition, of course, have been the "interruptions" of the civil war with the Communists, the retreat of the Nationalists to Taiwan, and, most important, its violent assertion of control on the island. Hence the institutionalized remembrance and careful preservation of a coherent "Chinese" tradition by the Guomindang government was coupled with an "organized forgetting"[4] that included the systematic suppression of the island's aboriginal past, of local history, and of Taiwan's complex heritage of non-Chinese colonization, particularly its development under the Dutch (1624–1662) and the Japanese (1895–1945). In short, any historical experience that would mark Taiwan's differences from China has long been downplayed or omitted altogether from the official culture of the island.

Just as its native identity was organized into oblivion by historical and sociopolitical discourse, "Taiwan," as a modern historical subject, was similarly absent from the island's literature and cinema, dominated for so long by escapist narratives that seldom dealt with sociohistorical realities unique to the island. One of the chief objectives of 1980s Taiwanese New Cinema (Taiwan xin dianying), therefore, was to challenge the narrow view of Taiwan's modern history institutionalized by civic education and official culture by describing the great diversity of experiences in contemporary Taiwanese life. Taiwanese New Cinema has contributed toward the definition of a distinctly Taiwanese "nation" through its groundbreaking attempts to construct historical representations of the "Taiwan experience" (Taiwan jingyan) on film, to claim cinematic space for Taiwanese "popular memory." Beginning with the 1982 anthology film *In Our Time* (Guangyin de gushi), which traced four decades of Taiwan's postwar socioeconomic change through the stories of four individuals, Taiwanese New Cinema has, with increasing attention to geographical and temporal specificity, brought to the screen distinctly Taiwanese stories of social, economic, and political change that had rarely, if ever, received cinematic representation in the past, focusing on historical developments such as the island's painful transition from Japanese to Nationalist Chinese rule, its postwar transformation from rural agrarian society to urban industrialism, and its entry into the global order as a growing economic power.

Of all the New Cinema directors, no one has been more concerned with Taiwanese history than Hou Hsiao-hsien (Hou Xiaoxian). His films take as their grand theme Taiwanese identity, looking to the island's past in order to better understand the complex historical relationships—with China, Japan, and the West—that have shaped modern Taiwanese society. His autobiographical *A Time to Live and a Time to Die* (Tongnian wangshi, 1985), for example, transcends its personal coming-of-age story to examine the roots of modern Taiwanese life; it is a graceful and elegaic tracing of Taiwan's history from the Nationalist government's exile to Taiwan in 1949, through its decades of quasicolonial rule, to the gradual relinquishing of the dream of returning to the Mainland. The film marks the beginning of Hou's construction of the Taiwanese nation as a hybrid space, shaped by multiple waves of refugees, immigrants, and colonials and characterized by linguistic and cultural diversity. Later films such as *Dust in the Wind* (Lianlian fengchen, 1986) and *Daughter of the Nile* (Niluohe nüer, 1987) have depicted the consequences of Taiwan's rapid urbanization and internationalization, as Taiwanese youths find themselves caught up in a society where traditional Chinese values are collapsing in the face of American and Japanese cultural imperialism. In the increasingly liberalized atmosphere of the post-dictatorship era, Taiwanese cultural discourse has been characterized by a resurgence of interest in aspects of local history that had, until the lifting of martial law, been suppressed by the Nationalist government. As part of this native reawakening, Hou's films since 1987 have been overtly historical interrogations into the Taiwanese past. Hou has said that he sees his film-making as the process by which he can try to understand the culture and history of the island he calls home. The three films that make up his ambitious and important "Taiwan Trilogy"—*City of Sadness* (Beiqing chengshi, 1989), *The Puppetmaster* (Ximeng rensheng, 1993), and *Good Men, Good Women* (Haonan haonü, 1995)—investigate three eras in Taiwanese history long considered politically taboo: the Japanese occupation; the violent transition years of 1945–1949, when control of the island passed from the Japanese to the Guomindang; and the "White Terror" (baise kongbu) anti-Communist witchhunts of the 1950s. It is precisely because these historical eras highlight the cultural differences and sociopolitical tensions between Chinese mainlanders and Taiwanese natives that they were excluded from official historiography. It is also for these reasons that their reexaminations have been critical for the formation of a "Taiwanese" national identity.

· Critical Historiography, Or, The Uses of The Past

In his "Theses on the Philosophy of History," Walter Benjamin says that "to articulate the past historically does not mean to recognize it 'the way it really was' (Ranke). It means to seize hold of a memory as it flashes up at a moment of danger."[5] Like much of modern historiography, Benjamin's philosophy of history rejects the claims to authority and objectivity that typified nineteenth-century historical writing and is instead emphatically critical and interventionist. In place of a single linear narrative, it aims to "blast open the continuum of history" (p. 261) by emphasizing rupture and fragmentation. Specific moments or events are wrenched out of the homogeneous order of history and reconfigured into monads, "pregnant with tension" (p. 262). While the classical historical narrative offers up a fixed " 'eternal' image of the past," Benjaminian historiography is based on an interactive principle that recognizes a dialectical relationship between past and present. The historical materialist "grasps the constellation which his own era has formed with a definite earlier one" (p. 263) and actively engages in the constant construction and reconstruction of the past.[6] All representations of the past, then, are shaped and defined by the political and cultural concerns of the specific moment from which they emerge.

Hou Hsiao-hsien's films are marked by a preoccupation with the Taiwanese past that might easily be seen in Benjaminian terms as an effort to find a sense of the past that is useable in understanding current crises in Taiwanese history. *City of Sadness*, for example, has been called Hou's "post-martial-law film,"[7] his response to the remarkable democratization in Taiwan launched by the lifting of martial law in 1987. The present moment marks a critical transition in the island's history, with optimism for continued cultural and political liberalization tempered by fear of a conservative backlash.[8] It is no accident, therefore, that the period of Taiwanese history depicted in *City of Sadness* (1945–1949) is another era of transition—from Japanese occupation to rule by the Nationalist government—that saw a brief moment of hope for political liberalization followed by disillusionment and harsh repression. The film tells of an extended family's experiences during this turbulent era but is at the same time an exploration of national identity, an attempt to recover a period in Taiwanese history that Hou considers crucial for understanding the dynamics of contemporary Taiwanese society—the antagonistic relationship between the government and the people and the continuing tensions between mainlanders and native Taiwanese.[9] Hou's film, then, might be seen as an attempt to "seize hold of a memory as it flashes up in a moment of danger," to articulate the Taiwanese past as a reference point for contemporary struggles.

The notion of "struggle" is central to an understanding of the role of historiography in *City of Sadness*. Hou has said that after centuries of invasion and colonial rule, Taiwan is finally, during this post-martial-law era, in the process of decolonization.[10] An important step in this process is the restoration of native memory and the reclamation of a Taiwanese position as subject—rather than mere object—of history. Walter Benjamin sees interventionist historiography as an important tool in the struggle against oppression by the ruling classes. "In every era," he writes, "the attempt must be made anew to wrest tradition away from a conformism that is about to overpower it" (p. 255). The goal is to "brush history against the grain" (p. 257), to challenge the official histories written by the victors. The historical materialist is not interested, therefore, in the lives of "the great minds and talents" of an era or in major political events but focuses instead on "the anonymous toil of their contemporaries" (p. 256).

Hou Hsiao-hsien's films can be seen as attempts to write such a "history from below," deliberately rejecting the vantage point of the rulers in favor of the perspective of the common people. Milestones of public political history are pushed away from the centers of his films, allowing the everyday experiences of ordinary Taiwanese families to come to the fore. *City of Sadness*, in particular, explicitly denies the Guomindang government representation and subjectivity. "Officialdom" exists in the film only as a disembodied voice, heard on a radio broadcast or as offscreen dialogue; a faceless police uniform, shot from behind; a pair of heavy military boots echoing down a prison hallway; or a shadowy figure brandishing a rifle in the dark. Instead, the film gives names and voices to those "anonymous toilers" un-acknowledged by official history, the ordinary citizens whose personal stories together make up Taiwanese "popular memory."

· Interweaving Public and Private: Narrative and the Open Texture of History

"History," writes Jean-François Lyotard, "is made up of wisps of narratives, stories that one tells, that one hears, that one acts out . . . a mass of millions of insignificant and serious little stories that sometimes let themselves be collected together to constitute big stories and sometimes disperse into digressive elements."[11] History here is no longer conceived of as a univocal, seamless narrative but as a complex dialogic web of multiple, heteroge-neous, and fragmentary stories that by chance touch, intersect, and some-times contradict each other. Lyotard's conception of history illuminates the way that "history" emerges from the overlapping stories of the individuals who inhabit Hou's *City of Sadness*. Hou's film challenges the "continuum of History" by forcing a dialogue between the kinds of texts admitted by con-ventional historiography—public accounts of political history—and those that are normally excluded: the private narratives of the Lim (Lin)[12] family and their friends. There are, to begin with, the personal narratives of the four Lim brothers: the eldest son of old Taiwanese hoodlum Ah-luk-sai (A Lushi/Ah Lu-shih),[13] Bun-heung (Wenxiong/Wen-hsiung), has carried on the family businesses, running a nightclub and gambling establishment called Little Shanghai and shipping goods between the Taiwanese port of Chilung (Jilong) and Shanghai on the Mainland. His involvement with the Shanghai underworld in shipping illegal goods eventually gets him killed by the Shanghai bosses. Second son Bun-hsim (Wensen/Wen-sen), family members recount, is a doctor who loves Beethoven but who has disap-peared after being conscripted by the Japanese and sent to the South Seas. Most of the family has given him up for dead, but his wife clings to her hopes and patiently awaits his return. Bun-leong (Wenliang/Wen-liang), the third son, was sent to Shanghai by the Japanese and returns from the battles there shellshocked and traumatized. After he recovers, he becomes enmeshed in underworld activities that lead to his arrest by government authorities. The beating he receives at the hands of the Nationalists leaves him a physical and mental cripple. Much of the film focuses on the young-est son, Bun-ch'ing (Wenqing/Wen-ch'ing), a deaf-mute[14] who works as a photographer and is the family intellectual. He often functions as a silent observer of events and is the family's chief witness to the political upheavals of the era. His friends include Hiroe (Kuanrong/K'uan-jung),[15] an idealistic young schoolteacher, Hiroe's circle of intellectual friends, and Hiroe's sister Hiromi (Kuanmei/K'uan-mei), a nurse who comes to the mining village of Kim-Kuei-chiu (Jinguashi/Chin-kua-shih)[16] to work in the hospital and who eventually becomes Bun-ch'ing's wife. Their narratives, together with those of the Lim brothers, weave a complex web of stories that offers a densely textured portrait of Taiwanese life between 1945 and 1949. Significantly, these personal stories are told neither in a chronological nor carefully emplotted manner but are gradually revealed in "wisps": snippets of conversation, fragments of diaries and letters, seemingly unrelated images and sequences of action that a viewer must attempt to piece together. The text is full of temporal disjunctions, gaps, and discontinuities, leaving audiences with a rich but ambivalent and incomplete sense of history. History is not narrated but evoked; it emerges not as a logical, univocal sequence of events but as a complex Benjaminian "constellation" that brings together fragments of individual life stories into a monad that remains open, ambiguous, and "pregnant with tensions."

The intertwining of public and political history with this network of personal narratives links the fates of the Lim family and their friends with the fate of Taiwan as a nation. Private and public events are woven together from the film's very first scene: images of an extremely personal event—the birth of a child[17] in the Lim family—are accompanied by the voice of the Showa emperor, announcing over the radio Japan's unconditional surrender and the end of its fifty-one-year occupation of Taiwan.[18] This use of intertitles and radio broadcasts in the opening sequence establishes a strategy that is continued throughout the film: the major political developments of this period in Taiwanese history are introduced into the narrative not through visual representation but through language, spoken and written. The activities of the government and its direct interactions with the Taiwanese people are rarely, if ever, depicted on the screen. Instead, public history enters the space of the film—and the private space of the family—through intertitles, through the sound track (radio announcements, music, and Hiromi's voice-over narration of her diary entries), and through the dialogue. There are, of course, the many serious political discussions in which Hiroe and his friends engage, but a great deal of political history also finds its way into the film through the grandfather Ah-luk-sai's rambling monologues, through humorous anecdotes, through the casual conversations Bun-heung has with friends in his nightclub, through the songs they sing, and through the written notes (intertitles for the film audience) that Bun-ch'ing and Hiromi use to communicate with each other. The significance of Hou's suppression of the visual in his filmic representation of his-

Fig. 10. *City of Sadness* (Beiqing chengshi), directed by Hou Hsiao-hsien, Taiwan, 1989. British Film Institute.

tory cannot be overestimated. As has often been noted, the rapid flow of images that make up film makes it a particularly powerful ideological tool, one that hinders rather than stimulates the critical faculties of the viewer.[19] The "reality effect" and "visual pleasure" associated with the cinematic image makes it an especially persuasive—and hence dangerous—medium for historical representation.[20] Film has the power to render the past visible, to make audiences feel they are eyewitnesses who can look directly at historical events. Film audiences for whom "seeing is believing" tend to forget that cinematic visualizations of history are not transparent windows on the past or mirror reflections but are, like verbal narratives, constructed re-presentations. Historical representation in *City of Sadness* is decidedly unfilmic: the voice-over commentary, intertitles, and written texts that contain most of the film's historical information are presented in an openly "unrealistic" manner. Hou's insistence on filtering all public historical events through language and the subjectivities of individual characters reminds us that all historical knowledge is mediated, underscoring the idea that "history" is, after all, storytelling.[21] This emphasis on the discursive and ultimately indeterminate nature of historical "truth" is an idea that Hou and his scriptwriters have frequently invoked as a response to those film critics and cultural pundits who stubbornly insist on treating *City of Sadness* as semi-documentary, endlessly debating the "accuracy" of its historical representations.[22]

By allowing "history" to emerge from multiple and heterogeneous "wisps of narratives," Hou's film avoids the limitations of conventional historiography, which insists on reducing the complexities of human existence into a single authoritative narrative. It also moves beyond a simple counternarrative to official history toward a more radical questioning of traditional historiographical methods. Like Bakhtin's "dialogic novel,"[23] *City of Sadness* is opened up by the forces of "heteroglossia" to accommodate the sometimes dissonant "polyphony" of voices that make up Taiwanese society. History is understood as an ongoing process, a continual play between heterogeneous forces that present options for different possible histories and for different potential futures.

• The Transition to Nationalist Rule and the February Incident

> *Forgetting, I would even go so far as to say historical error, is a crucial factor in the creation of a nation, which is why progress in historical studies often constitutes a danger for [the principle of] nationality. Indeed, historical enquiry brings to light deeds of violence which took place at the origins of all political formations. . . . Unity is always effected by means of brutality . . . .* ERNEST RENAN

> *[E]very narrative, however seemingly "full," is constructed on the basis of a set of events which might have been included but were left out. . . .* HAYDEN WHITE

The four years between the end of the Japanese colonial occupation in 1945 and the relocation of the Nationalist government from the Mainland to Taiwan in 1949 have, until very recently, been almost completely elided from official versions of Chinese history. Hou Hsiao-hsien's cinematic evocation of these chaotic years—one of the first attempts to examine this missing period—presents a clear challenge to official accounts. From the Guomindang perspective, Japan's surrender and the end of its occupation of Taiwan were a great victory that "liberated" the Taiwanese from oppression and exploitation and returned them to the "warm embrace of the Chinese motherland." It was to be the start of a new era of peace and prosperity for the Taiwanese people—a sense of hope and expectation for the future that is conveyed in the celebratory opening scenes of *City of Sadness*. Taiwanese jubilation and optimism, however, was short-lived, as the behavior and attitudes of the Nationalist officials sent to govern the island began to alienate and antagonize the native population. Dominant historiography has, of course, perpetuated the myth that the transition to Chinese rule was a joyous reunion of one people. While the ancestors of those who consider themselves native to Taiwan did come from China centuries ago, interaction between the island and the Mainland was in fact extremely limited throughout the eighteenth and nineteenth centuries, as the island was virtually ignored by the central Chinese government, which did not hesitate to cede Taiwan to Japan in 1895. The island's sense of separateness and difference was aggravated by its half-century under Japanese rule and again by the Nationalist government's arrogant behavior when it took over the island from the Japanese in 1945. Chinese officials did not welcome the Taiwanese populace as their own; instead, they adopted the attitude of a conquerer. In his first public address, Lt. Gen. Ge Jingen (Ko Ching-en), head of the Guomindang "advance team" that arrived in Taiwan in October 1945 to begin the transfer of power, unabashedly expressed his contempt for the island he considered to be "beyond the passes"—at best on the margins of true Chinese civilization. He publicly characterized Taiwan as "degraded territory" and the Taiwanese as a "degraded people,"[24] an insistence on the inferiority and savagery of native peoples that is typical of a colonizing force.[25]

Nor did the Taiwanese people welcome the new arrivals from the Mainland as their Chinese brothers and sisters.[26] In *City of Sadness*, the profound cultural, linguistic, and experiential differences that separate Taiwanese and mainlanders are underscored by the babel of mutually incomprehensible tongues—Japanese, Taiwanese, Cantonese, Mandarin, Shanghainese, and Hakka—spoken by the characters. A number of scenes foreground the multiple levels of translation necessary for Taiwanese and mainlanders to even communicate with each other,[27] an obstacle that clearly raises the potential for mutual misunderstanding between the two groups. Divisions between the mainlanders and native islanders worsened in the face of the economic disaster and social chaos precipitated by the system of state monopolies imposed by the Guomindang-appointed governor, Chen Yi (Ch'en Yi), and by the greed and corruption that characterized his administration. *City of Sadness* gives voice to the growing disillusionment and discontent expressed by all sectors of the native population,[28] angered by Chen Yi's authoritative rule and frustrated by their continued denial of a voice in determining their own fates. Says one of the intellectuals in the film: "The Qing court sold us out in the first place. Who ever asked us Taiwanese if we agreed to the Treaty of Shimonoseki?" Lim Bun-heung puts it in simpler words, but with equal eloquence: "We Taiwanese are the most pitiable. First come the Japanese, then come the Chinese. We're eaten by everyone, ridden by everyone, but cared for by no one at all." As Hou's film depicts, the tensions between the Nationalist government and the Taiwanese populace reached a feverish pitch and finally exploded on February 28, 1947, in a violent confrontation known as the February 28 or "Two-two-eight" Incident (Ererba shijian).[29] On that morning, a crowd of two thousand or more angry Taiwanese gathered at the Monopoly Bureau headquarters in Taipei to protest the brutal beating of a cigarette vendor by government agents the night before. Rioting erupted, and the Nationalist soldiers guarding the bureau headquarters sprayed the crowd with machine-gun fire, killing an unknown number of unarmed civilians and wounding scores more.[30] The brutal response of the government ignited the Taiwanese populace. In the days and weeks that followed, demonstrations and riots erupted all over the island, as Taiwanese patriots grew bolder and louder in their demands for economic and political reform.[31] Chen Yi's government retaliated swiftly and brutally, treating the Taiwanese not as protesters against maladministration in the provincial government but as insurgent rebels who threatened Nationalist rule. Though no one knows the exact death toll, it is believed that tens of thousands of Taiwanese may have died in the Nationalists' subsequent campaign to eradicate Taiwanese resistance throughout the island.

Chen Yi's government succeeded in suppressing the Taiwanese uprising, but the result of the bloody clash between the Mainland rulers and the native people was a deep and bitter enmity between the two groups that has poisoned Taiwanese politics and society for much of the last four decades. For many, the February 28 Incident is *the* symbol of the Guomindang's "foreign domination" over Taiwan's "native people," the defining event dividing "China" and "Taiwan" into two separate and irreconcilable entities.[32] From the beginning, the Nationalist government suppressed the facts surrounding the incident and, under the martial law that was imposed following the confrontation, any discussion of the incident was taboo. Due to the official silence on the incident, Hou Hsiao-hsien's *City of Sadness* is, for many people in Taiwan, an introduction to the historical event. It is no surprise, therefore, that although the February Incident lies in its background, much of the debate surrounding the film has focused on its representation of this historical event.

Like other major events in public political history, the incident itself receives no visual representation in Hou's film. Instead, it enters the film's narrative in purely verbal form: Chen Yi's radio broadcast, in which he seeks to downplay the incident and placate the Taiwanese people. Speaking in Shanghai-accented Mandarin, he uses soothing and conciliatory words which belie the ruthlessness of his subsequent response to the uprising. As Hiromi's diary entry for that day suggests, however, the Taiwanese people knew that a major political crisis was at hand: "The radio today reported an incident in Taipei: killing between Taiwanese and mainlanders. Taipei is under martial law. . . . everyone is afraid. A war just ended; how can another start again?"

The official Guomindang interpretation of the February Incident has always been that it was instigated by a handful of Taiwanese rebels who were influenced by communist agitators,[33] a point of view again represented in the film through a radio broadcast. Throughout the rest of the film, however, this official account is subverted by the forces of Bakhtinian "dialogism." First, by contextualizing dominant history as an "utterance"[34] produced by a specific person (Chen Yi) living in a specific historical period (a time when the Guomindang was in the process of consolidating power in Taiwan), belonging to a specific social class (the ruling class), and addressing a specific audience (the Taiwanese masses), Hou exposes the ideological biases of what has long been presented as objective truth. The official interpretation of the February Incident as a purely political struggle is further undermined in the film by the subversive effects of what Bakhtin refers to as the "centrifugal forces" of "heteroglossia": those discourses, normally considered to be outside the generic boundaries of "historical narrative"—nonpolitical "voices" like economic and sociological discourses, personal letters and diaries, and so on—that Hou incorporates to interrupt, complicate, and ultimately explode the monolithic view of Taiwanese history disseminated by the Guomindang. Hou suggests, for example, that the February Incident could also be seen as an economic, rather than political, battle: an inevitable outcome of the deep-seated resentment provoked by widespread corruption and exploitation by Nationalist officials. References to the tobacco monop-

Fig. 11. *City of Sadness* (Beiqing chengshi), directed by Hou Hsiao-hsien, Taiwan, 1989. British Film Institute.

oly and the smuggling activities of greedy government officials are made early in the film, foreshadowing the February Incident and the escalation of violence in its aftermath. The tragic fates of Hiroe and his friends and the experiences of Bun-ch'ing and the rest of the Lim family suggest that the goal of Chen Yi's government was not to eradicate "a tiny handful of traitorous rebels" but to indiscriminately punish the Taiwanese people for daring to resist Nationalist rule. The Lim family suffers greatly during the chaos and violence of the March massacres. Returning from a trip to Taipei, a wounded Hiroe reports the arrival of Nationalist troops from the Mainland: "They're arresting and killing people as they go." The Lim family is forced to shut down their business because of the fear and confusion; as Bun-heung's daughter explains to Hiromi: "[T]hings are too chaotic. People are getting killed everywhere and the neighboring houses are always being ransacked." The retaliatory reaction of the angry Taiwanese people is violent as well. In a tense scene that captures the irrational and impulsive anger of the Taiwanese toward mainlanders, Bun-ch'ing is approached by a group of Taiwanese youths on a train.[35] Unaware that he cannot hear them, they angrily ask him where he is from. When he fails to answer, they ask again, in Japanese. Since a Taiwanese would understand Japanese and Bun-ch'ing does not respond, one of the men yells "He must be a mainlander!" and they surge forward to beat him up. Hiroe arrives just in time to tell them Bun-ch'ing is a deaf-mute. Both Bun-ch'ing and Hiroe personally experience the brutalities of the government crackdown. Arrested for his association with Teacher Lin, Bun-ch'ing sees his prison mates taken away one by one and escorted to the execution grounds by Nationalist soldiers. Although he cannot hear them, the gunshots fired by the executioners echo on the film's sound track. Hiroe and his friends, like so many Taiwanese intellectuals and students at the time, are forced to hide out in the mountains. They too, are tracked down and summarily executed by Nationalist soldiers.

By the end of the film, the interpenetration of public history and private stories is total, as the tides of political change completely disrupt the Lim family order and their normal rituals of life. The final dinner scene reveals the toll that political history has exacted on the family: the bustling activity that characterized earlier family meals is replaced by a poignant silence. The Lim family men are all either dead, missing, or in Guomindang prisons;[36] the only ones left to carry on are an old man, a mental cripple, small children, and the women of the family.

· A "Look Back to the Future"

Today, fifty years after the violent events of 1947, Taiwan seems finally ready to reassess this controversial chapter in its history. The current government, with its Taiwan-born leaders, has demonstrated a willingness to reexamine the episode in order to "heal the wounds of history" and move toward easing tensions between the government and the people, between mainlanders and native islanders. In February of 1992, the government at last broke its silence on the February 28 Incident and issued a report[37] that contradicts the long-time official interpretation of events by acknowledging that government corruption and misrule were the fundamental causes for the uprising and by admitting to killing an estimated eighteen thousand to twenty-eight thousand native-born Taiwanese in the 1947 incident and the massacres that followed. The government has fulfilled its promise to erect a monument to the victims of the massacres; in February of 1995, a memorial was dedicated in Taipei, accompanied by a formal apology from President Li. In addition, the legislature has discussed the possibility of monetary compensation for the families of victims.

For Walter Benjamin, the writing of history is inextricably tied up with the possibilities of redemption, for "only a redeemed mankind receives the fullness of its past" (p. 254). Hou Hsiao-hsien similarly sees his exploration of the past in *City of Sadness* as a necessary catharsis for the Taiwanese people, without which the tensions and conflicts of society cannot be put to rest. Hou wants the healing process to begin and envisions his film as a new start for Taiwanese/mainlander relations and the beginning of a new phase in Taiwanese history:

> I hope that a renewed understanding of "Two-two-eight" will help everyone to finally cast away its dark shadow and to go on living with energy and vitality. What I most desire is for audiences who see my film to leave the theater not only with tears in their eyes, but with a new sense of pride, of empowerment, and with the determination to move toward the future. . . .[38]

• Play/Dream/Life: *The Puppetmaster* and the Theater of History

What is history for the elite has always been work for the masses.   HEINER MULLER

The Puppetmaster is the second installment of Hou's Taiwan Trilogy. While *City of Sadness* depicted the years following the end of the Japanese occupation, this film probes even further into Taiwan's past, focusing on the fifty years of the occupation itself. Since the lifting of martial law, there has been a revival of interest in Taiwanese life during the Japanese occupation, a period that was seldom, if ever, discussed under the Guomindang dictatorship. Hou Hsiao-hsien's film is among several recent films that have sought to reexamine the island's Japanese era and its lasting impact on Taiwanese life. Hou has expressed his belief that, in order to truly understand how Taiwan came to be what it is today and to gain a secure sense of belonging, one must dig beneath the many layers of the island's complex past; he sees the Japanese occupation as a crucial period to which many of contemporary Taiwan's sociocultural structures and attitudes can be traced.[39] In *The Puppetmaster,* Hou once again approaches public political history "from below," telling the story of Taiwan under Japanese rule through the colorful life story of Li T'ien-lu (Li Tianlu; Li T'en-luk in Taiwanese), the aged master of Taiwanese hand puppetry who has appeared as a grandfather in all of Hou's films since *Dust in the Wind.*

The Puppetmaster might best be described as anecdotal biography. The film traces Li's life and times from his birth in 1910 to the Japanese surrender in 1945, relying sometimes on vignettes with dramatizations by actors to tell its story, sometimes on the old master's own recollections, either heard in voice-over or spoken directly to the camera. Like *City of Sadness,* this film intertwines the public and the private, opening with an intertitle defining the historical parameters of the film—"1895, China loses the war and signs the Treaty of Shimonoseki, ceding Taiwan and the Pescadores to Japan. Thus, Japan ruled Taiwan for fifty years, until World War II." The scene that follows is not exactly a birth but a similar private moment: a family is seen sitting around a table, where a proud father and grandfather are toasting the birth of a son, Ah-luk (A lu/Ah lu). Into this celebratory scene is suddenly interjected the voice of the old man Li T'en-luk himself, who tells us the story behind this family gathering. Shortly after his birth, Li tells us, a fortune-teller predicted that he was destined to have a hard life. The difficulties began almost immediately, with his father and grandfather quarreling over which surname the baby should bear. The father thought it logical that the baby share his surname, Hsu (Xu; K'o in Taiwanese), but the superstitious grandfather insisted that Ah-luk call his parents Auntie and Uncle and take the surname Li, after the matchmaker who brought his parents together. "And so," explains Li, "That's how I was born." This pronouncement is followed by a shot of a hand-puppet theater set up in a field, then a shot of the performance itself. There is no dialogue or expository narration, only the songs and music of the puppet show. As the show ends and the puppets disappear behind the theater curtains, the screen fades to black and the film's title—literally, "Play, Dream, Life"—appears in bold red characters.

It is worth noting that in the opening scene of *City,* it is the voice of the Japanese emperor announcing Japan's surrender in a radio broadcast—the voice of public political history—that penetrates the private sphere of the Lim family. In this film, by contrast, there is only personal narrative on the sound track, the recollections of an old man looking back on the beginning of his life. Hence, despite the politically significant historical markers that open the film, *The Puppetmaster* deliberately pushes public history far into the background. Even more than *City of Sadness,* it valorizes the apolitical lives of the common masses by refracting major political events through the limited consciousnesses of ordinary people. While *City of Sadness* had its share of intellectuals, whose discussions and debates about the politics of the era were given significant screen time, *The Puppetmaster* leaves that world behind. Li T'en-luk, as puppetmaster, opera actor, and itinerant folk artist, is someone who truly lives on the fringes of Chinese society. By choosing Li's life experience as the prism through which to look at the Taiwanese past, Hou has said, he is searching for elements of Taiwanese culture that lie beneath the surface of history and beyond ideology. Li's story is not so much about the politics of the Japanese era but about the common person's adaptability in the face of historical events that are beyond his control or comprehension.[40]

From the private perspective, then, political history appears merely as a series of hurdles to overcome, pragmatic adjustments to be made in order to survive. In *The Puppetmaster*, for example, the massive and dramatic changes that marked the early stages of the Japanese takeover—a radical restructuring that overhauled every aspect of life on the island, from its political institutions, economic organizations, health, education, and transportation systems to the physical appearance of the island's cities and villages[41]—cause barely a ripple in Li T'en-luk's daily life. His memories of those years focus on everyday things: his boredom with traditional schooling, the consequent punishment he suffered at the hands of his parents, and finally his teenage rebellion, when he left his family to apprentice with a traveling puppet-theater troupe. In the early part of the film, the political reality of the Japanese occupation invades the private sphere of Li's family in a brief and notably undramatic scene: as part of the occupation's efforts to modernize and "Japanize" the Taiwanese, soldiers ask the family to cut off their traditional Chinese pigtails. The family does not even question the order, let alone reject it as a colonizer's act of forced cultural assimilation. For them, it is only a minor annoyance—alleviated by the soldiers' offer of opera tickets in exchange for their compliance. The entire episode is probably most significant for the fact that the family is given tickets to the opera, perhaps planting the seeds for Li's future career.

Throughout the film, the impact of Japanese colonization on Taiwanese life makes itself felt gradually, without unusual drama or commentary: here and there a Japanese word or phrase slips into the dialogue, a casual comment is made about a visit to a Japanese doctor, a Japanese song is heard on the sound track, or a Japanese-style house appears on the screen. There are, of course, instances when major political events have a direct impact on Li's life. Still, the historical events themselves are not given visual representation but only referred to in passing in Li's voice-over. Li tells us, for example, that in the wake of the 1937 Marco Polo Bridge Incident, he joined an opera troupe as an actor because the Japanese censors, ever fearful of subversive activity, felt it necessary in 1938 to ban popular puppet shows, which they found were caricaturing the Japanese and mocking their government.[42] Later, when the Pacific War escalated, Li was recruited by the Japanese colonial government to help the war effort and participate in the government's assimilation program by performing Japanese propaganda puppet shows.

As in *City of Sadness*, Hou's depictions in this film of the relationships between ordinary Taiwanese and the Japanese colonials living on the island during the occupation reveal a human side of Japan seldom acknowledged in official history. The impact of the occupation on the island's culture has been lasting, and even today, the Taiwanese attitude toward Japan and Japanese culture is deeply ambivalent—a mixture of wary antagonism, repressed nostalgia, and envy. It is a love-hate relationship that can only be understood by looking back to its roots in the Japanese occupation. While Japanese brutalities and discrimination against the Taiwanese were undeniable, the colonial government also laid the foundations of an infrastructure that made Taiwan's post–World War II economic boom possible. Moreover, though Japan was the political enemy during the occupation, at a personal level, many solid working relationships—even friendships—developed between Japanese colonials and Taiwanese natives. In *City of Sadness,* the Lim family counts among its closest friends a Japanese brother and sister, whose repatriation following the Japanese surrender is depicted in several poignant farewell scenes. Some of the Japanese soldiers and officials in *The Puppetmaster* are insensitive bullies, but there are also those who help Li and his family and who feel genuine affection for Taiwan, their "second home." For ordinary Taiwanese dealing with the everyday reality of living under the occupation, political antagonism rarely came into play. For a poor commoner like Li, moreover, political resistance was simply impractical. Flexibility and a cooperative spirit are often necessary for survival. Li, for example, agrees to join the Japanese government's propaganda puppet troop because, in the uncertainty of wartime, he was grateful for the promise of a nice apartment, a good salary, and, most important, security for his family.[43]

Japan's imperialist ambitions and her eight-year war against China and the Western Allies took its toll on the native Taiwanese population, not only on the Taiwanese youths who were conscripted and sent into battle all over Asia but also on the island's civilians. One of the casualties of the prolonged war was the public health system. As funds, supplies, and personnel were taken away from public services and put into the war effort, disease—particularly malaria—spread throughout the island. In *The Puppetmaster,* the war forces Li's family to move around constantly; eventually, the family is stricken by malaria. Li himself falls ill, but continues to perform puppet shows, resting on a bed behind the stage during his bouts of fever and chills. Li's father-in-law dies from the disease, as does his youngest child. When Li makes a tiny coffin for his dead child, though, it is without visible bitterness or resentment. As his voice-over suggests, Li's attitude toward the personal tragedies he has suffered as a consequence of political turmoil is one of stoic resignation: "One's fate can't be changed." Even after the Japanese are defeated and begin their retreat from the island, Li expresses no enmity toward the Japanese. At the end of film, Li even relates how, after the Japanese surrender, he helped to protect a group of Japanese soldiers from an angry Taiwanese mob. The final image of the film shows men, women, and children tearing apart planes that have been abandoned in a bombed-out airfield, salvaging the metal. It is an eloquent reminder that for ordinary citizens, the dramas of public political history mean very little. They have no time to contemplate the significance of Japan's surrender or Taiwan's "glorious liberation"; they are too busy with the everyday task of living.

The past can only be recaptured as memory and, as such, can never be fully reconstructed. The processes of memory seize hold of the past selectively, emphasizing and lingering over only those images and events that have special significance. In *The Puppetmaster,* the life story of Li T'en-luk is shaped by the often unreliable operations of memory; hence, while the film presents the experiences of Li's childhood and youth in more or less chronological order, it remains extremely elliptical and impressionistic. Li's retrospective look at his past seems to center on the various women in his life: his mother, the filial daughter-in-law who was willing to exchange her own health—and ultimately her life—to save Li's gravely ill grandmother; the stepmother who made Li's childhood miserable. One of the longest and most colorful stories Li tells is about his grandmother, who came to live with him after all the other relatives had decided she was hexed. Little is said about Li's wife and children; their entry into his life is suggested through brief, dialogueless vignettes: the sound of firecrackers and music in the distance hint at a marriage; the sounds of a woman screaming in pain and the sight of a servant scurrying by with a pan of water suggest the birth of a child. By contrast, Li tells elaborate tales about the prostitute, named Li-chu (Lizhu), whom he met during the war.

The film is also filled with lyrical images and suggestive details—a second-floor balcony, a tree towering over a temple, a puppet theater in an open field, a dirt road winding through rice fields, a fishing boat gliding silently across the water—which take on almost Proustian significance. The memory-laden details provide the texture of Li's recollected life, but because they are often presented without exposition or commentary, they do not "narrate" Li's life in the conventional sense. As in *City of Sadness,* where the personal stories of the Lim family members were revealed in "wisps of narratives" that the viewer must weave together, *The Puppetmaster* offers only fragments of Li's experiences, perhaps raising more questions about Li's life and times than it answers.[44] In the end, the film underscores the indeterminacy of identity, emphasizing the impossibility of fully reconstructing a life or of really "knowing" the man called Li T'en-luk.[45]

· Fiction or Document? Deconstructing the Past

One of the most persistent themes in classical Chinese literature and philosophy—from Zhuangzi's famous dream of the butterfly to Cao Xueqin's *Dream of the Red Chamber*—has been the interplay between illusion and reality. Hou Hsiao-hsien's *The Puppetmaster* is one of two recent Chinese films (Chen Kaige's *Farewell My Concubine* is the other) that once again take up this theme. Hou's film has been described as a blend of documentary and fiction, with "documentary" referring to the sequences in which Li T'en-luk speaks directly to the camera and "fiction" referring to the dramatic reenactments by the actors.[46] The film is actually much more complex, as it ultimately questions the very distinction between the two modes. Like *City of Sadness*, the film juxtaposes a polyphony of heterogeneous discourses and multiple perspectives. In addition to the discourse of official history—whether information presented through the intertitles or knowledge that the viewer is assumed to bring to the film—there are Li T'en-luk's own memories, which he narrates in voice-over and direct address to the camera, Hou's filmed restagings of the events in Li's life, and the many performances of opera and puppetry that appear throughout the film. All four of these "voices" are introduced in the pretitle sequence and interact throughout the film. Sometimes they complement each other: in one instance, for example, a puppet show about the sorrow of leaving home precedes Li's recounting, in voice-over, his decision to leave his family and apprentice with a traveling puppet troupe. More often, however, they contradict each other. Perhaps the best example is the characterization of the stepmother. The vignette that depicts the stepmother's introduction into Li's life is poetic and suffused with nostalgia: the child Ah-luk is called into the room to meet his new mother, who solemnly performs a belt-changing ritual to join her life with his. Li's impression of the woman, however, is quite different: in his own words, it is a "life made miserable by my stepmother" that drives him away from home.

The question arising from the contradictions between visual image and verbal narration is: which representation is more "real"? Which version tells the "truth" about Li's past? The title of Hou's film translates literally as "Play, Dream, Life." "Play" most likely refers to the puppet shows and opera performances in the film, but the associations of the other two are not so clear. One could argue, for example, that visual images are more "real" than words; hence the dramatic vignettes must correspond to "life" while Li's narrated memories, colored by his concerns and desires of the moment,[47] are associated with "dream." On the other hand, one could just as easily argue the opposite: that the actors, speaking dialogue written by Hou and his screenwriters, are reconstructing an illusion of the past within a closed fictional space, while Li T'en-luk as raconteur is "real," with the camera simply "documenting" him telling his story. If the actors reenacting Li's life are mere performers mouthing the words of others, are the dramatic vignettes in which they appear any more "real" than the "play" of the hand puppets? Hou offers no answers to these questions; the tensions and dynamic interplay between the different voices simply serve to undermine and blur conventional distinctions between life and dream, reality and illusion, document and fiction.

The disjunction between multiple perspectives and voices in the film—image versus text, the "narrating I" (Li's voice-over commentary) versus the "narrated I" (the actors who portray Li in his childhood and youth)—creates an ironic distance which challenges both the narrative continuity and naive referentiality associated with conventional historical representation. It forces the viewer into an active, critical stance and reminds us of the constructedness of all forms of representation. This is particularly apparent when the dramatization of an episode in Li's youth—the episode in the coffin shop, for instance—is jarringly interrupted by a shot of the old man Li himself sitting on the set where the action had been taking place. Li tells his story directly to the camera, further breaking the diegetic illusion. Hou's distanciation techniques are not unlike the strategies of Jean-Marie Straub and Danielle Huillet, the radical filmmakers who also sought to challenge the conventional assumptions of historical representation[48] and to whom some European film critics have compared Hou.[49] By incorporating long sequences of puppetry and folk opera, as well as numerous shots of audiences and of puppeteers working backstage, Hou further emphasizes the performative and the presentational, again reminding viewers of their role as spectators of a constructed film image, an illusion.[50]

Finally, the metaphor of puppetry raises a host of interesting questions about history, identity, and the possibility of apprehending the "truth" about the past. Puppets, after all, have no life of their own; they depend on someone to manipulate them and put words into their mouths. In Hou's film, the actors dramatizing scenes from Li's life can clearly be seen as "puppets," but who, exactly, is the "puppetmaster" of the film's title? The most obvious answer would be Li T'en-luk, since they are his memories that are being reenacted. Yet, as the contradictions between the dramatic vignettes and Li's narrated recollections remind us, the words spoken by the actors are not necessarily part of Li's memories but were imagined by the screenwriters. Li has even less control over the reconstruction of his past than it first seems, as even his monologues are subject to the whims of Hou Hsiao-hsien and his editors. So, who is the ultimate puppetmaster responsible for producing this performance of Taiwanese history? The very unanswerability of such a question points to the central lesson of Hou's cinematic explorations of Taiwanese history: that transparent "documentation" of historical "truth" is impossible. Knowledge of the past is always subjective and fragmentary, shaped by the needs and concerns of the individual writing in the present moment. As the film's English subtitle reminds us, "There is always someone pulling the strings. . . ."

· Updating the Cultural History of Taiwan

> *Once Upon A Time: that means, as in a fairy tale, not only something past, but also a brighter or happier someplace else.*   ERNST BLOCH

> *The work of memory situates experience in a sequence that keeps it alive, a story which can open out into free storytelling, greater life, invention.*   PETER HANDKE

Hou's original plan for the last installment of his Taiwan Trilogy was a film to be titled *Once Upon a Time There Was a Man Named P'u-tao T'ai-lang* (Congqian congqian you ge putao tailang), a Rip Van Winkle–like tale about a political prisoner, jailed in the aftermath of the February 28, 1947, incident, who suddenly finds himself released into Taiwan of the post-martial-law 1980s—a nation very much caught up in the postmodern network of transnational capitalism and global cultural exchange. The story of his adjustment to the island's modern, materialistic, and multicultural society was intended to bring Hou Hsiao-hsien's cultural history of Taiwan up to date. The title of the proposed project, which suggests a connection between history and fairy tales,[51] promised to continue the deconstruction of realistic historical representation begun in *City of Sadness* and *The Puppetmaster*. Although Hou altered his original plans, the film that he ended up making, *Good Men, Good Women* (1995), does indeed juxtapose past and present moments in the island's history in order to question the very nature of historical understanding.

Drawing on deconstructive techniques from both earlier installments of the trilogy, the film examines yet another critical era in Taiwan's repressed "popular memory": the "White Terror"—the anti-Communist witchhunts of the 1950s in which the Guomindang, fearing another February Incident, sought to eradicate dissident elements on the island by executing nearly five thousand people and imprisoning thousands more.[52] *Good Men, Good Women* focuses on a contemporary film actress who is preparing to star in a movie based on the lives of two Taiwanese patriots whose left-wing political activities during the 1930s and 1940s made them political targets of the

White Terror. Haunted by her personal past, the young actress also contemplates the historical experiences of the Taiwanese patriot she is preparing to portray. Like *City of Sadness*, the final installment of Hou's trilogy ponders the island's difficult historical relationship with the Mainland, suggesting that Taiwanese resentment of Chinese authority can, in part, be traced to the period of transition from Japanese to Chinese rule. The Taiwanese patriots depicted in the film-within-a-film, for example, make great personal sacrifices to travel to the Mainland to join the war of resistance against Japan—only to find themselves misunderstood, imprisoned, and mistreated by their Chinese "compatriots." Alternating between past and present, public history and personal narrative, memory and imagination, black-and-white and color, the film plays with multiple levels of "reality" in much the same way that *The Puppetmaster* sought to blur distinctions between "play," "dream," and "life." Like *City of Sadness*, *Good Men, Good Women* brings together fragments and snippets of personal stories—from the lives of the early patriots as well as the lives of the 1990s actress, her family, and her lovers—to evoke the sociopolitical atmospheres of two very different eras in Taiwanese history, contrasting the emotionally complicated but directionless existence of the contemporary actress with the idealism and single-minded dedication of the Taiwanese from the earlier era.

With the end of martial law and the emergence of an increasingly democratic society, Taiwan is poised at an extraordinary moment in its history. Sociopolitical liberalization and the end of Guomindang censorship has finally allowed Taiwanese to take an active role in asserting their own identity as a people. The restoration of the island's "forgotten" historical experiences has been a critical part of the ongoing process of self-definition. Hou Hsiao-hsien's "Taiwan Trilogy"—and similar films that have been made in recent years—have greatly contributed to the reexamination of Taiwanese history from which has emerged an entirely new picture of the Taiwanese "nation," one that challenges the Nationalist myth of Chinese consanguinity by revealing the complex multiplicity of heritages that make up contemporary Taiwanese identity. Through films like *City of Sadness*, *The Puppetmaster*, and *Good Men, Good Women*, long-silenced voices from the Taiwanese past have been resurrected to claim their place in Taiwanese nationhood—not only the ghosts of those who died as victims of the Guomindang's large-scale efforts to smother dissenting voices but also the memories of those from more intimate, familial pasts. By juxtaposing and blurring the lines between past and present, the films that make up Hou's Taiwan Trilogy challenge viewers to awaken their own historical imagination, to cast a retrospective glance at Taiwanese history as well as their personal pasts—to "seize hold of a memory" in order, perhaps, to participate in building a better and brighter future for Taiwan.

· Notes

1. Ernest Renan, "What Is a Nation?" (1882), trans. Martin Thom, in *Nation and Narration*, ed. Homi K. Bhabha (New York: Routledge, 1990), 19.

2. Cited in Marshall Johnson, "Making Time: Historic Preservation and the Space of Nationality," *positions: east asia cultures critique* 2, no. 2 (1994): 177–249. Johnson's article is a fascinating analysis of how the institutions of national historic preservation in Taiwan have been used to construct a "Chinese nation" under Nationalist rule and now, in the postdictatorship era, a "Taiwanese nation."

3. See Benedict Anderson, *Imagined Communities: Reflections on the Origins and Spread of Nationalism* (London: Verso, 1991), chap. 10. In this chapter, Anderson discusses the role of museums and two other institutions of power—the census and the map—that he feels profoundly shape the way in which a colonial state imagines its dominion. Significantly, the residents of Taiwan—even those born on the island and who have never been to the Mainland—are categorized on their identification cards by the Mainland provinces from which their ancestors originally came. See Johnson, "Making Time," 189, on *jiguan*. In geography classes, Taiwanese students are expected to recognize the location of not just Taiwan but of all China's provinces, mountains, and rivers. See, for instance, the textbook illustration reproduced by Johnson (p. 240) depicting China as a tree and Taiwan as a leaf.

4. Johnson, "Making Time," 206–210. Johnson emphasizes, in particular, the government's official edicts to destroy all traces of the island's Japanese past.

5. Walter Benjamin, "Theses on the Philosophy of History," in *Illuminations*, ed. Hannah Arendt, trans. Harry Zohn (New York: Schocken, 1969), 255. Further references to this essay will be cited parenthetically in the text.

6. Benjamin's philosophy of history is decidedly modernist, particularly in its emphasis on gaps, ruptures, and the dialectical relationship of past and present and in its tendency to disrupt linear narrative progression. Hayden White addressed similar issues of modernism and history in the Tenth Patricia Doyle Wise Lecture, titled "The Fact of Modernism: The Fading of the Historical Event," delivered on April 8, 1992, at the Univ. of California, Los Angeles.

7. See *"Beiqing chengshi ererba"* [*City of Sadness* and the February 28 Incident: A symposium], *Dangdai* [Contemporary] 43 (November 1, 1989): 111–130. Film scholar and critic Qi Longren (Ch'i Lung-jen) makes the comment on p. 116.

8. Even though some of the anxiety has dissipated following the success of the history-making presidential election of March 1996, tension and uncertainty were widely felt in the wake of the violent retaliation and subsequent repression that

shut down the prodemocracy movement in Beijing in June of 1989. The shadow of Tiananmen looms large over the contemporary Taiwanese psyche and lurks behind Hou's film as well. In an interview with Taiwanese film scholar Jiao Xiongping, Hou said that he was in the midst of editing *City* when the massacre in Tiananmen occurred. Hou immediately sensed the connection between Tiananmen and the massacres alluded to in his film, wondering "Why do such tragedies keep befalling the Chinese people?" and hoped that his film would evoke the same pain and anger in its audiences. See Jiao Xiongping (Chiao Hsiung-p'ing), "Jingtou saoguo lishi de anxiang" [The camera-swept back alleys of history: An interview with Hou Hsiao-hsien], *Zhongguo shibao* [China times], September 4–5, 1989. Audiences did indeed seize upon the parallels between events in the film and present-day events in Beijing. Lin Huaiming, for example, explicitly compares provincial governor Chen Yi's radio announcement of martial law in 1947 to Li Peng's radio broadcasts following the Tiananmen incident. See Lin Huaiming (Lin Huai-ming), "Wenren de guanzhao, shenchen de tanxi: Niuyue kan Beiqing chengshi" [Warm affections, deep sighs: On watching *City of Sadness* in New York], *Zhongguo shibao* [China times], October 18, 1989. European film festival audiences made the comparison so often that the Taiwanese government news agency became unsettled enough to pressure the film's distributors to carefully reword their overseas press materials. See "'Bei' haiwai xuancai yinqi zhenghan" [Overseas press materials for *City of Sadness* stir controversy], *Minsheng bao* [Min sheng news], August 30, 1989. Some have even argued that the film owes part of its success—winning the Golden Lion at Venice, for instance—to the coincidence of its release with the Tiananmen massacre. See Wu Qiyan (Wu Ch'i-yen)), "*Beiqing chengshi* xianxiangji" [Notes on the release of *City of Sadness*], in *Xin dianying zhi si* [The death of New Cinema], ed. Mi Zou (Mi Tsou) and Liang Xinhua (Liang Hsin-hua) (Taipei: Tangshan Publications, 1991), 84.

9. Says Hou: "The years between 1946 and 1949 constitute a special period in history, because they have important implications for political, cultural, and social change in Taiwan. Amidst change, people have tremendous survival instincts and determination to face the challenges which arise. . . ." See Jiao, "Jingtou saoguo lishi de anxiang." My translation.

10. Jiao, "Jingtou saoguo lishi de anxiang."

11. Jean-François Lyotard, *Instructions paiennes* (Paris: Galilee, 1977), 39, cited by Anton Kaes in "History, Fiction, Memory: Fassbinder's *The Marriage of Maria Braun* (1979)," in *German Film and Literature,* ed. Eric Rentschler (New York: Methuen, 1986), 281. The essay is reprinted as a chapter in Anton Kaes, *From Hitler to Heimat: The Return of History as Film* (Cambridge, Mass.: Harvard University Press, 1989).

12. Lim is the Taiwanese pronunciation of the family name.

13. These are rough transliterations of the Taiwanese—not Mandarin—pronunciations used in the film.

14. It is tempting to read a great deal into this character, seeing the deaf-mute as a metaphor for Taiwan's voiceless, marginalized existence. See, for example, Liao Binghui (Liao Ping-hui), "Ji long you ya de sheyingshi" [A deaf, dumb photographer], in *Xin dianying zhi si* [The death of New Cinema], ed. Mi Zou (Mi Tsou) and Liang Xinhua (Liang Hsin-hua) (Taipei: Tangshan Publications, 1991), 129–134. Hou, however, has coyly explained that the creation of this character was partially inspired by an encounter with a deaf-mute artist, Chen Tingshi (Ch'en T'ing-shih), and partially a pragmatic solution to the inability of the actor, who is from Hong Kong, to speak Taiwanese.

15. Hiroe and Hiromi are the Japanese pronunciations of Kuanrong (K'uan-jung) and Kuanmei (K'uan-mei) respectively. During the Japanese colonial occupation, most Taiwanese names were given a Japanese pronunciation. This would especially be true for people like Hiroe, who teaches in a Japanese-run school, and Hiromi, trained by Japanese doctors.

16. Marshall Johnson, "Making Time," 233–235, points to Jiufen (Chiu-fen), the real-life mining town where *City of Sadness* was filmed, as an exemplary illustration of the complex ideological struggles tied up in current projects of preservation in Taiwan. What Johnson finds most significant in the Jiufen campaign is that, unlike other recent campaigns to preserve local sites and buildings around the island, the project neither "substantiates the Taiwanese Nation and denaturalizes the Chinese Nation, or vice versa." Rather, the plan is to demonstrate how historically specific domination, autonomy, and commodification are integral to the struggle over historic preservation.

17. It is a common strategy of postcolonial writing to link the births, deaths, and other significant life events of characters directly to major events in national history. See, for example, Aruna Srivastava's essay on Salman Rushdie, " 'The Empire Writes Back': Language and History in *Shame* and *Midnight's Children*," in *Past the Last Post: Theorizing Post-Colonialism and Post-Modernism,* ed. Ian Adam and Helen Tiffin (Calgary: University of Calgary Press, 1990), 65–78.

18. As Anton Kaes notes in his essay on *Maria Braun,* Fassbinder similarly uses radio broadcasts to weave public, political history into the personal narratives of Maria and her friends.

19. For example, Max Horkheimer and Theodor Adorno, "The Culture Industry: Enlightenment as Mass Deception," *Dialectic of Enlightenment,* trans. John Cumming (New York: Continuum, 1988), 120–167.

20. *American Historical Review* 93, no. 5 (1988) features a forum of essays dealing precisely with the problems and possibilities of portraying history on film. Included are essays by Robert A. Rosenstone ("History in Images/History in Words"), David Herlihy ("Am I a Camera? Other Reflections on Film and History"), Hayden White ("Historiography and Historiophoty"), John E. O'Connor ("History in Images/Images in History"), and Robert Brent Toplin ("The Filmmaker as Historian"). On the

advantages and disadvantages of cinema's "reality-effect," see in particular the articles by Rosenstone (p. 1177) and Herlihy (p. 1187).

21. One Taiwanese critic has compared the treatment of the past in *City of Sadness* to *Rashomon*, Kurosawa's famous meditation on the relativity of truth. See Wen Gezhi (Wen Ko-chih), "'Bei'' de *Luoshengmen* benzhi" [The *Rashomon*-quality of *City of Sadness*], *Tzu-li Morning Post*, October 10, 1989.

22. Says coscriptwriter Zhu Tianwen (Chu T'ien-wen): "The representation of a historical era can never be more than what an author chooses to see in that era. It is always circumscribed by the author's own attitudes and motivations. A completely objective and comprehensive account of an era—whether in historical writing or fictional writing—simply does not exist." Zhu Tianwen, "*Beiqing chengshi shisanwen*" [Thirteen questions on *City of Sadness*]), *Tzu-li Morning Post*, July 11–13, 1989. Translation mine. The critical reaction to *City of Sadness* was not unlike the debate surrounding Oliver Stone's *JFK* (1991). Interestingly, Stone also invokes *Rashomon* in defense of his film, arguing that his film does not pretend to offer a single, comprehensive conspiracy theory but instead barrages the viewer with snippets of verbal and visual information—fragments of multiple theories that the viewer must then sort out. Oliver Stone, "The Flicker of an Eye Means Nothing in Print," *Los Angeles Times*, March 26, 1992, B7.

23. See, for example, Mikhail M. Bakhtin, *The Dialogic Imagination*, ed. Michael Holquist, trans. Caryl Emerson and Michael Holquist (Austin: University of Texas Press, 1981).

24. See George Kerr, *Formosa Betrayed* (Boston: Houghton Mifflin, 1965), 72. Kerr, who was U.S. vice-consul in Taipei during those years of transition, is clearly sympathetic to the Taiwanese people. Though his book may be somewhat colored by his sympathies and by American interests, his account of the events of the 1940s, based largely on personal experiences, correspondence, and eyewitness accounts, appears reliable.

25. See, for example, Albert Memmi, *The Colonizer and the Colonized*, trans. Howard Greenfield (Boston: Beacon Press, 1967), 79–85.

26. In the film, Taiwanese often refer to mainlanders using the derisive term *A shande (Ah-sua-eh/Ah-shan-te)*. Roughly translated as "the one from the mountains," it distinguishes those from the provinces on the Mainland from native islanders (who presumably are more closely associated with the sea).

27. The most notable of these is the scene in which eldest son Bun-heung pleads with the Shanghai bosses to use their influence to get Bun-leung released from a Guomindang prison.

28. The Lim family has been described as a microcosm of Taiwanese society, with many different socioeconomic groups represented: Patriarch Ah-luk-sai belongs to the older generation who lived through the entire Japanese occupation and can therefore measure the new regime against the old; eldest son Bun-heung repre-

sents the criminal low-life element of society; second son Bun-hsim stands in for the educated professional class; third son Bun-leung is an ex-military man; and the youngest son, Bun-ch'ing, represents the artist/intellectual. There are, of course, the women and children, but, with the exception of Hiromi, who serves as a sort of guiding consciousness throughout the film, most of them remain in the background.

29. A brief account of the major events of February and March 1947 appears in Gao Miaohui and Chen Jiuhui, ed., "Beiqing zen shi" [How is the sadness explained?], *Ying xiang (Ying hsiang)* [Imagekeeper monthly] I, no. 1 (November 20, 1989): 40. There are two collections of essays and documents dealing specifically with the "Two-two-eight Incident" and its aftermath. The volume edited by Wai Min, *Taiwan de ererba shijian* [The February 28 Incident in Taiwan] (Hong Kong: The Seventies Magazine Publications, 1975), reflects leftist views—not only the PRC response but also the views of overseas Chinese who support Taiwanese independence. A second three-volume collection is edited by Li Ao, *Ererba shijian yanjiu* [Research on the February Incident] (Taipei: Li Ao Publications, 1989). The first volume consists mostly of documents and articles from 1947; the second volume brings together testimonials, recollections, and essays by individuals caught up in the turmoil, including perspectives from mainlanders and aboriginal peoples; the third volume examines the life and career of Chen Yi. For the most comprehensive account in English of the February Incident and the violence that erupted in the weeks that followed, see Kerr, *Formosa Betrayed,* 254 310. Kerr and many of his friends—both Taiwanese and American—were eyewitnesses to much of the violence. A more recent book in English is Lai Tse-han, Ramon H. Myers, and Wei Wou, *A Tragic Beginning: The Taiwan Uprising of February 28, 1947* (Stanford, Calif.: Stanford University Press, 1991).

30. Kerr, who was nearby when shooting erupted, described what he saw upon rushing to the scene:

> As our jeep came into the intersection dominated by the Generalissimo's [Chiang Kai-shek's] gilded statue, we found ourselves running between a line of heavily armed Nationalist soldiers, before the Governor's gate, and a silent crowd of Formosans, facing them across the plaza.
>
> On the macadam roadway between lay the bodies of unarmed civilians who had been shot down as the demonstrators approached the entrance to Government grounds.
>
> The anticipated crisis had come at last. (p. 256)

31. In his account of the crisis, George Kerr repeatedly emphasizes that throughout, the majority of the Taiwanese protesters wanted reform, not revolution. It was the Guomindang government, seeking justification for its brutality in crushing the uprising, that painted the activists as traitorous rebels.

32. Huang Meiying (Huang Mei-ying), "Zaizhi de ererba" [The reproduction of 'February 28']," in *Xin dianying zhi si* [The death of New Cinema], ed. Mi Zou (Mi Tsou) and Liang Xinhua (Liang Hsin-hua) (Taipei: Tangshan Publications, 1991), 153–157.

33. For a full translation of Chiang Kai-shek's official speech defending Chen Yi's management of the affair (made in Nanking on March 10 and distributed in leaflet form in Taiwan's major cities on March 12), see Kerr, *Formosa Betrayed*, 307–309.

34. According to Bakhtin, in order for monologic texts to become dialogic, they must first be "embodied": "[T]hey must enter into another sphere of existence: they must become *discourse*, that is, an utterance, and receive an *author*, that is, a creator of the given utterance whose position it expresses." See M. M. Bakhtin, *Problems of Dostoevsky's Poetics*, ed. and trans. Caryl Emerson (Minneapolis: University of Minnesota Press, 1984), 184. Bakhtin defines *discourse* as "language in its concrete living totality" (p. 181).

35. The scene alludes to the practice of the Taiwanese, during the period following the February Incident, of stopping people in the street and asking, "Are you sweet potato or pig?" Anyone suspected of being a "pig"—that is, mainlander—was immediately beaten. See Kerr, *Formosa Betrayed*, 257, 279. Critics of the film who felt Hou did not go far enough in "restoring Taiwanese dignity" and comdemning the Nationalist authorities often cite this scene—with its unflattering portrayal of Taiwanese—as an example. See Huang, "Zaizhi de ererba," 156. To expect from Hou's film simply a "Taiwanese version of historical Truth," however, is to completely miss the point of the far more radical historiographical project Hou has undertaken.

36. The disintegration of the patriarchal family structure seems to be a recurring theme in Hou's films. In all of his films, the fathers are either absent (*Daughter of the Nile*), ill (*Dust in the Wind, A Time to Live and a Time to Die*), or otherwise debilitated (*The Boys from Fengg ui*). The strongest figures in his films are often women.

37. See David Holley, "Army Killed Thousands in '47 Massacre, Taiwan Admits," *Los Angeles Times*, February 24, 1992.

38. Cai Lingling (Ts'ai, Ling-ling), "Huanrao zhe 'Bei' de lunshuwu" [The critical fog surrounding *City of Sadness*], *Tzu-li Evening News*, October 10, 1989.

39. Xie Renchang (Hsieh Jen-ch'ang), "Wo shengming guocheng de yige baogao" [A report on my life], *Dianying xinshang* [Film appreciation] 64 (July/August 1993): 55.

40. See Xie, "Wo shengming guocheng de yige baogao," 58, and Jiao, "Jingtou saoguo lishi de anxiang." The Fifth-Generation Chinese director Zhang Yimou has made a similar observation about his latest film, *To Live* (Huozhe, 1994), which follows an ordinary Chinese family through nearly forty years of political turmoil on the Mainland—from the civil war between Chiang Kai-shek's Nationalists and Mao

Zedong's Communists, through the establishment of the People's Republic and the failed experiments of the Great Leap Forward, to the insanity of the Cultural Revolution. History, says Zhang, is full of stories about heroes and great deeds; what are missing are the stories about ordinary Chinese who, whatever the political drama of the moment, quietly go about the business of everyday living. His film is not so much about China's turbulent modern political history, which only provides a backdrop, as it is about the stubborn perseverance of Xu Fugui and Jiazhen, two "little people" who are politically uncommitted and unreflective. Their only concern is to face the challenges that each day brings, simply "to live."

41. For a useful overview of the Japanese occupation period, see George Kerr, *Formosa: Licensed Revolution and the Home Rule Movement (1895–1945)* (Boston: Houghton Mifflin, 1965). Kerr's focus is on the independence movement under the occupation.

42. See Kerr, *Formosa*, 196. Hou also mentions the suppression of puppetry in an interview with Jiao Xiongping in *Zhongguo shibao* [China times], June 13, 1993.

43. Contrast Hou's matter-of-fact treatment of this episode in Li's life with a parallel sequence in Chen Kaige's *Farewell My Concubine* (Bawang bieji, 1993) in which Cheng Dieyi's decision to sing for the Japanese is derided as an act of treason.

44. Hou has described his oblique and elliptical style technique as essentially Taoist in nature. See Xie, "Wo shengming guocheng de yige baogao," 52.

45. Recall, also, the very first sequence of the film, which underscores the arbitrariness of names.

46. See, for example, Vincent Canby's review of the film in the *New York Times*, October 11, 1993, B5.

47. The processes of memory are always unpredictable and unreliable. Hou notes, for example, that during filming, Li T'en-luk's stories about his past changed every time he told them. See Xie, "Wo shengming guocheng de yige baogao," 46.

48. Kaes, *From Hitler to Heimat*, 19–21.

49. See Jiao Xiongping's interview with Hou, *Zhongguo shibao* [China times], June 9, 1993.

50. Hou's emphases on the theatrical and the illusionary harken back, in a sense, to the often forgotten nonmimetic origins of the film medium in the fantasy and trick films of George Méliès. It is the other cinematic tradition—the realistic narrative tradition initiated by the Lumière films—that has dominated mainstream filmmaking.

51. This is not unlike Hou's deliberate blurring of "play," "dream," and "life." For thoughts on the relationship of history and fairy tales, see Kaes, *From Hitler to Heimat*, 123–127.

52. See Li Taipeng (Li T'ai-p'eng) and Ge Guangyu (Ke Kuang-yu), ed., "Buduan xianying de lishi yu jiyi" [The continual reappearance of history and memory]," *Dianying xinshang* [Film appreciation] 77 (September/October 1996): 64–78, two round-

table discussions of *Good Men, Good Women* and *Why We Don't Sing Songs.* The latter film is a documentary about the White Terror produced at the same time as Hou's film. The two films—one a supposedly "factual" account, the other supposedly "fictional"—were intended to be released simultaneously. The juxtaposition of the two raises precisely the kinds of complicated questions about historical understanding that Hou has explored in his trilogy.

Chapter 6
·
The Diaspora in Postmodern Taiwan and Hong Kong Film
Framing Stan Lai's *The Peach Blossom Land*
with Allen Fong's *Ah Ying*
·
Jon Kowallis

I define *postmodern* as incredulity toward metanarratives.
Jean-François Lyotard, *Postmodern Condition*

Born in the United States but educated in Taiwan after the age of twelve, Taiwan "mainlander" Chinese director Stan Lai (Lai Shengchuan) might be better described as an American Asian than an Asian American. Already noticed by *Newsweek, Time,* the *Los Angeles Times, Far Eastern Economic Review,* and the *Asian Wall Street Journal,* he is certainly one of the most prominent theatrical innovators in East Asia today.[1] Recently, he turned from stage to cinema to produce his first full-length feature film, *The Peach Blossom Land* (Anlian Taohuayuan; lit., "Secret Love: The Peach Blossom Spring").[2] The film won first prize in the young filmmaker's division of the Berlin Film Festival and the Silver Medal at the Tokyo Film Festival (where a $100,000 prize enabled him to finance a second film). *The Peach Blossom Land* later took first place in the Asian Film Festival in Singapore. This was a wholly unexpected response to a film most American critics would probably write off as "an art house hit." Who is Stan Lai and why all this fuss over what might seem, at first glance, an experimental film by a theater director?

After graduating from Furen (Fu-jen) University in Taiwan, Lai earned his Ph.D. at the University of California, Berkeley, in the Department of Dramatic Art, with a dissertation titled "Oriental Crosscurrents in Modern Western Drama" in 1983, a time when the term "Oriental" was still au courant at Berkeley. In 1982 he studied new techniques of actor-training under Shireen Strooker of the Amsterdam Werkteater, who was then visiting at Berkeley. Enthused about the techniques[3] he had learned and armed with the vital qualification of the Ph.D., he returned to Taiwan to serve as artistic director and professor at the newly founded National Institute of the Arts, where he "did everything anew the right way" (according to Dunbar

Ogden, his old adviser at Berkeley) and currently teaches his own graduate students. Lai writes:

> What drew me to Shireen's work was precisely the process of "making" a play that was radically opposed to conventional methods of approaching theatrical production. In a nutshell, I see conventional practice in America, in general, to be an attempt to assemble the divided pieces of production—acting, lighting, scene design, sound, etc.—into a final, cohesive whole. This process involves lots of unknown factors and chance—can an actor attain the certain quality of a certain role? Is the "chemistry" right? Will the scenic designer's ideas conflict with the director's? How will the actors adjust to makeup and costumes? The Amsterdam Werkteater's techniques employed by Shireen Strooker invert this process: Instead of pieces toward a whole, she takes the essence—some guiding thought or emotion—first, and from this genuinely heartfelt essence, the form and pieces of production begin to take shape. Though the end product is never predictable, this process eliminates much of the chance factors of conventional means. From the standpoint of the actors, they are not asked to "inhabit" a role, but rather to use *themselves* to *create* a role. From the standpoint of the designers and technicians, the ideas come by necessity, from the process itself.[4]

Lai also founded his own professional troupe in Taiwan, which he calls, with an American matter-of-factness, Performance Workshop (Biaoyan gongzuofang) and directed numerous plays before making the switch to film. He still intends to "move back and forth between theater and film," but judging from the unlikely critical success of *The Peach Blossom Land* and my hopes for his second feature, *The Red Lotus Society* (1994), chances are that his future will be more and more in cinematic arts, despite temporary protestations to the contrary. I say "unlikely" only because *The Peach Blossom Land* is so avant-garde and innovative, particularly when compared with the work of Mainland filmmakers such as Zhang Yimou and even Chen Kaige. In *The Peach Blossom Land*, historical and temporal frames are constantly switched on the audience to an almost irritating degree of frequency. Some of the sets are so contrived and theatrical that the audience is continually slapped with the "reality" that life is stage and stage is life, while all the time a pseudo real-life drama unfolds, much of it from a hospital bed in Taipei. Regarding this technique, Roswitha Mueller once observed:

> The inorganic work of art, the object constructed out of fragments, has its own history. In an article "On Brecht and Eisenstein," Rainer

Friedrich pointed out that Brecht often used the term "montage" to contrast modern art with traditional art. The traditional Aristotelian concept of art, argued Friedrich, centers on the concept of mimesis as *natura naturans,* the productive process of nature. The rise of modern subjectivity in the Renaissance, Friedrich continued, did not do away with the concept of mimesis, but instead merely altered it. The artist was now considered *ut alter deus,* another god. The implication was that the artist no longer imitated nature but was the creator of another nature, the realm of art. The latter was subsequently considered a higher form of reality. Insofar as the aesthetic realm still presented itself as natural and the organic work of art was the norm, the moment of construction first entered on the basis of negating its own artificiality, its constructedness: "For the practical principle of the organic work of art is *ars est celare artem,* art as the concealment of art."

The hallmark of the modern work of art, on the other hand, is divesting itself of the pretense of being nature and freely displaying itself as artifact. In that sense Friedrich contended that montage is the principle of the modern work of art. The emphasis montage places on the separateness of elements and on heterogeneity prevents the formation of an organic unity. In film, as Sergei Eisenstein has pointed out, it is the mechanical process itself that requires the cutting and juxtaposition of shots.[5]

In Brechtian fashion, Lai's film begins in a theater (sans overbearing "stage manager"). Sleek female figures grope their way through the dark walkways behind the stage. We are shown the empty seats of an auditorium, as the director and actors talk to one another. Then we are presented with a mock-up set of a play about two new lovers in Shanghai at the end of the Second World War, titled *Anlian,* or *Secret Love.* The young woman, Yun Zhifan (actress Lin Ching-hsia) has family in Guilin and needs to return home just once more to see them, while the man, Jiang Binliu (played by Chin Shih-chieh) is from Dongbei (Manchuria) and longs to see his own family but cannot easily go there.[6] The world for Chinese people has been radically uprooted, and even greater changes (the Communist victory in 1949 and the Taiwan diaspora) are clearly in store. These events separate the lovers, who both go to Taiwan, but each mistakenly believes that the other has remained on the Mainland.

Another set of actors then intrudes on the stage, insisting that the facility has been rented to them for the evening for a dress rehearsal of a play to take place the next day (a Brecht-inspired if not Brechtian device). Much argument ensues, and we are unclear which side will be victorious (perhaps

Fig. 12. Taiwan actors just don't seem to "get it right" in portraying a scene from late 1940s Shanghai. From Stan Lai's film *The Peach Blossom Land* (Anlian Taohua-yuan), 1992.

an analogy to the Chinese civil war, which goes on and on with no final resolution?). The lines of dialogue in the Shanghai scene are delivered in high northern-style stage Mandarin, but the intrusion of the actors from the second troupe abruptly brings in the southern Mandarin "Taiwan *'si bu si'* accent," another dose of reality for both the audience and the members of the first group of actors.

We are then introduced to the recurring reenactment (by the second troupe) of Tao Yuanming's (A.D. 365–427) fifth-century story, *Tale of the Peach Blossom Spring* (Taohuayuan ji), in which the classical Chinese language intrudes amid a predominantly farcical vernacular *(baihua)* narrative. Premodern stage techniques from traditional opera are used (such as waving blue paper to simulate a river's waves) in the protagonist's upstream journey by boat to a magical Never-never Land called the "Peach Blossom Spring," where he discovers other-worldly refugees "who have known nothing of the outside world since before the Han dynasty."[77] Questions like:

Fig. 13. A parody of Chinese antiquity and the "alternative reality" of Taiwan's phantasmagoric existence as doppelgänger for Mainland China. From Stan Lai's film *The Peach Blossom Land* (Anlian Taohuayuan), 1992.

"Do you know where Wuling[8] is?" are met only with bemused incredulity. To make matters worse, the protagonist, an impotent fisherman called Old Tao (Lee Li-chun) feels that his disloyal young wife, Spring Flower (Ismene Ting), and her lover, Master Yuan (Ku Pao-ming), may have been reincarnated there to torment him (in the form of a white-gowned man and woman who look surprisingly like their counterparts back in the "real" world), so the traditional ideal of the bucolic and peaceful Peach Blossom Spring, far away from the troubles and strife of the world, has been skewed into a kind of self-made (or at least uncontrollable) hell, much like what Taiwan became for a number of the refugees from the Mainland. Then there is the hopelessness of finding any direction back: to the question "Where's Wuling?" the incredulous woman in Peach Blossom Land responds: "What's 'Wuling'? Why would you want to get to Wuling?" The protagonist despairs of even describing Wuling to someone who has never been there.

Even though they both speak Chinese, all of the referents are different; just as Taipei has a Jingmei, but Taiwan has no Shanghai, Taiwan unintentionally became, for many people, something of a phantasmagoric doppelgänger for or an ersatz version of China.[9]

Even the name of Taohuayuan is continually questioned throughout the film, when different accents are placed on one of the Chinese characters that make up the name: "Tao HUA Yuan, TAO Hua Yuan, Tao Hua YUAN." One thinks, perhaps of Tai-WAN Sheng, TAI-wan sheng, Tai-wan SHENG ("Taiwan Province," the official Mainland designation for the island, skewed) and the perceived spiritual, if not intellectual, need for the "rectification of names"—is it really what it purports to be? And what say, if any, do its people have over this? Many of Lai's word plays are a form of postmodern anarchistic linguistic play. Old Tao decides eventually to return "home" to ask his wife to join him in the Peach Blossom Land. Although the protagonist has enjoyed a prolonged period of uneasy physical safety there (one cannot call it a "life" in any real sense of the word), how much of a refuge is a refuge if you can never go back? Of course, this is the dilemma of modern man as well, not just the mainlanders on Taiwan. Lai writes:

> [This] interruption creates chaos on the stage. The person in charge of the theatre cannot be found and each troupe tries to assume authority of the stage by performing fragments of the plays. As it goes, scenes of the tragic and the comic start to interact with each other, and opposite themes and styles begin to mesh and blend.[10]

Shortly thereafter, a young woman in her twenties wanders onto the set, ostensibly from off the street, continually calling the name of her boyfriend in Taiwan-accented Mandarin, which is not recognized by the actors of either troupe, although each assumes him to belong to the other. The viewer gradually begins to suspect that she and her elusive friend may represent Taiwan's Generation X, members of which are attempting to lead their own lives outside of the reality created by their parents, but nevertheless must do so with the risk of either being engulfed by that reality or constantly marginalized by it.

Meanwhile, as *Secret Love* continues, now in the Taipei of the early 1990s, the aging Jiang Binliu, who was deeply in love with the woman in Shanghai and, despairing of ever finding her, has married a Taiwanese woman in 1963, now languishes in a hospital. An impetuous Taiwanese nurse discovers that he has run a front-page ad in *Zhongguo shibao* (*The China Times,* a popular centrist newspaper) asking for information on the whereabouts of the woman from Shanghai. Concealing it from his Taiwanese wife with some effort, the nurse presses him for personal details of the romantic attachment and prods him about the failure of the Shanghai woman, Yun Zhifan, whom both of them now know to be somewhere in Taiwan, to appear. More time-frame switches back to the Peach Blossom Land, where characters degenerate into slapstick reminiscent of the Three Stooges (one wonders whether Stan Lai saw them as a child on television in Washington, D.C., where he spent his formative years). With frustration mounting upon frustration in the land of refuge—one also begins to wonder if the metaphor of the Peach Blossom Land might not extend to America, as well, the "new mainland"[11] to which many mainlanders wandered from Taiwan in the later 1950s and 1960s and continue to end up now.

After we have seen the protagonist's Taiwanese wife lifting him into bed out of a wheelchair and caring for him tirelessly without complaint, after we have heard her describe to the nurse how he would never drink the Taiwan tea she prepared for him and how he would lapse for years into long, unexplained silences and pensive moods, finally the woman from Shanghai appears at the hospital room door, asking for "Mr. Jiang" (a homonym: Mr. "Rigor-mortis"? Mr. Jiang as in Jiang Jieshi—Chiang Kai-shek from the Mainland? We don't know what the surname means, really, but the informed audience member probably has suspicions at this point, for the seasoned reader of Chinese literature often looks for double entendre).

At that point the nurse suggests that she accompany the wife downstairs to "pay the bill" (although the hospital stay is not over). The protagonist and the woman from Shanghai then compare notes on the last forty-plus years. She tells him she thought he remained in Shanghai and continually wrote him letters, which she must have had smuggled to the Mainland, since there was no legal mail service from either side of the Taiwan straits. Never receiving a response, her brother persuaded her to marry, "as one will grow old" without having done so. He gives her his own account, which is strikingly similar, questioning her on why it has taken so long (five or more days) for her to respond to his running ad, about which the nurse has goaded him repeatedly. She starts to fib: "I just saw it today—" but breaks off in mid-sentence, telling him she has always loved him, but that her current husband "is a good man," whereupon she takes her leave. Jiang is left with his Taiwanese wife to face up to the question of his own mortality and his place in the world, with greater clarity, we hope.

Despite his skillful employment of the Brechtian techniques of "distancing" (*Verfremdungseffekt*), montage, and the trappings of the postmodern stage, what Stan Lai has produced still comes thematically, at least, under the rubric of the "literature of exile" produced by Bai Xianyong and other skilled Mainland exiles in the 1950s and 1960s. This is not to say that his film is dated or already passé but rather a reflection of the basic reality that although the Chinese civil war may be over as an armed conflict, its consequences are far from resolved. The diaspora that has been created has spilled over not only to Taiwan but also to America and elsewhere.[12] Just as the Lai brothers in their youth tried to bring different Americans together, Stan has continued to bring the "two Chinas" closer. There is a somewhat Quixotic element in his endeavor, but that does not make it any less admirable.

Ah Ying (Banbian ren), a Mandarin film from Hong Kong[13] by Allen Fong (Fang Yuping; Cantonese: Fong Yuk-ping) released in 1984 and based loosely on the life of the all too short-lived Taiwan director Ge Wu (Koh Wu), whom Allen Fong knew, deals with the intellectual diaspora in a way that exhibits more consciousness of class and educational differences between Chinese from both Taiwan and Hong Kong and introduces ruminations on the "applicability" of graduate study in America, as well, which some viewers may wish Stan Lai had done. For example, what does it mean, *Ah Ying* proposes, to live out one's youth abroad in order to acquire knowledge that will supposedly benefit one's own society and then find that knowledge inapplicable or only partially applicable on one's return years later. Zhang Songbai, the character based on Ge Wu, is hard-pressed to use his knowledge of acting and theatrical sophistication to help Ah Ying, the young lower-class Hong Kong girl student who falls in platonic love with him. His own mortality (he was infected by a needle used for mass inoculations in the Taiwan army) prevents him from marrying her and benefiting her in that way as well.[14] Just as his parents were deprived of a country, the diaspora has deprived this middle-aged intellectual of a family and a livelihood, despite his scholarly achievements, which are a result of his patience, and his own hard work. As the two protagonists of *Ah Ying* watch his Volkswagen bug (the ideals of the international youth movement of the 1960s?) being crushed into a small metal block in a Hong Kong junkyard, we get a sense of foreboding concerning Ge Wu's own fate. These issues of the intellectual diaspora are also broached in modern Chinese literature in a number of the short stories by Lu Xun and other Chinese writers as well. How can the "returned" intellectual make use of what he has learned in a country where nothing he has learned from abroad applies?[15]

In a way, Lu Xun and Allen Fong extend the inquiry where Stan Lai cuts it off. On a personal level, the moral dilemma of the diaspora is how we deal with others while coming to terms with our own displacement (e.g., in *Schindler's List*, Schindler is not really a "pure" German but comes from Moravia in the former Czechoslovakia[16] and finds himself in Poland at the outbreak of the war. But the dilemma is how he places himself vis-à-vis other people, not the map). As T. S. Eliot's confused speaker's voice reminds us: "Bin gar keine Russin, stamm' aus Litauen, echt deutsch."[17] Rather than

Fig. 14. Would-be actress Ah Ying's life in "real world" Hong Kong, where she works as a fishmonger. From Allen Fong's film *Ah Ying,* 1984. Photo courtesy of Steve Horowitz and Fenghuang Motion Picture Company (Hong Kong).

conclude "there is no going back," which Stan Lai's own life disproves, his film concludes, we need to tell ourselves "our *qi* is here" and live as *Menschen* with that.[18] The question of "going back" is largely irrelevant, which is what I think *Peach Blossom Land* demonstrates.

Ah Ying is also similar to *The Peach Blossom Land* in that it contains a play within the movie. The Cantonese-speaking actors put on a Mandarin-language play adapted from the short story "Jiangjun zu" (A race/people of generals) by Taiwan dissident writer Chen Yingzhen. "Jiangjun zu" is something of a Lu Xun-inspired story about members of a private marching band, which played at funerals, people from the lowest strata of Taiwan society.[19] The fact that director Allen Fong (born in Hong Kong in 1947) included it within the movie says as much about his own goals in filmmaking at the time as it does about his own analysis of the role of the film itself. It is a tragedy based on the lives of unfortunates in a sick society. Fong and

The Diaspora in Taiwan and Hong Kong Film   *177*

Chen Yingzhen, like Lu Xun, hoped to "draw attention to this sickness and suffering, so that a cure might be sought."[20] In a way, that is also what Stan Lai does, but Lai operates on a less graphic and more existential level. That is where we see more Brecht and less Lu Xun, at least in terms of technique, if not inspiration. As Peter Brooker defines it:

> *Verfremdung* has been described as 'the key concept' of Brecht's theory of theatre. . . . Brecht's term itself has been variously translated as 'alien-ation', 'estrangement', 'eloignement', 'distanciation', and 'defamiliarisa-tion'. As he described it, it employed elements of stage design, music and lighting as well as a gestic acting style in a conscious—and in some ways self-conscious—attempt to historicise characters and events. In this way the theatre-goer's practically instinctual tendency to empathise with supposedly 'eternally human' characters and 'universal' situations would be frustrated, and the 'single chain' of a 'timeless' narrative nec-essary to a conventional illusion of reality would be interrupted. Instead of a unified and pacifying, or even simply 'entertaining' work of art, with all its aesthetic and ideological concomitants, Brecht wished for an epic theatre in which acting, music and design, conceived as a 'bundle of separate elements', would operate autonomously, but at the same time in a relation of commentary and contradiction with each other. The immediate effect of this separation (principally of actor and audience from theatrical character and incident) would be one of sur-prise, dismay and perhaps discomfort, as the audience's unexamined assumptions about art and society took a jolt. Brecht's audience would then be 'verfremdet', and would react, so Brecht says, in the following way: 'I should never have thought so—That is not the way to do it.—This is most surprising, hardly credible.—This will have to stop. This human being's suffering moves me, because there would have been a way out for him. This is great art: nothing here seems inevitable—I am laughing about those who weep on stage, weeping about those who laugh.'[21]

This technique, in turn, becomes Stan Lai's tower of strength (though he employs this modernist technique in an ironic patchwork and, I would argue, a definitively postmodern way)—the device that successfully forces his audience to contemplate the drama, on one level or another, in a detached manner.

Of all its reviewers, David Thomson, in the announcement of the 1984 San Francisco International Film Festival, provides the most insightful assess-ment of *Ah Ying* when he writes: "*Ah Ying* is a film of much promise and many virtues—it is gentle, funny, observant, compassionate; it has a fine sense of the great varieties of Chineseness in the world today, and of the precarious poise of Hong Kong; but it is most acute in its feeling for actuality turning inevitably into a composed story, of the raw seeming chosen." Other reviewers, however, were all too quick to misunderstand the film as being "too realistic" and therefore less than satisfactory. In this, they failed to grasp the irony of its postmodern pastiche critique, which goes beyond simple realism. Some prominent critics, missing the various levels of intertextuality embedded in the film, produced accounts that were simply laughable to anyone who had even a rudimentary appreciation of the movie or had read Chen Yingzhen (the story had already been translated into English),[22] such as Janet Maslin's review in the *New York Times*, which concludes:

> Like his own filmmaker-character, Mr. Fong seems convinced that merely transposing real experience to the screen is enough to hold an audience's interest. The scenes involving Ah Ying's family seem less artificial than the film school episodes, and have somewhat more drama to them. A family of about eight lives in a two-room flat, and in this setting Ah Ying is addressed simply as "Third Sister." It's not surprising, then, that she seeks the wider and more personalized recognition that an actress commands. By the end of the film, Ah Ying is triumphantly co-starring in a play with her revered teacher, he playing an old man and she a prostitute who, for some reason, seems to be dressed as a drum majorette.[23]

Of course, Ah Ying is "dressed as a 'drum majorette' " because she was portraying, on stage, a character in Chen Yingzhen's short story "Jiangjun zu" who made her living in a for-hire marching band that played primarily at funerals. But I am reminded here of Rey Chow's observation, "it remains the case that the 'people' of the 'third world' are invoked only in the form of an indistinguishable mass, while the 'first world' intellectuals continue to have names"[24] because I would submit that there is more to Ah Ying's would-be acting career than a quest for "personal recognition."[25] In part Ah Ying is seeking a way out of the class and gender traps of Chinese society in 1980s colonial Hong Kong;[26] in part she is facing an existential crisis and a star-crossed platonic love affair. Her solution is the attempt to redefine herself as a member of a larger Chinese community (i.e., one that embraces the cultural heritage of Taiwan, the international overseas Chinese community, and, by extension, that of Mainland China as well): this is part of a spiritual/intellectual development process that transforms her from an ordinary Hong Kong girl-fishmonger into a Chinese artist and intellectual and will ultimately remain with her longer than the material benefits accrued

Fig. 15. The art of survival at their first lesson: Zhang Songbai (Peter Wang) warns his drama class that to be actors, they may have to wait tables first. From Allen Fong's film *Ah Ying*, 1984. Photo courtesy of Steve Horowitz and Fenghuang Motion Picture Company (Hong Kong).

from a potential acting career. In a way, this is the crux of liberation from colonial status: identifying with a larger whole that is beyond the power of one's colonial masters to define. It is also the reason she learns to speak in Mandarin.

For these reasons, the "public" response to these two films was also markedly different. As already mentioned, mainstream critics have a hard time coming to terms with Fong. Although the two directors share an enthusiasm (Fong on screen and Lai off) for method acting, one critic even misinterprets this, writing off Zhang Songbai as "a knowing hipster who leads the class through encounter-group exercises and the like, and whose own ambition is to become a film maker."[27] And this was not the first time

Allen Fong had difficulties with the reception of his films. As a news item in the column "This Week" in the supplement to the *South China Morning Post* revealed:

> A new, first feature film by a local director which has excited world interest would seem the ideal choice to open Hong Kong's fifth International Film Festival. Or so you'd think. Unfortunately, there was an embarrassing snag to Allen Fong's *Father and Son* [*Fu zi qing*]. It was produced by Feng Huang, which is a left-wing motion picture company, and that, decided the Urban Council, really wouldn't do. So extreme was the reaction, in fact, that it was decided that *Father and Son* shouldn't be included in the festival at all.
>
> Apparently this riled many involved in the HKIFF, who considered the ruling arbitrary, unjust and more than a little ridiculous considering *Father and Son* had already been shown at the prestigious Berlin Film Festival and been invited to screen at the Melbourne, London—and possibly Cannes—Film Festivals later in the year. Eventually, emotions became so heightened that the Urban Council did an about-turn and lifted the ban—but by then it was too late. Insulted to the core, the Feng Huang people decided to withhold the film from the HKIFF and arrange their own local premiere and showings instead.

Fong was clearly made to suffer for his frankness and his associations, even in the "democratic" climate of Hong Kong. One wonders if the current slump in the career of this world-class and pioneering Chinese director may not be at least partially attributable to just such a reception. It is precisely that reaction which Lai seeks, successfully, to avoid through his use of the *Verfremdungseffekt*.[28] For although Lai does not challenge the status quo in Taiwan on the basis of class, he does do so, like his Mainland predecessor Cao Yu, on the basis of interpersonal relations (a key concept in Confucianism) and, unlike Cao Yu, identity (the linchpin of much of twentieth-century Chinese political rhetoric). To pull this off as well as he has is no small accomplishment, albeit that his timing was certainly better than Chen Yingzhen's. As Lai has written:

> Taiwan in 1983, when I began creative work in the theatre, was pregnant with contradictions that were soon to evolve into political confrontations and acute social and cultural changes. Foremost among these contradictions was (and still is) the question of identity, not only the gross political questions, but the subtle questions of cultural identity and direction as well. . . . The precept for using improvisation as the key creative tool was, given the influx sociopolitical environment of

Taiwan, ready-made forms of arts were inadequate; art had to define and continually redefine itself, just as did the individual and Taiwan society as a whole. The philosophy behind the technique used was that improvisation would become a channel for one's inner concerns, and that under proper direction, individual concerns would give shape to collective concerns, and collective concerns, once discovered through the process, would give shape to the performance piece.[29]

Central to Lai's approach to the Chinese identity crisis in Taiwan is his belief that political currents are external manifestations of more internal and personal contradictions. He continues:

> Political events always effect the way we work as well as with what we work. In many ways, I feel that in a given society, political events are often the gross-externalized manifestation of issues that have been internalized on an individual level. In Taiwan, the "independence movement" hasn't affected the way we work as much as the inner forces that this movement expresses. In my view, the movement is a struggle to be independent not from anyone else but from ourselves. This attempt to break away from ourselves constitutes another way of searching to redefine who we are. This is happening on gross and subtle levels, in all facets of life in Taiwan, not just politics.[30]

Given that even a mention of the Taiwan Independence Movement (Taidu) was once taboo in the controlled press of Taiwan, Lai's statement is certainly an indication of the political liberalization in process on the island today. Nevertheless, Lai's privileged position as a member of the Mainland elite gives him the license to do so with a minimum of controversy and to view the "independence movement" as an outgrowth of personal identity issues sidesteps the political ramifications of treating it as the outcome of historical forces and geopolitical events, which would seem more objective. It is clearly an intellectualized approach, one which harks back to Confucian notions of *neisheng waiwang* (an internal sage/an external king), which suggests either genuinely changing political climes or the ability to successfully "distance" oneself from the actualities of politics—an approach once a luxury for anyone on the island to adopt.

To conclude, then, it seems possible to say that although Allen Fong was the first, or one of the very first, directors to come to terms with changing perspectives on identity among the Chinese living on the periphery of the People's Republic of China, and did so with a degree of realism that has been thus-far unequaled, Stan Lai has brought the debate onto another level by viewing the question from a postmodern perspective of personal past/

present and self/society interplay. He invents a comical historical "other," which allows the audience to redefine the present by contrasting it with the past, but he eschews the Brechtian question of how to move from art to collective action. In the way that he employs the *Verfremdungseffekt* to demand both the actors and the audience come to terms with this as an existential dilemma, rather than just relating a story they may or may not personally "identify" with, he may in fact come closer to striking a more responsive chord in his Asian viewers than Allen Fong. Just as Fong's dying character, Zhang Songbai, the ghost of Ge Wu, given to soliloquies on his days as a struggling graduate student in America, attempts to address an international as well as a Hong Kong predicament, Stan Lai, with his resurrected and parodied Chinese past, addresses the hopes and fears of the Taiwan and also the overseas Chinese audiences with his multilayered rereading of history. But in the end Lai insists: "Basically, we aspire to channel the Taiwan experience, and the Chinese experience as a whole, toward the goal of revealing the human condition on a universal level."[31] Only time will be the judge of who speaks with greater immediacy in that regard. That is the ultimate paradox for all literature and film produced during a situation of flux which attempts to address that situation with timely and meaningful relevance.

· Notes

Special thanks to Steve Horowitz, an unsung founder of Chinese film studies in the United States, for the stills from *Ah Ying*.

1. For a sample of articles, see *Newsweek,* February 29, 1988, 48; *Far Eastern Economic Review,* July 26, 1990, 20; *Los Angeles Times,* November 9, 1991, F1.

2. Stan Lai wrote and directed the film. It was produced by his wife, Ding Naizhu, with light and camera work by Christopher Doyle and original music composed by Fumio Itabashi and Kazutoki Umezu. The film opened in New York in 1993 as part of the New Directors/New Films series. It was reviewed (favorably) in the *New York Times* on March 25, 1993, C20, by Janet Maslin. A book on the making of the play and film has been published in Taiwan under the title *Wo anlian de Taohuayuan* [The peach-blossom spring I loved in secret] (Taipei: Yuanliu, 1992). The script and photos of the play were also published as a book, *Anlian Taohuayuan* [Secret love: The peach-blossom spring] (Taipei: Huangguan, 1986).

3. These resemble the Russian director Constantin Stanislavsky's (1863–1938) technique of psychological realism.

4. As quoted in Dunbar H. Ogden, *Actor Training and Audience Response* (Berkeley, Calif.: Oak House, 1984), 25.

5. Roswitha Mueller, *Bertolt Brecht and the Theory of Media* (Lincoln: University of Nebraska Press, 1989), 67.

6. We assume that the Northeast is already occupied by the Communists, as "the land routes are all closed," although this is never stated specifically.

7. In the original classical-language tale they are said to have "fled the chaos of Qin times" (*bi Qin shi luan*). See *Jianzhu Tao Yuanming ji* [An annotated collection of Tao Yuanming's works] (Shanghai: Hanfenlou, 1922), *ce* 2, *juan* 5, 1b6. The authoritarian Qin Shi Huang (First Emperor of the Qin) is sometimes used as a stand-in for Mao Zedong or the Communist revolution. Certainly "chaos" can be a reference to the civil war of the 1940s between the Guomindang and the Communists.

8. Wuling, in the present-day province of Hunan, was the place of origin for the protagonist of Tao Yuanming's *Taohuayuan ji* (lit. ,"Record/Tale of [a trip to] Peach Blossom [Stream's] Source").

9. Compare the perspective of the narrator in Maxine Hong Kingston's novel, *China Men,* when her Chinese American brother is steaming toward Taiwan on a U.S. army troop carrier during the war in Vietnam and the voice of the narrator tells us: "He watched the real China pass by, the old planet his family had left light years ago. Taiwan was not China, a decoy China, a facsimile." Maxine Hong Kingston, *China Men* (New York: Knopf, 1980), 294.

10. Stan Lai, *The Peach Blossom Land: A Synopsis* (Taipei: Performance Workshop, 1992).

11. *Na shi yige xin dalu* (that is a new mainland), I recall reading of America in the Chinese literature produced by exiled mainlanders in the 1970s on Taiwan when I studied there and first met Stan when he and his brother hosted the only St. Patrick's Day party in Taipei, to which they naively but good-heartedly invited Americans from both the Stanford Center and the Mandarin Center, always the cordial ambassadors of a divided China to a divided America, refusing to notice the division of the latter, just as the American government refused to recognize the division of the former.

12. Lai even says at one point: "Almost from the beginning it is obvious that the story of the play may in fact be the Director's (Ding Chung) own love story. [He is] subconsciously trying to re-enact his lost dream." Lai, *The Peach Blossom Land: A Synopsis.*

13. *Banbian ren* (lit., "Persons from the space along the sidelines") was distributed in the United States, beginning in 1983, with the title *Ah Ying,* the name of its female protagonist. Wang Zhengfang (Peter Wang) plays the male lead, and Xu Suying (Cantonese: Hui So-ying), the female. The film is linguistically quite sophisticated, using Mandarin, Cantonese, and Chaozhou dialects and English as well. Within the story, the Cantonese-speaking actors are moreover forced to struggle with learning Mandarin for the play performed within the film.

14. The close of the film hints that what he has taught her may ultimately help her get a career in acting, but this is only implied; we do not see it actually take place.

15. The narrator in "In the Wine Shop" exclaims: "I had become a complete stranger." Lü Weifu, who ends up a private tutor to the children of a wealthy family, where he teaches only the Confucian classics, tells the narrator: "I don't even teach mathematics; it's not that I don't want to teach it, but rather that they don't want it taught." See Lu Xun, *Lu Xun quanji* [Complete works of Lu Xun], vol. 2 (Beijing: Renmin wenxue chubanshe, 1991), 33.

16. "You have to remember," said a boy whom Oskar would later save, "that Oskar had a German side but a Czech side too. He was the good soldier Schweik. He loved to foul up the system." See Thomas Keneally, *Schindler's List* (New York: Simon and Schuster, 1993), 233.

17. "[I'm] hardly a Russian . . . [I] come from Lithuania—pure German." From *The Waste Land* (1922), part I, "The Burial of the Dead," in T. S. Eliot, *The Complete Poems and Plays: 1909–1950* (New York: Harcourt, Brace and World, 1971), 37 (my translation).

18. I am using *Mensch* in the Yiddish sense of the word, meaning people who are decent human beings in that they treat others in a generous and understanding manner, regardless of personal stakes. *Qi* refers to life (lit., "life's breath").

19. For the text of the short story, see *Chen Yingzhen xiaoshuo xuan* [Selected stories of Chen Yingzhen] (Fuzhou: Fujian renmin chubanshe, 1983), 50–63. Chen Yingzhen was sentenced to ten years' imprisonment in Taiwan in 1968 for sedition. He was released as part of an amnesty following the death of Chiang Kai-shek in 1976. In an interview granted me in Jingmei in 1976, Chen Yingzhen stated: "One of the reasons I became a writer had to do with my reading Lu Xun when I was in my early teens. Although I did not really understand him, I read him over and over again. And this also eventually accounted for my imprisonment."

20. Lu Xun, *Lu Xun quanji*, vol. 4, 512.

21. Peter Brooker, *Bertolt Brecht: Dialectics, Poetry, Politics* (London: Croom Helm, 1988), 62–63. I prefer the translation "distancing" for *Verfremdung*. Regarding cinematic adaptations of Brecht, see the study by Soviet woman scholar M. I. Turovsakaia, *Na granitse iskusstv: Brekht i kino* (Moskva: Iskusstvo, 1985).

22. The first English translation of "Jiangjun zu" appeared in *Renditions* 19/20 (1983) under the title "A Couple of Generals." It was reprinted in a substantially different version in Lucien Miller, *Exiles at Home: Short Stories by Ch'en Ying-chen* (Ann Arbor: Center for Chinese Studies, University of Michigan, 1986), 69–82.

23. Janet Maslin, review of *Ah Ying, New York Times*, March 30, 1984, C7.

24. Rey Chow, *Writing Diaspora: Tactics of Intervention in Contemporary Cultural Studies* (Bloomington: Indiana University Press, 1993), 20.

25. Richard Springer notes: "Like Brocka, Fong is interested in the lives of the downtrodden who are trying to escape the poverty of the ghetto. Brocka slashes at his theme like an angry participant in the drama. Fong feels the oppression as much, but he sits back calmly and more objectively, painting his canvas with delicate

strokes. Both are bucking the power structure, but Brocka is living more dangerously this year." *East-West Journal* (San Francisco), April 18, 1984.

26. Rey Chow errs in saying "Hong Kong currently has a democracy" (*Writing Diaspora,* 23). Hong Kong, at the time of her writing, was a British crown colony with very little pretense of actual self-government.

27. Maslin, review of *Ah Ying,* C7.

28. Bertolt Brecht (1898–1956) was himself quite accomplished in this as well (both on stage and off), slipping by persecution in Nazi Germany and the United States during the McCarthy period, when he was called to testify before the House Committee on Un-American Activities in 1948. Despite his support of the East German workers' strike in 1953, he managed to continue to operate his own theater ensemble for eight years in East Berlin, winning the Stalin Peace Prize in 1954.

29. Stan Lai, "Specifying the Universal," *The Drama Review* 38, no. 2 (1994): 33–34.

30. Lai, "Specifying the Universal," 37.

31. Lai, "Specifying the Universal," 37. Lai, as a creative artist, seems to be articulating precisely what Yingjin Zhang would term the "Liberal, Humanistic Position" on Chinese literature. See Yingjin Zhang, "Re-envisioning the Institution of Modern Chinese Literature Studies: Strategies of Positionality and Self-Reflexivity," *positions: east asia cultures critique* 1, no. 3 (1993): 826–827.

Chapter 7

Breaking the Soy Sauce Jar
Diaspora and Displacement in the Films of Ang Lee
·

Wei Ming Dariotis
Eileen Fung

Ang Lee's films are powerful evocations of cultural preservation as well as intercultural (mis)communication. Lee's work illustrates the inevitable conflicts and negotiations between individuals bound by familial and societal obligations. These familial and social dramas are often set in scenes where the infiltration of Westernization is in direct conflict with orthodox Chinese ideologies. The overall philosophy of Ang Lee's films demonstrates the struggles of individuals within and between cultures. Lee's struggles to place Chinese culture within today's progressive societies—both in the "East" and in the "West"[1]—echo a long tradition of Chinese negotiation with the influences of Western culture. In contrast to the supposedly liberating possibilities of Western culture, the (also supposedly) oppressive nature of traditional Chinese culture has been criticized by many Chinese scholars. One of the most controversial critiques has been that of Taiwanese novelist and cultural critic Po Yang (Bo Yang),[2] beginning in the 1960s. Our use of Po Yang to begin our analysis of Ang Lee's films is a deliberate attempt to acknowledge the continual efforts of participants from multiple disciplines in the current discussion of transcultural and transnational interactions. Lee's films consistently negotiate among cultures, nations, generations, and genders—illustrating the repressive as well as revitalizing forces of Chinese traditions in the intersection of the residual past and emerging future. Po Yang and Ang Lee have in common a belief in the positive power of change. The difference between them is Ang Lee's recognition of the possibility of change within Chinese societies, as well as from without. In contrast, Po Yang argues for a view of Chinese culture that emphasizes its stagnant qualities:

> The soy sauce jar *(jianggang)* represents a confused society in which the forces of erosion and the forces of stagnation are at their most powerful. It also represents a kind of politics of enslavement. It is a mal-

formed morality, a distinctive philosophy of life, and a snobbishness that has been destructive over a long period of time. It has created a confused society in which the intelligence peculiar to man [*sic*] is put out of action or made to vanish without a trace.[3]

Po Yang envisions Chinese cultural traditions as a massive "soy sauce jar." In Po Yang's characterization, soy sauce is a body of stinky, stagnant, dead water (*zhuoshui*); it also has a strong preservative aspect such that, after the fermentation process is complete, it stagnates. Soy sauce has a powerful odor and taste which strongly flavors any food with which it comes into contact. With this image, Po Yang criticizes the homogenizing forces of traditional Chinese culture which have assimilated even its conquerors into the cultural hegemony of the Han people. More recently, the rigidity of Chinese tradition, in Po Yang's analysis, has prevented the acceptance of exciting and progressive thoughts and practices emanating from the West. Po Yang's suspicion of Chinese traditional culture mirrors that of his literary predecessors in the early part of the twentieth century. For example, one of Lu Xun's highly respected texts, "The Diary of the Madman," characterizes Chinese traditions as being cannibalistic. The story insinuates that the self-destructiveness of the oppressive traditional past can only harm the awakening present.

Po Yang's works, particularly the controversial *Ugly Chinese* (Choulou de Zhongguo ren), as well as his earlier works, created enormous controversy in both China and Taiwan in the 1980s. His comparison of Chinese tradition to a dead and repressive "soy sauce" culture closely follows Lu Xun's criticism of Chinese culture at the turn of the century. Such attacks on traditional Han Confucian beliefs and practices became the central driving force behind communist ideology by attracting the socially underprivileged who had always been at the bottom of the metaphorical "soy sauce vat." Traditional Chinese culture, Po Yang suggests, tends to foster a love of power, which may command respect but also breeds fear. Thus, fear tends to govern the relationship between individuals in the family and in society. In his article "Life or Death at the Mercy of a Cough" (in *Si bu rencuo ji*), he discusses such concomitants of fear as suspicion, jealousy, and sycophancy— features demonstrably in evidence in both imperial and republican China.

The counter criticisms to Po Yang, especially by scholars from Taiwan, were immense and immediate. While the scope of this paper does not allow for a full analysis of this criticism, a brief elaboration of the arguments of two respected scholars, Sun Guodong and Li Ao, is useful here. They argue that the problems of Chinese society, resulting from specific political and historical situations, are nevertheless transitory and circumstantial. Furthermore, if China is truly as fatally diseased as Po claims, then its demise would be indisputable and soon in arriving. Instead, its five-thousand-year survival and its continual adaptation deconstruct the validity of Po's prediction, analysis, and—some would argue—curse.

As we approach the end of the twentieth century, these binary oppositional characterizations of the relationship between Chinese tradition and "Western" modernity appear more than naive. Cultural critic Rey Chow theorizes about this reaction of twentieth-century Chinese intellectuals to Chinese traditions. She writes:

> China, perhaps because it is an exception to the rule of imperialist domination by race, land, and language involving a foreign power, in fact highlights the effects of the imperialistic *transformation of value and value production* more sharply than in other "third world" cultures. . . . The obsession of Chinese intellectuals remains "China" rather than the opposition to the West. The cultural production that results is therefore narcissistic, rather than simply oppositional, in structure. Whatever oppositional sentiment there exists is an oppositional sentiment directed toward itself—"China," "the Chinese heritage," "the Chinese tradition," "the Chinese government," and variants of these.[4]

This "obsession" with "Chinese tradition" as a static symbol of hegemony has been eroded by the increasing ability of people to cross national borders with relative frequency. As contemporary Chinese and Taiwanese negotiate an increasingly transnational sense of self and nation, the "soy sauce jar" has begun to crack. Filmmakers like Ang Lee may use "soy sauce" to flavor their dishes, but they juxtapose it with unexpected ingredients. There may be a danger, as bell hooks argues, that "[w]ithin commodity culture, ethnicity becomes spice, seasoning that can liven up the dull dish that is mainstream white culture,"[5] but Lee's understanding of the "soy sauce jar" of Chinese culture largely avoids such reductive commodification. In many ways, Lee, like Po, recognizes the undeniable significance of cultural traditions in everyday political organization, societal expectations, and family interactions; yet Lee's films indicate a much more ambivalent and nuanced interpretation of the significance of Chinese traditions for contemporary populations.

Unlike Po Yang's total disillusionment, Lee's films reenvision "tradition" in a much more sympathetic light as something that is highly versatile and adaptive. The "soy sauce jar," which both represents and contains Chinese and Taiwanese national and transnational identities, is figuratively "broken" to reveal a new sensibility, but the fluid "soy sauce" within the "jar" is not discarded. Recognizing the unfinished nature of intercultural processes endows individuals with a sense of agency and consequence: the past we reconstruct will shape the future in which we must live. Ang Lee's films depict the intersection between individuals and cultures as a Derridean "always already" interpolated space that constantly challenges and changes the course of those who seek to find their places within the micro- and macro-cosmic social (dis)orders.

Lee's characters, whether they are members of a Taiwanese or Chinese diaspora, or they are merely undergoing smaller forms of displacement, are each affected by the difficulty of negotiating identity not only as individuals moving from place to place but as members of families that become dislocated—literally and figuratively. When the family boundaries are expanding—through both marriage and migration—a crisis is created within the intergenerational relationships. This crisis is resolved in Lee's films by dramatic end moments, or final shots, which both reinscribe normative heterosexual bonds—thus insuring the continuation of the family into the next generation—and simultaneously destabilize these familial relations.

Ang Lee was born and educated in Taiwan. Although he went to New York in 1977 to study theater at New York University, he switched to film, and his career has developed quickly since the debut of his first film, *Pushing Hands* (Tui shou), in 1992. Does Ang Lee's shifting transnational identity destabilize the identification of his films? Is identity ultimately about sameness (identifying with something) or difference (identifying against something)? The question of how to label him as a director and his films—Taiwanese, American, or some kind of Asian American—is in some ways best answered by the content of the films themselves. His first two films, *Pushing Hands* and *The Wedding Banquet* (Xiyan), both deal with older Chinese/Taiwanese parents coming to an understanding with the European American mates of their sons. There is a need to renegotiate personal identity through the changes caused by immigration and relocation. Lee's third movie, *Eat Drink Man Woman* (Yin shi nan nü), appears to be the least problematic in terms of identifying labels. The entire film is set in Taiwan, and Taipei is clearly the spatial locus of the film. The interactions that occur within the Chu family have been read by several film critics as metaphors for the interactions within the larger Taiwanese society between traditional Chinese culture and the emerging modernization of the "West,"[6] but this interpretation simplistically positions Chinese tradition as a monolithic guardian of the past and the artificial construct called "the West" as the sole repository of progressive thought. We would argue that Lee's treatment of these issues is much more nuanced, as should be the categorization of his films.

In terms of subject matter, *Sense and Sensibility* does not fit into any of the

Fig. 16. Director Ang Lee. British Film Institute.

categories mentioned above. On the surface, it is simply an adaptation of a Jane Austen novel and therefore is a very British period costume drama. How does Ang Lee's presence as director complicate this simple identification? Is he simply a part of the mechanism that produced the film, his sensibilities and concerns—as displayed in his previous work—completely overridden by a purely technical participation in the project? Or is he an auteur whose personality was not completely subsumed by that of Emma Thompson? These questions of identity have serious consequences. Despite the transnational nature of contemporary cinema, the way a film is identified and labeled still has real meaning (distribution, awards, viewership, location on the video store shelf). This "real world" concern with multiple and shifting identities mirrors the complexities of Lee's cinematic world. These tensions are generally manifested in various characters who must come to terms with how the identities of family members and friends shift their own identities. However, this does not mean an easy melding into an unproblematic universalism. Film critic Donald Lyons says of Lee's work that "[h]e's no sentimentalist: generations and cultures do not compromise, coalesce, fuzzily melt, but rather achieve a tense, polite, somehow bracing remove."[7] *Pushing Hands* shows early signs of Lee's preoccupation with the conflict between traditions and contemporary life and the ways individuals learn to redefine their relationships to them.

· Pushing Hands

> *The overriding fear is that cultural, ethnic, and racial differences will be continually commodified and offered up as new dishes to enhance the white palate—that the Other will be eaten, consumed, and forgotten.*   BELL HOOKS, *BLACK LOOKS*

The negotiation for space between dislocated relations in *Pushing Hands* (screenplay by Ang Lee, Ted Hope, and James Schamus) is enacted primarily between a Mainland Chinese father and his European American daughter-in-law when he moves to upstate New York to spend his retirement with his son's family. This film focuses on the cultural, as well as personal, maturation of all the major participants. Though the film begins with a strict binary opposition between "East" and "West," by the end of the film the representatives of this opposition have learned to accommodate one another on a personal level. They have also learned to appreciate and integrate each other's culture into their own daily lives. This effect is most noticeable for Alex (Bo Z. Wang), Mr. Chu's son, who must act as a cultural translator between his father and his wife.

According to film critic Mal Vincent, "Ang Lee has done more to unveil the mysteries of the East than anyone since Marco Polo. His films about Chinese people, whether in America or in their native land, have reached huge audiences and proved that people, after all, are merely people."[8]

The specificities of the identity crisis of an Asian man encountering his Asian American family are indeed "unveiled" by Ang Lee in his first feature film. But do the specific differences of this family and these experiences as depicted by Ang Lee *merely* demonstrate that people are "merely people?" What kind of anxiety is hidden behind such a statement? Why is it necessary that Lee be characterized as an explorer returning from foreign lands with consumable riches to sell? The comparison of Marco Polo and Ang Lee is undoubtedly quite problematic. Marco Polo's role as explorer, merchant, and adventurer in Mongolia elicits issues about imperialist and colonialist practices that began as early as the twelfth century. Marco Polo materialized the "Orient" into consumable merchandise, which he brought back to a "Western" market, while Ang Lee does not overtly engage in this kind of imperialist ethnography. Lee is not an ethnographic observer. He sees the "East" from the perspective of the "native." In other words, he presents to his audiences alternative cultural histories that attempt to challenge the consuming hegemonic views of the "West." Of course, one must question why Vincent would make such a comparison of Lee's portrayal of his "native land" and Polo's exoticization of the "foreign land." It raises the question, does Lee deliberately create stereotypic images to buy into the American (and Americanized) movie marketplace, or does the very process of making Hollywood narrative-style films necessarily engage in "Western" exoticization of the "East"?

Lee's use of Chinese traditions does occasionally venture close to Vincent's Marco Polo comparison as Lee negotiates his position vis-à-vis his multiple audiences, but ultimately, the cultural differences of his characters are not merely consumed and subsequently "forgotten" like the consumable merchandise of stereotypes. *Pushing Hands,* which was released first in Taiwan and became available in the United States only after the successes of *The Wedding Banquet* and *Eat Drink Man Woman,* displays a distinctly Asian American sensibility. Lee does not cater solely to a Taiwanese mass audience, nor to that of America. The relational difficulties of the Chinese immigrant and his European American daughter-in-law are not simplified by purely binary oppositional characterizations, even when the film threatens, on occasion, to slip into precisely this kind of static relationship.

Mr. Chu, played by veteran Taiwanese actor Sihung Lung (Lang Xiong), is the Chinese tai chi master whose "pushing hands" martial arts technique provides the metaphor around which this movie is organized. The movie opens with the silent images of Mr. Chu practicing tai chi in the morning. These scenes are intercut with shots of a blond woman, whom we eventually discover to be his European American daughter-in-law, typing at her computer. The motions of her hands are incongruent with his. She seems agitated, and subsequent scenes are constructed in such a way as to demonstrate that even when they are both engaged in writing—she at the computer, he practicing calligraphy—they may share the same space, but they live in separate worlds. The difference in their daily activities as well as their division of the space of the home complicates even further the issue of silence both as a linguistic absence as well as visual nonrecognition. As Donald Lyons notes, Lee's work in this film demonstrates "a mastery of the visual dynamics of interior spaces and their psychic pressures."[9] As she works at her computer, he watches Chinese videos, and their backs are to one another. Even culturally specific sounds are controlled when the daughter-in-law tells Mr. Chu to use headphones when he listens to Chinese opera. She silences him, not only because she cannot understand him but also because when he speaks in Chinese—to her husband and to her son— she is prevented from engaging in the community of her own family.

The issue of translation epitomizes the drama of cross-cultural tension in this film. The Chinese American Alex must translate his father for his wife and vice versa. Ironically, the truth is never circulated because Alex must often "mistranslate" in order to avoid direct conflicts between the two most important people in his life. The son's role as the negotiator or middleman begins as a means of mediation, but he later loses himself in his bicultural triangulation between father and wife. His violent outburst when his father gets lost signifies the hidden problem of "mistranslation" as a way to mediate between two cultures. Alex frantically looks for his father and not finding him, comes home and destroys the kitchen, symbolically the heart of the home. Mr. Chu had asked his daughter-in-law to go for a walk with him. Her fear that he will get lost fails to be communicated. Eventually they are yelling over each other, and her question, "Don't you understand what I'm telling you?" seems heavily ironic, since neither of them can understand the other. Mr. Chu is eventually returned by the police, and he and his daughter-in-law work together to clean up the kitchen destroyed by Alex. Their hands are finally working in cooperative harmony. Alex returns home after some heavy drinking. Finally united in their concern for Alex, Mr. Chu and Alex's wife carry him between them up the stairs. His frustration causes him to bang his head against the wall, which awakens his son Jeremy, whose concern "awakens" him to his responsibilities as the father of his own family.

Ironically, when Alex does manage to translate correctly, the consequences are no more promising. One of the most interesting scenes displaying this cross-cultural difficulty is when the multiracial grandson, Jeremy, naughtily runs away from his mother after his bath, wearing only a towel. His grandfather picks him up and tickles him while jokingly checking Jeremy's "family jewels" to make sure his family will have a next generation. After Alex explains to his wife the meaning of his father's actions, she angrily grabs her son away from his grandfather. This leaves Alex once again having to (mis)translate her actions for his father: "She is worried Jeremy will catch a cold." This type of cultural friction—on the one hand, Chinese tradition demands the assurance of the family's continuity; on the other, U.S. culture is highly anxious about children's sexuality—underscores the irresolvability of subtle and sometimes unintelligible cultural differences.

There are perhaps a few too many obvious cross-cultural misunderstandings, such as when the daughter-in-law eats from the cake in the refrigerator with her fingers while her Chinese father-in-law performs his silent exercises or puts aluminum foil in the microwave; but the moments during which they try to communicate are more subtle and more real. She is eating at the kitchen counter; he moves past her to eat at the table but changes course to eat with her. But the gesture is not fulfilled; they are still not eating "together." Later, we see them both in the kitchen cooking dinner, but they are always at odds. Their hands perform the same tasks in preparing the meal, yet they are unable to work with one another. What is so striking about these early moments in the film is that they are filled with silence. But unlike later in the film, when silence functions as a kind of communication, at the beginning, it is only the silence of two people who cannot understand each other, and even more, who are competing to communicate with someone who is absent throughout most of the day—Alex Chu.

While the film is centered primarily on the displacement of the Chinese father-in-law, it also illustrates the cultural disorientation of the European American wife when her work space in the home becomes dominated by cultural signs of China. Her frustration is made heavier by Alex's refusal to borrow money from her mother in order to buy a larger home, one that would have room for all of them to have their own space. Cultural differences come into play here as well; as Alex says, the home they have could house four families in China. As she notes, those people all speak the same language and can thus occupy the same space without dislocating one another. Her (dis) "orientation" is further signified when she must be hospitalized for an ulcer—a physical manifestation of the stress she is experiencing. During the scene right before her hospitalization, her mistrust of the "other" culture is intensified when Mr. Chu attempts to practice tai chi on her and increases her pain rather than alleviating it. She rejects, at a physical level, his outreach to her. Even when she returns from the hospital and he tries to reach across the table when he sees her in pain, she flies back in an emotionally disturbing echo of a humorous previous scene where his hands caused his Chinese tai chi student to fly across the room at the community center where he teaches. This rejection by the daughter-in-law is also in contrast to a later scene where Mr. Chu successfully treats a middle-aged Chinese woman, Mrs. Chang, for a sore shoulder. Clearly, trust and faith are at issue here; Mrs. Chang's complete acceptance of Mr. Chu's philosophy and tradition builds a successful relationship, as well as treatment, which is denied and unwanted by the daughter-in-law.

This juxtaposition brings forth the problematic issue of generational reversal, which is magnified by the father's physical displacement from his homeland. While Mr. Chu represents the residual traditions of the Chinese culture, his son Alex represents the "new" patriarchy. Even his wife says, "your father is more and more like a child" and that she is his "baby-sitter." Soon Alex decides he has to tell his father they will find him an "old people's apartment," but in the morning when he goes downstairs to find his father, instead of practicing tai chi, Mr. Chu is still in bed. Under his father's pillow Alex finds a photo of his father and mother, and Alex asks his father why he does not wish to look at his mother's picture. Mr. Chu says it is because he has so many regrets toward her. Because he was a kung fu master, when the Red Guards came during the Cultural Revolution, they dared not beat him up, but instead attacked his son and wife. Because he had to protect his son, Alex, his wife was beaten so badly that she later died from it. This history makes clear the lines of obligation that run between father and son but also shows the contrast in values between China and America. Mr. Chu put his son before his wife; Alex, in his American context, does not know how to put his father before his wife. Mr. Chu must find a way to negotiate his new position with grace rather than allowing himself to be displaced.

Mr. Chu's friendship with Mrs. Chang (Lai Wang), a widowed cooking instructor at the Chinese community center, is not only a way for them to reminisce about the past. More importantly, their friendship helps them negotiate both their new positions in their children's families and their new identities in a new world. During a picnic scene that is significant for the absence of Alex's European American wife and the presence of Mrs. Chang's Chinese daughter and granddaughter—forming a perfect mirror of the Chu men—there appears to be no conflict between generations. There seems to be a perfectly balanced racial harmony and every sign of filial piety. After a long uphill climb that leaves the older couple lagging behind, however, Mrs. Chang breaks down and cries to Mr. Chu that her daughter wants to get rid of her. By the end of the movie, Mr. Chu and Mrs. Chang seem to have found a way to live in America without abandoning their Chinese traditions and identities, but also without maintaining a stubborn hold on those traditions.

Their ability to assimilate without the loss of the strength of their traditions is shown in contrast to the Chinese restaurant owner Mr. Chu works for when he "runs away" from his son's home. This man's contempt for the Chinese culture he sells in his restaurant signifies the negative consequences of the commodification of tradition for consumption by dominant culture. The restaurant owner's capitalist greed, which leads him to short-change Mr. Chu of his dishwasher's wages, is combined with his extreme aversion to China and things Chinese (although he runs a Chinese restaurant). Repeatedly he shouts, "This is America!" and while this acknowledgment of his new location would seem to signal a positive adjustment, his refusal to bring with him a sense of his own past or traditions leaves him fundamentally unstable in his new home. Visually, this is signified by Mr. Chu's rootedness in the face of adversity. When the owner wants to throw him out, Mr. Chu cannot be moved, even by ten cooks and waiters. Finally they—who are also Chinese immigrants—recognize Mr. Chu for the tai chi master he is and leave the owner in his blindness. Tellingly, the owner then summons a Chinese American street gang, the leader of which speaks English with no accent (as opposed to the Chinese of the previous scene).[10] When the leader says, in English, "Yeah, I seen his kind before," we cannot help but be struck by the irony, because it is clear this child has no recognition of the man he sees before him and the tradition he represents. If Mr. Chu signifies the residual dignity of the traditions of the past and their adaptability for the present, the restaurant owner's disrespect and his unwillingness to acknowledge the value of tradition result in his ultimate humiliation and disgrace.

The film's resolution between Mr. Chu and his family in America, though a bit quick and superficial in some ways, becomes clear in the expression of regrets on the part of the son and his wife. Her acceptance and understanding of Chinese tradition becomes a process of resolution depicted through her performance of cultural signs: she cooks egg rolls and expresses an interest in writing a novel about the history of the Chinese railroad workers in America. There is some danger in the simplicity of this resolution, which reduces cross-cultural understanding to the consumption of stereotypical Chinese cuisine—the "chung-king" style of diplomacy. As bell hooks argues,

> Currently, the commodification of difference promotes paradigms of consumption wherein whatever difference the Other inhabits is eradicated, via exchange, by a consumer cannibalism that not only displaces the Other but denies the Other's history through a process of decontextualization.[11]

What is significant is that she does not attempt to recreate herself in an imitation of a stereotype of a traditional Chinese woman. Her understanding of Chinese traditions is clearly located in her position as a European American woman married to a Chinese American man. She does not decontextualize that understanding. This understanding is aided by her husband's ability to finally fulfill his role as translator. Alex's final act of translation is to explain to her Mr. Chu's philosophy—his particular brand of tai chi, the pushing-hands technique. This philosophy is "a way of keeping balance while unbalancing your opponent." In some ways, this method of "using the force of others to your own advantage" appears to be a defense mechanism that mirrors the father's way of life. Alex's explanation of his father's philosophy of life is significant; he believes his father uses the method of "pushing hands" to move beyond the painful memories of the past as well as the troubles of the present. The ending reflects not only the children's reeducation in bicultural communication but also the father's realization that he must not rely on an opponent for his balance; he must learn to establish a sense of peace within himself. His final decision to live on his own rather than in his son's new house and his self-initiated friendship with Mrs. Chang signify his discovery of a newfound vigor and hope. The film's conclusion thus represents a renegotiation of cultural practices and beliefs on both sides, "West" and "East," young and old, man and woman.

Although the film seems to end with a burgeoning sense of hope, it nevertheless leaves several problematic issues unresolved. The resolution of bicultural tensions is superficial and even slightly ambiguous. Linguistic and cultural barriers still remain between the wife and her father-in-law. Despite Alex's protestations that his home is his father's home, by the end of the movie Mr. Chu is living in an apartment in Chinatown and has a thriving tai chi school because of his notoriety. Mrs. Chang is also living on her own, and the final scene of the movie is the two of them exchanging addresses and a long shot of them standing in the bright winter sun on a street in Chinatown. The resigned tones of Mr. Chu and Mrs. Chang in the final scene in front of the door of the community center display their dissatisfaction with their current circumstances. While they share comfort in their friendship, they still live alone and expect only limited visitation from their children, "once every two, three weeks." Their new independence still leaves them culturally isolated in Chinatown while the rest of the United States remains unintelligible to them. Yet by that very token Lee has avoided a simplistic "universal humanist" approach, which would have made his film and its characters easily consumable but just as easily forgettable. Mr. Chu and Mrs. Chang are not located in a stereotypical universalized "American" locale, they are in Chinatown and they interact within the auspices of a localized ethnic community. While the film ends with the two speaking of getting together later, their isolated figures are nevertheless both physically and psychologically alienated as the camera pulls back to frame them looking solemnly into the space around them. Simultaneously this shot both reinscribes heterosexual, monoracial bonding in the Hollywood tradition and yet suggests the dissolution of other familial bonds. According to traditional Chinese society, these two elders should not be living on their own but should be living with their multigenerational families. Yet it would be unfair to characterize this as simply an "American" ending that emphasizes the individual's needs and drives over that of any familial community. Rather, Lee manages to break the paradigm of the confining "soy sauce jar," while retaining the useful specificity of the "sauce" itself. The fluidity of Chinese tradition—as represented here by Mr. Chu—is not without moments of interruption. But the "soy sauce" need not be an overpowering ingredient in the lives of those moving outside of the "jar" of their original homeland. Members of the diaspora, Mr. Chu included, can learn to enjoy all of the flavors their new homes have to offer, although they must at the same time resist commodifying and being commodified by those whom they encounter.

• The Wedding Banquet

> *A complex signifying chain is introduced in place of the lack which can never be made good, suturing over the wound of castration with narrative. However, it is only by inflicting the wound to begin with that the viewing subject can be made to want the restorative meaning and narrative.* KAJA SILVERMAN, *SEMIOTICS AND SUTURE*

The movie *The Wedding Banquet* (screenplay by Ang Lee, Neil Peng, and James Schamus) brings forth several critical issues. It most obviously deals with Asian parents grappling with the reality of their gay Asian American son. It thus forces an examination of the crossroads between traditional Taiwanese and American gender ideologies and transgressive sexual behaviors. Furthermore, it compels an investigation of the issue of immigration and the body of the immigrant woman who is caught between the transgenerational and transsexual identity crisis of men in *The Wedding Banquet*. Several secondary issues complicate these primary concerns. First, what types of cross-cultural and cross national issues does this film raise between the heterosexual parents and their gay Asian American son and his gay white lover? Second, the representation of homosexuality appears to be connected with the "West"—Wai-tung is thought by his mother to have "turned" gay after his immigration to America, and this "symptom" of homosexuality is situated far away from the "homeplace" of Asia. Third, the semiotic constructions of homosexuality and heterosexuality become confused and contained, especially when paternal authority and masculine ideology continue to exert themselves in the heterosexual paradigm of the gay couple and the ultimate preservation of Wei-wei's baby. Finally, the international politics of Taiwan, China, and the United States are subtly inscribed in the characterization of Wei-wei and her immigrant status.

"In Hannah Arendt's view," Homi K. Bhabha writes, "the society of the nation in the modern world is 'that curiously hybrid realm where private interests assume public significance' and the two realms flow unceasingly and uncertainly into each other 'like waves in the never-ending stream of the life-process itself.' "[12] The language Arendt uses evokes particular images, the "waves in the never-ending stream of the life-process itself" suggests "waves" of immigration as well as the "life process" of pregnancy and birth. The liminality of the sense of national identity described by Arendt is particularly in flux for the gay male immigrant, because so much of national

Fig. 17. *The Wedding Banquet* (Xiyan), directed by Ang Lee, Taiwan, 1993. British Film Institute.

identity is based on mythic (male) heterosexuality. The male homosexual immigrant threatens this in several ways. As a homosexual, he signifies castration and lack of potency, the ability to generate more "national identity" in the form of children. Paradoxically, as an immigrant, he invades the now feminized body of the nation. He throws into flux, therefore, the gendered identity of the nation. In order to resolve this tension in *The Wedding Banquet,* the "castrating wound" of male homosexuality must be "sutured over" by a reinscription of heterosexuality and ultimately the presence of a male baby who must have a "white father" to naturalize him into the identity of the ("white-identified") nation.

In this case, the "wound of castration" is literally a homosexuality that castrates the potential for national regeneration; this wound is then "sutured" over with the structure of the narrative, which reinscribes a heterosexuality and national identity, particularly in the bodies of the Chinese baby boys

Wei Ming Dariotis and Eileen Fung

with white fathers. As Eve Sedgewick makes clear in the introduction to *The Epistemology of the Closet,* her work has shown that "men's same-sex bonds" have been immanent in English literature since the nineteenth century.[13] We would argue that the homosocial (and the threat it carries of the homosexual) has long been a narrative commonplace precisely because it provides the castrating wound that requires suturing, which in fact sets up heterosexuality as its answer. Lee, however, by making explicit that which has previously been only implicit (and closeted) has added new dimensions of complexity to the "wound." The suture is not entirely successful perhaps because the "wound" was too obvious. The "threat" of the homosexual is the threat of disrupting the necessarily heterosexual national identity. Though, as Homi Bhabha says, "[t]he 'locality' of national culture is neither unified nor unitary in relation to itself, nor must it be seen simply as 'other' in relation to what is outside or beyond it."[14] A good deal of national identity is constructed according to false binary oppositions. Bhabha clarifies this by explaining that "the subject is graspable only in the passage between telling/told, between 'here' and 'somewhere else', and in this double scene the very condition of cultural knowledge is the alienation of the subject."[15]

Semiotic film theory is less openly concerned with this "passing" back and forth, though ultimately it is the negotiation between terms which reveals the meaning of binary opposites. In her chapter on "suture," Kaja Silverman discusses the lack of intrinsic value of any term: "They are fully contained within the closed system of signification: 'I' always derives its value from 'you,' and 'here' from 'there,' just as 'black' refers to 'white,' or 'male' to 'female.' "[16]

Within the context of *The Wedding Banquet* this binary is transmuted into "East" versus "West," old and young, and female versus male. Interestingly, just as the terms Black/white evacuate terms which cannot be accommodated within this binary (yellow, for instance), so the terms East and West likewise eliminate a good deal in their division of the world; Africa and South America, for example, simply disappear. The only constant that remains is the image of the "white man," the center of all equations, because it is this culture which is the primary generator of concepts of binary opposition.

Ang Lee plays with, and sometimes reproduces, the stereotypes based on these binary oppositions. In *The Wedding Banquet,* an Asian man is constructed as silent. General Gao's voice is seldom heard, while in contrast Mrs. Gao's voice is heard even in her absence on the tapes she sends her son, full of her and her husband's expectations, to play while he exercises. General Gao's silence is strategic. The night of the wedding banquet swiftly leads to a morning breakfast exploding with tensions unleashed as Simon discovers Wei-wei's pregnancy and Wai-tung's infidelity (not only person-ally, but in terms of sexual identity, the ultimate threat of the bisexual in biphobic discourse is that their identities are unstable). Though we do not know the sex of Wei-wei's baby, it functions as a male in that it has assured General Gao of the continuance of his family line in a mirroring of his own experience of needing to return to the family fold in order to continue the line with his own son, Wai-tung. Interestingly, the very survival of the baby is predicated on General Gao's deliberately hiding his ability to speak English and thus to move freely within the national boundaries (this is sym-bolically alluded to in the final moment of the film as he and his wife walk down the long hallway in the airport for their departure from America and return to Taiwan, only to be stopped by an apparently "white" security guard who requires General Gao to raise his hands for a security check). The resulting gesture is captured in slow motion and rendered as a gesture of surrender, of one generation's sacrifice for another. Yet, ultimately, it is a selfish sacrifice; it is the Gao family, and thus in a sense himself, which the general wishes to perpetuate. Paradoxically, because of his son's homosexu-ality, which could not be expressed in Taiwan in a naturalized nuclear family without a descent in class status,[17] General Gao's family line could only be continued by a shift in location. The act of immigration (not neces-sarily from a "more repressed" to a "less repressed" locale) is what permits Wai-tung to be gay, but it is also what requires him to have a child because this child who will be born in the United States fixes his identity as an Asian American. By the conclusion of the movie, Simon has been ritually asked by Wei-wei to be the baby's second father. Although this seems to be done in order to validate the homosexual relationship between Wai-tung and Simon, the effect is also to secure a white father for the baby while maintaining a nonthreatening racial purity. Within the schema of immigra-tion, having a white father for one's child can be seen as the closest non-European immigrant parents can get to assimilation and thus validation for their children as well as themselves.

The version of *The Wedding Banquet* released in France is called *Garcon D'Honneur* (The Best Man). The photograph accompanying a review of the film in the October 1993 issue of *Studio Magazine* features Mitchell Lichten-stein and May Chin sitting next to one another and slightly back to back, with Winston Chao (Zhao Wenxuan) rising slightly above, behind, and between them. He is holding Lichtenstein's hand, and all are attired as for a formal wedding portrait. The caption places Lichtenstein first. The signifi-cance of this retitling is that, like the title of David Henry Hwang's play, *M. Butterfly,* it ultimately refers to the white man in the story and his strug-gle with sexuality and manhood. The U.S. release title, on the contrary, refers to a specifically Chinese cultural signifier and also to the crux of the movie, for it is after the tensions of the wedding banquet that Simon is left to drive General and Mrs. Gao home, while Wei-wei rapes/seduces Wai-tung and thus becomes pregnant with his child, the child that will root the immigrants in America and into a normative nationalist heterosexuality, thus "suturing" the original castrating wound.

When we examine the body of the immigrant woman in this film, we find that she is eventually caught between the transgenerational and transsexual identity crisis of men in "The Wedding Banquet." The film's Cinderella formulation and the deceptively happy ending bring in the issue of the semiotic function of a somewhat aggressive, yet apparently victimized, "China doll" whose illegal-immigrant status drives the subsequent actions of the film. While her immigration status directs the cinematic avenues of the narrative action, the urgency and the problem of her "illegitimacy" in America are gradually replaced by the sexual and cultural crisis between the gay man and the Chinese father.

The identities of the two main female characters are built upon their roles as transmitters, as catalysts, and as translators for their male counterparts. The film literally begins with the mother's voice on tape translating—and literally speaking for—the father and giving voice to his wish that Wai-tung would marry and procreate. Even when they arrive in the United States, the mother continues to act as the (gift) bearer of the Chinese customs, while the father remains mostly silent (aside from the speech about his own escape from marriage). Most importantly, the mother becomes caught between the lie of the son to the father; she is the bearer of guilt and a secret that, on the one hand, has made her role more significant; yet on the other hand, her agency/identity is completely disintegrated by the overwhelming importance of the connection between father and son. Even her identity as translator is obliterated as everyone realizes that the father himself speaks English and that he was never in need of a translator or transmitter (in fact, he says that he "sees and hears" everything). He reveals to Simon that he knows of his son's homosexuality; this scene represents an acknowledgment of his son's homosexual relationship as well as a reinforcement of a different type of male friendship.

Like the mother, Wei-wei also occupies an "in-between" space within the male milieu. While at one moment she becomes literally the translator between Simon and Mrs. Gao, her pregnancy also makes her a transmitter of a male legacy to the extent that a male identity is implied in her unborn child. Wei-wei's role, however, is much more complicated than that of her mother-in-law. Although her Cinderella transformation from starving illegal immigrant artist to financially stable married legal resident appears to be a product of male generosity and beneficence—a result of Mr. Gao's invest-ment in America, Simon's suggestion, and Wai-tung's cooperation—her ini-tial appearance as a poor, beautiful but driven illegal immigrant/artist never-theless represents a different type of "womanhood" from that of her later mother-in-law. Her origin in Mainland China, furthermore, creates a certain kind of stereotypical discourse around her identity—both artistic and impov-erished. Of utmost importance is her illegal immigrant status; she is now homeless, without a national identity, living under constant threat of being deported to China. She occupies both an economically and socially inferior status, which causes even her female "sexuality" to become somewhat com-promised. On the one hand, she seems to be quite liberal and free-spirited; on the other hand, to some viewers, her hypersexualized behavior with Wai-tung might seem quite transgressive (particularly in the scene where she might be said to have raped him). The first view of Wei-wei is her sweating back and her aggressive drinking—a sensationalized and sexual-ized moment that becomes further emphasized with her casual behavior toward her young and handsome landlord, Wai-tung. However, through her "Cinderella" experience—from poor to rich, from illegal to legal, from desperately single to her marriage to a handsome and educated, though gay, husband—one can argue that Wei-wei is becoming domesticated through-out the movie. She moves from a place she herself describes as not fit for human habitation to sipping cool drinks in Simon's middle-class house, and then she moves from acting the part of a desirable fiancée and wife to her decision to become a mother. Donald Lyons notes that in this film, as in his others, "Lee's spaces are clear sites of moral struggle."[18] She is domesticated, tamed, and desexualized. The scene at the airport when she first meets Wai-tung's parents clearly illustrates her physical domestication: her conserva-tive dress, the closing of her legs and the correcting of her aggressive arm posture, the lowering of her hair, and finally her eagerness to comply with "female" duties as a submissive daughter-in-law by struggling with the lug-gage are all part of her domestic transformation.

Of course, one should not overlook the deliberate construction of Wei-wei as a liberated woman as well as an educated and ambitious artist. Her learned knowledge of Chinese writing and her passion for impressionist art on the one hand represent certain stereotypes about China as a land of op-pressed scholars versus Wai-tung's stereotypical role as a cheap apartment owner from Taiwan;[19] on the other hand, they also connote female inde-pendence and intelligence. Interestingly, even her name, Wei-wei, in Chi-nese transmits a certain masculinity. However, her aggressivity becomes the very element which, ironically, completes the process of her domestica-tion. Her seduction of Wai-tung borders on sexual violence: Wai-tung's saying "no" and the positionality of Wei-wei could qualify this as a "rape" scene. Her sexual aggressiveness toward Wai-tung leads to the pregnancy which ultimately (re)locates her permanently into Simon and Wai-tung's domestic milieu.

The complexity of this scene deserves closer examination. The relationship between Wei-wei's female (hetero)sexuality and Wai-tung's male homosexuality and their respective roles as members in Chinese families are at odds. As the good Chinese daughter, she is expected to do what she does, marry a wealthy, preferably Chinese, man in America. She is not expected to be the sexually liberated starving artist she is at the beginning of the movie. Wai-tung's role as a good Chinese son is to do what his father eventually did: marry and have sons. His homosexuality does not function well in this regard, and considering the pivotal moment in the plot of the wedding-night scene, one has to wonder if his homosexuality is here being shown as an impediment to his fulfillment of his cultural and familial responsibilities. Given our earlier discussion of the strong association of homosexuality with the "West" in this film, is a dichotomy being created between "modern" Western values and "traditional" Chinese values, or is a more subtle negotiation being enacted which recognizes that although Wai-tung could not be openly homosexual in Taiwan, his familial duties need not be opposed to his personal preferences? Likewise, Wei-wei's participation in a "marriage" with Wai-tung and Simon seems to preclude her sexual happiness, while it fulfills her filial obligations.

These interactions are made even more intricate when the role of Simon, Wai-tung's European American lover, is questioned. In light of the heterosexual duties that Wei-wei performs, Simon seems to be the other semiotic construction of a female counterpart. The first dinner scene between Wai-tung and Simon connotes a typical family scene of an overworked masculine figure who strives to appease the agitated feminine counterpart who desires to go on vacation. Simon's "wifely" mastery over Wai-tung's everyday habits and his cooking ability further "feminize" him as the "woman" to Wai-tung's man. This seems to be a reinscription of a heterosexual paradigm where one appears to be more "masculine" and the other more "feminine." Indeed, the kitchen scenes where Wei-wei and Simon cook (or in Wei-wei's case, attempts to cook) show two potential "daughters-in-law," where one fulfills the expectations of the traditional Chinese parents and the other satisfies the sexual desires of the gay husband. However, the issue of race cannot be ignored within these constructions of gender. The fact that Wai-tung is more stereotypically masculine than Simon reverses the stereotype of the feminized Asian man (atypically for American films in general, neither the Taiwanese American man nor the Chinese woman is able to cook), but at the same time it reinscribes the notion that homosexuality, understood erroneously as the feminization of the male, is a particularly "Western" construct.

The question of whether homosexuality is a social construct or a biological determinant is brought up in conjunction with the question of Western influence in the scene between Wai-tung and his mother in the hospital corridor. Wai-tung, faced with the possibility of his father's impending demise, confesses he must tell his mother a secret. Thinking he means Wei-wei's pregnancy, Mrs. Gao sets her herself up for an extreme shock. When he tells her that he is gay, his mother does not understand him to mean that he has always been gay but rather that he has been "turned" homosexual by the influence of being "dislocated" in America.

While this scene is sensitively handled and the mother's point of view is seen as both culturally and generationally determined, another moment in the film raises further questions. In the translation of a line during the English-language fight between Wei-wei, Simon, and Wai-tung at the breakfast table about Wei-wei's pregnancy, the Chinese subtitles show Wei-wei calling the two men "vampires," though she does not say this in English. Is this a deliberate choice, a scribal error, or a translational mistake? It reflects a moment of anxiety and bias about homosexuality that is difficult to reconcile with the otherwise positive light in which the relationship between Simon and Wai-tung is depicted. If the issue of homosexuality is dealt with more positively elsewhere in the film, then what about the uneasy knowledge both the mother and the father bring back with them when they return to Taiwan? What of the sign of "surrender" when the father raises his hands in the final moment of the film? Is it one of acceptance or one of emasculation? And can we call this a "gay" movie when the subject is treated in this ambiguous fashion? At least one reviewer saw *The Wedding Banquet* as "notable for being the first Chinese movie to problematise reactions to a gay relationship rather than the relationship itself,"[20] but the complexity of these reactions is belied by the simplicity of this statement. The very consciousness of the film's construction of the relationship between "gayness" and the reaction to it is revealing of a certain tension surrounding this issue.

In the actual scene of the wedding banquet, followed by the intrusion to the newlyweds' room, both heterosexual union and orthodox tradition are renegotiated. The dramatic irony at play here is quite interesting. As viewers, we recognize an extremely mixed crowd of whites, Asians, heterosexuals, and gays. (Significantly, all the Chinese people appear to be heterosexual while the white male couples upon which the camera quite often focuses appear to be gay.) The white gay onlookers who always look amused, the Chinese heterosexual "jokers" who continually emphasize the past brotherhood shared by the groom and themselves, the exasperated gay groom and his lover, and the heterosexual bride all make this wedding-banquet scene one of the most ironic moments in the film. In a way, the banquet signifies an ongoing containment of homosexuality; even at the end of the film, it is the photo album of the heterosexual tradition of marriage which brings all of the characters closer together, literally and figuratively. The wedding banquet functions as a repeating trope not unlike the always-sleeping, deathlike image of the father throughout the film which continually reinforces the parental pressure on the gay son to procreate. For example, Wai-tung's liaison with Simon can only be transmitted through technology—the cordless phone and one of the pictures in the album. Even at the moment when they are about to perform the sexual act, the camera discovers the father struggling to try on the blood-pressure measuring system. If the wedding banquet and the shadow of the father's mortality act as means to contain the "transgressions" of homosexuality, then can the father's revelation to Simon of his ongoing knowledge, and acceptance, of Simon and Wai-tung's true relationship disrupt this almost homophobic formulation within the film?

• *Eat Drink Man Woman*

> *Identity: the singular meaning of a person, a nation, a race, has undergone a reversal of values. Effacing it used to be the only means of survival for the colonized and exiled; naming it today often means declaring solidarity among the hyphenated people of the Diaspora.*

> *It is hardly surprising then that when identity is doubled, tripled, multiplied across time (generations) and space (cultures), when differences keep on blooming within despite the rejections from without, she [the Diasporic traveler] dares—by necessity. She dares to mix; she dares to cross the borders to introduce into language (verbal, visual, musical) everything monologism has repressed.* TRINH MINH-HA, *WHEN THE MOON WAXES RED*

Eat Drink Man Woman (screenplay by Ang Lee, Hui-ling Wang, and James Schamus) can be read as a kind of sequel to *The Wedding Banquet* given the implied return to Taiwan at the end of that film. As a sequel, it is a comment on the specificities of transnational interactions as well as on the particular vagaries of contemporary Taiwanese society. The scene that opens the film—an empty intersection soon filled with the chaos of motorbikes and cars unleashed by a changing traffic light—becomes a metaphor for a Taiwan growing in many different directions at once. This image of the technological mobility of this society is immediately contrasted with the

Fig. 18. *Eat Drink Man Woman* (Yin shi nan nü), directed by Ang Lee, Taiwan, 1994. British Film Institute.

deceptively harmonious domestic space occupied by Mr. Chu (Sihung Lung) and his three daughters. The violence with which Mr. Chu captures the fish in the small container to prepare it for dinner signals that these dinners, "the Sunday torture ritual," are not the nurturing feasts they appear to be but that the violence of unresolved relations underlies the struggle to maintain domestic harmony. The orgy of cooking belies the repression of appetites ("All the Chu family, one way or another, have their appetites suppressed"[21]) which is slowly resolved in a slightly formulaic fashion. This resolution comes as first the youngest daughter gets pregnant and marries, then the eldest daughter breaks through her "old maid" demeanor and gets married, and finally the father both finds love (with a younger woman) and regains his taste buds through the cooking of the middle daughter, whose culinary talents he had years earlier refused to encourage. The middle daughter's sexual liberty, her subsequent disillusionment with love, her decision to remain within Taiwan instead of taking a job abroad, and finally her "replacement" of the father in the kitchen all speak to issues about the interactions between female independence and familial as well as patriotic loyalties. The end results of these relationships ultimately sum up Lee's message about the inevitable codependency of domestic and national allegiances.

The identity of Taiwan is far from singular in meaning. To name it, we must declare the specifics of its multiplicity. In *The Geopolitical Aesthetic: Cinema and Space in the World System,* Frederic Jameson explores the transcultural spaces of Taipei as they are being reconfigured through cinema: "Taiwan is somehow within the world system as its citizens are in their city boxes: prosperity and constriction all at once; the loss of nature . . . ."[22] Jameson asserts that "if . . . it no longer makes much sense to talk about such cities [as Taipei] in terms of an opposition between the Western and the traditional, then it would seem to follow that . . . notions of national or ethnic identity (of the modernist type) are equally threatened by postmodernity."[23] Thus it would be simplistic and inaccurate to argue that the tension in the film is between a traditional Taiwanese man, Mr. Chu, and his "Westernized" daughters, particularly the middle daughter, Jia-chien, whose work as an airline executive both literally and symbolically transnationalizes her identity. Yet some critics, like John Powers, argue that this is exactly how we are to see the film: "[e]ach daughter embodies one facet of a culture that's surging wildly forward, just like the swarms of motorbikes whose restless, apparently chaotic motion becomes one of Lee's defining images of Taiwanese modernization."[24] In Powers' estimation, the father does not figure as a "facet of a culture that's surging wildly forward"; this energy is reserved for the next generation. Jonathan Romney agrees with this assessment, arguing that "[c]onventional though it is, the most effective strand is the one about Jia-chien, who embodies the new cosmopolitan Taiwan. . . . The twist on Western sexual conditioning is that the one thing she's never been allowed to do is cook."[25] Lizzie Francke argues similarly that the return of Jia-chien to the kitchen "makes manifest the various needs that bind a family by setting a mother back at the heart of it,"[26] suggesting that it is Jia-chien's womanly skills as a cook that are needed to recenter the family, which has only been (mal) nourished by a male for too long. As Romney notes, "[t]here's this discrepancy between the ritual of food presented with love and the difficulty of actually tasting the love in it."[27] Of course, what Romney and the others do not recognize about Jia-chien is not only that she is not allowed to cook but that she has not been allowed to become a chef, which is a male preserve not only in China and Taiwan but in Europe and America as well. Thus the clear divide between "West" and "East" is really less than the transparency to which they attest.

This issue of Jia-chien's cooking is a significant site of contestation in the film—not only in terms of Powers' and Romney's suggestion that Jia-chien and her cooking represent the new wave of "cosmopolitan" Taiwanese culture as opposed to the old stinky "soy sauce jar" of stagnant Chinese traditions represented by her father, Mr. Chu. Jia-chien's identity is indeed caught up with the identity of Taiwan, whether that is traditional or modern, Chinese, native, or "Western." But the answer is more complex than her modern sensibilities (as demonstrated by her sexual freedom) overtaking those of her father. Her decision not to flee but to remain rooted at the heart of the home and her decision to cook are matched by her father's decision not only to marry and start a new family but to share the cooking space with her. When she helps him rediscover his sense of taste through her cooking, she is demonstrating the fluidity of the "soy sauce" of Chinese culture. But it is her father's decision to marry the young divorcée, rather than the woman's older mother, that breaks the confining "jar" of traditions. And it is her father's marriage that leaves Jia-chien able to make a choice that is not based on binary oppositional structures. Had she left the family home rather than take care of her elderly father, she would have been acting in opposition to traditional expectations. Likewise, had she remained, she would have opposed the "modern" sensibilities of the "West," which place individual satisfaction over the welfare of the family. Instead, at the end of the film she has neither abandoned the past as represented by her father nor embraced it, because even her father's traditionalism is not confined to the past. He has finally been able to move beyond his wife's death to embrace a young wife and her young daughter. Jia-chien's position as the new family chef is an "in-between" terrain from which she can move in many directions. Though she seems in some ways to have been left behind, in actuality she has been let free. But this is not the easy "freedom" of modern sexuality that she practiced at the film's opening; this freedom requires slow and deliberate movements to work through it. In recentering herself in her identity as chef, Jia-chien charts the path of the new Taiwan. Trinh Minh-ha says that "[i]dentity is a way of re-departing. Rather, the return to a denied heritage allows one to start again with different re-departures, different pauses, different arrivals."[28] Now that Jia-chien has returned to her "denied heritage," she can begin again. In this sense, although she and the film never leave Taiwan, she is clearly situated as a member of the diaspora.

The relationship between Jia-chien and her older sister, Jia-jen, is fraught with miscommunication and displacement and is significantly revealed in the scene where they are washing dishes—or, metaphorically putting their home in order. The early death of their mother had left Jia-jen feeling responsible for filling that role for Jia-chien, but in doing so she abdicated her position as sister. Jia-chien laments being abandoned by her sister in that way. Furthermore, as they grew older, Jia-jen became a sexually conservative Christian (perhaps to match her role as mother-figure), while Jia-chien became a sexually liberated executive. Each suspects the other of disapproving of her morals. What makes their relationship even more complex, however, is that Jia-chien begins to fall in love with one of her colleagues, a man named Li Kai (Winston Chao), whom she suspects to be the chemistry student who jilted her older sister in college. This wound appears to be what caused Jia-jen to retreat from the world, but we eventually discover that Jia-jen made up the whole story in order to create a barrier against intimacy—even with her family. "Since identity can very well speak its plurality without suppressing its singularity, heterologies of knowledge give all practices of the self a festively vertiginous dimension."[29] Although the plurality of Jia-jen's identity is largely a plot device, the revelation of her desire to be a mother to her sister ironically relocates her outside of the repressed atmosphere of her father's home. Critic Lizzie Francke's observation that "[t]he vision of food being prepared provides the mise en scene of desire deferred"[30] can also be read backwards such that the vision of Jia-chien and Jia-jen doing the dishes "provides the mise en scene" of desire satisfied. It is when Jia-chien reveals her desire for a sister rather than a mother in Jia-jen that the latter is able to become who she really is with all the complexity that entails (a modern, conservative, Christian, sexually aggressive Taiwanese woman), rather than being who she thought her family needed her to be.

Unlike the formulation of the "spinster turned sensual woman" story of Jia-jen, the story of the younger sister—Jia-ning—is one of naïveté and immature love. The construction of the "melancholic" boy-in-love and the overdramatization of the love triangle among three "teenagers" is in many ways a parody of comic book romance.[31] Their innocence, or perhaps even ignorance, belies the danger and tragedy of Jia-ning's unexpected pregnancy. Furthermore, her boyfriend comes from a clearly "dysfunctional" family—his parents are abroad most of the year, leaving him in a nearly empty house with few signs of habitation. His "fatherhood" seems to be built upon invisible financial resources that no one in the film questions. This lack of inquiry is endemic of this story line. In fact, it is with little ceremony or question that the Chu family sees Jia-ning off after her announcement that she is pregnant. The superficial treatment of Jia-ning's story is quite disturbing. While it is clear that the focus of the film is the relationship between Mr. Chu and the middle daughter, Jia-chien, the depictions of "innocent" love and the spinster finding a husband remain not only flat but also dangerously uncomplicated.

The last moment in this film is the image of Jia-chien and Mr. Chu sitting in the kitchen, which has become hers. She stands up slightly and feeds him with her chopsticks. The last words of the film are *nüer* and *ba:*

"daughter" and "father." This moment is highly enigmatic. It appears at one level to be a simple reaffirmation of their familial relationship to one another. But as they verbally reaffirm their relationship as father and daughter, they also visually reverse their roles. Jia-chien now is the provider of food and stability; her father is the one who faces the challenges and uncertainties of a new life and a new family. The two have resolved the tension that began the film: Jia-chien being trapped by her feelings of responsibility toward a man she thought was in his declining years, and Mr. Chu negotiating his own identity as a member of a changing society. He is no longer living in the past but has moved out of the house, which is filled with memories of his dead wife and the life they never lived together. He is no longer merely a representative of the traditional past.

What makes this scene even more resonant is the fact that earlier, when we see a photograph of Mr. Chu's dead wife, she is depicted by the same actress who plays Jia-chien. Thus Lizzie Francke's observation that the return of Jia-chien to the kitchen "makes manifest the various needs that bind a family by setting a mother back at the heart of it" has multiple meanings.[32] The oedipal significance of the relationship between Mr. Chu and Jia-chien is complicated not only by Jia-jen's confessed attempts to fulfill the role of mother but also by Jia-chien's "tomboy" wish to be a chef like her father. In this sense Jia-jen is trying to be the son her father never had. One troubling aspect of Ang Lee's revision of traditional culture is his continual glorification of fraternal love. When Mr. Chu's old cooking companion, the man Jia-jen affectionately refers to as "Uncle," dies, this motivates the dénouement of the film. His death causes so much anxiety for Jia-chien about her own father's health that she decides to stay close to home and assume the role of "mother" in the kitchen. Ironically, it is in fulfilling her wish to be "like her father," that is, to be a chef, that Jia-chien is reinscribed into the domestic role she had tried so hard to escape. The "Uncle" in this film is matched by the army driver turned restaurant owner in *The Wedding Banquet*. His unswerving loyalty to General Gao motivates the central action of the film—it is he who offers to give a wedding banquet for the marriage of the son of his former commander. All of this is based in uncomplicated heterosexual male bonding. All three of Lee's films starring Sihung Lung have been loosely categorized as his "father knows best" trilogy.[33] Lee's failure to problematize "brotherhood," not unlike his unwillingness to deconstruct heterosexual tendencies in all his films (though he cannot be held as accountable for the inevitable ending of *Sense and Sensibility*), remains a disappointing element in his otherwise complex vision of social interactions. In other words, his Hollywood-like endings—one must not forget that he is heavily influenced by his education in U.S. cinema—invite criticism about his concern for marketability in the "West." Ironically, Lee's adaptation of Jane Austen's novel, *Sense and Sensibility,* is both very marketable and very "Western."

• *Sense and Sensibility*

Sense and Sensibility at first appears to be diametrically atypical of Ang Lee's films. Of course, there is the obvious difference that Lee did not coauthor the screenplay with writer and actress Emma Thompson, and therefore we should have little expectation that the concerns manifested in his earlier films should make themselves known here. And indeed, on a superficial level, little of this film of nineteenth-century English manners and romance seems related to Lee's concern with contemporary transnational Chinese and Taiwanese generational interactions. There is, to begin with, no strong father figure—unlike the ubiquitous and profoundly present father portrayed by Taiwanese actor Sihung Lung in Lee's earlier films. Furthermore, the film is set in rural, aristocratic nineteenth-century England, as opposed to the United States or Taiwan. However, the intimacy and complexity of relationships between parents and children, between siblings, and between those who will come together to form new family configurations remain consistent throughout Lee's oeuvre even as the old social dynamics are changing. As in Lee's earlier works, the displacement of the individual and the family is a central concern of *Sense and Sensibility,* both in the original novel and in Lee and Thompson's adaptation. The heroine must move away from home in order to discover the truth of her situation. Being at home somehow blinds her, as well as the rest of Lee's protagonists, to what they can discover about themselves when they are forced to cope with the displacement of their identity.

Because Lee did not participate in writing the screenplay for *Sense and Sensibility,* as he did with his earlier films, a close reading of the details of the plot and themes of this film would serve less purpose than such an examination of the previous films. We therefore focus instead primarily on the conflict over Lee's identity and his identification with the film. References to the plot will largely act to clarify this argument.

Richard Corliss, in his review of *Sense and Sensibility,* speculated that Ang Lee "will probably be the first Asian to receive an Oscar nomination for best director."[34] Corliss' prediction would seem to have been a safe one given that Lee received such a nomination from the Golden Globe Awards. Given the critical and popular acclaim of his last two films, it seems only reasonable that the even more popular *Sense and Sensibility* would win him an Academy Award nomination. But despite the overall success of the film in Academy Awards nominations—one for Emma Thompson as screen-writer and another as lead actress, in addition to five others, including Best Picture—Lee did not receive the expected nomination.

We would speculate that it is Lee's apparent "difference" in identity from the "identity" of the film which made such a nomination unlikely. More than simple "difference," however, we would argue that it is Lee's position as a non-Westerner directing a film about such an inimitably British subject which prevented his recognition by the Academy. Trinh Minh-ha discusses the problem of non-Western filmmakers who step outside the boundaries of their "own" culture as subject matter for their films:

> Non-Westerners may or may not want to make films on their own societies. . . . Any mutation in identity, in essence, in regularity, and even in physical place poses a problem, if not a threat, in terms of clas-sification and control. If you can't locate the other, how can you locate your-self?[35]

No article or interview about *Sense and Sensibility* passes without some comment about Ang Lee's difference of identity from the understood iden-tity of the film. These comments are generally in the form of an argument about why Lee, a late twentieth-century Taiwanese American man, is in fact (despite all unspoken expectations to the contrary) the perfect director for such a project. Lee's struggles to deal with complex familial and societal interactions and obligations, according to both Emma Thompson and pro-ducer Lindsay Doran, are concerns that address all cultures. They both agree that Ang Lee was the correct choice to direct *Sense and Sensibility*.

> After she [Thompson] saw *The Wedding Banquet,* directed by Lee, she discovered that Ang Lee's meticulous talent for details and candor in family dramas made him the most appropriate candidate to direct and bring forth the complexity of emotions and relationships central to the English family drama [by Austen]. . . . He also helped to interject many Eastern cultural expressions in a world renown English novel . . . in expanding and articulating interpersonal relationships, a topic inher-ently congenital and intrinsic to all cultures. . . . Doran [agreeing with Thompson] also pointed out that although the geographic background of *Sense* was England, its central topics would be appropriate for any nation. Thus, she realized the film needed a director who understood intricate human emotions and romantic entanglements. . . . Lee was not only a Taiwanese director but also a man. Both his Eastern as well as masculine perspectives broadened and redefined a work which has traditionally been labeled as Western and feminine.[36]

Film critic Donald Lyons argues that Lee's sensibilities are in perfect synch with the demands of nineteenth-century British fiction. Lyons calls Lee "an artist of family and society,"[37] and indeed *Sense and Sensibility* is an affirmation of that characterization. The Confucian principles of *ren* (humanity) and *li* (etiquette) are a perfect match, in Lyons' view, for Jane Austen's concern with emotional sensibility and social sense. Can we therefore call this film "British Taiwanese"? Or "British Taiwanese American"? In dealing with this film, we begin to see the difficulty and perhaps even the absurdity of this kind of labeling. Trinh Minh-ha understands this issue of labeling as the need to divide between "outside" and "inside"—in other words, between axes of power rather than merely between neutral "differences." The difficulty, she argues, is in the very process of definition and identification itself: "Where should the dividing line between outsider and insider stop? How should it be defined? By skin color . . . ? By language . . . ? By nation . . . ? By geography . . . ? What about those with hyphenated identities and hybrid realities?"[38] "Hyphenated identities and hybrid realities" are caused by violations of boundaries. Whether sexual or national, "[v]iolations of boundaries have always led to displacement, for the in-between zones are the shifting grounds on which the (doubly) exiled walk."[39] To use an image from *Sense and Sensibility,* when Marianne violates the boundaries of decorum by openly expressing her regard for Willoughby, she suffers by a displacement from the regard of her society—a displacement that could have the very real consequence of causing her untimely death, as illustrated by Colonel Brandon's story of the girl he once loved, whom he identifies with Marianne. Marianne's transgression is not merely one of decorum; her actions cause a disruption in her identity as an English lady. Her wild ride with Willoughby through town and her later highly visible approach toward him at the ball identify her as something less than a "lady." Her reinstatement into this identity is allowed only after she has walked through "the in-between zones [of] shifting grounds" (the land between Willoughby's home and the Palmers') and submitted her identity to Colonel Brandon's auspices. Insofar as she "reminds" him of his lost love, however, she will always be marked by his identification of her. In contrast, Eleanor's union with Edward Ferris, while it does save her from her identity as a "spinster," need not function to alter her identity as a lady, for her sense has allowed her to maintain that label throughout the film. The end shot of this film stresses the shower of money thrown by Colonel Brandon into the crowd; thus, ironically, it is Marianne who reaps the financial rewards of her elder sister's propriety, while we are reminded that Edward Ferris' fortune resides in the hands of Colonel Brandon. The ending, as depicted by Ang Lee, is highly enigmatic. Eleanor's "ladylike" behavior does not serve to maintain her class standing. The image of the golden coins emphasizes Marianne's good fortune, while her sister appears almost poor in contrast. The stress between the proprieties of tradition and the freedom of emotion is a major theme in each of Ang Lee's films.

With Lee's previous films, his identity seems to be less at issue than it is with *Sense and Sensibility*. *Eat Drink Man Woman* is set entirely in Taiwan, and although Lee has lived in the United States since 1977, he is still identified (by the placement of his films in film catalogues and video stores as well as in movie reviews) as a Taiwanese director. *The Wedding Banquet* did raise the issue of whether it could indeed be called a "gay" film given that the filmmaker professed to be "heterosexual." However, Lee's "authenticity" as a Taiwanese American man making a film largely about a Taiwanese American man and his parents was never in question. Although his first film, *Pushing Hands,* is primarily about an elderly man from Mainland China and his European American daughter-in-law, neither of which Lee can claim to be, his distance from the subject matter does not seem to be worthy of comment in any article we have found on the film. In fact, Lee's "authenticity" and his identity with the films he produces have seemed to be fairly transparent until the question of *Sense and Sensibility* arose. But the issue of "identity" is itself never fully transparent, as Rey Chow notes: "In the politics of identifying 'authentic' natives, several strands of the word 'identification' are at stake: How do we identify the native? How do we identify with her? How do we construct the native's 'identity'? What processes of identification are involved?"[40]

Indeed, what processes of identification are involved, and are at stake, in identifying Ang Lee? What threat is made to the existing order of cinema personalities? For the Hollywood establishment, as represented by the Academy of Motion Picture Arts and Sciences, the lines between insider and outsider must remain clearly defined. But these lines are continually eroding. The small-budget independent niche films that used to enjoy obscure cult status are now gaining increased popularity—and commensurate financial success. While "foreign" (particularly European, but more recently Japanese and even Chinese) directors have long been given a "status" location in the cinema hierarchy, they nevertheless remained "outsiders" in Hollywood. The anxiety caused by the increased popularity of independent and foreign directors, is not, however, the same as the displacement of identity caused by Ang Lee's work on *Sense and Sensibility*. This anxiety over Ang Lee's "identity label" is much more profound, for it indicates the dissolution of national boundaries that Hollywood has been so fundamental in maintaining.

And yet, despite all of this discussion of difference, *Sense and Sensibility* is more like Lee's other films than one would imagine. One primary element linking all the films is the (dis)placement of the father figure. While the first three films, the "father knows best" trilogy, begin with anxiety about the position and power of patriarchy, the major action in *Sense* is also driven by problems that arise from the displacement (in this case the death) of the father. In some ways, all four films are about attempts to restore the patriarchal order so as to recuperate the dislocated familial and societal harmony. For Ang Lee, the "restoration" of patriarchal positions is in actuality both a recreation and a reconstruction. The new patriarchy, although still within the bounds of heterosexual culture, is nevertheless a renegotiation of the old with the new rather than a mere reinscription or an overturning of traditions.

Ang Lee's close scrutiny of cultural and generational differences, in each of his films, once again raises the issue of the conflict and renegotiation between the supposedly spiritual tendencies of the "East" and the materialistic tendencies of the "West." Lee continues to uphold the value of the traditions of Chinese culture through his depiction of the three fathers portrayed by Sihung Lung while retaining a sense of the contemporary locations of those fathers and their families. Simultaneously, Lee remains quite realistic in his portrayals of the everyday lifestyles of Taiwan as well as of the Chinese diaspora communities worldwide. The emergence of a transnational sensibility, not only in the films of Ang Lee but in other Chinese and Chinese diaspora cinemas as well, represents a symbolic breaking of the "soy sauce jar" that Po Yang criticizes as the restricting force of Chinese culture. Insofar as the "soy sauce" itself represents the binding force of Chinese culture—that is, that which makes it Chinese, no matter its temporal or spatial location—in breaking the "soy sauce jar," these transnational cinemas have demonstrated the viability rather than the stagnation of the "soy sauce." This revaluation contradicts the binary oppositional construction of Asian "tradition" as opposed to European "modernization." As Shoichi Saeki writes, "[m]odernization seems to be a term applicable only to non-European countries, which experienced a radical kind of transformation under Western impact. 'Modernization' [in Japan] was, in large measure, 'Westernization.' "[41] This is as equally true of Taiwan as it has been of Japan. Debaters over the "East-West" controversy retain a deep concern over the role of Chinese traditions in the modern world. Ang Lee's boundary-crossing cinema offers new methods of brewing and mixing the sauce to meet the changes and challenges offered in contemporary global cultural economies.[42]

· Notes

1. Although we would argue that the cultural constructs known as "East" and "West" engage in a false binary oppositional structure, we use the terms both to question the binary structure inherent in the arguments we outline as well as for lack of better generalities.

2. Although we use the Westernized version of Ang Lee's name, Po Yang's name is presented in the Chinese order, surname first, given name last. Po Yang is the pen name of Guo Yidong.

3. Po Yang, "Zhuyao chengfen" [An important ingredient], in *Si bu rencuo ji* [Stubborn to the end] (Taipei: Pingyuan chubanshe, 1967), 25–27. Translation by Eileen Fung. All other translations here are also by Eileen Fung.

4. Rey Chow, *Writing Diaspora: Tactics of Intervention in Contemporary Cultural Studies* (Bloomington: Indiana University Press, 1993), 9.

5. bell hooks, *Black Looks: Race and Representation* (Boston, Mass.: South End Press, 1992), 21.

6. See John Powers, "Wine, Song and Right-Wing Humor," *Vogue* 184, no. 18 (1993), and Donald Lyons, "Passionate Precision: Sense and Sensibility," *Film Comment* 32, no. 1 (1996): 36–42.

7. Lyons, "Passionate Precision," 40.

8. Mal Vincent, "Pushing Hands," *The Virginian-Pilot,* August 10, 1995.

9. Lyons, "Passionate Precision," 40.

10. The Chinese American's accentless English is an ironic reversal. Instead of signaling his ability to "fit in" to contemporary culture, in this case, it signals his lack of knowledge, which will lead inevitably to his defeat.

11. hooks, *Black Looks,* 31.

12. Homi K. Bhabha, "Introduction: Narrating the Nation," in *Nation and Narration,* ed. Homi K. Bhabha (New York: Routledge, 1990), 2.

13. Eve Kososfsky Sedgewick, *The Epistemology of the Closet* (Berkeley: University of California Press, 1990), 15.

14. Bhabha, "Introduction," 4.

15. Homi K. Bhabha, "DissemiNation: Time, Narrative, and the Margins of the Modern Nation," in *Nation and Narration,* ed. Homi K. Bhabha (New York: Routledge, 1990), 301.

16. Kaja Silverman, *Semiotics and Suture* (London: Oxford University Press, 1993), 196.

17. On this topic, see Pai Hsien-yung's novel, *Crystal Boys* (San Francisco: Gay Sunshine Press, 1990).

18. Lyons, "Passionate Precision," 40.

19. The reviewer for *Sight and Sound* noted that, "[t]hanks to this backstory, the fake marriage could be taken as a ruinous parody of the reunification of China and Taiwan." Tony Rayns, "Xiyan," *Sight and Sound* 3, no. 10 (1993): 59.

20. Rayns, "Xiyan," 56.

21. Jonathan Romney, "Food Glorious Food," *New Statesman and Society* 8, no. 336 (January 20, 1995): 33.

22. Fredric Jameson, *The Geopolitical Aesthetic: Cinema and Space in the World System* (Bloomington: Indiana University Press, 1992), 155.

23. Jameson, *The Geopolitical Aesthetic,* 117.

24. Powers, "Wine, Song and Right-Wing Humor," 139.

25. Romney, "Food Glorious Food," 33.

26. Lizzie Francke, "Yin Shi Nan Nu (Eat Drink Man Woman)," *Sight and Sound* 5, no. 1 (1995): 63.

27. Romney, "Food Glorious Food," 33.

28. Minh-ha Trinh, *When the Moon Waxes Red: Representation, Gender, and Cultural Politics* (New York: Routledge, 1991), 14.

29. Trinh, *When the Moon Waxes Red,* 14.

30. Franke, "Yin Shi Nan Nu," 53.

31. The word *teenage* here is metaphorical as well as literal. Although we never find out their exact ages, their student status and their employment at Wendy's (which is surely also a comment about U.S. imperialist food culture consuming the father's Chinese cultural heritage) create a picture of a stereotypical teenage lifestyle. The immaturity of their actions and their lack of understanding about love, particularly in juxtaposition with the worldly second sister, deliberately create an image of innocence that seems to have little purpose in the film other than to fulfill a Taiwanese cultural expectation of a story about the loves of three sisters.

32. Francke, "Yin Shi Nan Nu," 63.

33. Vincent, "Pushing Hands."

34. Richard Corliss, "Ang Lee: Persuasion," *Time International,* January 29, 1996.

35. Trinh, *When the Moon Waxes Red,* 71, 73.

36. Lindsay Doran and Emma Thompson, review of *Sense and Sensibility, Guoji ribao* (International News), January 22, 1996, translated by Eileen Fung.

37. Lyons, "Passionate Precision," 41.

38. Trinh, *When the Moon Waxes Red,* 73.

39. Trinh, *When the Moon Waxes Red,* 70.

40. Chow, *Writing Diaspora,* 28–29.

41. Shoichi Saeki, "The Role of Western Literature in the Modernization of Japan," in *Thirty Years of Turmoil in Asian Literature,* lectures delivered at the Fourth Asian Writers Conference, April 25–May 2, 1976, Taipei (Taipei: Taipei Chinese Center, International P.E.N., no date), 188.

42. Reports vary about Lee's future film projects. Richard Corliss mentions that Lee's plans include a U.S. family drama called *Ice Storm,* and Taiwanese newspapers claim he will begin work on a martial arts costume drama based on Wang Dulu's novel, *Sleeping Tiger, Hidden Dragon* (Wohu canglong).

Chapter 8

Transnational Action
John Woo, Hong Kong, Hollywood
.
Anne T. Ciecko

Hong Kong cinema poses a number of interesting problems for film scholars. A comprehensive film history remains to be written, and the work that has been done by Hong Kong film critics and historians has yet to be translated.[1] Meanwhile, old prints of films (and collective memory) are disappearing.[2] Without proper documentation, collection, and preservation, it is as if Hong Kong cinema exists only in the present—and its future is unknown. Who knows how 1997 will change the shape of Hong Kong cinema? Another thorny issue is that of identity: Who is a Hong Kong director, and what constitutes a Hong Kong film? In discussing Hong Kong cinema, as Paul Fonoroff has asserted, one must always consider cultural and linguistic crosscurrents (the language of the current Hong Kong output is almost exclusively Cantonese, subtitled in English and Chinese[3]) and the interrelationships between Hong Kong production and the industries of Mainland China and Taiwan,[4] not to mention the global audiences in Africa, Latin America, Japan, Asian communities in Europe and North America (especially the Chinese diaspora—"Chinatowns" around the world). Finally, to the Western spectator, Hong Kong film is often perceived as synonymous with the popular in its most degraded sense, for example, "chopsocky" martial arts films as opposed to the "art" films of the Chinese Fifth-Generation filmmakers (although, as Nick Browne has suggested, the highly commercial "action" mode in Hong Kong cinema can be viewed as the most directly "political"[5]). In this essay, I will explore the status of John Woo (Wu Yusen) and action cinema in a transnational context. Born on the Mainland, reared in Hong Kong, and now expatriated to the United States (living in Los Angeles) for political and practical reasons, Woo is an émigré director in the process of becoming.[6]

· Hong Kong Action: Visual Pleasure and the Transnational

For much of his American audience, John Woo's name is synonymous with "action" films, which, according to Richard Dyer, promote an active—even erotic

—engagement with the world: "going out into it, doing to the environment; yet enjoyment of them means allowing them to come to you, take you over, do you."[7] Indeed, Woo's films, specifically his 1980s Hong Kong romantic gangster thriller films[8] and his Hollywood debut, *Hard Target* (1993), invite the movement of this sort of highly charged spectatorial pleasure from identification to active manipulation and interaction. However, his films move and act through the world in other ways, through the hybridity of genre as cultural representation.

"Transnationalism" has been defined as "a process of global consolidation."[9] The United States leads the world in the transnational spread of commercial media, especially entertainment products (e.g., films), which suggests the global hegemony of Hollywood film styles, genres, and so forth. Films from major Asian production sites like Hong Kong, however, have established audiences in the United States as well as Asia. The implication of this fact is that crossover Hong Kong films must somehow embody "transnational culture." The Hong Kong movies that visit international festivals (e.g., films from Tsui Hark's Film Workshop and from Golden Harvest Films) "are far from typical of the industry as a whole."[10] Presumably, these texts are open enough that even specific film genres "allow different audiences to fill in desired and potentially distinct meanings."[11] During the 1980s and early 1990s, the popularity of Hong Kong films at home surpassed that of overseas and even Hollywood imports. For example, John Woo's *Once a Thief* (1991) was more of a local box-office success than the Hollywood blockbuster *Terminator 2*. However, historically (after 1945), the local industry was not geared exclusively to the Hong Kong market. Exceptions to the local production and consumption dynamic have included internationally successful action films, such as those starring Bruce Lee and Jackie Chan. John Woo's films are genealogically linked to these martial arts vehicles, but they also tap into other local and imported genres. Their visual stylistics suggest art-house aspirations as well as (local and international) popular appeal. Woo's *The Killer* (1989) demonstrates the influence of Chinese and Hong Kong genres such as the martial chivalry films and swordplay epics, as well as Hollywood genres such as the western, the gangster film, the hardboiled detective film/film noir/thriller, and melodrama. The film can be read as a supremely nostalgic (and gun-loving), self-conscious commentary on genre.

The actual world (or more accurately, the topos of "nation") depicted within the diegesis of a John Woo "Hong Kong" film is a constructed image, an illusion. In the ironically titled *A Better Tomorrow* (1986), one of the all-time successes of Hong Kong cinema, John Woo's ubiquitous star, Chow Yun-fat, as Mark, face bloodied and bandaged, puffs on a cigarette and observes: "I never realized Hong Kong looked so good at night. . . . Like most things, it won't last; that's for sure." The character's wistful musings resonate with a sense of imminent change, which, Ackbar Abbas has argued, becomes a marker of the emergence of a new Hong Kong cinema. A defining moment is signaled by the 1984 Sino-British Joint Declaration returning Hong Kong to China in 1997. It won't last. Hong Kong is seen with nostalgia, "with new eyes. It is as if the possibility of the disappearance of this social and cultural space led to seeing it in all its complexity and contradiction for the first time: an instance Benjamin would have said, of love at last sight."[12] The gangster society of *A Better Tomorrow* is not "real," as Woo himself has asserted in an interview, but the product of memory and personal and international cinephilia: "It's a hybrid of all the worlds of all the films I loved, an imaginary place recreated from the [American] gangster films I saw when I was young. I'm a dreamer."[13]

Similarly, the opening images during the title sequence of Woo's breakthrough international success (despite its X rating for violence), *The Killer,* offer a few establishing glimpses of the city as iconic spectacle, as a postcard. Hong Kong, the setting for the narrative, is also a fantasy space—the location for an action film about a hired gunman, with a most generic title. Baudrillard's concept of the simulacrum and his famous example of Disneyland ("a perfect model of all the entangled orders of simulation"[14]) are evoked by the extreme artificiality of the mise-en-scène. Perhaps the most striking examples are scenes with an almost cartoon-like hyper-realism within a chapel filled with white birds, a waxen-white plaster Madonna, and brightly lit by white candles (and ultimately splattered with much red blood). Even more explicit are the mock pet names the hired killer and the cop give each other—Mickey Mouse and Dumbo—as their good guy/bad guy typology is blurred. It is a not uncommon practice in contemporary Hong Kong action films to borrow cartoonish American names for (anti)heroes—for example, King Kong in *Aces Go Places* and Wonder Woman in *Heroic Trio.*

Hard Boiled (1992), Woo's follow-up film to *The Killer,* also participates in an explicitly represented discourse of hybrid identity. For example, this exchange occurs between Inspector Yuen (Chow Yun-fat)—nicknamed Tequila —and the cop Tony (Tony Leung) in a restaurant filled with caged birds:

> You ever thought about leaving Hong Kong, emigrating?
> No, not me, Tequila. I'm a true Hong Konger. I'll live and die in this town. I don't want to go anywhere else. How could I get a fantastic breakfast like this?
> At a Chinese restaurant anywhere.
> But it's better right here.

The dialogue is telling in a number of ways. Tony defines his "true" identity by the town where he plans to spend his entire life, as a part of a social-

Fig. 19. *The Killer* (Diexue shuangxiong), directed by John Woo, Hong Kong, 1989. British Film Institute.

economic nexus. His words are spoken like a true capitalist; yet implicit in his remarks is a recognition of the ways local Hong Kong culture, in this case cuisine and eating rituals, is tied to China. Tequila (nicknamed after his favorite drink, a mixture of tequila and 7-Up, a Hong Kong favorite) reminds him of the cultural currency of Chinese culture in the global economy; a "Chinese" restaurant could conceivably exist anywhere. However, Tony desires to fix Hong Kong as a cultural site, as home. Yet visually and iconographically (via the birdcages), this sense of borrowed or reinterpreted culture is represented as potentially confining and restrictive.

A number of critical characterizations of Hong Kong New Wave cinema suggest that it emerged from a general lack of sociopolitical and cultural certainty. For example, Li Cheuk-to states,

> Although a modern consciousness took root in the 1970s, there was an attempt at the same time to develop a local culture to fill the vacuum

left by the demise of traditional ways. From this perspective, the popularity of the "romantic-hero" genre and the resurfacing of the idea of a new paradigm reflect the crisis of confidence felt by Hong Kong people in the late 1980s, as does the genre's preoccupation with such themes as betrayal of friendship and fatalism.[15]

The possibility of narratives of national identity (or national allegory in the Jamesonian sense) is muddied by Hong Kong's pre-postcolonial status as a British crown colony (peopled by many refugees from China and their families) on the verge of the 1997 return to the People's Republic of China. Esther Yau describes this as "colonial-Chinese cultural syncretism": "The economic environment of Hong Kong is the result of international collaboration. . . . The political identity of Hong Kong is . . . the product of a pragmatic kind of complicity conducive to ideological ambivalence or dubiety."[16] One might read Hong Kong films, then, as responding to an existential dilemma, demonstrating, as Yau describes, "a skillful adaptation of the ideological codes and functions of Hollywood to a context in which the public's preoccupations are survival and upward mobility."[17] However, as Li Cheuk-to explains, the rise of the Hong Kong New Wave films had much to do with a sense that these filmmakers were indeed "genuinely local"—that is, born, reared, and educated in the territory—and thus apt to represent things from a Hong Kong perspective or aesthetic, albeit an often Westernized (or internationalized) one.[18]

For American audiences during the 1980s, John Woo occupied a primarily cult status, as a fan culture, albeit largely an underground one, developed.[19] The director's fame as an action auteur increased after festival acclaim and after European and American distributors circulated *The Killer* and other Woo gangster films. A bootleg—then legitimate—video market for his films was established in the 1980s and early 1990s. Finally, Hollywood invited Woo to become the first Asian to direct a major Hollywood studio picture. The landmark significance of this offer is underscored by its coverage in the trade papers. In an article in *Variety* Frank Segers described the situation: "A rare helmer from the territory surfaces in the U.S. to take charge of modestly budgeted specialty market pics, such as *Slam Dance* and *Chan is Missing* by Hong Kong-born Wayne Wang. Until now commercial pics have been *off limits*" (my emphasis).[20] With his Hollywood debut as "helmer," in *Variety* parlance, Woo asserted his transnational status by virtue of his integration into—or within the limits of—the American filmic matrix of commercial film production via a major studio, (appropriately named) Universal.

• Hollywood and Hybridity: *Hard Target*

The popular cinema, according to Yvonne Tasker in her book-length study of gender, genre, and the action cinema, "forms one space in which identities can be affirmed, dissolved and redefined within a fantasy space."[21] However, this process is complicated by national, ethnic, racial, and gender identities. During the summer of 1994, one of the biggest film hits in Hong Kong was an American import, the action flick *Speed* starring Keanu Reeves. As a reassertion of the hegemony of Hollywood, this was, according to Tony Rayns, "the first time since the mid-60's that Hollywood imports . . . outgrossed local hits."[22] Reeves-as-star, however, is arguably also a rather atypical action hero, an unconventional and destabilizing figure of masculinity (overtly "Orientalized" as Bertolucci's *Little Buddha* [1994]).

Examining the Hollywood action output of the 1980s and the stars who emerged—especially Arnold Schwarzenegger and Sylvester Stallone—one gets an overwhelming sense of how action stars were constructed according to standards of racially and politically encoded masculinity: white and conservative. The persona of Vietnam veteran Rambo and the public politics of Schwarzenegger came to personify Reaganism and Republicanism, even neofascism and the new right wing. In Hollywood, few 1980s big-budget action pictures centered on a non-Caucasian hero, although the Black "buddy" became a common figure. In the Hollywood tradition, a villain might often be marked by signifiers of "otherness" and marginality.

In the 1990s, Jason Scott Lee has come to typify the all-purpose Asian (indeed the all-purpose ethnic) in adventure epics, most notably in the biopic of a Hong Kong action superstar, *Dragon: The Bruce Lee Story* (1993).[23] His body is often eroticized for filmic consumption as the exotic—even androgynous—"other." (An extreme case of this is his recent role in Disney's live-action adaptation of *Jungle Book*.) I would argue, however, that the figure of Hong Kong superstar Chow Yun-fat does not perform the same function in Woo's action films, as screened by American audiences. In a country with a notorious aversion to foreign-language films and affinity for American remakes (indeed, the story of the would-be remake of *The Killer* now is the stuff of myth), Woo's Hong Kong films will probably always occupy a cult or novelty status—and a lucrative specialty video market. Xenophobia has a delimiting effect on transnational representations in the global economic exchange.

Within the Hollywood sexual politics of representation, the action star is traditionally larger than life, an iconic "pin-up" with superior physical capacities.[24] Chow Yun-fat is never imaged/imagined in Woo's films according to this visual/syntactical paradigm of near-naked musculature.[25] More emphasis is placed on his stylized clothes—and the bloodstains they acquire. Facial closeups abound, as Chow Yun-fat's visage rather than his body is used expressively to develop character (via "acting"); he is certainly not a "poser" à la bodybuilding culture and aesthetics (the passive-aggressive Schwarzenegger-Stallone model of self-display). Throughout the 1980s romantic gangster films, he is singularly "oral" (i.e., psychosexually immature), constantly putting things into his mouth—fingers, food, gum, cigarettes, matches even. Physical affection with female characters ("love interests") are rare, minimizing the representation of the action hero as spectacle within the narrative of heterosexual romance and emphasizing chivalry and sentimentality. Male bonding (sanctioned homosociality), however, is enormously important in these films, as in their Hollywood generic precedents, such as the classical western. Likewise weaponry.

In an important essay on "Masculinity as Spectacle," Stephen Neale describes such a dynamic in terms of the genre of the western, in particular Sergio Leone's shoot-outs:

> We see male bodies stylized and fragmented by close-ups, but our look is not direct, it is heavily mediated by the looks of characters involved. And those looks are marked not by desire, but rather by fear, or hatred, or aggression. The shoot-outs are moments of spectacle, points at which the narrative hesitates, comes to a momentary halt, but they are also points at which the drama is finally resolved, a suspense in the cumulation of the narrative drive. They thus involve an imbrication of both forms of looking, their intertwining designed to minimize and displace the eroticism they each tend to involve, to disavow any explicitly erotic look at the male body.[26]

(The connection to Leone's "spaghetti" genre is particularly appropriate. As James Wolcott has noted, "John Woo has become the most exciting cult-icon director from overseas since Sergio Leone put Clint Eastwood in a poncho."[27])

By rendering his star sexually unthreatening and literally "generic" and even parodic, Woo enables Western audience identification (predominantly white, male, young) that elides race. Focus is on the star(s) as agency for excessive violence and destruction, for "action," both potential and realized. For example, in Woo's famous scenes of choreographed (pas de deux) gun-to-the-head conversations between Jeff (the Killer a.k.a. Mickey Mouse) and Inspector Lee (Dumbo), played by Chow Yun-fat and Danny Lee in The Killer, the intimacy between cop and killer further blurs their identities and thus opens up multiple possibilities for "identification."

As Yvonne Tasker asserts, "Beyond Hollywood it is the Asian stars, both male and female, of the Hong Kong industry who have defined and developed the action genre."[28] Within the representational nexus of the popular Hollywood action film, however, non-Asian actors trained in the martial arts have more star currency than their Asian counterparts. Steven Seagal, Chuck Norris, and Jean-Claude Van Damme are exemplars of the 1980s and 1990s Hollywood martial arts performer. Their transnational currency is also indicated by their work in Asia. For example, Van Damme had previously made films in Hong Kong and was an admirer of Woo's work before he and the director decided to work together.

Their collaborative film is constructed in such a way as to retranslate the Hong Kong action idiom. The narrative of *Hard Target* takes place in New Orleans and focuses on rich foreigners who design human hunting trips. Van Damme plays a marginalized character who is a poor, un(der)-employed vet. He picks up work as a merchant seaman whenever available, and during off-times he performs odd jobs, for example, handing out flyers for a phone-sex operation. He is recruited by a young woman (played by Yancy Butler) in search of her missing father. His real-life European accent is given a diegetic explanation, as he is represented as creole and this serves to further alienate him from mainstream society. Van Damme's character (Chance) was reared, we are informed, in the swamps.

The creolization of the Muscles From Brussels (as a Ragin' Cajun, right down to the predictable use of John Fogerty's anthem, "Born on the Bayou," as the credits roll) gives him a hybridized American identity and separates him from the "generic" villains. He seems to share an affinity with the Chow Yun-fat antiheroes of Woo's Hong Kong films, as he is extremely chivalrous in his relations with women. For example, he apologizes for the sex-service marketing contents of the flyers that he and the young woman's father had distributed, and he saves her from would-be muggers, advising her not to display her money in public. The only real physical contact between the two is a chaste embrace and a kiss on the cheek that she gives him.

However, Chance's own superior bodily defense skills are put on display, and he does strip down to a muscle-enhancing tee shirt during a crucial battle. His body is a weapon as much as the firearms he wields, which are, for the most part, rather primitive. In fact, his uncle, curiously played by Wilford Brimley, comes to his assistance with an archery kit. Even more striking is the scene in the wilds of the swamps where Chance restrains an about-to-strike snake with his bare hands, saving the woman (and thwarting a filmic moment of potential romance, as he's just asked her to trust him and close her eyes), and then creates a booby trap for the hunters. Thus the film seems to bridge the gap between the "primitive" hyper-masculine 1980s action hero (similarities to Vietnam vet John Rambo cannot be ignored) and the alternatives suggested in the Hong Kong gangster films. The Van Damme character is both physically confident and self-effacing. His sense of humor, outcast status, and relatively unkempt physical appearance (especially his long hair and rather ragged clothes) serve to undermine or even parody representation of conventional "macho" masculinity.

Extratextual information about the film provides some interesting perspectives on the question of transnationalism and cultural exchange. During the production of *Hard Target,* a number of factors influenced or hindered the transnational enterprise—including budgetary scale, communication (language), and censorship. At approximately twenty million dollars, *Hard Target* cost five times as much as Woo's last Hong Kong–made film. Woo contended that it was easier to make a film with a larger budget, but the hard part was fitting into a new studio system without his usual production crew. Reputedly, the language barrier was crossed via the "international language of films." That is, Woo would explain his shots as "Scorsese" or "Peckinpah," and his crew apparently understood what he was looking for. In fact, a technician dubbed a certain kind of close-up a "John Woo shot." Woo claimed,

> To me the most important thing is to come up with something which is *tong-yi*—consistent, complete and in a spiritual sense reunited. . . . If an artist's work is screened and his original passion is ignited in the audience, he comes full circle. He rediscovers his original expression as God.[29]

However, the director was forced to edit *Hard Target* seven times before it received an R rating. He has asserted in interviews that these changes profoundly affected the finished product, and as a result, the film does not express his personal vision or bear his authorial mark. The censorship and rating of levels of violence are things Woo comments on intertextually, even within his Hong Kong films. Perhaps the most comic example occurs in *Hard Boiled* when Chow Yun-fat exclaims appreciatively (to a baby he's managed to save from a hospital under siege and is carrying beneath his arm as he continues to shoot): "Hey, X-rated action!"

· Rethinking Auteurism and Questions of Value in a Transnational Context

What does it mean to assert that *Hard Target* is *not* a "John Woo" film? The mechanics of auteurism in relation to Woo's films, and to new Hong Kong cinema in general, needs to be reconsidered. According to Ackbar Abbas, "It [new Hong Kong cinema] is both a popular cinema and a cinema of auteurs, with directors like Ann Hui, Tsui Hark, Allen Fong, John Woo, Stanley Kwan, and Wong Kar-wai gaining not only local acclaim but a certain measure of international recognition as well in the form of awards at international film festivals."[30] However, the means of film production complicate the already problematic notion of the auteur.

It is interesting to note that the *politique des auteurs* originally emerged from a desire to canonize American cinema and, as Peter Wollen has stated, "a whole range of authors whose work had previously been dismissed and consigned to oblivion."[31] Referring to Hong Kong directors as auteurs validates their work and, in turn, a cinema that has often been critically viewed as debased and degraded. Furthermore, the circumstances that gave rise to the intellectual discourse of auteur theory were in practical terms transnational ones, including the banning of American films from France under the Vichy government and their reemergence after the liberation. Now, in the mid-1990s, auteurism retains currency as a means of extolling the virtues of American independent filmmakers and essentially mainstreaming them, and it seems predicated on international acclaim (not to mention commercial potential). Quentin Tarantino—who incidentally has acknowledged John Woo as a major influence—is one such example. After winning the Palme d'Or at the 1994 Cannes Film Festival, the tag's relevance became apparent. (Peter Biskind's profile of Tarantino in the November 1994 issue of the film magazine *Premiere* is titled, appropriately, "An Auteur is Born.")

When examining John Woo's career and critical discussions of the development of his styles and genres, auteurism almost becomes synonymous with pastiche, parody, and influence/derivation, thus providing critical points of reference. For example, a scene in a Woo film such as the exploding Madonna sequence in *The Killer* might be described as "more Scorsese than Scorsese."[32] (In fact, Woo is often critically linked with American "movie brat" directors.) Or Woo's suggestion that he was influenced by Hollywood musicals like *Singin' in the Rain* and *West Side Story* (and that, in addition, he loves ballet and was a high school dance teacher) might color a choreographic reading of his famous gun-to-the-head action scenes. As with critical discourse of a director like Tarantino, postmodern "synthetic" modes would be thus deemed auteurist. In contrast, the application of the term in discussions of Fifth-Generation Chinese filmmakers such as Zhang Yimou and Chen Kaige seems to conform to nostalgic and outmoded models of the (European) director of the "art" film. The idea of new cinemas promotes the persistence of tropes of invention such as auteur.

What needs to be considered further is an issue that I can only hint at here: the ways generic and stylistic modes are transformed and complicated by specific local, national, and global industry-based concerns. Woo trained as a filmmaker *within* the Hong Kong film industry, beginning at Shaw Brothers and Golden Harvest. Consider, for example, Woo's association during the development of the romantic gangster cycle with producer Tsui Hark, widely referred to in Western discourse of Hong Kong cinema as the "Steven Spielberg of Hong Kong." Tsui Hark's company, Film Workshop, has been characterized as at once encouraging directors to produce an original style but also intensely interested in a collective aesthetic: spectacularity (i.e., special effects, extravagant mise-en-scène) and mass-entertainment appeal. In critical practice, an auteur is still often thought of as "the single dominant personality behind a work of film art, a creative personality whose imprint should be discernible throughout the body of his or her films."[33] (Like Spielberg, Tsui Hark, the producer-director-writer-actor, is himself also labeled an auteur.) Woo's classification seems, at least in part, rooted in a recognizable or signature style, and his frequently multiple roles as writer and director—ultimately a rather regressive and reductive emphasis on the individual and aesthetic, leading to the elision of specific ideological and industrial concerns and to the promotion of the illusion of autonomy. As I have attempted to demonstrate, the idea of autonomy is especially bankrupt when it comes to Hong Kong cultural productions, and it is at odds with a reading of film production and consumption as "transnational."

In conclusion, Hong Kong has managed to maintain a flourishing local and culturally specific (and, paradoxically, culturally "hybrid") film industry. Many of its films, however, via their status as genre films have managed to become exportable products; action films are envisioned as having a potential international audience. Awareness of the global market has reinforced the reflexivity of genre. And one might argue that John Woo-as-auteur has a similar transnational exchange value.[34]

• *Broken Arrow,* Epilogue . . . (1997 Approaches)

Hong Kong may be in a state of disappearance—culturally, temporally, and spatially—as Curtis K. Tsui has recently argued, but its cinematic styles, genres, and talents are reappearing in Hollywood.[35] The blockbuster status of John Woo's enormously successful *Broken Arrow* (1996) marks a new stage in the development of his career and cross-pollinated action cinema. The hybridization process described above is further complicated by the conflation of categories like "auteur" and "genre" (as in the "John Woo action film") and the blurring of boundaries of Hollywood and Hong Kong. Regarding the anxiety of influence: witness Hollywood's ever-warming embrace of

Fig. 20. Park Ranger Terry Carmichael (Samantha Mathis) with a gun in *Broken Arrow,* directed by John Woo, USA, 1995. Twentieth Century Fox.

Hong Kong action, exemplified through appropriations (homage, pastiche, rip-off), extreme self-reflexivity, and a paradoxical quest for style-making "authenticity" (e.g., Quentin Tarantino's now-notorious borrowings from Ringo Lam, and Robert Rodriguez' choreographed gunplay quotations from Woo's now-canonical *The Killer* in his 1995 film, *Desperado*). In 1996, Jackie Chan—whose physical stunts were long imitated by Hollywood action filmmakers—finally made a real impact at the multiplex with his *Rumble in the Bronx,* a cross-cultural version of his own generic trademark martial arts action-comedy.[36]

In contrast to the reception of *Hard Target, Broken Arrow* is celebrated by many critics as true Woo and an effective translation of Hong Kong action.[37] For example, David Denby wrote in his review: "If you've never experienced a Hong Kong action movie, you might as well see John Woo's lightning-fast *Broken Arrow,* because it represents the wave of the future as well as a significant style of the recent past. (You will also have a very good time.) John Woo has moved to Hollywood . . . ."[38] *Broken Arrow* is profoundly inter-

Fig. 21. John Travolta as Vic Deakins and Christian Slater as Riley Hale in *Broken Arrow,* directed by John Woo, USA, 1995. Twentieth Century Fox.

textual in Hollywood–Hong Kong terms. Its casting plays on John Travolta's second coming to movie stardom via Tarantino. (Terrence Rafferty titled his *New Yorker* review of *Broken Arrow,* "Pulp Fission"). As Vic Deakins, a demented-but-charming Air Force pilot who steals a pair of phallic-shaped nuclear warheads, Travolta takes on some of the props and mannerisms of the Chow Yun-fat persona with his sunglasses and endless cigarettes. His relationship with copilot Riley Hale (Christian Slater), a friendship turned murderously confrontational, fuels the film's action and its many spectacular chase scenes through the sprawling desert landscape. The film makes abundant use of Hollywood's arsenal of special effects.

While *Broken Arrow* broadly addresses typical Woo themes like loyalty and betrayal, it also offers a potentially broader perspective on gender relations and representations. Scripted by Graham Yost, the screenwriter of *Speed, Broken Arrow* features a strong female character, the feisty-yet-vulnerable park ranger Terry Carmichael (played by Samantha Mathis), who knows how to handle a gun. Ultimately shifting the focus from codes of brotherhood to the dynamics of sexual politics, *Broken Arrow*'s last exchange between Hale and Carmichael about being "taken in" slyly echoes the ending of Woo's *A Better Tomorrow,* the filmic catalyst that marked the emergence of a truly transnational action genre.[39]

· Notes

I would like to thank Sheldon Hsiao-peng Lu and Tony Williams for animated discussions of Woo's films. Earlier versions of this paper were presented at the Cultural Studies Colloquium at the University of Pittsburgh, April 1995, and the University Film and Video Association Conference, August 1995.

1. Recent books by Li Cheuk-to, coordinator of the Hong Kong International Film Festival, have yet to be translated into English. These include: *Bashi niandai Xianggang dianying biji* [Notes on Hong Kong cinema of the 1980s], 2 vol. (Hong Kong: Chuangjian, 1990), and *Guan niji (Xianggang dianying pian: Zhongwai dianying pian)* [Viewing against the grain: Hong Kong cinema; Chinese and foreign cinema], 2 vol. (Hong Kong: Ciwenhua tang, 1993).

2. According to Tony Rayns, progress has been made in Chinese archival work with the recent establishment of the Hong Kong Film Archive, but the future of the Hong Kong Film Festival is unstable. See his "Hong Kong Notes" in *Sight and Sound* 5, no. 6 (1995): 5, and 6, no. 5 (1996): 5.

3. Ackbar Abbas explains that Hong Kong Cantonese is itself a hybrid: "sprinkled with snatches of Mandarin, English, and barbarous sounding words and phrases—a hybrid language coming out of a hybrid space. It is by being local in this way that the new Hong Kong cinema is the most international." See his essay, "The New Hong Kong Cinema and the Déjà Disparu," *Discourse* 16, no. 3 (1994): 69.

4. Paul Fonoroff, "Orientation," *Film Comment* 24, no. 3 (1988): 52–56.

5. See Nick Browne's introduction to *New Chinese Cinemas: Forms, Identities, Politics,* edited by Browne with Paul G. Pickowicz, Vivian Sobchack, and Esther Yau (Cambridge: Cambridge University Press, 1994), 6.

6. John Woo was born Wu Yu-sum in Guangchou (Canton), China, in 1946 and came to Hong Kong with his family at age four. Prior to his relocation to Hollywood, Woo amassed twenty-six feature directing credits in Hong Kong.

7. Richard Dyer, "Action!" *Sight and Sound* 4, no. 10 (1994): 10.

8. Abbas, "The New Hong Kong Cinema," 70, states that these films are known in Hong Kong as "hero" films, after the Chinese title for John Woo's *A Better Tomorrow.* In his excellent book, *Hong Kong Action Cinema* (London: Titan Books, 1995), Bey Logan employs the term "heroic bloodshed" films to describe this subgenre of action films in which gunplay replaces kung fu. He explains that the label was first coined by British fanzine editor Rick Baker. See Rick Baker and Toby Russell, *The Essential Guide to Hong Kong Movies* (London: Eastern Heroes Publications, 1994).

Woo's Hong Kong gangster films include *A Better Tomorrow* (1986) and its sequel, *A Better Tomorrow* 2 (1987) (in which Chow Yun-fat returns as his previous character, Mark Gor's identical twin brother), *The Killer* (Diexue shuangxiong, 1989), and *Hard Boiled* (Lashou shentan, 1992). Woo's *Bullet in the Head* (Diexue jietou, 1990), which moved away from the gangster genre with an epic scope and the incorporation of historical events like the Vietnam War, failed to make an impact on American audiences. This film was followed by a "romantic caper comedy," *Once a Thief* (1991).

9. Mohammed Bamyeh, "Transnationalism," *Current Sociology* 41, no. 3 (1993): 1. This article provides an overview of the concept of transnationalism as well as a brief discussion of global media and cultural exchange.

10. Tony Rayns, "Hard Boiled," *Sight and Sound* 2, no. 4 (1992): 22.

11. Bamyeh, "Transnationalism," 62.

12. Abbas, "The New Hong Kong Cinema," 66.

13. Maitland McDonald, "Things I Felt Were Being Lost" (interview with John Woo), *Film Comment* 29, no. 5 (1993): 52.

14. Jean Baudrillard, *Selected Writings,* ed. Mark Poster (Stanford: Stanford University Press, 1988), 171.

15. Li Cheuk-to, "The Return of the Father: Hong Kong New Wave and Its Chinese Context in the 1980s," in *New Chinese Cinemas: Forms, Identities, Politics,* ed. Nick Browne, Paul G. Pickowicz, Vivian Sobchack, and Esther Yau (Cambridge: Cambridge University Press, 1994), 177.

16. Esther Yau, "Border Crossing: Mainland China's Presence in Hong Kong Cinema," in *New Chinese Cinemas: Forms, Identities, Politics,* ed. Nick Browne, Paul G. Pickowicz, Vivian Sobchack, and Esther Yau (Cambridge: Cambridge University Press, 1994), 183–184.

17. Yau, "Border Crossing," 181.

18. Li, "The Return of the Father," 161.

19. Woo fandom in the United States is chronicled by articles in fanzines and specialty film magazines such as *Asian Trash Cinema, Film Threat, Hong Kong Film Connection, Hong Kong Film Magazine,* and *Oriental Cinema* (the recent issue no. 11 [1996] is a "John Woo Issue"), as well as compendiums such as *Sex and Zen and a Bullet in the Head: The Essential Guide to Hong Kong's Mind-Bending Films* (New York: Simon and Schuster, 1996) by Stefan Hammond and Mike Wilkins. See also the proliferation of Internet news groups and web sites devoted to John Woo and Hong Kong cinema.

20. Frank Segers, "A Trans-Pacific Crossover: Woo at the Helm for Universal," *Variety,* August 24, 1992, 49, 52.

21. Yvonne Tasker, *Spectacular Bodies: Gender, Genre and the Action Cinema* (London: Routledge, 1993), 165.

22. Tony Rayns, "Chaos and Anger," *Sight and Sound* 4, no. 10 (1994): 14.

23. See Jonathan Romey's review of *Jungle Book* in *Sight and Sound* 5, no. 3 (1995): 50–51.

24. See Richard Dyer's formulations of the male "pin-up" and stars in general in his books, *Stars* (London: British Film Institute, 1979) and *Heavenly Bodies* (London: British Film Institute, 1987).

25. Chow Yun-fat, dubbed "the coolest actor in the world by the *Los Angeles Magazine* (March 12, 1995), has committed to several projects in Hollywood; his debut will be *The Replacement Killers* for Columbia Pictures. He hopes to collaborate on future projects in both Hollywood and Hong Kong, including ones with John Woo (who will not be doing a Hollywood remake of *The Killer*) and Wong Kar-wai. See the interview with Chow Yun-fat by Beth Accomando, "Eat My Bullet," *Giant Robot* 6 (1996): 44–48.

26. Steve Neale, "Prologue: Masculinity as Spectacle: Reflections on Men and Mainstream Cinema," in *Screening the Male: Exploring Masculinities in Hollywood Cinema*, ed. Steven Cohan and Ina Rae Hark (London: Routledge, 1993), 18.

27. James Wolcott, "Blood Test," *The New Yorker*, August 23 & 30, 1993, 63.

28. Tasker, *Spectacular Bodies*, 5.

29. Jonathan Penner, "Wooing America," *Harper's Bazaar*, October 1993, 146.

30. Abbas, "The New Hong Kong Cinema," 65.

31. Peter Wollen, "The Auteur Theory" [from *Signs and Meaning in the Cinema*], in *Film Theory and Criticism*, ed. Gerald Mast and Marshall Cohen (New York: Oxford University Press, 1992), 589.

32. See the review of *The Killer* by Tony Rayns in *Monthly Film Bulletin* 57, no. 680 (1990): 260.

33. This working definition comes from Jeffrey Chown, *Hollywood Auteur* (New York: Praeger, 1988), 9, a study of the career of American director Francis Coppola. For a challenging critical reconsideration of the notion of the author/auteur, see John Caughie, *Theories of Authorship* (Boston: Routledge and Kegan Paul, 1981).

34. Wong Kar-wai has been critically constructed as the next big Hong Kong auteur. According to Terence Chang, producer of *Broken Arrow* and Chow Yun-fat's manager, "Hong Kong films have seen their better days. Now, because of the uncertainty of the political situation and Hong Kong about to revert back to China, most of the good writers and directors have left." See Jerry Roberts, "Hollywood's New Pacific Strategy," *Face* 19 (1996): 64.

35. Curtis K. Tsui, "Subjective Culture and History: The Ethnographic Cinema of Wong Kar-wai," *Asian Cinema* 7, no. 2 (1995): 95–96.

36. Gary Dauphin suggests that Jackie Chan is "trying to sell *back* a cultural aesthetic, specifically one that looks and sounds lifted straight out of an '80s r&b crossover video. This cross-cultural circulation of proto-gangster fantasies is ultimately *Rumble in the Bronx*'s lasting irony and perhaps even the source of its outsized hilarity." See Gary Dauphin, "Chan is Missing," *Village Voice*, February 27, 1996, 72.

In addition to Chan's breakthrough, 1996 marked Hong Kong director Ringo

Lam's Hollywood debut, *Maximum Risk,* an action film starring Jean-Claude Van Damme. Tsui Hark's *Double Team* (1977) also stars Van Damme.

37. *Broken Arrow* was made for Twentieth Century Fox in association with WCG Entertainment (based on the Twentieth Century Fox lot), the company Woo formed with partners Terence Chang and Christopher Godsick.

38. David Denby, "Movies: *Broken Arrow* directed by John Woo," *New York,* 29, no. 8 (1996): 126.

39. Woo's television debut, *John Woo's Once a Thief,* a two-hour made-for-TV movie that aired on Fox television in September 1996, was ostensibly auteur-confirming (see Rick Schindler, "Woo's the Boss: Hong Kong's Celebrated Action Auteur John Woo Choreographs His First TV-Movie," *TV Guide* 44, no. 39 [1996]: 5–6). An action thriller set in Hong Kong and Canada with an entangled subplot featuring libidinal dynamics as well as filial loyalties among Asian and Caucasian characters, this television film is a radically divergent remake of Woo's 1991 Hong Kong film, *Once a Thief. John Woo's Once a Thief* (1996) marks a significant further development in Woo's transnational career.

Chapter 9

•

Jackie Chan and the Cultural Dynamics of
Global Entertainment

•

Steve Fore

In early 1996, as Hong Kong's 1997 reversion to the control of Mainland China loomed ever closer, the precise mechanism and meaning of this transition remained maddeningly indistinct. Hong Kong citizens, political interests, and business entities still didn't know exactly how reversion to China would be manifested. Of course, the city had been living in this state of suspended animation since the signing of the Joint Declaration in 1984, but as the deadline approached, individuals, families, and corporations alike were furiously concocting contingency plans that ranged from maintaining the status quo to overnight evacuation.

For the Hong Kong movie industry, which boomed throughout the 1980s and early 1990s, this uncertainty had destabilizing effects both on the infrastructure of the business itself and on the tastes and interests of the local moviegoing audience. Movie attendance fell 30 percent between 1992 and late 1995;[1] the number of films produced annually dropped from a steady 135–150 a few years ago to well under 100 in 1995 (and the critical consensus was that proportionately fewer "good" movies were being made); the local exhibition market, dominated since the late 1970s by homegrown product, increasingly was swamped by Hollywood films; and a number of prominent producers, directors, and performers acquired overseas passports, work permits, and even citizenship. Some of these people have remained in Hong Kong and are continuing to work for the time being, while others have either "retired" from the movie business, relocated regionally (to Singapore or Malaysia, for example), or, in a few instances, left Hong Kong to pursue success in that Holy Grail of global commercial media production, Hollywood.

The first highly publicized defection to the United States was that of the director John Woo (and his producer, Terence Chang), whose second U.S.-produced film, *Broken Arrow,* was released in February 1996 and proved a moderate hit in the U.S. market, grossing in the vicinity of $70 million in first-run release. As of early 1996, two other well-known Hong Kong directors, Ringo Lam and Tsui Hark, were also shooting or preparing U.S. projects. The conventional wisdom in Hollywood was that the groundwork for this modest influx of behind-the-camera talent from Hong Kong had to do with the acknowledged influence of Woo and others on influential young Hollywood filmmakers such as Quentin Tarantino and Robert Rodriguez, who have professed in numerous interviews their infatuation with the wildly kinetic and exuberantly, playfully excessive visual and narrative pyrotechnics associated with the best Hong Kong–based action filmmakers. For these young American directors, and for the sizable non-Asian cult audience for Hong Kong movies that has developed especially in large cities and on college campuses all over the United States, these films have provided a controlled setting in which to be exposed to and (perhaps) examine certain notions of linguistic, racial, and cultural difference. They have also provided a legitimate alternative entertainment film aesthetic appealing particularly to an adolescent and young adult male audience—a way out of the prison house of Stallone. As Hong Kong critic Li Cheuk-to has suggested,

> Even though today's Hollywood is still the world's greatest dream factory, neither its filmmakers nor its audience can return to their past innocence. . . . Self-consciousness about genres and formulas often makes films reserved and inhibited. Hongkong films on the other hand believe in a no-holds-barred approach to action, gags, and stirring up emotions, even to the point of loss of control and total overload.[2]

It is significant that Woo, Lam, and Tsui are all directors; for decades, Hollywood has welcomed behind-the-camera talent from some parts of the world (e.g., the many European émigrés of the 1920s and 1930s and the string of defectors from the Australian New Wave during the 1980s), as long as those new arrivals were willing to adapt themselves to the rules of the Hollywood system. On-screen performers—numerous stars from Great Britain and the Commonwealth, plus second-language learners from Greta Garbo to Arnold Schwarzenegger—also have made the transition successfully. The current wave of Chinese directors in the United States (including, of course, the Taiwanese-born Ang Lee, who has "assimilated" to the point of adapting Jane Austen's *Sense and Sensibility* to the screen) is, however, the first ever of non-Anglo/European émigrés, and not only is it too early to tell whether Woo and others ultimately will make it in Hollywood (much less whether the circumstances associated with "making it" add up to an aesthetically advantageous career move), the crystal ball is even cloudier with regard to on-screen talent imported from Hong Kong. Chow Yun-fat, the suave romantic and action star of several Woo and Lam films (among many others), has a project in the works with Fox, but it remains starkly true that the Hollywood movie industry has not seriously attempted to market an Asian performer (male or female) as a marquee name since the brief but spectacular success of Bruce Lee in the early 1970s.[3] Lee, whose revisionist kung fu films revitalized the genre in Hong Kong and were wildly successful elsewhere in East Asia, rode into the U.S. market on the wave of low-budget action films (blaxploitation and otherwise) that found a market niche especially among young, urban African American and Latino audiences. After Lee's death in 1973 (just before the release of his first U.S.-produced film, *Enter the Dragon*), the Hong Kong movie industry became synonymous in the United States during the 1970s with "chopsocky" entertainment, the period martial arts films produced most successfully on the Shaw Brothers assembly line. These movies, some of which are eminently worthy of restoration and serious critical reevaluation, came to bear the mark of pure camp among the small number of U.S. viewers who saw them at all, thanks to their release in truncated, badly dubbed English-language versions.

The shabby Far Eastern exoticism of the mutilated Shaw films was the dominant image in the United States of the Hong Kong film prior to the post–*Better Tomorrow* (Woo's deliriously violent and melodramatic 1986 breakthrough film) wave of movies that excited some Western critics and generated a new cult audience. Over the last few years, the signals emanating from the Hong Kong movie industry have been edging closer to the threshold of popular consciousness in the United States, but while some Hong Kong directors are now seizing the opportunity to go Hollywood (on Hollywood's terms), no earlier films by these directors (or any others) have received a U.S. release.[4] At first, this seems like a curious phenomenon; after all, Chinese film was *the* hot ticket on the international festival circuit in the late 1980s and early 1990s, and that success has led to a small number of respectably profitable U.S. distribution deals for movies from Taiwan (Lee's *The Wedding Banquet, Eat Drink Man Woman,* and *Pushing Hands*) and the People's Republic of China (all of Zhang Yimou's films since *Ju Dou,* Chen Kaige's pan-Chinese coproductions *Farewell My Concubine* and *Temptress Moon,* Tian Zhuangzhuang's *The Blue Kite*).[5] But until early 1996, no films from Hong Kong were able to climb aboard this modest bandwagon, and the reason as I see it is this: while the above examples from Taiwan and the PRC fit comfortably enough within the conventionalized marketing and reception paradigms under which foreign films enter the United States (based especially on locating a "comfort level" of linguistic, racial, and cultural difference), most Hong Kong films do not (including most of the Hong Kong films that have generated the strongest cult buzz in the United States).[6]

And this brings us to Jackie Chan, who since the late 1970s has been the most phenomenally popular and successful movie actor—and producer, and director, and stunt coordinator—in Hong Kong. The details of Chan's early life and career have been recounted in numerous articles: born into a poor family in Hong Kong in 1954,[7] he was indentured by his parents at the age of seven to a Peking opera academy, where he spent the next ten years rigorously training in the martial arts and gymnastics skills required of opera performers. He made a handful of movie appearances as a child and entered the Hong Kong industry full-time in the early 1970s as a stuntman and fight choreographer. After moving into lead roles in a series of ordinary (and commercially unsuccessful) kung-fu melodramas, Chan—with the assistance especially of director Yuen Woo-ping—finally registered a breakthrough hit in 1978 with *Snake in the Eagle's Shadow*. This was the film in which Chan began to explore the potential appeal of adding elements of verbal and slapstick comedy to the usual kung fu narrative structure of a generic moral tale held together by elaborate sequences of violent hand-to-hand combat. While he has been credited in some Western sources as the originator of "comedy kung fu," Chan's experiments actually occurred in a context in which other stars and producers, including most prominently the Hui brothers, Karl Maka, and Samo Hung, were also coming up with comic variations on the martial arts formula.[8]

Since 1980's *Young Master,* Chan has released his martial arts–action–comedy films through Raymond Chow's Golden Harvest, the best-established and largest movie production and distribution company in Hong Kong.[9] In an industry in which film budgets typically range from a few hundred thousand to a little more than a million U.S. dollars, where stars often are expected to work on several films simultaneously, and where production schedules are typically hectic and brief, Jackie Chan's films have been and are exceptions. His production budgets are by far the largest in Hong Kong (*Thunderbolt,* his 1995 Chinese New Year's release, was, at US$20 million, the most expensive Hong Kong movie ever). His shooting schedules would be considered luxurious on many big-budget Hollywood productions, and Chan himself earns a reported US$5 million per film these days. He gets these perks, quite simply, because his films are consistent box-office blockbusters, and not just in Hong Kong. While moviegoers from the Middle East to Latin America know his work, Chan's primary audience base has been in East Asia. In this sense, his films have represented the best-case scenario of the Hong Kong movie industry's general marketing strategy: in a home market with only six million people, for a film to achieve profitability, overseas audiences are a necessity.

And now, with the uncertain long-term status of Hong Kong as a base market and production center, backed by his own management team and Golden Harvest, Chan has made a serious bid for entry into the high-dollar, high-stakes world of the U.S. movie marketplace. (There's also Mainland China, which has become a more viable consumer market and a less tightly controlled exhibition situation for Hong Kong films, and where Chan's last three films have been released to wild popular acclaim, but which still poses substantial questions for would-be movie entrepreneurs, ranging from political pressure to video piracy.) This isn't the first attempt to break Chan into the U.S. market; he starred in two low-budget, U.S.-produced, English-language movies in the early 1980s (*Battle Creek Brawl* and *The Protector*), and he had small roles in the two *Cannonball Run* films (in which Golden Harvest had an investment interest). But those early efforts to sell Chan to U.S. audiences fizzled, thanks to the fact that Chan was not in control of the productions, resulting in distinctly substandard movies (the comparison has been made with MGM-era Buster Keaton), and to the fact that Hollywood distributors were at that point much less savvy than some are today in the marketing of entertainment films that do not necessarily fit within the paradigms of mainstream Hollywood.[10] In any case, since the early 1980s Chan has been content to be a top-shelf action film star to rival Schwarzenegger and Stallone in most of the world *except* the United States.

In February 1995, though, Chan and Golden Harvest signed a deal with the U.S.-based distributor New Line Cinema (a successful independent absorbed in 1995 by Turner), through which New Line acquired the North American rights to Chan's then most-recent film, *Rumble in the Bronx,* and first negotiation rights on his next two films (these were *Thunderbolt,* which is set in the world of international auto racing, and the cop/spy adventure *First Strike,* which was released simultaneously in Hong Kong, Taiwan, and the PRC in mid-February 1996 as a Chinese New Year "event"). Subsequently, Miramax, the savvy New York–based distributor of mostly European art-house fare (e.g., *The Crying Game* and *The Cook, the Thief, His Wife, and Her Lover*) later acquired by Disney, bought the North American rights to Chan's *Crime Story* (1993) and *Drunken Master 2* (1994). The first large-scale U.S. release of a Jackie Chan movie in more than a decade (and the first ever with the backing of a substantial promotional apparatus) was launched on February 23, 1996, when a reedited, shortened (by about ten minutes), and English-dubbed version of *Rumble in the Bronx* opened in multiplexes all over the United States. Like his early-1980s U.S. ventures, *Rumble* places Chan as a Hong Kong émigré trying to make his way through, and make sense of, U.S. culture. This is a typical Chan role in that his character from film to film is usually a "typical" Hong Kong resident who finds himself between cultures, sometimes overseas (e.g., Mainland China in *Police*

Fig. 22. Jackie Chan, star and director of *Police Story* (Jingcha gushi), Hong Kong, 1986. British Film Institute.

Story 3: Supercop, Russia and Australia in *First Strike*) and sometimes in his own backyard (e.g., *Project A* and its sequel, the first two *Police Story* films, and *Crime Story*). More complex issues associated with the sojourner-exile experience, though, are not central to the story told in *Rumble*. The themes of extreme dislocation and loss chronicled in some other Hong Kong films that focus on the immigrant experience (*Crossings, Farewell China, An Autumn's Tale*) in fact would be out of place in a Jackie Chan vehicle, in which broader, feel-good themes of optimism, industriousness, and the value of familial and fraternal bonds are emphasized. In *Rumble,* Chan plays a Hong Kong cop who comes to New York to visit an uncle who runs a grocery store in the Bronx and finds himself embroiled in a gang war and a diamond-smuggling operation. The particulars of the plot are much less carefully articulated in this film than in some of Chan's earlier efforts (including his two previous films, *Crime Story* and *Drunken Master 2*), but *Rumble* does include solid examples of the elaborately staged fight sequences and death-defying stunts that are Chan trademarks. In any case, whatever its deficiencies relative to much of his previous work, after the opening weekend of release, *Rumble* was the number one box-office attraction in the U.S. market, accumulating more than $10 million in revenues.[11]

The U.S. marketing of *Rumble in the Bronx* is especially interesting in that it represents an attempt to define "global cinema" as something other than the Hollywood entertainment film.[12] The U.S.-based movie industry, of course, has long-established economies of scale and scope that for decades have provided Hollywood companies with the clout to inundate national and regional markets all over the world; packaged entertainment is now the United States' second-leading export commodity. The reverse—sustained, mass commercial success by foreign-made entertainment films in the United States—has never occurred.

As Richard Dyer has pointed out in numerous essays published over the last two decades, the notion of "entertainment" is notoriously difficult to define with precision. Dyer himself steers clear of, and is not especially concerned with, locating broadly applicable, concrete markers of identification, instead suggesting the ways in which "entertainment" has been linked with other concepts such as "leisure" and "escape." For my purposes here, Dyer's key observation is that its precise nature is, among other things, dependent on the particulars of specific social and cultural contexts: "Entertainment is not simply a way of describing something found equally in all societies at all times."[13] Dyer's most famous work focuses on the idea of entertainment in relation to the fictive worlds created in the Hollywood musical; that is, he is most directly concerned with the nature and function of entertainment in a capitalist-consumerist setting. And in that setting, he argues, entertainment has a strongly utopian inclination:

> Entertainment offers the image of "something better" to escape into, or something we want deeply that our day-to-day lives don't provide. . . . Entertainment does not, however, present models of utopian worlds, as in the classic utopias of Sir Thomas More, William Morris, et al. Rather the utopianism is contained in the feelings it embodies. It presents, head-on, as it were, what utopia would feel like rather than how it would be organised.[14]

I am invoking Dyer's ideas here apropos Jackie Chan less because the martial arts sequences and stunts he supervises in his films often have been equated by Western critics with the elaborate, stylized choreography of classic Hollywood musicals (and with the artfully arranged slapstick of U.S.

silent comedy stars)[15]—although these correlations are useful to an extent—than because the marketing of a Jackie Chan film and the Jackie Chan persona in the United States represents an interesting case study of the dynamics involved with introducing non-U.S. mainstream entertainment into the United States, and doing so in a way that reverses the conventional direction of that movement (i.e., from outside the United States into that market, rather than emanating from the United States across national borders all over the world). What kind of meanings, that is, were associated with the image produced of Jackie Chan through his promotion (by way of print and television ads, theatrical trailers, profiles in national and local magazines and newspapers, and feature stories and guest appearances on network television programs) to non-Asian U.S. audiences, who were assumed as of early 1996 to have no image of him at all? While Chan has developed a significant cult audience in the United States (a factor that helped to convince New Line and Miramax to pull the trigger on the current distribution deals), in early 1996 he was not yet a "star" in the United States, and the selling of the Chan persona in that market necessarily started from this central fact. And, by way of illustrative contrast, what does Jackie Chan as a maker and star of entertainment films "mean" to Chinese and other Asian audiences, for whom Chan is already a mega-superstar?

In an important essay published in 1991, Joseph D. Straubhaar provides a useful revisionist model of the phenomenon of media imperialism in a world of increasingly interdependent economies and increasingly dispersed and polyglot cultural geographies. He refines the standard definition of "asymmetrical interdependence" in light of the daunting complexities involved with the movement of capital and culture today, suggesting that the term refers "to the *variety* of possible relationships in which countries find themselves unequal but possessing variable degrees of power and initiative in politics, economics, and culture."[16] While recognizing the marketing advantages that U.S. entertainment exports continue to enjoy in most parts of the world, Straubhaar points out that the growth of viable indigenous commercial media industries in some regions has presented Hollywood product with ever stiffer competition in some countries for screen time, air time, market share, and advertising revenues, and that significant export markets have developed for some of this non-U.S.-produced, non-English-language entertainment (e.g., television programming from Brazil, Mexico, and Hong Kong, movies from Hong Kong and India).

Significantly, Straubhaar also takes pains to build a consideration of the nature and preferences of media audiences into his model (his focus is on broadcast television audiences). He introduces the notion of "cultural proximity" as a means of delineating the broad parameters of mainstream tastes across national, regional, and transnational situations, arguing that

> we must look at how media are received by the audience as part of cultures and subcultures that resist change. . . . [W]e propose that audiences make an active choice to view *international* or *regional* or *national* television programs, *a choice that favors the latter two when they are available,* based on a search for cultural relevance or proximity.[17]

While Straubhaar's analysis focuses on the strategies of media production and the conditions of reception among audiences in the developing world,[18] the notion of cultural proximity is also useful, I think, to a consideration of the attempt to introduce Hong Kong entertainment films into the mainstream U.S. market.

What it illuminates most immediately is the difficulties faced by Jackie Chan and New Line in their attempt to break *Rumble in the Bronx* in U.S. shopping mall multiplexes. In East Asia, where Chan is already a major star, the "Chineseness" of his persona is, of course, more closely aligned with the cultural heritage and life experiences of the average moviegoer, whether at a primary level of cultural proximity (for audiences in Hong Kong, Taiwan, and the PRC[19]), or at a secondary level (for non-Chinese audiences in Asian countries where Hong Kong movies are widely distributed). In the United States, though, where the level of cultural proximity to Chan's "Chineseness" is low, New Line found itself faced with a double dilemma.

First, there was the long-term difficulty of marketing *any* kind of "foreign" film in the United States (even English-language films from the United Kingdom and Australia[20]). Since the 1950s, domestic distributors have almost always equated "foreign" films with the niche market of the "art film," which Peter Lev describes as "feature films made in the post–World War II period (and continuing to the present) which display new ideas of form and content which are aimed at a high-culture audience."[21] From the 1950s until the 1980s, most such films imported into the United States were made in Europe, with an occasional Kurosawa film also managing a North American art-house release. More recently, art films from Australia, Latin America, the Middle East, and Asia also have found their way into the United States (although in some instances not venturing beyond New York and Los Angeles theaters).[22] Lev offers a useful discussion of the industrial aspects of this kind of filmmaking:

> [T]he art film is intended for an *international* audience. Its marketing strategy depends on reaching a relatively small, culturally elite audience

in several countries, rather than serving the local market alone. A low-to medium-budget film can make a reasonable profit if it reaches art theater audiences in Western Europe, the United States, and Canada. These audiences are not well-served by Hollywood films, so the art film can be seen as a kind of counter-programming.[23]

Lev suggests further that in positing an audience that is somewhat more amenable to being intellectually and ideologically challenged or flattered by a movie-viewing experience, another aspect of the art film's "brand identification" in the U.S. market is its relatively strong foregrounding of linguistic and cultural difference and of narrative and stylistic experimentation.

A further international aspect of the art film is that it assumes a cosmopolitan, non-chauvinist spectator who can empathize with characters from many nations. Subtitling, not dubbing, is standard for the art film, and this requires a spectator who is tolerant of other cultures.[24]

This construction of difference as a marketing strategy is, however, strongly regulated. That is, when dealing with movies from other countries, U.S. distributors tend: (1) to buy the rights to films perceived to be similar in form or content to other films that previously have been marketed successfully, plus occasional flyers on films that exploit a high-visibility topic of interest to the target audience; and (2) to promote these films using graphical and rhetorical conventions that emphasize their similarity to earlier examples of movies from the same country or of a similar style (e.g., the Merchant-Ivory "look"). In many instances, this regulation of difference in the promotional apparatus amounts to a reliance on cultural stereotypes. For example, it has been noted by some Chinese and Western critics that most of the PRC films that have received wide art-house releases in the United States—mainly Zhang Yimou's—are set in (and implicitly promoted as) a visually and narratively exoticized representation of China's past that does not challenge white, Western stereotypes of the "Orient."[25] Beyond that, there has been a tendency to efface, if not erase, aspects of cultural specificity in the U.S. marketing of Chinese films. *The Wedding Banquet,* for instance, was sold (very successfully) to U.S. audiences as a "gay film," ignoring the traditional-Chinese-family-in-crisis theme that would be more likely to stand out for Chinese audiences,[26] and Zhang's *To Live* was marketed in the United States as a straightforward, David Lean–style historical epic, without any suggestions in advertisements and trailers of the vein of darkly absurdist, "postsocialist" comedy that permeates the film. In one respect, these marketing strategies make plenty of sense; in order to get the viewer into the theater, you need a hook, and that hook needs to involve something familiar *and* provocative to the viewer's sensibilities. In the above examples, the better hooks—for the U.S. art-house audience—are more likely to involve *Doctor Zhivago* and considerations of multicultural queerness rather than the nuances of the Chinese family structure and bitterly satirical looks at the Great Leap Forward. In another sense, though, these marketing strategies point indirectly but clearly to the lingering presence of high boundaries between cultures, to the severe limitations that still exist (everywhere, not just in the United States) in the area of intercultual understanding (or even comprehension), and to the rather cramped prevailing definition of "acceptable" cultural difference under which we (including the media industries) continue to operate.

And this brings us to Jackie Chan's and New Line's second dilemma. The entrepreneurial and ethical quandaries involved with the marketing of "foreign" art films in the United States have at least been recognized (though to my knowledge not at all self-consciously) and contained within the institutional apparatuses of this segment of the distribution-exhibition business; that is, over several decades, strategies within the industry have been developed and deployed for confronting or, more commonly, circumventing these quandaries. But no such strategies are in place for "foreign" motion pictures that don't fall within the art-film paradigm, a situation that required New Line to look for alternative marketing models. As I see it, those models have involved complementary efforts in the areas of the promotion of and postproduction on *Rumble in the Bronx,* activities intended to reduce the anticipated viewer experience of cultural difference well beyond the already modest standards allowable within the conventions of marketing "foreign" art films in the United States. The very fact that *Rumble* was chosen as the film to break Jackie Chan in the United States is indicative of this, as the decision seems to have been based largely on the fact that the story takes place in (what is purported to be) New York City,[27] ignoring the critical and cult-fan consensus that *Rumble* was in many ways a much less satisfying movie than several other recent Chan vehicles.[28] Also, New Line's redubbing, rescoring, and reediting of the film were clearly part of the strategy designed to take advantage of and strengthen the anticipated level of viewer familiarity with the *kind* of moviegoing experience provided by *Rumble.* The fact that mainstream Hong Kong action movies, including Jackie Chan's, show the influence of Hollywood visual and narrative conventions (realistic representation, continuity editing, plot linearity, emphasis on character relationships) meant that *Rumble in the Bronx* was less likely to be intimidatingly exotic to viewers who never before had seen an Asian-made film.

While the film already contained some English dialogue, the majority was originally recorded in Cantonese.[29] Under the assumption that the average multiplex audience has no patience for subtitles, almost all of the dialogue was dubbed into English, with Chan doing his own looping (the logic behind the choice to dub seems identical to that employed more than twenty years earlier in pursuit of the goal of "mainstreaming" Bruce Lee for the U.S. entertainment-film market). The original score was replaced by incidental music that more poundingly adheres to the conventions of musical styles used in Hollywood action films, and, to promote ancillary sound track sales, by the addition of songs by currently popular U.S. bands (e.g., Ministry). The scenes and shots that were cut involved especially the kind of self-deprecating physical comedy that has long been a crucial part of Chan's persona for Asian audiences—his mugging and pratfalls help to soften the harder edges of the character shown in the elaborate fight and stunt sequences (although these too usually include comic elements and overtones). Also, the role of the female lead, played by Anita Mui, has been substantially reduced in the U.S. release version. Mui is a star in her own right in Asia, but she is largely unknown in the United States, and her on-screen relationship with Chan apparently was considered expendable—especially since the nature of the relationship involves matters of personal obligation and loyalty rather than romance.

The U.S. version of *Rumble in the Bronx,* then, consists substantially of a series of action sequences of varying duration and elaborateness; a semblance of narrative exposition has been retained, but in all the movie's basic story makes even less sense and carries even less weight than it did in the original Hong Kong version. What was being sold in the United States was the *action,* period, and the rationale underlying the distributor's decision[30] to go that route arose, ironically, from precisely those aspects of Jackie Chan's persona that appealed to New Line executives in the first place and convinced them that Chan had commercial potential in the U.S. market. At the same time, the decision to concentrate on his physicality (which is a significant part of his persona, but by no means the only part) had to do also—in keeping with the conventional wisdom that violent action movies are globally marketable—with the belief that it is this aspect of his persona that can more easily cross linguistic, racial, and cultural boundaries. New Line saw Chan as a different kind of action-film star, but an action-film star nevertheless (and only that), and the promotional apparatus constructed for *Rumble in the Bronx*'s U.S. release followed the conventions already established for marketing that kind of film. There was an emphasis (in the theatrical and television trailers and in the visual images and pull-quotes in print ads) on Chan's physical presence and style, which New Line promoted as

Fig. 23. Jackie Chan in *Armor of God* (Longxiong hudi), Hong Kong, 1987. British Film Institute.

the new wrinkle about this particular action hero. The trailers especially emphasized the kinetic visual appeal of Chan's body, using a highly compressed montage of kicks, leaps, and falls to convey his grace, his toughness, and his willingness to take apparently life-threatening risks to accomplish his most spectacular stunts. In this setting, Chan's body becomes an object

The Cultural Dynamics of Global Entertainment   *251*

of fascination, a source of visual spectacle as it flies through the air, as it interacts with other human bodies and inanimate objects.

A taxonomy of contemporary Hollywood action heroes constructed by Yvonne Tasker in her book *Spectacular Bodies* makes clear that Jackie Chan has been positioned by New Line within the conventions associated with the visual and narrative world of this kind of film. Tasker identifies three general categories of action heroes, each of which bears "very different connotations of both masculine and artistic identity": stars, performers, and actors.[31] "Stars," says Tasker, tend to be bodybuilder types: literally and figuratively larger-than-life cultural presences (Schwarzenegger and Stallone are the obvious examples), physically and conceptually excessive, "complex personas made up of far more than the texts in which they appear."[32] "Performers" (e.g., Chuck Norris, Stephen Seagal, Jean-Claude Van Damme), meanwhile, are identified primarily through their ability to demonstrate particular physical skills and especially talents deriving from the martial arts tradition. Finally, as Tasker points out, there doesn't seem to be much room for the category of "actor" in action films, given that "within western traditions the definition of a 'good' cinematic actor centres largely on the ability to develop the sustained portrayal of a complex character," and action films are not generally interested in constructing complex characters.[33]

Within this framework, it seems clear that Jackie Chan was positioned throughout the promotion of *Rumble in the Bronx* as a "performer," as signaled by the emphasis on Chan's athleticism and on the spectacle of danger associated with his showpiece stunts. This strategy has to do in part with Chan's relative unfamiliarity to the mainstream U.S. audience and partly, I think, with different cultural definitions of the concept of the "star." Tasker, in fact, draws a useful distinction between the Hollywood male action star and his Hong Kong counterpart, in terms of differences in physiognomy that in turn lead audiences to different expectations with regard to the nature of performance and spectacle provided.

> [T]he figure of the bodybuilder as star can be contrasted to the male stars of the Hong Kong action tradition, in which an elaborate, quick-fire, physical performance has come to form a central part of the visual pleasure that is on offer. The distinction is that between images of the body in action, so central to fight-films, and images of the top-heavy, almost statuesque, figure of the bodybuilder who essentially strikes poses within an action narrative. This distinction clearly has implications for the kinds of action, and the sorts of display, that action films offer.[34]

Within Tasker's model, for Asian audiences Chan is both a star and a performer—a star in part *because* he's such a spectacular performer. But his star status comes not only from his willingness to throw his body around with abandon, and this returns us to the notion of cultural proximity. In the world of the entertainment film, a star becomes the personification of characteristics that are considered positive, or at least interesting, to the culture within which she or he emerges as a star, and as Jenny Kwok Wah Lau has pointed out, "To interpret a gesture or an event or a symbol within its cultural context, we have to think in terms of the system of meanings by which a given group of people perceive, interpret and act or react with respect to different phenomena."[35] That is, before seizing the opportunity to become a star on U.S. cultural terms, Jackie Chan had to establish himself as a Chinese, and even more specifically, a Hong Kong star. He did so in part by developing a screen persona that corresponds in important ways with traits and behaviors that are considered virtuous in Hong Kong, a hybrid culture that incorporates both traditional Chinese values and aspects of Western modernity (e.g., consumerism, materialism, individualism). In her comparative analysis of some of the narrative emphases of PRC and Hong Kong films, Lau draws on the ideas of Mainland Chinese anthropologist Sun Longji, who has proposed that

> the Chinese view of a person can be dichotomised into the "body" *(shen)* and the "heart" *(xin)*. The physical body is what contributes to the physical life of a person, while the relationships with fellow human beings defines the spiritual realm of existence. The task of a person in the context of Chinese culture is to preserve his/her body and to keep the spiritual alive by maintaining proper relations with associates.[36]

In this setting there is an emphasis on the virtue of establishing interpersonal and intragroup relationships based on principles of loyalty, mutual aid, and selflessness; that is, says Lau, these relationships

> are shaped by the activities of the person's "heart." The "heart" generates an emotion called "*qing*" (emotive feeling). When this is directed towards another person, it should result in empathy and concern. This is called "having heart". . . . In contrast, the concern for the preservation of the body results in pragmatic survivalism of which the attitude of "*jing*" (cleverness) is an example. A "*jing*" person calculates his/her tactics to gain advantages, which may result in his/her refusal to "have heart" for others.[37]

Lau proposes further that Hong Kong films tend to emphasize the practicality and pragmatism (in pursuit of survival, of the "preservation of the body") characteristic of *jing* over the empathy and selflessness associated with *qing*.

I would suggest that a guiding principle of Jackie Chan's screen persona (and his films) involves an effort to strike a more equal balance between *jing* and *qing* and that a key aspect of his popular appeal in Hong Kong involves his character's respect for the value of nurturing a group orientation based on altruism and humility.[38] This is a desirable virtue precisely because of Hong Kong's chronic crisis of identity, a crisis that has intensified because of the 1997 issue; Chan's films suggest that unified, cooperative action in a chaotic, violent, and unjust world is the only means of achieving individual *and* collective survival and self-definition. Certainly, the intricacy and spectacular nature of his trademark fights and stunts speak metaphorically to the principle of preserving the body (under situations of extreme duress), and his resourcefulness, grace under pressure, daring, and luck attest to the cleverness of his character. For example, in *Rumble in the Bronx,* in order to disable a runaway hovercraft, he comes up with an improvised approximation of an ancient knight on horseback by employing a purloined Italian sports car and an old sword swiped from an antique store; and in *Drunken Master 2,* he drinks wood alcohol in order to sharpen his "drunken boxing" skills in the climactic fight sequence, which also features Chan falling into and crawling across a bed of red hot coals.

Some of these spectacular fights and stunts emphasize self-preservation (as well as Chan's individual skills as a performer), but the narrative contexts in which they occur also stress that Chan has found himself in his current predicament because of his selfless pursuit of more community-oriented goals. *Project A* (1983), for example, includes one of his most famous stunts, a Harold Lloyd homage in which Chan, attempting to escape a group of evil smugglers, finds himself dangling from the minute hand of a clock tower several stories above the street below. Unlike Lloyd, he falls, in slow motion (and in two successive unedited takes shown back to back), through three flimsy awnings and crashes to the ground. He gets up, grimacing in pain, but manages to stagger away. This is certainly a spectacular enough fetishizing of Chan's body, but within the story line of *Project A,* the event occurs because of Chan's efforts to maintain and preserve the Hong Kong coast guard community of which he is a part.

Another way of looking at this is to suggest that the heightened emphasis on *qing* in Chan's persona amounts to a way of resolving certain contradictions characteristic of Hong Kong culture. On the one hand, his movies emphasize individual action in the sense that he sometimes is compelled to break the rules and antagonize his superiors in order to accomplish his goals (and his stunts and acrobatics call attention to Chan's own physical agility and skill). On the other hand, what makes Chan a heroic, admirable figure has to do with the fact that he always asserts himself by identifying with the group, by showing a primary consideration for the physical and emotional needs of others. He is self-effacing even in the context of the martial arts combat at which he is so obviously accomplished. In keeping with fundamental principles of the martial arts tradition, he is never the aggressor; he fights in defense of his body, in defense of the social community of which he is a member, and, frequently, in order to demonstrate the superiority of his community's value structure; and (unlike U.S. movie action heroes) he never gloats over a fallen opponent, and may even offer the opponent an opportunity to redeem himself by acceding to the values of Chan's community. This pattern occurs in *Rumble in the Bronx*. After the biker gang has trashed the grocery store that Chan is obligated to protect, he enters the warehouse lair of the bad guys and proceeds to balletically pound some sense into them. At the conclusion of the fight, instead of delivering a "hasta la vista, baby" coup de grâce, Chan *lectures* the beaten bikers about their socially irresponsible behavior and departs with the words (preserved in Cantonese in the U.S. release), "I hope that the next time we meet we can sit down and have tea together." After getting a translation from a gang member who conveniently knows Cantonese, the leader of the bikers is so impressed that he decides on the spot to change his and the gang's ways. (In the two screenings of the U.S. version of *Rumble* that I have attended, this turn of events proved so unlikely to the mostly non-Asian audiences that it stimulated quite a bit of laughter.)

With the U.S. release of *Rumble in the Bronx*, New Line and Jackie Chan successfully scaled the wall of popular success that previously has been considered all but impregnable to assaults by non-Hollywood renditions of the "entertainment" film. This success was relative, however, and if the case of *Rumble in the Bronx* is indicative, what we call global entertainment will continue to be defined "asymmetrically" and equated primarily with Hollywood-produced fare. But there are constraints and limits even on the clout of that dominant force. Because audiences are active producers of meaning, definitions of entertainment are not universal, and very real cultural boundaries (of taste, of interest, of understanding) still exist in virtually every market situation around the world. While the conventional wisdom continues to be that action films are the safest bet in the global market, even in mainstream Hollywood these are not the only kinds of films produced, and some of these U.S.-made nonaction films do not export especially well.[39] Still, the magnitude of the alterations worked on *Rumble in the Bronx*—a movie made within an action-film paradigm that parallels but also differs in significant ways from the Hollywood model—for the U.S. release shows that U.S. distributors still perceive a high level of resistance among mainstream North American movie audiences for "foreign" films, and for cultural otherness in general. It is also true, of course, that Hollywood-produced entertainment films are dubbed into different languages around the world and that these films may be similarly reedited to suit the vicissitudes of national or regional tastes, values, and beliefs. But I would suggest that these situations—an "alternative" entertainment film seeking entry into the U.S. market versus a Hollywood entertainment film released into the global market—are not equivalent. Hollywood is selling a presold product with a strong brand identity overseas, while the distributor of a "foreign" entertainment film in the United States operates at a disadvantage in this regard. The U.S. movie industry's domination of screen time and box-office revenues in national and regional markets all over the world first emerged in the 1920s, and while the rules governing this hegemonic arrangement have evolved since then, the phenomenon itself has demonstrated remarkable staying power and adaptability, thanks especially to the "enforcement mechanisms" provided by the U.S. entertainment industry's huge advantage in available investment capital for production and marketing (an advantage due in part, of course, to Hollywood's long-term track record.)[40]

"Foreign" entertainment films by definition operate from a position of relative weakness in this situation. Golden Harvest, Jackie Chan, and Chan's management team have played their cards adroitly in the attempt to add the United States as the flagship (in terms of box-office receipts) of the roster of national and regional markets in which Chan is already a household name. And this was an optimum time to make this move, in that the U.S. distribution business is now populated with several companies (including some of the old-line majors) that are capable of marketing nonmainstream movies more successfully than ever before. New Line's handling of the release and promotion of *Rumble in the Bronx* was indicative of this new savvy. The film opened on fifteen hundred screens simultaneously and was supported by a substantial and well-orchestrated prerelease campaign of theatrical trailers, television ads, feature stories on Chan in sources as diverse as the *New York Times Magazine, Detour,* and *Entertainment Weekly,* high-profile appearances by Chan on David Letterman's and Jay Leno's late-night talk shows, a mini-biography and interview on the ABC news magazine show *Prime Time Live,* and a cross-country tour of preview screenings of *Rumble* with Chan in attendance.[41] This attention to detail was rewarded well: in its first-run U.S. release, *Rumble* grossed approximately $30 million, which constituted a substantial addendum to the $40 million the film had taken in during its initial 1995 release elsewhere in the world. This rate of return was pleasing to the Chan management team, since *Rumble* already was well into profit at the time of the U.S. run, and to New Line, which had invested only rights fees and marketing expenses in the project. In fact, the bottom-line figures were sufficiently encouraging to New Line that the company optioned the U.S. rights to Chan's next five films while *Rumble* was still in the theaters.[42]

At the same time, the cultural connotations of some aspects of that marketing (the retooling of the film, the general obscuring of the "Chinese-ness" of Chan's screen persona[43]) remain unsettling. In the film, Chan plays a visitor to the United States who finds himself adrift in social and cultural settings with which he is unfamiliar, and the editing and marketing of the U.S. version of *Rumble* in a way reproduce that scenario with regard to the Chan persona. In the United States, that is, his character seems similarly without mooring in some of the more important contextual factors that inform it and that in turn help to dictate the logic of Chan's (and other characters') actions in *Rumble*. Some of these actions, which may be perceived as logical enough, I think, within a Chinese cultural context, are much more likely to play as overly sentimental, naive corn to non-Asian U.S. audiences.

This is the sort of dilemma that will continue to confront filmmakers and film marketers hoping to generate mainstream U.S. success for foreign-made entertainment movies, especially when the degree of cultural proximity is relatively modest. It is the converse of the situation enjoyed by Hollywood entertainment in national and regional environments around the world, where U.S. product often has substantial asymmetrical marketing advantages. Even under those highly desirable circumstances, this imported material still is not guaranteed easy access to popular success because of the continuing preference of local audiences for comparable locally produced entertainment (when it is available). As Ien Ang has suggested with regard to television transmissions, while the transnational media companies have pretty successfully (but provisionally, temporarily) established an electronic global village in purely economic terms, local tastes and interests still matter with regard to both the generalized acceptance of imported mass-market entertainment and the constellation of meanings assigned to particular examples of that entertainment by particular audiences.

> The emphasis on speed of delivery and immediacy of transmission does indeed produce a structure of temporal synchronicity which makes space irrelevant. . . . At another level, however, the spatial dimension cannot be discounted when it comes to what happens to those images once they arrive in specific locations. At this cultural level, at once more mundane and more fluid local realities can themselves present an unpredictable interpretive screen through which the

intruding electronic screen images are filtered. At the level of the day-to-day, space cannot be annihilated because the social specificity of any locality is inevitably marked by its characteristics as a place.[44]

Reversing the polarities here—moving externally generated information and entertainment images into the United States—puts a different spin on the cultural and economic ramifications of the situation, as I've suggested. The "mundane" and "fluid local realities" of U.S. audiences for mainstream entertainment historically have included a substantial resistance to non-Hollywood product and a tendency to make sense of "foreign" images largely in terms of cultural and racial stereotypes that (unwittingly) help to preserve existing inequalities of access and acceptance. In a sense, that is, the dominance of Hollywood in its *home* market both helps to produce and is a product of the industry's global hegemony. But as usual, hegemony leaks, and the modest success (by U.S. movie box-office standards) of *Rumble in the Bronx* suggests the parameters of the U.S. entertainment industry's adjustment mechanism in the era of economic globalization. It remains true enough that a relatively universal marketability is the signature of the international blockbuster, the kind of product that has been recognized as a major component of Hollywood's ever-growing interest in rationalizing its business practices on a global scale. And if this universality constitutes the holy grail of mass entertainment salesmanship, the present success of Jackie Chan in the United States represents an as yet small-scale but significant revision of the master narrative of global marketing. It may be that the concept of mainstream entertainment is in the process of being revised to include the apparently paradoxical notion of "niche mainstream" product, in response to a growing realization even on the part of the wide boys who run the transnational media companies that at any given time and place in the world today there is likely to be more than one applicable (and potentially profitable) zeitgeist at work.

· Notes

1. David Ansen, "Chinese Takeout," *Newsweek,* February 19, 1996, 68.

2. Li Cheuk-to, "Tsui Hark and Western Interest in Hongkong Cinema," *Cinemaya* 21 (1993): 51.

3. There is also, of course, the eerily similar "what-if" scenario involving Lee's son, Brandon, whose accidental death during the filming of *The Crow* in 1994 tragically paralleled his father's in that each died just as he was achieving a new level of stardom in the United States.

4. The one quasi exception is Woo's 1989 film *The Killer,* which was picked up

for U.S. distribution by a small independent company, Circle Releasing. Only a few theatrical playdates were ever arranged.

5. For a discussion of the ramifications of (self-conscious) production for the international market, see Jenny Kwok Wah Lau, "*Farewell My Concubine:* History, Melodrama, and Ideology in Contemporary Pan-Chinese Cinema," *Film Quarterly* 49, no. 1 (1995): 16–27.

6. A recent exception was the limited U.S. release of Wong Kar-Wai's *Chungking Express,* which landed a distribution deal because Quentin Tarantino is a fan of the film.

7. His given Chinese name is Chen Gang Shen; to Chinese audiences he is known as Sing Long ("Be the Dragon"), a name he was given by director Lo Wei in the mid-1970s. Grant Foerster and Rolanda Chu, *Jackie Chan Star Profile* (San Francisco: Hong Kong Film Monthly, 1994), 14.

8. Useful English-language accounts of Chan's career include the chapter devoted to his work in Bey Logan, *Hong Kong Action Cinema* (London: Titan Books, 1995); Foerster and Chu, *Jackie Chan Star Profile;* and Craig Reid, "An Evening with Jackie Chan," *Bright Lights* 13 (1994): 18–25. A good summary of the history of the Hong Kong martial arts film is Sek Kei, "The Development of 'Martial Arts' in Hong Kong Cinema," in *A Study of the Hong Kong Martial Arts Film,* ed. Lau Shing-hon (Hong Kong: Urban Council, 1984): 27–38.

9. For additional discussion of Golden Harvest, see Steve Fore, "Golden Harvest Films and the Hong Kong Movie Industry in the Realm of Globalization," *The Velvet Light Trap* 34 (1994): 40–58.

10. See Justin Wyatt, "*The Wedding Banquet,* Independent Cinema, and Cultural Identities." Paper presented at the Ohio University Film Conference, November 1994.

11. This is by no means a record opening, but it is a splashy debut for a film released in (what the movie industry perceives as) the doldrums between the Christmas and Easter holidays, when more high-profile, high-expectation releases are scheduled. John Woo's *Broken Arrow* also opened in this "downtime" (on February 9) and did even better—more than $15 million in the opening weekend.

12. See also Joey O'Bryan, "A Rumble in Hollywood," *Austin Chronicle,* March 22, 1996, 34–35, 38.

13. Richard Dyer, *Light Entertainment* (London: British Film Institute, 1973), 9.

14. Richard Dyer, "Entertainment and Utopia," in *Genre: The Musical,* ed. Rick Altman (London: Routledge and Kegan Paul, 1981), 177.

15. For instance, Richard Corliss writes: "In American terms he's a little Clint Eastwood (actor-director), a dash of Gene Kelly (imaginative choreographer), a bit of Jim Carrey (rubbery ham) and a lot of the silent-movie clowns: Charlie Chaplin, Buster Keaton and Harold Lloyd." Richard Corliss, "Jackie Can!," *Time,* February 13, 1995, 82.

16. Joseph D. Straubhaar, "Beyond Media Imperialism: Asymmetrical Interdependence and Cultural Proximity," *Critical Studies in Mass Communication* 8, no. 1 (1991): 39. Emphasis mine.

17. Straubhaar, "Beyond Media Imperialism," 39. Emphasis mine.

18. For a discussion of these issues in a Hong Kong context, see Paul S. N. Lee, "The Absorption and Indigenization of Foreign Media Cultures—A Study on a Cultural Meeting Point of the East and West: Hong Kong," *Asian Journal of Communication* 1, no. 2 (1991): 52–72.

19. There are, of course, also significant differences in life experience across and within the populations of the three Chinas as well. I have placed the word "Chineseness" in quotation marks throughout this analysis to remind both readers and myself that I am attempting to steer clear of essentialist definitions of Chinese identity.

20. Recall that the original *Mad Max* was dubbed into "American" English for its U.S. release.

21. Peter Lev, *The Euro-American Cinema* (Austin: University of Texas Press, 1993), 4.

22. For example, the Australian New Wave of the 1980s, *Strawberry and Chocolate* from Cuba, *Like Water for Chocolate* and *Cabeza da Vaca* from Mexico, *Through the Olive Trees* from Iran, Ang Lee's Taiwanese films, Zhang Yimou's PRC films, and *The Scent of Green Papaya* from Vietnam (by way of Paris).

23. Lev, *The Euro-American Cinema,* 5.

24. Lev, *The Euro-American Cinema,* 5.

25. For an example of this kind of criticism from a Chinese perspective, see Dai Qing, "Raised Eyebrows for *Raise the Red Lantern,*" *Public Culture* 5, no. 2 (1993): 333–337. For a provocative response to that criticism, see also, however, Rey Chow, *Primitive Passions: Visuality, Sexuality, Ethnography, and Contemporary Chinese Cinema* (New York: Columbia University Press, 1995).

26. See the discussions of this issue in the following: Nick Deocampo and Chris Berry, "On Questions of Difference," *Cinemaya* 23 (1994): 40–43; Jim Hwang, "Cross-Cultural Resonance," *Free China Review* (February 1995): 16–17; and Jim Hwang, "On Being Gay in Taipei," *Asiaweek,* December 1, 1993, 45.

27. In fact, except for a handful of pickup shots, *Rumble* was shot entirely in Vancouver. Numerous U.S. critics and viewers have pointed out the presence of snow-capped mountains in the background of several scenes—glitches in topographical verisimilitude that are of much less consequence for audiences outside the United States.

28. It is also significant that New Line opted to buy the rights for one of Chan's Hong Kong–produced films rather than bring him to the United States to make a movie. The logic here, I think, was that New Line is a company that has gone the pick-up route frequently, that Chan was considered to be a risky property in the

U.S. market (in light of the commercial and critical failure of his early-1980s U.S.-produced vehicles, not to mention the "risk" that New Line would associate with his racial heritage), and New Line may have recognized as well that to make an "authentic Jackie Chan film" full of expensive, time-and-money-consuming stunt and fight sequences would have been prohibitively expensive in the United States, at least at this point.

29. Chan's (and other Hong Kong) films are regularly dubbed into other languages for the regional Asian market and into Spanish for Latin American release.

30. Chan himself has said that he prefers the original Hong Kong cut of the film.

31. Yvonne Tasker, *Spectacular Bodies: Gender, Genre, and the Action Cinema* (London: Routledge, 1993), 74.

32. Tasker, *Spectacular Bodies*, 74.

33. Tasker, *Spectacular Bodies*, 75. Still, suggests Tasker, there are stars such as Harrison Ford, who has demonstrated an ability to exhibit both physical and verbal agility on screen, and who on a sustained basis has been able to move between character-driven and action-driven roles—frequently in the course of a single performance (e.g., *The Fugitive*, the Tom Clancy films).

34. Tasker, *Spectacular Bodies*, 73.

35. Jenny Kwok Wah Lau, "A Cultural Interpretation of the Popular Cinema of China and Hong Kong," in *Perspectives on Chinese Cinema*, ed. Chris Berry (London: British Film Institute, 1991), 166.

36. Lau, "A Cultural Interpretation," 167.

37. Lau, "A Cultural Interpretation," 167.

38. I am grateful to David K. Joplin, a graduate student in my course on Chinese film in spring 1994, for writing an excellent essay on Jackie Chan which stimulated my interest in these ideas.

39. In the People's Republic of China (a market which only recently has been opened to a limited number of Hollywood films), for instance, *True Lies* and *The Fugitive* were hits, while *Forrest Gump* was not, apparently because of the cultural specificity of *Gump*'s themes and narrative threads. On the other hand, *The Bridges of Madison County* was enormously popular with Mainland audiences, and this success may help to add mythic melodrama to the short list of export-friendly genres.

40. See Janet Wasko, *Hollywood in the Information Age* (Austin: University of Texas Press, 1994), 219–240.

41. For a sample of this coverage, see Ansen, "Chinese Takeout," 66–68; Chris Nashawaty, "Kong Kings," *Entertainment Weekly*, March 8, 1996, 28–29; Lawrence Schubert, "Just for Kicks," *Detour*, February 1996, 28–32; and Jaime Wolf, "Jackie Chan, American Action Hero?," *New York Times Magazine*, January 21, 1996, 22–25.

42. As I type this in the summer of 1996, other strategies designed to break Jackie Chan as a U.S. action-movie icon seem to be in the works. *Daily Variety* reported recently that "Wesley Snipes and Jackie Chan are making deals with Uni-

versal to develop *Confucius Brown,* 'an action-comedy reminiscent of 48 *Hours,'*
which would bring them into an unlikely teaming as cousins who battle Chinatown gangsters." Michael Fleming, "Snipes, Chan Say *Confucius," Daily Variety,* April
9, 1996, I. Also, it has been reported that Chan's current project, *Mr. Nice Guy* (an
Australian location shoot that reunites him with childhood friend and fellow Hong
Kong martial arts star Samo Hung), will be filmed entirely in English. Clyde Gentry
III, *"Mr. Nice Guy:* Jackie and Sammo Reunite!," *Hong Kong Film Connection* 4, no. 2
(1996): 3.

43. This tendency carried over into the visual design of the primary one-sheet
poster used to promote the film, which featured a fist ripping through the title;
Chan's face was conspicuously absent. By contrast, a full-page advertisement for
Rumble in *A* magazine, which is niche-marketed to a primarily Asian American reader-
ship, prominently featured a portrait of Chan's face.

44. Ien Ang, *Living Room Wars* (London: Routledge, 1996), 151.

Part III

·

Engendering History and Nationhood:
Cross-Cultural and Gendered Perspectives

Chapter 10

•

Reading Formations and Chen Kaige's *Farewell My Concubine*

•

E. Ann Kaplan

Third World texts, even those which are seemingly private and invested with a properly libidinal dynamic—necessarily project a political dimension in the form of national allegory.
Fredric Jameson

Edward Said was prescient in pointing out the importance of theories circulating from one culture to another. In an essay titled "Traveling Theory" in *The World, the Text, and the Critic,* Said wrote:

> Like people and schools of criticism, ideas and theories travel—from person to person, from situation to situation, from one period to another. . . . There are particularly interesting cases of ideas and theories that move from one culture to another, as when so-called Eastern ideas about transcendence were imported into Europe. . . . Such movement to a new environment is never unimpeded. It necessarily involves processes of representation and institutionalization different from those at the point of origin. This complicates any account of the transplantation, transference, circulation, and commerce of theories and ideas.[1]

Since Said's essay was written, theories have traveled with increasing rapidity. This is partly because of the new global networking—usefully analyzed by Arjun Appadurai in terms of a series of "scapes" that include mediascapes, financescapes, and ideascapes.[2] Electronic mail, the Internet, CD-ROMs, as well as the increased frequency of literal international traveling by Eastern and Western theorists with their new ideas, has meant increasingly complex phenomena of "the transplantation, transference, circulation, and commerce of theories and ideas" that Said mentions.

Said's comments have relevance for the much-debated and now fraught issue Fredric Jameson raised of "national allegory" in "Third Cinema" versus "something else" in Western films. It is an issue that cannot be addressed outside consideration of the context within which Other World films are produced. As is obvious from the case of America, however, it is not necessary for film studios to be state-controlled for them to be ideologically restricted; nor is it true that all state-produced films are mere "propaganda." The issue is more complex, more nuanced.

In the 1980s, the interesting questions had to do with what film ideas arose, which were accepted for production, and which made it through the final review process. All film production in China was (and still basically is) organized through state-run film studios and training academies, where directors, producers, actors, actresses, and so on are employees of the state. In the 1990s, the situation is more complicated than it was in the 1980s: filmmakers like Chen Kaige obtain international funding, and their films are exhibited in the international film-festival circuit, often winning prestigious awards. Nevertheless, as the case of *Farewell My Concubine* itself shows, censorship still exists within Mainland China.

As I argued in 1990, cross-cultural analysis is difficult—fraught with danger, because the critic is forced to read works produced by the Other through the constraints of one's own frameworks, theories, ideologies.[3] In saying this, I meant to refer to both Western and non-Western critics, although Western critics' dilemmas remained central since that is what I knew something about.[4]

I addressed anxieties that analyses by critics trained in the West were in danger of becoming a new form of cultural imperialism in much the same way as Gayatri Spivak has argued. Quoting an example from a Marxist academic writing on Garcia Marquéz "as a paradigmatic case of Third World literary production," Spivak pointedly asked, "What are the implications of pedagogic gestures that monumentalize this style as the right Third World style?"[5] Specifically to be avoided, I implied, was the danger that Trinh T. Minh-ha has since explicitly named as the critic "grasping the native's point of view" or aiming "to realize *his* vision of *his* world."[6] I referred to reactions by some not only to the possible imperialism of Western critics' analyses of Chinese films but to the *content* of what Western critics said.

Feminists might be tempted to argue that questions about the viability of cross-cultural research do not apply to their research because they are women and feminists and thus bring to their meetings frameworks that avoid power/knowledge axes. However, research by women of color—from African Americans like bell hooks, Barbara Christian, and Hazel Carby to Asian scholars like Amy Ling, Chandra Mohanty, and Sau-Ling Cynthia Wong to Chicana writers like Cherri Moraga and Gloria Anzaldua—has long shown the (albeit unconscious) white feminist colonizing habits of thought that I have briefly addressed elsewhere.[7] It is, thus, in full awareness of the Eurocentric bias of my brief reading of *Farewell My Concubine* that I offer it: Eurocentrism includes ways Western critics are trained to be self-conscious about the emotional impact of a film on the individual spectator and to focus on subjectivity. In relying (to some extent) on my subjective responses to the film, I am implicating my subject-formation as a white, European woman trained in the West to use feminist theories, psychoanalysis, and Western cultural studies in specific ways. What is interesting to me in undertaking cross-cultural analysis is precisely finding out what *others* will make of my responses.[8] Reading formations inevitably shape film interpretation. What's fascinating is the debates that follow the laying out of interpretations: I am interested in how others understand and "decode" what gave rise to this, that, or the other reading. I am interested in the differences among readings.

· The Film: Defining the Problem

How may a feminist critic trained in the West begin to enter this film? Where should she start? What tools are appropriate? And why? Should she begin by studying the history of Chinese opera? Or find out more about Chinese politics between 1927 and 1977, given the film's focus on fifty years of dramatic political and social changes? Should she start by locating the film in Chen Kaige's filmography or personal career moves from his role in the short, exciting late 1980s intellectual thaw and new film movement it permitted to his making an expensive epic film partly outside Mainland China and with Western funding?

Any or all of these might have been sensible, useful. But I decided to turn to my own discipline and ways in which U.S. feminist film studies might make a cross-cultural contribution. I thought that feminist research on melodrama might be useful as part of an exploration of the genre's formations across a wide diversity of cultures. For women, the sphere of the private, the domestic, in its constructions vis-à-vis male public spheres (which have all the power and value in most cultures) offers important insights into what it means to be female in many cultures. Such investigation is particularly appropriate as women begin globally to move out of the domestic spaces, to challenge male public spheres, and to engage in the public sphere themselves. As they empower themselves in government and public policies, so women internationally may better bring about urgently needed changes in matters central to women in the domestic sphere, such as childbirth, child care, health care, divorce law, equality of job opportunity, and so on.

A recent Chinese film like *Farewell My Concubine* raises interesting issues *for the Western-trained feminist critic* in relation to the representation of gender. While the film is a drama rather than specifically a *melo*drama, it nevertheless has melodrama elements that I find useful to focus on. As noted, studying melodrama can tell the critic much about a culture's imaginary constructions of women and of men, of gender, class, and racial difference and may illuminate paths toward change. Stressing the way *Farewell My Concubine* deals with mother-child and male-female relations may illuminate larger issues to do with the family and with constructions of male and female sexualities as they are impacted upon by the public sphere.

I hope my brief comments will stimulate debate, for that, as I have argued, is one of the main purposes of cross-cultural film analysis.

· An Analysis

I start with the simplest of levels, namely, my responses as I watched the film. These responses, I thought, might lead me to underlying assumptions in the film about sexual difference, gender, familial relations—assumptions glossed over by the riveting epic male narrative of the impact of wars and changes of regime on two male opera stars.

I was interested in the film's impact on my emotions: Early on in viewing *Farewell My Concubine*, I found tears streaming down my face. It's not that I never cry watching films; but it's rare for me to feel so choked up.[9] I wondered if my response might direct me toward some of the underlying traumas, emotions, and psychic conflicts that the narrative addresses.

The scene that first evoked tears was that when Douzi's (Cheng Dieyi) mother begs the itinerant Chinese opera company's master to keep her boy child, born in the brothel where the mother works, because she cannot rear him there. The mother's desperation is obvious not only in her being impervious to the cruelty to the children she witnesses in the company quarters but also in her own ability to brutally cut off her child's extra finger, which the master had declared ruled out an acting career. I gasped as I saw her do this, but I felt the tears flow in a contrastingly silent moment—that when Douzi, trying unsuccessfully to run away, bends down beneath a table. His mother says goodbye, but he keeps his head turned away. Realizing she means it, he calls out "Ma!" and turns his head. I expected to see the mother in the doorway, turning back to her child. Instead, Chen cuts to the huge doorway, where no one stands, and through which white snow can be seen falling on an empty field. The camera holds on that silent image for what seems like an age.

It is a shocking visual metaphor for abandonment. The emptiness, the coldness, the whiteness all conjure up absence, loss. It was the unusual combination of violence and loss that produced the scene's powerful impact on me. The scene is important because it establishes one of the main emotional strands of the film as far as one of the protagonists, Douzi, is concerned.

Fig. 24. Leslie Cheung (Zhang Guorong) as Cheng Dieyi in *Farewell My Concubine,* directed by Chen Kaige, 1993. British Film Institute.

Douzi (played as an adult by Leslie Cheung) becomes, in Freud's terms, an "abandonment neurotic," ever seeking to refind or replace the mother who left him but always anticipating rejection. As a child, full of hate, anger, and vengeful feelings, he finally bonds with Shitou (nickname for Duan Xiaolou), who takes care of him in the terrible days of learning opera skills through brutal, heartless, inexorable beating. Tellingly, Douzi plays the concubine to Shitou's king once they are adult and successful: In the ancient Chinese opera *Farewell My Concubine* (set in 200 B.C.), which doubles with the film's title, the concubine stays with the king when he is surrounded by enemies; she then kills herself with his sword before he is captured and killed.

The title *Farewell My Concubine* resonates across many passionate yearnings, longings, unitings, and severings apart that happen in the film. It stands as a metaphor for everyone's loss, all characters' inability to fulfill their desires. But it is Douzi's double transference onto Shitou—his making him stand in for the loss of his mother and his literalizing the concubine-king relationship offstage—that produces the tragedy.

Douzi and Shitou become famous actors in their joint roles mainly because Douzi's performance is not only so perfect but also so moving and "real." Of course, it is "real" because Douzi in fact lives inside the concubine role all the time. For a while, it is a viable transference-defense mechanism against his loss: "living" the concubine role enables him to forget the traumatic double shock of castration (the finger) and of abandonment—both by his mother.

But when Shitou, his mother-substitute, tries to free himself of Douzi's dependence through marriage to Juxian (Gong Li) and starting a family (Juxian soon becomes pregnant), Douzi undergoes a traumatic crisis in which his moral structures are eroded: in revenge, he takes up with the "decadent" opera patron, Master Yuan, and he sings for the Japanese to bring about Shitou's release—Juxian has promised to leave Shitou if Douzi does this.

Here, the film seems to follow a fairly stereotypical representation of homosexuals that gay and queer studies have exposed.[10] The male aesthete as necessarily queer, the male queer as necessarily a feminized aesthete—these are well-worn Western images. In addition, the psychoanalytic paradigm I am using encourages a reading such that male homosexuality emerges as resulting from a problem with the mother (Douzi cannot relate to women because of the trauma with his mother, for example). Perhaps the film needs to be criticized from a gay/queer-studies perspective for perpetuating such negative gay stereotypes as the effete, seductive, and narcissistic opera patron, and for apparently utilizing an underlying traditional psychoanalytic understanding of queerness as a result of overidentification with the mother. On the other hand, Chinese cinema has only just begun to deal with gay sexualities, so Chen's introduction of these should be recognized as progress.

I have not hesitated to use traditional psychoanalytic concepts in analyzing the crucial opening scenes and my response to them, despite the fact that *Farewell My Concubine* was made in Mainland China, was produced by an ex-kung fu Hong Kong actress, Xu Feng, and concerns an ancient Chinese art form with specific cultural, historical, and social traditions. I do this partly for reasons I elaborated a few years ago and have already referred to.[11] As I noted earlier, I accept that critics trained in the West are, indeed, only able to bring to works from other cultures the frameworks and theoretical paradigms they know and to respond out of their own psychic "sets," as I have done here. But I also believe, with Frantz Fanon, that abandonment neurosis, like that I argue Douzi suffers, is not peculiar to Western cultures.[12] Indeed, the case of the Antillean Jean Veneuse that Fanon describes in *Black Skin, White Masks* very much parallels that of Douzi in this film.[13]

Psychoanalytic concepts only become dubious within specific complicated social-political-economic contexts. The applicability or not of psychoanalytic paradigms has to do with context. Fanon remarks of the Malagasy, for instance, that there never was a case of oedipal rivalries or problems. This was partly due to the strength and centrality of the community in the typical Malagasy child's psychic and social development. Fanon also notes that in the Antilles black children were "normal" (not exhibiting oedipal or other neuroses) until contact with white culture.[14] It was precisely this contact that seemed to produce oedipal problems, particularly for black male children confronted with denigration, scorn, and lack of respect from the white authoritative father, symbolized in state power.

It is possible that within the relatively ethnically homogenous Chinese culture manifest in the film oedipal scenarios may be relevant. Or else Chen Kaige, as a Chinese director who spent time at New York University film school and who has had extensive exposure to Hollywood film, finds Western constructs useful: Perhaps he chose to tell his story in a way that stimulates the Western viewer to perceive oedipal processes at work despite his not necessarily having them in mind.

But the psychic traumas alone could not, I think, produce the sort of powerful, almost Shakespearean, impact the film ultimately has. For all its much-discussed aesthetic and spectacle qualities, this is a deeply felt film. It is never sensational because psychic pain is always linked to economic need, class war, revolution, or international invasion. While many critics have discussed the film's demonstrating that art cannot remain a transcendent space beyond economics, politics, and the social sphere, none has noted the

Fig. 25. Gong Li as Juxian in *Farewell My Concubine,* directed by Chen Kaige, 1993. British Film Institute.

way the film shows how the family and the supposedly private, domestic sphere also cannot be transcendent or unaffected by political, social, and historical changes.

The "family" then becomes an allegory for the larger Chinese situation. Here Fredric Jameson's theory about allegorical readings is quite appropriate (as it surely is also for many Hollywood films).[15] The painful love triangle, its oedipal suffering, mimics the suffering China as a whole endures in different ways in the periods the film covers. Oedipus is never reduced to the social; nor is the social reduced to Oedipus. But the two levels within which humans live, suffer, and enjoy are inextricably linked. The family is not a sacrosanct entity but is prey to international warfare and also to state tyranny, state legislation.

In addition, the film is sensitive to gender issues even if it cannot produce a specifically "feminist" analysis of Juxian's predicament. Juxian is apparently the "strong" one—the one who is active, who initiates. But a Western feminist reading enables one to see that, in fact, her life trajectory is severely limited by the social construction of her desire. Isn't Juxian's entire desire to win Shitou's love and protection? Where is any "autonomous" or self-fulfilling desire? Once the revolution happens, she cannot associate herself with the new communist heroines, who are entirely new kinds of women constructed to be loyal to the state—to have the state as their desire (not necessarily any better a location than a single male). None of the three protagonists in *Farewell* is able to break prerevolutionary modes of thought. Shitou stands between life (Juxian) and art/the aesthetic sphere (Douzi): the battle takes place *across* his body but *inside* Juxian's. No critics I read mentioned Juxian's tragic loss of the baby that meant so much to her and that symbolized her and Shitou's union. It is a union that Douzi despises and fears, for it reminds him of the loss of his mother, of what he never had, and it consolidates Shitou's relationship to Juxian. It is a union that, within the terms of her socialization, Juxian dearly longs for and has, so to speak, earned.

Given this interlacing of the psychic and the social, Oedipus and politics, let me speculate on what may have been the underlying *political* passion in *Farewell*. Chen Kaige was one of the several brilliant young directors who came into adulthood just at the moment when the Chinese regime was loosening its hold on cultural productions. The years from 1983 through 1988 were heady ones in which freshly trained directors working in remarkable film studios like those at Xi'an, Shanghai, and Beijing were making beautiful films tentatively critical of Chinese regimes from before and up to the Cultural Revolution. Already then, filmmakers had found an excellent strategy in producing narratives with double meanings—the specific narrative about a family or individual was often intended to be read as an allegory for the Chinese political scene. The power of *Farewell My Concubine* possibly derives from something similar: that is, the passion and power in the film seem to be fueled by grief over Tiananmen Square: the epic quality of the film, in which the central protagonists' lives are caught up in a series of violent national disruptions from the 1920s warlord era, through the 1937 Japanese invasion, the victory over the Japanese by Chiang Kai-shek, Mao's defeat of the Nationalists in 1949, to, finally, the devastating 1966 Cultural Revolution. It seems that the pain and tragic series of losses that Douzi sustains are meant also to represent the tragic losses to Chinese culture wrought by the wrenching from one regime and politics to another. But, as I hope I have made clear, Chen has managed to create powerful links between individual abandonment neurosis and traumas in the public political and historical sphere.

· Notes

1. Edward Said, "Traveling Theory," in *The World, the Text, and the Critic* (Cambridge, Mass.: Harvard University Press, 1983), 226.

2. See Arjun Appadurai, "Disjuncture and Difference in the Global Cultural Economy," *Public Culture* 2, no. 2 (1990): 1–17.

3. See E. Ann Kaplan, "Problematizing Cross-Cultural Analysis: The Case of Women in the Recent Chinese Cinema," *Wide Angle* 11, no. 2 (1989): 42; reprinted in *Perspectives on Chinese Cinema,* ed. Chris Berry (London: British Film Institute, 1991), 141–154.

4. When I say "Western and non-Western critics," I mean to differentiate critics *trained* in the West from those *trained* in the East. It's not so much that any ideas per se "belong" to a specific nation or part of the world but that how ideas are deployed, within what discourses they are situated depends very much on other aspects of a particular culture. How knowledge is organized, codes relating to knowledge use, habits of scholarship, and so forth all differ from nation to nation. Within the Eurocentric cultures that I am familiar with, certain ways of using knowledge prevail, and it is these that I intend to reference with the phrase "Western critics."

5. Gayatri Chakravorty Spivak, "Marginality in the Teaching Machine," *Outside in the Teaching Machine* (London: Routledge, 1993), 57–58.

6. See Trinh T. Minh-ha's essay, "Outside In/Inside Out," in *Questions of Third Cinema,* ed. Jim Pines and Paul Willemen (London: British Film Institute, 1989).

7. I discuss some of these problems in my essay, "The Couch-Affair: Gender and Race in the Hollywood Transference," *American Imago* (winter 1993): 481–514. I explore issues further in my book, *Looking for the Other: Feminism and the Imperial Gaze* (London: Routledge, 1997).

8. For example, Yoshimoto Mitsuhira has a detailed response to Western film scholars' work on Japanese (and in my case, Chinese) cinema. See "The Difficulty of Being Radical: The Discipline of Film Studies and the Postcolonial World Order," *boundary* 2 18, no. 3 (1991): 242–257. I believe his intervention has been useful in stimulating further thoughts about these complex issues. Elsewhere, I respond to Yoshimoto's reactions in some detail. See E. Ann Kaplan, "Who's Reading What Signs and Why," unpublished paper.

9. My husband, incidentally, was not so moved: while gender constructions may partly account for our differing responses, it may also be true that, in psychological terms, the film struck one of my "hot cognitions" (that is, one of the emotional registers that fit my particular psychic makeup). The reading formation involving the "hot cognition" for me has to do with abandonment fantasies having figured heavily in my own childhood.

10. See, for instance, Parker Tyler, *Screening the Sexes: Homosexuality in the Movies*

(New York: Holt, Rinehart and Winston, 1972); Richard Dyer, ed. *Gays and Film,* 2nd ed. (New York: Zoetrope, 1984).

11. See Kaplan, "Problematizing Cross-Cultural Analysis."

12. See Frantz Fanon, *Black Skin, White Masks,* trans. Charles Lam Markmann (New York: Grove Press, 1967).

13. Fanon, *Black Skin,* 74–81.

14. Fanon, *Black Skin,* 142–143.

15. This shows that it is not Jameson's insight about allegory being a necessary element in Third World literature and film that is, per se, wrong. What's wrong is his limiting this insight *to Third World texts.*

Chapter 11

·

The New Woman Incident
Cinema, Scandal, and Spectacle in 1935 Shanghai

·

Kristine Harris

When the silent film *The New Woman* (Xin nüxing) opened in Shanghai during the lunar new year festival of 1935, one newspaper reviewer applauded
"the number of films with 'the woman question' as their subject over the
past few years" and declared that "in a time when the women's movement
is being noticed once again, it is inevitable that this kind of film will go on
to influence many aspects of the women's movement to come."[1] This passage suggests just one way in which *The New Woman* was a striking conver-
gence point for the cinematic, journalistic, and social construction of gendered
subjectivity in 1930s Shanghai. Periodicals and studio publicity drew attention to the centrality of gender in the film, championing the eponymous
"New Woman":

> Women have been shackled down and treated like non-persons for sev-
> eral thousand years. They have gradually climbed out from the abyss
> of suffering during the past hundred years, but archaic customs and eco-
> nomics still block the passage for women.
>
> *The New Woman* is aimed at precisely this state of affairs—it is a call
> to arms for humanity and society. It offers a model for the spirit of new
> women and opposes suicide which is an action that is not as new as it
> may seem. The film characterizes classic archetypes of women and ad-
> vances a new kind of woman.
>
> Having seen *The New Woman* you will feel that the "Old" Woman is
> pathetic and pitiable. Watching this film is like suddenly being offered
> a glass of brandy after a lifetime of drinking plain water—it will stun
> and provoke even the most complacent person; it is encouraging and
> inspiring.[2]

The film's title also attracted audiences for the same reason. One viewer in
a province as distant as Guizhou recounted his movie date with a young
woman from work this way: "I think that I can easily guess the reason she

Fig. 26. Actress Ruan Lingyu (1910–1935).

wanted to see this movie. Naturally, she wanted to understand what the 'New Woman,' as presented by the movie company from the big city, was all about."[3] Certainly the film accommodated such curiosity by profiling the life and death of Wei Ming—a schoolteacher and aspiring author who experiences the challenges and confusions facing educated, independent women in the big city, until she is ultimately implicated in a tragic suicidal confrontation with the Shanghai news media. In this sense, *The New Woman* resembled some of Hollywood's "fallen woman films" of the 1920s and 1930s, or its "woman's films" of the 1940s, in "documenting a crisis in subjectivity around the figure of woman—although it is not always clear whose subjectivity is at stake."[4]

But in Shanghai's *The New Woman,* the disturbing representation of Wei Ming's suicide was accompanied by a critique of contemporary urban society that alluded to class revolution. The film provoked a debate in the Shanghai news media over the status and symbolic significance of the New Woman, and the protagonist's "crisis in subjectivity" was profoundly magnified when the lead actress, Ruan Lingyu, committed suicide in reaction to the press slander just a month after the premier. The "New Woman Incident" (as it was later dubbed) became the nexus of a controversy over the responsibility of the urban news media—as the modern creators of "public opinion" *(yulun)*—toward women and society.[5] For historians, the film and the suicide expose Chinese popular culture at a moment of crisis over the degree to which women would be agents, symbols, or victims of modernity.

Criticism on *The New Woman* has appeared under two rubrics. It is either cited as an example of the complications in the leftward developments of director Cai Chusheng's politics,[6] or it serves as the tragic climax to hagiographies of its star, Ruan Lingyu.[7] These approaches pinpoint biographical correspondences to the narrative scenario; they do remark on gender and politics in the film but elide the complex interaction between the two. The present essay examines how that interaction was constructed within the film's frame and beyond it, in the scandal and spectacle of the New Woman Incident.

The New Woman could be read narrowly as a text in terms of pyschoanalytic theory to render an analysis of issues that have become central to feminist film criticism in Europe and America, and also in China, today—such as the relationship between cinematic images and spectators or the function of the star. I have chosen to broaden the scope, however, working on the premise that, like any cultural text, a film is an artifact of specific social conditions, as well as of certain technological capabilities.[8] I investigate the changing position of filmmakers and the notion of the New Woman in 1920s and 1930s Shanghai; the film's narrative sources, publicity, direction, script, and iconography; the manner in which it was exhibited and received among contemporary audiences; and Ruan Lingyu's own actions and role in the media circulation of her star image. These factors all came together in an incident that exposed the shifting status of women and the media in the political economy of urban China.

· Cai Chusheng and the Politics of the Image

Cai Chusheng and his scriptwriter, Sun Shiyi, based the plot of *The New Woman* on the life and death of Ai Xia. Earlier in 1934, this fledgling Shanghai actress had committed suicide shortly after starring in a movie she had also written, *A Modern Woman* (Xiandai yi nüxing).[9] Taking off from the question of woman and modernity posed by Ai Xia's film and suicide, *The New Woman* was initially conceived as a twofold critique. Cai and Sun targeted traditional constraints on women and the mistreatment of women in mass media and urban society. But while depicting the precarious position of women in contemporary China on the cusp of modernity, they also inflected the film with a sense of national urgency. Only a year earlier, the twenty-seven-year-old Cai had become acquainted with a group of young left-wing film critics and joined their patriotic Association for Film Culture as an administrative member. The association had been organized in solidarity against the Japanese invasion of Rehe that February, and it opposed the Nanjing government's policy of targeting domestic "enemies" rather than external ones. As its manifesto proclaimed, "we are being invaded from the outside and oppressed on the inside."[10]

Following the association's call for national salvation, Cai published an essay denouncing his own earlier filmmaking style prior to 1933 as "divorced from reality."[11] Dedicating himself to "facing the strong morning light" and "starting a new future," he made a tragedy about the fate of small fishing villagers forced to scrape out a living in modern Shanghai, *Song of the Fishermen* (Yu guang qu). This film broke local box-office records with a run of eighty-four days in 1934, and in Moscow it earned China's first international festival prize. Cai planned a study trip to the USSR immediately after completing *The New Woman*, but censorship complications with this latest movie prevented him from going.

Viewed in the context of growing film censorship under the Nanjing government's Central Propaganda Committee, a key theme in *The New Woman* is the (im)possibility of public voice. Wei Ming is an aspiring author, and the film calls attention to her as an enunciative subject through psychological flashback sequences and point-of-view structures. The spoken and visual articulations that constitute this silent film's narrative "voice" belong primarily to its female characters—Wei Ming, her sister, and her friend Li Aying. These women possess privileged narratorial knowledge in the film, and they initiate nearly all the subjective point-of-view shots and flashbacks.

The possibility for a strong female narrative voice exists in *The New Woman*, even though in many respects the main protagonist appears confined and silenced. For instance, she is cinematically circumscribed by a series of flat, one-dimensional images. In the set design, Wei Ming's own apartment walls are decorated by mirrors and photographs of herself. Does this confirm contemporary presumptions that New Women were just modern ornaments, shallow image-conscious narcissists? The excess of recurring images in the mise-en-scène do prompt the spectator to see Wei Ming as a kind of star and, by extension, to identify the fictional character with the star *playing* her, Ruan Lingyu. Like the commodified image of a star, Wei Ming is vulnerable to and even complicit in a kind of voyeuristic look.

But unlike her flashy former classmate, Zhang Xiuzhen (another kind of New Woman in the film), Wei Ming's daily life is modest and mundanely familiar. She ordinarily wears a somber black *qipao* dress and rides rickshaws instead of automobiles. In this way, the film resists categorizing Wei Ming as wholly alien. Instead, her neutral silent image (cinematic, photographic, or mirrored) is a kind of tabula rasa that will be charged with meaning only after it has been appropriated by others. Wei Ming submits a manuscript to a publisher who only accepts it after he sees the author's photograph. He uses the picture without Wei Ming's consent to publicize her book as the work of an attractive young woman writer. The image serves to transform this young schoolteacher into a best-seller author, a star. The figure of Wei Ming is thus split between agency and passivity, between critical distance and emotional intimacy, between object and subject.

The tension between external, objective images of the protagonist and her internal subjectivity gradually erupts in a series of startling visual effects. Halfway through *The New Woman*, Wei Ming becomes unemployed and reluctantly considers prostitution to support her daughter, Xiao Hong. As she is being adorned with makeup and jewels in front of a mirror, the camera zooms in on her distraught reflection and then suddenly exchanges places with the mirror in a reverse shot. This effectively positions the spectator within the film in a dual capacity: we are invited, on the one hand, to identify sympathetically with Wei Ming's visual perspective and emotional state, and on the other, to stand in the place of an objective mirror or camera, reflecting on the image of this fictional character. The mirror allows Cai Chusheng to self-consciously invest the silent, visual image with a double significance. On the one hand, it reflects the female protagonist's confinement and commodification as image; on the other hand, the mirror inverts and unsettles that image.

Xiao Hong, a kind of double for Wei Ming, experiences a similar transformative encounter through the image. The child sees a photograph of her parents and learns about her absent father from her aunt (Wei Ming's sister). The aunt's explanation dissolves into a montage of brief narrative scenes, which display for Xiao Hong (and the film viewer) her mother's romance and elopement with a college sweetheart, their simple home, and the father's dissatisfied abandonment of mother and child. The flashback appears to be a morality tale about the pitfalls of modern love. But it also demonstrates that the young woman's passionate defiance is also the source of strength that enables her to endure; in that same rebellious vein, the disillusioned daughter now takes the image of her father in the photograph and destroys it.

In two sequences, Cai's composition of highly subjective flashbacks and point-of-view shots compel a spectator to participate emotionally, and yet also critically, in Wei Ming's "split" subjectivity. The first occurs early in the film when the manipulative, wealthy school director, Dr. Wang, persuades Wei Ming to accompany him to a dance hall cabaret. As Wei Ming sits in the back seat of his car, she gazes sadly through the frame of the window. Over her shoulder we watch a landscape of poverty pass by—a landscape that serves both to illustrate the impoverished condition of the city (in contrast to the luxurious car) and to express metaphorically Wei Ming's own sense of dislocation and bankruptcy.

Through the car window, a restaurant facade appears, and then suddenly a scene of Wei Ming herself at a party inside the restaurant. Once again Cai Chusheng makes use of the tension between surface images and contrasting content: the lush decor and Wei Ming's attractive dress seem to suggest a certain decadence, but the school principal is introducing Wei Ming to Dr. Wang as a respected music teacher, not a prospective dance hall date. Wei Ming now watches her own memory being projected in the car window and shakes her head regretfully. The memory dissolves to the passing cars and city lights, and Wei Ming glares angrily at Wang.

Essentially the car window has become another mirror, or a screen for a film within a film which reflects and replays a dramatic moment from Wei Ming's memory. She becomes, in effect, a spectator within the movie, watching herself critically. The camera aligns our perspective with Wei Ming's, as if to encourage us to identify with the protagonist, but the visual transformation of the car window is disorienting enough to interrupt that identification. This produces a double Brechtian alienation effect, creating ironic distance between the character's past expectations and her present situation, as well as between the objective spectator and the character's pathos.

This tension between the cathartic and the didactic was often present in left-wing Chinese cinema of the 1930s. A second illustration is the dance hall cabaret sequence. Seated at a table, Wei Ming and Wang are the audience for two dance shows performed by Caucasians. In one show, a man dressed as a cowboy whips his female partner during a theatrical burlesque. Wei Ming flinches in pain, while Wang breaks into applause. In the following show, a woman dressed in a stylized striped prisoner's uniform saunters among the tables until she drops to the floor while looking up at Wei Ming. Her eyes meet Wei Ming's, and ours, and suddenly, we see the enthralled Wei Ming on the floor, now dressed in the prisoner's costume. Instantly this image of Wei Ming on the floor is replaced with that of the dancer. Dizzied, Wei Ming stands, knocks over a glass, and leaves the table, pushing Wang aside.

The vertigo of this sequence is even more unsettling than the previous example. The seductive glow of neon lights and the fascinating performance enacted on stage (and on film) are mesmerizing. Then, sudden alarming distortions and the sheer perversity of the show—with its mock subversion of the colonial and patriarchal gaze—disengage and alienate the viewer from the stylized spectacle. The image of shackles was a stock metaphor in early twentieth-century Chinese feminism and literature, illustrating the oppression of women and even the nation.

As in the car scene, dislocating cinematic techniques again complicate the film spectator's identification with the protagonist's psychological preoccupations—her social enslavement to a controlling employer. Here, in place of a reflective window on her past, Wei Ming transposes her anxiety onto a much more immediate and active presence, the dancer-as-prisoner performing directly before her. Yet immanent though that presence may be, it is also a charade. Wei Ming looks back only to see the swaggering "prisoner" pull off her manacles and break into a jitterbug. Wang tries to defuse the incident by proposing to her, though in fact he is already married—to her former classmate Xiuzhen. In the wake of their contrasting reactions to the performance, his facetiousness is all the more glaring. With a new sense of clarity and rage Wei Ming retorts, "What can marriage give me? 'Lifelong companionship'?!—just a lifetime of slavery!" (Dr. Wang later retaliates against her resistance with blackmail and gets Wei Ming fired.)

Wei Ming sees that she has identified with a figure in a masquerade of extremes, but she maintains the insights of this new perspective. The stunning artifice of the stage show, with its grotesque overlay of pleasure and pain, only seems to have sharpened Wei Ming's own sense of "impersonation." She watches herself perform the role of a woman subjugated to social conventions—just as the film, with its mixture of pathos and edification, encourages the spectator to do.

• "True Reflections"

A series of encounters with hospitals, doctors, and journalists emphasizes the pathology of Wei Ming's professional and private dissolution, from teacher, author, and mother to unemployment and near prostitution. She is unable to pay a medical doctor to cure her ailing daughter and cannot bear raising the cash as a call girl after discovering that the proposed client is Dr. Wang. Xiao Hong lies dying, and the broken, grieving mother consumes a handful of sleeping pills.

The film culminates in the melodramatic crisis of Wei Ming's suicide, after friends rush her to the hospital. While she is confined to bed, a reporter stands in the wings making notes for sensational stories and then conspires with her book publisher and Dr. Wang to capitalize on her death. The publisher exclaims, "Such a shame we didn't have her write two novels! . . . Why don't we have a memorial service for her?! Not that we really feel anything for her. It just makes sense—it'll stir up a little news material!" Until this juncture, the film has allied the viewer's visual perspective with Wei Ming's. But now that Wei Ming has attempted suicide and fallen unconscious, she loses the power of representation: the authority of her vision is qualified, and it no longer guides the viewer. The female character's enunciative position in the film is now displaced with various male figures of authority associated with the publicity and (mis)information of the journalistic print media.

Wei Ming's friends wake her from this unconscious state and force her to confront the media distortions by showing her an array of newspaper columns, which are also are displayed for us as close-up inserts—among them:

THE SUICIDE OF WOMAN WRITER WEI MING
The Decline of the Romantic Woman [*langman nüzi*]
The True Reflection of the Modern Girl [*modeng guniang*]

BIG REVELATION: HER SECRET LIFE
A Fallen Woman and Unwed Mother

A CRITIQUE OF WEI MING'S SUICIDE
Women Really are Weak

Each viewing of these headlines alternates with a close-up of Wei Ming's anxious reaction, until she sits up and exclaims, "I want revenge!"

As in earlier scenes, Wei Ming and the spectator witness the ironies of her life from a disembodied distance, projected onto scenes passing before her. Here, she recognizes herself as different and separate from the journalists' representation of her in print—and this recognition is amplified in a haunting death scene. Wei Ming struggles to sit up in the hospital bed and directly confronts the camera and spectator, exclaiming, "Save me! I want to live!"

Each instance of despair in the film has been characterized by a visual, specular event (her view of herself as a prostitute in the mirror, her reading of the newspapers' representation of her suicide, even her daughter's "glimpse" of scenes from her own past). These events are constructed through objective shots of the protagonist intercut with subjective views of things she is told about, shown, or remembers, from her own perspective. The content of the subjective images is unsettling, and in form they appear as inserts, flashbacks, and mirror images that interrupt the continuous flow of action. Here, in the last act, that disruption is taken one step further. The imaginary "wall" dividing the audience from the world of the film breaks down, and the film becomes self-consciously theatrical—acknowledging the presence of an audience and allowing the protagonist to appeal to that audience in a bold confrontation. Since the film is silent, the confrontation is all the more arresting when her words "I want to live!" emerge not as intertitles but as animation superimposed directly on the screen, "growing" straight from Wei Ming's mouth.

Cai Chusheng opens up a number of spaces for progressive possibility beyond Wei Ming's suicide. Parallel editing, for instance, emphasizes the simultaneous yet contrasting experience of Wei Ming's teaching colleague, Li Aying, who composes her own class-conscious adaptations of popular songs to teach workers in a labor union night school. The scene of Wei Ming at the dance hall listening to the big-band tune "Peach Blossom River" is crosscut with one of Li Aying in the classroom teaching "Huangpu River," her overtly political version of the same song. Just as Li teaches a lesson through subversive mimicry of mainstream entertainment songs, the film's use of a polished Hollywood-style surface and familiar silent "star" image for its protagonist Wei Ming served a similarly covert, instructive purpose in the film at a time when openly dissenting images and speech were being regulated. Although "Huangpu River" was cut from the film in order to pass the government's censors, one other song, at the end of the film, survived.

This single recorded sound sequence was crosscut into the death scene of Wei Ming and presents us with a stark contrast to her mute "voice" appearing on screen. Outside the hospital, women workers emerge from a factory to flood the streets with their triumphant voices singing out the proletarian

"Song of the New Woman," composed for the film by Nie Er, a young musician who also wrote the melody later chosen for the national anthem of the People's Republic of China. Describing the toiling life of a woman factory worker, the song culminates in a revolutionary verse which envisions the simultaneous dissolution of class and gender divisions:

> New women are the masses of women producers;
> New women are the labor of society;
> New women are the vanguard in constructing a new society;
> New women want to roll forth the stormwinds of the times together
>   with men!
> The stormwinds! We must use them to awaken the nation's people
>   from their comfortable elusions!
> The stormwinds! We must use them for the glory of women!
> We won't be slaves,
> This earth is for all of us!
> No divisions between men and women,
> A great world unity!
> New women, bravely charge forth;
> New women, bravely charge forth!

The only sound in the film is synchronized to the collective voices of these anonymous urban working women marching forth combatively as they sing. The silent written cry "I want to live!" uttered by the music teacher and fallen literary celebrity indoors is starkly different from the unison of sound and action outdoors.[12] Sound is used to a contrapuntal effect here, implying that the problems posed by "the woman question" and the forces of class revolution are at odds with one another—and even that the "I" of Wei Ming's subject position, a despairing individual new woman, has been eclipsed by the collective "we" of utopian new women who will destroy "divisions between men and women" and build a "great world unity." At the same time, the two simultaneous episodes are edited together into a frenzied exhibit of sound and words, binding the women outside with the woman inside: slanderous castaway tabloids about Wei Ming litter the streets, trampled under the workers' feet as if in victory over the injustice and tragedy of her death. Through shifting point-of-view structures and crosscutting at key moments of crisis, Cai Chusheng created an equivocal, split female subject that masked the film's political content. This ambiguity extended beyond the limits of the film itself to fuel intense debates in the press and public opinion over the film, its star, and the category of New Woman.

· "After the Chinese Nora Leaves Home"

Newspapers and audiences were consumed by the debate over which of the three female leads might be considered a real New Woman and whether Wei Ming's suicide was a "correct" ending for a film called *The New Woman*. The term New Woman itself evoked an imported concept that had first been translated into Chinese during the May 4th period. During this period, a "New Culture Movement" began in 1917 among young urban intellectuals who sought to strengthen the new republic and its people by defining the freedoms, rights, and responsibilities of men and women in China. Their ideas about independence, novelty, and identity eventually extended into popular culture, with gender and sexuality in the foreground. "The woman question," or *funü wenti,* centered on love, marriage, education, and employment for women but also developed into a potent symbol for modernist discourse in China. Key modern thinkers and authors such as Hu Shi and Lu Xun looked to Europe and the United States for examples of independence and found the New Woman, which they translated as *xin nüxing* or *xin funü.*[13] In 1918, Hu Shi wrote,

> "New Woman" is a new word, and it designates a new sort of woman [*xin pai de funü*] who is very intense in her speech, who tends towards the extreme in her actions, who doesn't believe in religion or adhere to rules of conduct [*lifa*], yet who is also a very good thinker and has very high morals. Of course amongst them there are plenty of fake New Women. Their words don't match their intentions: what they do is completely at odds with what they say. But among New Women there are some who really are very good thinkers and have very high morals. . . . Although there aren't many [true New Women] in America, they best express one of the recent directions for American women.[14]

In the United States, European nations, and Japan during the 1890s, "New Woman" at first referred primarily to educated, politically active public women with women's rights agendas such as suffrage, labor, or birth control. This definition was blurred by the popularization of the New Woman's marital and financial freedoms, so that successive generations entered the cultural vocabulary as "Gibson Girls," "flappers," "gold diggers," and "modern girls" (or *moga* in Japan) during the following three decades. These subsequent generations came to be characterized by their apolitical image and function in consumer society—short hair, modern fashion, and free love—but "New Woman" did retain the distinct connotation of politically vocal feminism.[15]

Even though "New Woman" was an imported term in China that precluded strict nativist definitions, the appearance of the New Woman in contemporary Chinese discourse on "the woman question" did have its own chronology and significance. The New Woman Hu Shi introduced to his Chinese audience in 1918 was not a woman with political goals but someone who could maintain her positive "extremes" of independence and selfhood (zili) in marriage. A translation of Ibsen's A Doll's House had appeared earlier that year under the title Nora (Nala) in the May 4th flagship magazine New Youth (Xin qingnian), underscoring the way concepts of marriage freedom and equality (and reactions to that freedom) played a large role in shaping the definition of the New Woman in China during the 1920s. The riddle of closure in A Doll's House had prompted Lu Xun to speculate, in a 1923 address to a women's college, "what would become of the Chinese Nora after she leaves home?"[16] In contrast to the romantic ideal Hu Shi had described a few years earlier, Lu Xun considered the prerequisites for a woman's independence once she was out on her own and spoke in economic terms: instead of "dreams," Lu Xun argued, "what she needs is money." Lu Xun's approach laid the groundwork for later class-based formulations like The New Woman.

Beyond an independent spirit, education, and financial resources, Cai Chusheng and Sun Shiyi added a further necessity for the New Woman: social conscience in the form of proletarian politics. This recent addition to the New Woman formula derived from the urban left wing's approach to feminism that had developed after the May Thirtieth Labor Movement of 1925, where the emphasis was shifted from the category of gender to that of class. By the mid-1930s, well-known filmmakers like Xia Yan (a founding member of the League of Left-Wing Writers) were voicing their concern for women working in factories—for example, in Xia's reportage on female contract laborers.[17] Cai Chusheng explored the new variety of confusing social meanings "New Woman" could invoke in China during this period by incorporating three very different female leads into a visual narrative, each representing a different image of the New Woman.

Film reviewers in Shanghai's press dissected these various possibilities for the New Woman. For example, left-wing critic Tang Na saw the three main female characters as New Women at different developmental stages, following a historical progression from feudalism, through capitalism, to socialism. First, there is the school director Wang's wife, Zhang Xiuzhen (a rather minor character in the narrative). Tang Na believed that she was "a 'new style' of educated woman, the wife of a compradore and a capitalist woman poised to enjoy a life full of all kinds of pleasures" and represented the "feudal woman who seems to be a New Woman." Then there is Wei

Ming, "the petty bourgeois New Woman [who] opposes the power of this ancient feudalism—a Nora who has left home." The dialectic progression of characters culminates in a third educated woman who uses her skills and independence to benefit the proletariat: "Finally, it goes without saying: the intellectual Li Aying among workers is the real New Woman."[18]

Wei Ming's escape from an arranged marriage and, more symbolically, the iconic "woman who never falls" *(budao nüxing)* doll she has bought for Xiao Hong, which presides over her apartment, prompted reviewers to cite *A Doll's House* and call Wei Ming a "Chinese Nora who has left home."[19] The play also presented itself for convenient and timely comparison since that very spring a stage production of *Nora* at the Golden City Theater (Jincheng daxiyuan) was getting a fair amount of press attention (in part thanks to the efforts of Tang Na, who was dating the actress playing Nora, Lan Ping—or Jiang Qing, a future wife of Mao Zedong). *A Doll's House* was so ubiquitous in 1935 that the year of the New Woman Incident was also known in theatrical circles as "The Year of Nora."[20] Even attacks on women's liberation would take *A Doll's House* as their starting point. Articles like "The Woman Question in China," published some months earlier in *The New Life Weekly,* made liberal use of the vocabulary of Marxist class analysis, but in the service of a conclusion—that women should remain in the sheltered space of the home rather than face commodification under capitalism—more analogous to the rhetoric of National Socialism in Germany at the time:

> Mr. Ibsen didn't point out very clearly what happens to Nora after she's left home. . . . Actually, Nora is still a doll; the doll has just changed its style and name. Before she may have been a personal doll for her husband in the home, but now she has become a doll for all society—no, she is, directly or indirectly, a doll for capitalists. This is because the society into which Nora has stepped is a capitalist formation where she, and anyone else, will be sold as a commodity.[21]

Critics and audiences of *The New Woman* were speculating on Wei Ming's options within the framework Lu Xun had proposed a decade earlier when he determined that, "By logical deduction, Nora actually has two alternatives only: to go to the bad or to return to her husband."[22] Unless, he added, she had the tenacity to attain economic freedom that would enable her to move forward. What shocked some audiences of *The New Woman* was that, unlike Nora, the character Wei Ming *does* (however briefly or marginally) attain the economic independence to move forward, but then she does not fulfill this promise. Another movie critic, Chen Wu, argued that none of the film's characters were real "New Women," although Li Aying could qualify to be the New Woman of the film's title if she had been featured more prominently. Chen Wu believed that neither a Wei Ming nor a Nora qualified for the name New Woman:

> This so-called "China's Nora after she has left home" is the most vex-ing group of our times. This sort of woman is born in the capitalist middle class and then begins to vacillate. She has been subjected to all kinds of pain by capitalist society, yet . . . she has no way of reforming the very society that gives her so much misery.[23]

Even the viewer from Guizhou reported,

> After seeing the film, [my date] said to me dejectedly: "How can a person like Wei Ming qualify to be called a New Woman? She's sim-ply a weak girl! A New Woman would surely never have died except for a cause. Nor would she ever have dealt with an issue by merely say-ing 'I want to live.' "[24]

Similarly Chen Wu wrote, "Instead of committing suicide, Wei Ming could have moved forward or 'sold her soul'; it's inconceivable that she would go back home."[25] Of course, Wei Ming nearly "goes to the bad," as Lu Xun put it; but when she refuses to go through with "selling her soul," she trans-gresses even that taboo by committing suicide.

If critics conceived of Wei Ming's status as a New Woman within the framework of the "Chinese Nora" (a desire for independence from author-ity, rather than any particular feminist goals per se), they were also dis-turbed by her symbolic victimhood and her inability as an intellectual to change society. In debating the significance of Wei Ming's suicide, literary film critics worried that the death of the film's protagonist—as a young teacher—"advocates that the only ending for intellectuals is suicide."[26] The intensity of their uneasiness becomes all the more poignant when we recall that many prominent May 4th writers, including Mao Dun and Yu Dafu, had imagined a New Woman position from which to iterate their own desire for emancipation.[27] Wei Ming's suicide was a disquieting denoue-ment to a drama of complicated victims and villains, accompanied by gender and class struggles. By resisting closure and an easy moral, *The New Woman* had kindled a wide range of critical responses.

• Public Spectacle and the Modern Woman

The New Woman was a silent picture made at a time when movies in China were being politically censored and morally censored. Cai Chusheng self-consciously advanced an alternative silent visual "show" as a kind of pantomime with moral or didactic potential. The film's visual composition managed to insinuate a subversive challenge to the social order that had driven Wei Ming to suicide, and its ambivalent open ending also dramatized the potential contradictions for a left-wing filmmaker—aspiring to speak for the oppressed underclass through a mass medium generated by capitalism.

The conflicts surfaced when the film opened in Shanghai. The commercial press took the film's narrative to task for depicting the news media as slanderous and the potential New Woman as suicidal. The Journalists' Union loudly protested the dismal characterization of their trade and the specter of negative publicity coaxed Lianhua studio into making an open apology, much to the director's chagrin.[28] Second, in an attempt to clear away accusations that the movie was "condoning" the suicide of New Women, the producers made a public relations show of their virtue by agreeing to screen the film at a fundraiser for a women's educational center on International Women's Day, March 8th.[29] But on the day *The New Woman* was to be presented at the Women's Day festival, the actress Ruan Lingyu herself took an overdose of sleeping pills and died.

Not only did Ruan's suicide add a layer of meaning to the film's reception, apparently duplicating the death of the fictional character she had played, but it was also immediately transformed into a citywide spectacle which exhibited—to borrow a phrase from Thomas Pynchon—"an extended capacity for convolution." Five kilometers of mourners—one hundred thousand people, almost a tenth of inner Shanghai's population—followed her funeral cortege through the metropolis on March 11, 1935.

Tributes from the press, the film studio, government representatives, and colleagues were followed by souvenir memorial books, storytellers' songs, even a lucrative stage show. Cinemas ran retrospectives of her work for at least another year. Precisely because the compelling intimate details are at once so accessible and yet so contradictory, the mythmaking continues even today with a steady flow of biographical novels, television shows, and movies. All this fictionalization and theatricalization teased out the enigma of, as one headline put it, "Who Killed Ruan Lingyu."[30] This articulated the same fascination with the question of who had killed Wei Ming—the character Ruan had embodied on film—and with the riddle of "what would become of the Chinese Nora after she leaves home."

To cite but a few powerful examples, one Shanghai storyteller's *kaipian* sung in the Wu style opened with the stark lines "When the shocking news arrived, it startled the nation: / Lingyu of the Ruan family had suddenly committed suicide." The song melodramatically conveyed the details of Ruan's background—a misguided youthful love for Zhang Damin and a true devotion to her acting career and Tang Jishan—and continued,

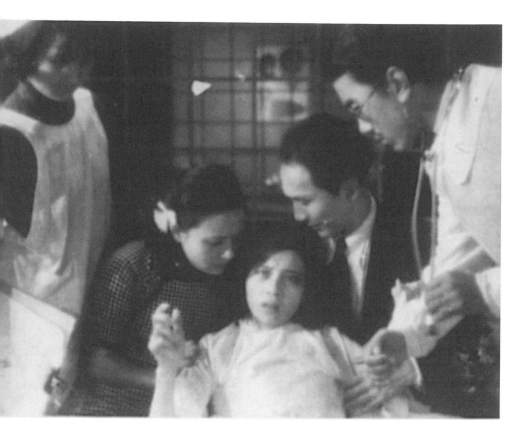

Fig. 27. Ruan Lingyu in *The New Woman* (Xin nüxing), directed by Cai Chusheng, Lianhua Studio, 1934.

> Recently she appeared in *The New Woman*,
> It only exacerbated her feelings and brought what years she had left to
>   a close.
> To calm her spirit she took three bottles of sleeping pills,
> And spelled out her hatred for Damin.

This rendition of Ruan Lingyu's suicide concludes with the admonition that "Love and social relations are truly fearsome / Young men and ladies must take care / Getting into this kind of trouble ends in suicide."[31] Another souvenir booklet also saw the root of Ruan's problem in her marriage dispute and devoted more than thirty-five pages to topics ranging from the pseudo-analytical to the unabashedly voyeuristic—among them: "The Social Significance of Ruan Lingyu's Suicide," "Marriage Issues under Discussion since Ruan Lingyu's Suicide," "Ruan Lingyu Died Because of the Philandering and Coercion of Others," and "A Look Inside the Funeral Home."[32]

The studio and press coverage of the funeral accentuated the circle of correspondences between the star's personal life and her roles. Where the film's opening scene had enmeshed Wei Ming in the spectacular and mechanized infrastructure of the modern city as she rides a streetcar home from downtown Shanghai, the same urban landscape of Nanjing Road served as the stage for Ruan Lingyu's elaborate funeral cortege. But now the audience, as mourners, became actors in this public theater staged by the same studio that had produced the film. Even as Lianhua proclaimed that it would not capitalize on the star's death to sell tickets, within weeks the respectful promises were evidently forgotten and her entire oeuvre began to resurface in venues across the nation.

The theatricality of the funeral was intensified by the use of the same photograph of Ruan Lingyu that had circumscribed Wei Ming and represented her rise to fame in *The New Woman*. Newspaper articles asking "Who Killed Ruan Lingyu?" echoed the headlines in *The New Woman* that Wei Ming reads about herself as she is dying; at the same time, they self-referentially called attention to the journalistic excess within, and surrounding, both the film and its star. And finally, the photographs of Ruan's wake were taken from the same angles used to shoot Wei Ming's death in the film. Ruan's act of suicide appeared to duplicate *The New Woman*'s final refusal to gratify with a happy ending. In this sense she had posed a transgressive threat to the order of the fictional and the real—a threat that was simultaneously acknowledged and disavowed through the exaggerated scale of the obsequies. The fetishized spectacle served as a form of containment and control, with the materiality of the funeral ritual reifying certain correspondences between the star and the roles she played, and finally enforcing a sense of closure. Exorcised, the star could be returned to a realm of harmless, tragically passive figures. The film's director, scenarist, and star all played their parts in blurring the line between the real world and the fictional one of the film. As mentioned earlier, Cai Chusheng and Sun Shiyi had based *The New Woman* on the story of *A Modern Woman*'s author and actress, Ai Xia. Publicity profiles for *that* film and its star had emphasized its autobiographical quality, saying that from it, "readers will have no trouble seeing that she's a modern woman."[33] Likewise, before Ruan Lingyu's death the press depicted her not so much as a New Woman in the feminist sense but as a somewhat threatening *modeng nüxing* or *modeng guniang* (modern woman). Ruan was separated from her common-law husband, Zhang Damin, had adopted a little girl on her own, and was living with a different man. By 1935, she had already arranged for a legal separation from Zhang and paid him alimony for two years, but a month before the payments were to conclude, Zhang sold a story to the press accusing Ruan of adultery. Even established newspapers like *Shi bao* and *Shen bao* bought the scandal, printing columns without bylines titled "A Page from Ruan Lingyu's Life Story" and "I Lived with Ruan Lingyu for Eight Years," framed by fineprint disclaimers like "in Zhang Damin's own words" and "the defendants have already discussed the issues of the lawsuit with their lawyers and deny the plaintiff's allegations."[34]

Since Ruan Lingyu had starred as a Shanghai telephone operator escaping arranged marriage in a film called *Three Modern Women* only two years earlier, *Shi bao* featured a jocular article titled "Three Modern Women" after Ruan's own rift with Zhang Damin was revealed. The terms for "New Woman" *(xin nüxing)* and "Modern Woman" *(modeng nüxing* or *modeng guniang)* were occasionally used interchangeably in 1930s China. But "Modern Woman" more often carried additional negative associations of superficial Westernization, hedonism, even avarice—similar to the cunning "gold digger," or *wajin guniang*, described by Lin Yütang, or the "so-called *modan garu* [or *moga*] types" in Taisho Japan, who, according to Barbara Hamill Sato's quotation from one 1926 women's magazine, were "just shallow, 'bean brains' who have been influenced by American motion pictures."[35] The *Shi bao* article "Three Modern Women" depicts the film's three actresses shrewdly arranging for the dissolution of their own marriages and calls them *modeng*—something in a realm entirely beyond the familiar: "Modeng means 'MODERN.' But in China, the definition of *modeng* can sometimes be even broader than the word 'that' *[neige]*. . . . My dictionary defines *modeng* as inscrutable *[moming qimiao]* and abnormal *[fanchang]*." The actresses may have been exercising the tenacity and economic rights that Lu Xun had once commended to the "Chinese Nora," but this columnist depicts them buying off discarded husbands. He banishes them to the outside margins of *modeng,* concluding with the exasperated diagnosis for women: "Now that's just far-TOO-mod-ern *[mo-TAI-deng-le]!*"[36] Another column in *Shi bao,* "Even Women Movie Stars' Love Accounts Don't Add Up," chastised the actress for privately hiring a modern lawyer to settle her marriage dispute, lamenting the entry of women into the rationalized world of legal self-defense and claiming that's "not like the old days; nowadays it's all plaintiff and defendant."[37]

After Ruan Lingyu's suicide one detects a certain tone of relief. The obituaries, whether by critics or by supporters, almost unanimously represented the actress (like her character Wei Ming) as helpless and weak.[38] Ruan's "modern" legal efforts were eclipsed by her public reticence about the

Fig. 28. Ruan Lingyu in *The Goddess* (Shennü), directed by Wu Yonggang, Lianhua Studio, 1934.

slander. In the tabloids and other popular interpretations, her reluctance to address the press directly was read as passivity, or even guilt. Suicide in the face of ignominy also fit neatly with traditional expectations of how a humiliated wife should properly assert her virtue—wronged spirits were thought to possess the power to return and wreak vengeance. It was in this framework of traditional mores, rather than more recent ones, that Ruan's defenders chose to reclaim her from the kind of accusations of self-pity and modern immorality leveled against the character she had played in *The New Woman*. Lu Xun and Cai Chusheng both remembered Ruan as a silent and powerless victim of gossip and unjust persecution.

Ruan Lingyu's star persona was based on the expressive, tragic roles she played, and her very livelihood was, for better or for worse, predicated on her silent image. When the Shanghai "talkies" adopted *putonghua* (standard Mandarin) as their standard, this Cantonese native was thrown into fatal competition with popular actresses like Hu Die who were already fluent in Mandarin. When at last Ruan did "speak" out, hers was a disembodied, posthumous "voice." She wrote three letters before committing suicide, one of which was an open statement "to society" in which she repudiated the spoken word and reiterated the film's challenge to the press. Using the chilling phrase *renyan kewei* (commonly translated as "gossip is a fearful thing," *renyan* also evokes, more broadly, "things people say" or "talk"), Ruan condemned Zhang Damin for selling calumnious stories about her to the press. In the same stroke, she described the indirect pressure of gossip that *he* had instigated, lamenting, "You may not have killed me with your own two hands, but I have died because of you."[39] Condemning the unaccountability of her lovers' talk, Ruan's suicide note effectively supplies a plot for the novel penned by the silent film protagonist, titled *Lian'ai de fenmu* (The tomb of love).

Lu Xun later went on to make the phrase "gossip is a fearful thing" famous in his memoir of Ruan when he issued a battle cry against the kind of "gossip" or "talk" journalism that had victimized Ruan Lingyu and her character Wei Ming. Lu Xun (along with others) condemned columnists who manipulated the print media's power of representation to their own advantage and to the disadvantage of others, particularly women:

> The "society news" articles in Shanghai's newspapers and tabloids are simply cases digested by the authorities and turned over to the public safety and works ministries. But there is a bad tendency to tack on some description, especially of women; since this kind of case does not involve great gentlemen or high ministers, it's even more susceptible to added description. In a given case, the age and appearance of a man are generally described honestly, but as soon as we come across a woman, the embellishment comes into full play.[40]

His attack on the "talk" press was ostensibly prompted by his defense of Ruan but may also be traced further back to May 4th intellectuals' disdain for the "black curtain" (*heimu*) scandal exposés popular since the late Qing.[41] This strain persisted through the Republican period, until we see the "progressive cinema's" cast of supporting intellectuals on the one hand (authors like Lu Xun and film critics like Chen Wu) and the circulation-conscious commercial press on the other, polarized over public opinion-making in the case of *The New Woman* and Ruan Lingyu's suicide.

The film's scenarist, Sun Shiyi, had already questioned the role and responsibilities of the media, including cinema, in society. Some years earlier Sun had explored the social significance of the cinema in a magazine article, quoting American sociologists on the "destructive and constructive power of indirect suggestion" in the movies.[42] His work with Cai Chu-sheng on *The New Woman* further refined this concept. In the film, cinematic cues such as point-of-view structures fortify the constructive "power of indirect suggestion," while the journalistic medium is explicitly relegated to the destructive end of this continuum.

The film does put the print media on trial, indicting journalists as ruthless and libelous. But *The New Woman* works within left-wing Chinese film-making practices, quietly using a commercial medium to undermine that very commodified culture of privilege in contemporary urban China. The motion picture and Ruan Lingyu's suicide both privilege the silent visual gesture of cinematic and theatrical "showing" as more reliably authentic than the journalistic "telling" of gossip and public opinion. The actress, like the final character she played, spoke publicly through the cinematic image and gesture. Just as the silent, written characters *Wo yao huo,* "I want to live," must serve as Wei Ming's final utterance, the voice Ruan Lingyu's Shanghai audiences heard was her silent performance enacted on celluloid.

This "silent speech" emerged as a useful strategy, born of necessity, for left-wing filmmakers in Republican China of the 1930s.[43] On a purely narrative level, the disillusionment and tragic death of an isolated young woman at the "Tomb of Love" could not have been more clearly melo-dramatic. But cinematically, the enunciative subject of the film is full of complex ambiguities. Cai constructed the New Woman as equivocally split between word and image, speech and silence, class and gender, subject and trope. These clefts leave open the possibility for alternative, subversive interpretations of the narrative, especially during the concluding proletarian "Song of the New Woman." The New Woman may be a victim of the status quo, or a threat to it; she may be silent by necessity, or by choice; she may speak out as an individual woman or as a member of a class. In its open ending, the film articulated the kind of plurality that became increasingly untenable under the Nationalist government's "unification" policies.

The New Woman Incident that erupted in 1935 persists as legend in China more than fifty years later. It symbolizes something approaching an irrecoverable loss of public innocence. On a local level, this was an instant of recognition that the press, film studio, star, and audience were mutually implicated in the production and circulation of images—a process of com-modification and consumption that could strip away or reconfigure what-ever fragile boundaries exist between artifice and nature, romantic and real, public image and private life. For Mainland Chinese of the 1980s and 1990s, the disillusionment defining the New Woman Incident may strike a familiar chord for anyone who experienced a sense of being duped by, and yet complicit in, the larger national-scale publicity machine behind the Cultural Revolution. In the late twentieth century, economic liberalization policies have fed the popular revival of interest in a prior golden age of Shanghai consumer culture. The recovery of Ruan Lingyu has come mainly in the form of biographical novels, a genre whose turbid lines between fact and fiction manage to accommodate the mythology of this actress particularly well.[44]

In Hong Kong, the attraction of prewar Shanghai culture has taken on a special meaning. Growing economic ties between the two ports are an obvious factor. On a psychic level, the splendor and fear of 1930s semicolonial Shanghai on the eve of war match the sense of fin-de-siècle uncertainty accompanying the British colony's imminent reunification with Mainland China. Will Hong Kong's energetic local film industry, which has thrived on commodified stars and all manner of action, romance, and fantasy films since 1949, perish under unfamiliar new censorship regulations? The death of Ruan Lingyu in the New Woman Incident has become a site where these apprehensions have crystallized for Hong Kong film critics and filmmakers such as Shu Qi and Guan Jinpeng.

In early 1988, the Hong Kong Arts Centre conferred international classic star status on Ruan in a series called "Three Goddesses of the Silver Screen from the Thirties," bringing together major works of Marlene Dietrich, Greta Garbo, and Ruan Lingyu. The series inspired Guan Jinpeng's semi-documentary, semifictional film *Ruan Lingyu* (a.k.a. *Centre Stage*), a self-reflexive attempt to sort out and preserve the legacy of two golden ages of world-class Chinese cinema—early twentieth-century Shanghai and late twentieth-century Hong Kong. A sense of transience pervades Guan's film, from the intentional inclusion of disintegrating footage to the interviews with octogenarian stars of the 1930s; from the manic repetitions and reenactments of Ruan playing a New Woman crying "I want to live" as she lies dying to the closing shot of decaying rubble where the Lianhua film production studio once stood. *Ruan Lingyu/Centre Stage* suggests that the Cantonese actress' silent death was partly a result of her frustrated attempt to speak Mandarin for Shanghai cinema; Guan's documentary lament is shot mainly in Cantonese, accentuating a bleak parallel with the fate of contemporary local filmmakers as they confront a Mainland Chinese film industry dominated by Mandarin and Beijing. Today, as in 1935, the New Woman Incident invokes the dramatic memory of an individual and a community perilously positioned on a line between the new and extinction.

· Notes

An earlier version of this chapter, titled "The New Woman: Image, Subject, and Dissent in 1930s Shanghai Film Culture," appeared in *Republican China* 20, no. 2 (1995): 55–79.

I. *Shishi xinbao* review reprinted in *Lianhua huabao* 5, no. 5 (1935).

2. *Xin nüxing* publicity sheet (Lianhua studios, n.d.).

3. Huang Ming, "Seeing *New Woman*," in *One Day in China: May 21, 1936*, trans. and ed. Sherman Cochran and Andrew C. K. Hsieh, with Janis Cochran (New Haven: Yale University Press, 1983), 64–66.

4. Mary Ann Doane, *The Desire to Desire* (Bloomington: Indiana University Press, 1987), 4. Doane's examples include *Mildred Pierce, Letter from an Unknown Woman, Kitty Foyle, Daisy Kenyon,* and *Rebecca.*

5. The term in Chinese is *xin nüxing shijian.* Cai Hongsheng, *Cai Chusheng de chuangzuo daolu* [Cai Chusheng's creative path] (Beijing: Wenhua yishu chubanshe, 1982), 33.

6. Cai Hongsheng, *Cai Chusheng.* Cai Chusheng (1906–1968) became an apprentice to the seasoned director Zheng Zhengqiu at the age of twenty-three and worked on nine films at Mingxing, China's largest film company at the time. In 1931, he moved to the newly formed Lianhua, where a number of "left-wing" filmmakers had congregated. There he made six more films before release of *The New Woman.* During the Second World War Cai continued working in Hong Kong and returned to the Mainland in 1945 to make one more major film, the box-office hit *A Spring River Flows East* (Yijiang chunshui xiang dong liu). Although his films were popular and often patriotic (many of them enjoying success abroad), Cai's position in PRC film history has been an uneasy one. He entered the Chinese Communist Party fairly late, in 1956, and died during the Cultural Revolution.

7. Like Cai Chusheng, Ruan Lingyu (Ruan Fenggen, 1910–1935) was born in Shanghai of working-class Cantonese parents. Newspaper accounts, obituaries, and popular "biographies" disagree on many details of her life, but the following narrative is common to them all: Shortly after the early death of her father, she and her mother lived with another Cantonese family named Zhang, as servants. By the age of sixteen, the Zhangs were on the decline, and Ruan was withdrawn from school to become the common-law wife of their fourth son, Zhang Damin. A year later, she quietly screen-tested into Mingxing studios and began a decade of steady work there and at Lianhua studios, making nearly thirty films before her suicide in 1935. In counterpoint to the consistency and success of her working life, Ruan's turbulent relationship with Zhang forced her to change addresses annually, or even twice a year. One attempt at separation had culminated in a failed suicide attempt at the age of nineteen. Only at the height of her popularity, in 1933, was Ruan able to formalize the separation through a lawyer, and a few months later she moved in with

another man, Tang Jishan. But when Tang and Zhang began suing each other over property division and slander, the press placed Ruan at the center of the scandal, driving her to a suicide that seemed to reenact the narrative of the film she had just completed, *The New Woman*. See, for instance, the chronological appendix to Huang Weijun, *Ruan Lingyu zhuan* [Biography of Ruan Lingyu] (Changchun: Beifang funü ertong chubanshe, 1986), 243–247.

8. While acknowledging the momentous contribution that psychoanalytic theory has made to the way we think about the spectator, gender, and the cinematic medium—see, for example, the essays in *Psychoanalysis and Cinema*, ed. E. Ann Kaplan (New York: Routledge, 1990)—my overall approach here owes a debt to recent work on women and stars by historians of early cinema such as Janet Staiger, Lea Jacobs, and Richard deCordova.

9. This film is no longer extant.

10. "Dianying wenhua xiehui jiji jinxing" [The Film Culture Association energetically moves forward], *Chen bao*, March 26, 1933.

11. Cai Chusheng, "Zhaoguang" [Morning light], *Xiandai dianying* 1 (1933), quoted in Cai Hongsheng, *Cai Chusheng*.

12. The original film was silent but included this one recorded song. However, the extant film also includes voice dialogue dubbed over the images and intertitles. This latter dubbing project was carried out under Cai Chusheng's supervision during the 1960s. Chen Ye, *Zhongguo dabaike quanshu, dianyingji* [Great Chinese encyclopedia, film volume] (Beijing: Zhongguo dabaike quanshu chubanshe, 1991), 429.

13. For example, Hu Shi, "Meiguo de furen" [American ladies], *Xin qingnian* 5, no. 3 (1918): 213–224.

14. Hu, "Meiguo de furen," 222–223.

15. On the New Woman in the United States, Europe, and Japan: Kate Flint, *The Woman Reader, 1837–1914* (London: Oxford University Press, 1994); Sumiko Higashi, *Cecil B. DeMille and American Culture: The Silent Era* (Berkeley: University of California Press, 1994); Atina Grossmann, "The New Woman and the Rationalization of Sexuality in Weimar Germany," in *Powers of Desire: The Politics of Sexuality*, ed. Ann Snitow et al. (New York: Monthly Review Press, 1983), 153–171; Barbara Hamill Sato, "The *Moga* Sensation: Perceptions of the *Modan Garu* in Japanese Intellectual Circles during the 1920s," *Gender and History* 5, no. 3 (1993), 363–381; Laurel Rasplica Rodd, "Yosano Akiko and the Taisho Debate over the 'New Woman,' " in *Recreating Japanese Women, 1600–1945*, ed. Gail Lee Bernstein (Berkeley: University of Cali-fornia Press, 1991), 175–198.

16. Lu Xun, "Nala zouhou zenyang" (December 26, 1923), translated as "What Happens after Nora Leaves Home?" in *Silent China: Selected Writings of Lu Xun*, trans. Gladys Yang (London: Oxford University Press, 1973). On *A Doll's House* and May 4th feminism in China, see Kazuko Ono, *Chinese Women in a Century of Revolution*,

1850–1950 (Stanford: Stanford University Press, 1989 [1978]), 97–100, and Elisabeth Croll, *Feminism and Socialism in China* (New York: Schocken, 1978), 87.

17. "Baoshengong" [Indentured laborers] (1936), in *Xia Yan xuanji* [Selected works of Xia Yan] (Beijing: Renmin chubanshe, 1980). A number of studies on the relationship between feminism and socialism in China have examined the broader implications of the subordination of gender to class in Chinese Communist Party policy—for example, Judith Stacey, *Patriarchy and Socialist Revolution in China* (Berkeley: University of California Press, 1983) and, more recently, Christina Kelley Gilmartin, *Engendering the Chinese Revolution: Radical Women, Communist Politics, and Mass Movements in the 1920s* (Berkeley: University of California Press, 1995).

18. Tang Na, "Guanyu jixielun: Xianshi zhuyi yu *Xin nüxing*" [On mechanism: Realism and *The New Woman*], *Zhonghua ribao,* March 2, 1935.

19. For example, Tang, "Guanyu jixielun"; Chen Wu, "Guanyu *Xin nüxing* de yingpian, piping, ji qita" [On the film *The New Woman,* criticism, and beyond], *Zhonghua ribao,* March 2, 1935. The title for *A Doll's House* was often rendered in Chinese simply as *Nala* (Nora) but also translated more literally as *Wan'ou zhijia.*

20. Ye Yonglie, *Jiang Qing shilu* [The real Jiang Qing] (Hong Kong: Liwen, 1993), 59.

21. Tie Xin, "Zhongguo funü wenti" [China's women's issues], *Xinsheng zhoukan* I, no. 20 (1934): 386–387.

22. Lu Xun (1923) in Yang, *Silent China,* 149.

23. Chen, "Guanyu *Xin nüxing* de yingpian, piping, ji qita."

24. Huang, "Seeing *New Woman,*" 64–66.

25. Chen, "Guanyu *Xin nüxing* de yingpian, piping, ji qita."

26. Tang, "Guanyu jixielun"; Chen, "Guanyu *Xin nüxing* de yingpian, piping, ji qita."

27. For one recent treatment of this topic in literature, see Ching-kiu Stephen Chan, "The Language of Despair: Ideological Representations of the 'New Woman' by May Fourth Writers," in *Gender Politics in Modern China: Writing and Feminism,* ed. Tani Barlow (Durham: Duke University Press, 1993), 13–33.

28. Cai Chusheng, "Xi ru rensheng" [Art imitates life], *Zhongguo dianying* 2 (1957). In the PRC film history narrative, the Journalists Union was an arm of "reactionary rule" and Lianhua's studio head, Luo Mingyou, being at best a fellow-traveler, acted in his own capitalist interests and in collusion with the journalists when the studio issued the formal apology.

29. "'San ba' guoji funü laodong jie: *Xin nüxing* canjia nüjiaoguan kaimu dianli" [International Women's Labor Day, March 8: *The New Woman* takes part in the opening ceremony for a women's education center], *Lianhua huabao* 5, no. 6 (1935): 16.

30. "Shei shahaile Ruan Lingyu?" *Zhonghua ribao,* March 16, 1935.

31. Li Taiyan, *Li Taiyan kaipian ji* [Collected *kaipian* of Li Taiyan] (Shanghai: Li Taiyan, 1937), 2. I would like to thank Carlton Benson for bringing this *kaipian* to my attention.

32. Anonymous souvenir booklet (n.p., n.d., ca. March 1935), 36 pp. Private collection, China.

33. "Ai Xia," *Mingxing yuekan* I, no. 2 (1933).

34. *Shi bao,* January II, February 15, 1935; *Shen bao,* January II, 1935.

35. Lin Yütang, "Wajin guniang" [The gold-digger girl], reprinted in *Ai yu fengci* [Love and satire] (Taibei: Jinlan wenhua chubanshe, 1984), 176–180; Sato, "The *Moga* Sensation," 373.

36. "San'ge modeng nüxing" [Three modern women], *Shi bao,* January 17, 1935.

37. "Nü mingxing de lian'ai zhang ye suan bu qing" [Even the stars' love accounts don't add up], *Shi bao,* January 17, 1935.

38. Cai Chusheng, "Xi ru rensheng"; Lu Xun, "Lun renyan kewei" [On gossip being a fearful thing], *Taibai banyue kan,* May 20, 1935, reprinted in *Lu Xun quan ji* [Complete works of Lu Xun], vol. 6 (Beijing: Renmin wenxue chubanshe, 1981), 331–334.

39. Ruan Lingyu's letters addressed to Tang Jishan and to society, all dated March 7, 1935, and reproduced on pp. 21–22 of the anonymous souvenir booklet booklet cited above.

40. Lu Xun, "Lun renyan kewei," 331–334.

41. For description in English of *heimu,* see Leo Ou-fan Lee and Andrew J. Nathan, "The Beginnings of Mass Culture: Journalism and Fiction in the Late Ch'ing and Beyond," in *Popular Culture in Late Imperial China,* ed. David Johnson, Andrew Nathan, and Evelyn Rawski (Berkeley: University of California Press, 1985), 383.

42. Sun Shiyi, "Yingju zhi yishu jiazhi yu shehui jiazhi" [The artistic and social value of film drama], *Guoguang tekan* 2 (January 1926).

43. "Silent speech," the Shanghai star system, and the actress as modern woman are the central topics of my current book project, based on my Ph.D. dissertation. (Columbia University, 1997).

44. One might also say that the blurred lines of this genre appear as an antidote to the Manichean division of subjectivity and objectivity during the Cultural Revolution and that after a decade of glorifying the heroic collective, these biographical novels also work to recuperate the individual psyche.

Chapter 12

•

Gendered Perspective

The Construction and Representation of Subjectivity

and Sexuality in *Ju Dou*

•

Shuqin Cui

Since its release in 1990, Zhang Yimou's *Ju Dou* has drawn intense interest from film critics, academic scholars, and general audiences. Reading *Ju Dou* against the difficulties and errors that often occur in cross-cultural interpretations of non-Western texts, Jenny Lau finds qualities of "Chineseness" fundamental to the film's textual and conceptual meanings, especially as inherent in the cultural notions of *yin* (excessive eroticism) and *xiao* (filial piety).[1] W. A. Callahan, by contrast, reads *Ju Dou* as a political allegory invoking both communism and Confucianism. These systems of patriarchal domination, he argues, define the film narrative as a "woman's struggle against her social placement" and as a father-son embodiment of Confucian ideology.[2] The image of Ju Dou has become iconographic in Chinese film criticism: a still of an impassioned Gong Li dominates the cover of Rey Chow's *Primitive Passions*. Chow describes *Ju Dou* as "the sign of a cross-cultural commodity fetishism," and, indeed, the appetite for viewing—and writing about—new Chinese cinema is strong. One can, as Chow does, see the director in the role of exhibitionist, displaying his "exotic" female protagonist, and thus engaging in the "Oriental's orientalism."[3]

This article supplements the growing body of broadly cultural and political analyses of *Ju Dou* by concentrating on cinematic analysis to show how the film produces meaning—more specifically, gendered meanings. As the central image in the film, the figure of Ju Dou exposes the oppressions that issue from social traditions. But behind her entrancing visibility lies the shadow of a patriarchal unconscious. In other words, a hidden male subjectivity is projected onto the sexualized heroine of the film, which throws open the question of whose subjectivity and sexuality is being represented. To address this question, I rely first on a textual analysis of the meanings embedded in cinematic language and, second, on how the representation of woman occurs through gendered perspectives. Finally, I argue that representations of woman can convey a desire to reassert a repressed male subjectivity and sexuality. While placing women in the foreground of a film may display a humane concern for exposing social oppression, the gendered perspective that relates women to men may reveal a longing for a lost masculinity.

Cinematic representation involves the construction of gendered meanings. In this film narrative, the female figure is entangled with three character triangles. The first triangle of relations (hereafter, the first narrative order) comprises the husband Jinshan, the wife Ju Dou, and the nephew Tianqing. A struggle to possess the woman and thus restore a masculinity threatened or suppressed defines the first narrative order. Elements of off-screen sound effects render the husband's social ownership of the wife, while a structure of point-of-view shots unfolds the nephew's sexual engagement with the aunt. As Ju Dou shifts her role from Jinshan's wife to Tianqing's lover and initiates a second set of relations, or narrative order, a sense of entrapment emerges. A closed film form, with a subjective mise-en-scène rich in symbolic meaning, places the forbidden love affair under an aura of confinement. Relations among the mother, the two fathers, and the son constitute a third narrative order, which ends the film with an unresolved questioning of the interplay between social structure and human nature.

• The Story of *Ju Dou*

Set in a small village of northern China in the 1920s and involving the tangled relationships among husband, wife, lover, and son, *Ju Dou* is a film about a social system that produces repressed human beings. The dye-house owner, Yang Jinshan, an old and cruel man, purchases a beautiful young woman, Ju Dou, in expectation of her bearing him a male heir. Impotent and hostile, however, he uses his new wife as slave labor during the day and abuses her at night for failing to bear him a child. Her nightly, tormented cries arouse the sympathy and affection of Tianqing, the owner's adopted nephew, who has eyes for her the moment he sees her. The old man's mistreatment and the young man's secret passion lead Ju Dou and Tianqing to long for the death of the sadistic Jinshan. The "aunt" and the "nephew" consummate their love affair and soon after produce a son, Yang Tianbai, whom the old man initially believes to be his own.

Under the roof of the dye house and within the walls of the courtyard, secret lives and unlawful relations carry on. The old victimizer, now paralyzed by a stroke, becomes the victim as he watches his wife and nephew openly having an affair. The passionate lovers, in turn, suffer psychologically and physically from their transgressions. The angry son, reared in confusion as to who his father is, accidentally drowns his acknowledged father and willfully kills his actual father, whose love relation with Ju Dou the boy deeply resents. With no way out from under the blanketing power of the feudal system, Ju Dou sets a fire that sends the dye factory and her years of longing for liberation up in smoke.

· Off-Screen Sound Effects

Ju Dou is a subjective film in that off-screen sounds and point-of-view structures powerfully carry the process of narration. The sound track is beautifully constructed, yet the sound itself is shrill and striking. Functioning as a cinematic and narrative apparatus, the off-screen sound effects in *Ju Dou* not only produce the meaning of the drama, but also help control the way in which meaning is produced. The narration can be viewed as a mode of representation rich with implicit meaning, with the relations between sound and space, sound and image, and sound and the viewer's imagination as primary elements in the process of representation. Each element conditions and is conditioned by the others; the analysis of the sound effects is a dialectical process focusing first on the nature of the sound and then its intermingling with space, image, and the reader's imagination.

Ju Dou employs a number of moments when off-screen sound effects bring the viewer's imagination into play by suggesting off-screen space before revealing images. We hear Ju Dou before we see her. Consider, for instance, sound cut one: a static medium shot of Tianqing lying in his bed is accompanied by an off-screen sound track of a woman screaming and a man shouting. As Tianqing sits up to listen, the screams grow louder and the man's words become decipherable: "you'll never bring the Yang family a male heir. You are not good for anything." Sound cut two: after two close-up shots of Ju Dou with her mouth gagged and her hands tied behind her back and a medium shot of the husband sitting on a saddle astride Ju Dou's body, the scene cuts to a closely framed exterior setting where Tianqing enters screen right as the off-screen screaming and whipping roars in. Sorrowful music accompanies the woman's cries. Sound cut three: suddenly the same screaming again emanates from off-screen. Tianqing enters frame right, picks up a knife, and runs toward the staircase. A dialogue between Tianqing and the man off-screen ensues.

As off-screen sound effects function to create off-screen space, the film image expands beyond the confines of the frame in the viewer's imagination. In its volume and distance, the sound source acts as a narrator directing the drama. Since what is suggested by the sound source is audible but invisible, however, viewers are forced to imagine what is happening in the off-screen area. For instance, the first application of the off-screen sound track in *Ju Dou* (the verbal commotion) evokes suspense—something terrible is taking place beyond the screen—and creates viewer anticipation through the mystery of what compels the altercation. The audience conjures visual images of the sound's source.

The discomfort of hearing without seeing is mediated in terms of diegetic transmission—the sound passes from film to spectator, filtered through character.[4] In other words, the presence of an on-screen figure forms a character narration or point of view, connecting the off-screen space and the viewer's imagination, as we watch the face of a listener while we hear voices, sound, or music whose source is hidden. Among the three sound cuts, Tianqing is the primary channel through whom off-screen sound passes to the audience and through whom the viewer's involvement is connected to the off-screen space. Since the off-screen sound can only be approached from the on-screen character's point of view, the character narration becomes subjective. The transmission through Tianqing actively interrelates the audience with the fictional world within the frame. One listens tentatively as Tianqing listens and one worries intensely as Tianqing worries. From Tianqing's perspective on the off-screen sounds, we come to realize that the husband sexually abuses Ju Dou because she has not borne him a male heir.

Unlike visual images, the off-screen images are not rendered directly or concretely. The significance of this distancing and fluidity, which requires imagination and involvement, resides in its power to arouse curiosity in the audience, which tends to be especially alert to what it can imagine but not see.

The images concealed in off-screen space are often revealed with the use of shot/reverse shot editing: a retrospective and self-reflective style. By converting an off-screen space that was imaginary in the initial shot into concrete space, the reverse shot mediates between an invisible world and the audience's concern for knowing that world. For instance, the enigma of Ju Dou's screams and the husband's tirade remains unsolved until the camera translates the off-screen sound into on-screen images. In shot one, the mise-en-scène, which reveals Ju Dou's condition (mouth gagged, hands tied), discloses the reason for her distress. Shot two, the composition of "horse riding" with Jinshan mounted on a saddle across the almost naked Ju Dou, highlights the violence inflicted by husband on wife. A return to the close-up of Ju Dou struggling to avoid hot tea poured from off-upper frame to her shoulder indicates the continuation of the abuse.

With just enough revelation of the image to satisfy the viewer's curiosity and expectations, a cut from the interior shot to the exterior mise-en-scène, again to the backdrop of off-screen whipping and screaming, uses closed framing to suggest a sense of confinement. Allowing the audience to witness the action and then to hear the off-screen sound track again provokes the viewer's involvement so that fictional world and audience space are commingled. To further provoke audience interest, the anticipatory camera introduces Tianqing as he enters frame right toward the staircase. The direction of Tianqing's movement suggests a subjective narration: we want to follow Tianqing upstairs and intervene forcefully. However, Tianqing appears trapped within the tightly framed columns, the image emphasizing his impotence to act. When the shot of Tianqing shifts to a medium shot of the husband ready to disrobe, we hear the sound of lash on flesh and the cries of pain, while the image of abuse disappears from us again. In sum, the off-screen sound effects in *Ju Dou* constitute a process of narration by creating off-screen space and image.

In the marital relation, Jinshan, as head of the household and the owner of the dye mill, symbolizes an ultimate economic and sociocultural authority. His position permits him to possess Ju Dou as if she were an animal purchased at market, to violate her body as if she were a reproductive machine, and to practice his power like a master riding a horse. The socially assigned relation between Jinshan and Ju Dou is simply but powerfully presented in the cinematic composition of horse riding. Sitting on the saddle, Jinshan whips, tortures, and enjoys the pleasure of riding the female animal and ploughing the woman's body so as to plant the seed for a male heir. The sounds from Ju Dou's gagged mouth and the bruises on her abused body utter a painful yet powerless cry. A Chinese woman's chief function in life was to further her husband's lineage. Attempts to swerve from that path were dealt with harshly.[5] Thus, social position provides Jinshan the authoritarian right to pursue lineal continuity by abusing Ju Dou. But *why* does Jinshan brutalize Ju Dou in his hunger for a male heir?

While social position offers Jinshan the right to purchase and possess Ju Dou, his sexual impotence haunts him with the psychological fear of not having posterity. To mediate the conflict between his need for social power and his sexual lack, he engages in violence toward woman's body. The contradiction between social power and sexual anxiety sets male violence against female sexuality. The fear of impotence drives Jinshan to find an object against which he might transform and reduce his anxiety.

Ju Dou is represented as an agent within the text of the film whereby Jinshan's fear and sadism are brought to light. It is in Ju Dou that Jinshan is faced with the recognition of his lack; it is in Ju Dou that his fear of impotence might be transformed; and it is in Ju Dou that his desire to restore his patriarchal power might be fulfilled. For Jinshan, therefore, violence is a way of covering his lack, reducing his fear, and asserting his power by destroying the body of the other. In torturing Ju Dou, he enjoys neither pleasure nor her pain but transmits his fear and proves his power at her expense.

• Point-of-View Structure

In examining the relationship between the aunt, Ju Dou, and the nephew, Tianqing, we encounter the cinematic point-of-view structure and the concept of the male gaze in a Chinese sociocultural context. In a cinematic point-of-view shot, the camera assumes the spatial position of a character. The camera eye becomes the eye of the character and of the audience. The significance of point-of-view structure in *Ju Dou* is not only to show us what we would see from the viewpoint of the character but how we would see it as well. A point-of-view shot, for instance, introduces an unstable relation between Tianqing as the subject and Ju Dou as the object of the look. First, a close-up of the eye of a donkey leads our vision to Tianqing, who is looking through a peephole: the establishment of the man as the viewing subject. Second, a subjective view occurs through a medium shot of the female figure with her back toward Tianqing and the audience: the revelation of the object being looked at from Tianqing's point of view. The donkey's sudden braying interrupts Tianqing's anxious peeping and stealthy desire: temporal condensation destroys the possibility of visual pleasure. Furthermore, low-key lighting and enclosed framing—which confines the back of the female figure behind bars and in shadow—suggest a spatial limitation that makes seeing difficult. The second point-of-view structure reinforces the unstable relation between the subject and the object of the look by alternating the distance through different shots, camera angles, and high-key lighting effects. The shots that alternate from extreme long shot to medium shot and then to close-up suggest a distance between the two characters. While low camera angles distort the distance, high-key lighting invests the female character with a sense of unreachability. In a close-up, Tianqing, positioned at the corner of the foreground and blocked behind the lines of the wooden wheel, looks up. He sees Ju Dou, who is presented in a series of subjective point-of-view shots. The first is a long and low-angle shot combined with extreme high-key lighting. The long shot distances Ju Dou at the far background framed by lines of hanging pieces of cloth. The high-key lighting places Ju Dou in a halo and the overexposed space suggests her unapproachability. Then, the long, low-angle shot is replaced by a low-angle medium shot where Ju Dou is bathed in the golden rays of the sun and the color of the fabric: a sense of closeness yet still out of reach. Finally,

Fig. 29. Ju Dou (Gong Li) and Tianqing (Li Baotian) in *Ju Dou,* directed by Zhang Yimou, 1990. British Film Institute.

when Ju Dou looks back, Tianqing fails to control the notch of the wheel and the collapse of the machine interrupts the looking.

The third point-of-view shot develops a gender shift between viewing-subject and viewed-object. Ju Dou finds the peephole. In the same position that Tianqing used to spy on her, Ju Dou composes the look through the peephole. What the reverse shot reveals is her private bathing space. However, she sees no female body: an erasure or denial of the male look. Hence, by alternating the trajectory of the look, Ju Dou does not allow herself to be observed unaware. The transformation from object being looked at into subject possessing the look establishes a female subjectivity in relation to and with emphasis on vision. Ju Dou finally stops up the hole with straw, hoping to eliminate the possibility of being looked at.

The final point-of-view shot is a silent yet powerful answering vision to the male gaze that erases the thrill of secret looking. The destruction of pleasure in looking is effected through the sound track, the turning of the body, and Ju Dou's confrontational gaze. Ju Dou attracts Tianqing to the peephole by closing the door and beginning to wash. Responding to the sounds, Tianqing peers through the peephole again. The return of his gaze is completed with three takes highlighting the moment of "turning." The first take is a long shot with Ju Dou's back toward the camera. The contrast between light and shadow highlights the bruises on her body. The long shot shifts to a medium shot as Ju Dou slowly turns her naked body toward the camera. Finally, a close, deeply focused, and high-key lit shot of Ju Dou directly confronts the eyes of Tianqing, the camera, and the audience. She turns to look over her shoulder toward the camera, seizing and fixing the viewer. Ju Dou thus reverses the visual dynamic back on the male look, yet leaves the viewing situation unaltered. The wordless expression on her face and the powerful visual image of her body change Tianqing's pleasure into discomfort and the audience's as well.

· Male Gaze and Female Sexuality

The cinematic representation of looking and being looked at, of course, typically evokes concern about the male gaze and female sexuality. And while one finds that a Third-World film text may be interpreted in terms of Western film theories, notions of feminism that seem self-evident in one context may become problematic in another, due to different cultural, social, historical, and political codes. The concept of the gaze and the structure of the look have been among the most important elements in Western feminist film criticism. Relying on Freud's theories of voyeurism and fetishism, Laura Mulvey defined the system of the look as a basic cinematic structure of active/male as bearer and passive/female as object of the look.[6] As the active male gaze dominates both the narrative and the woman, the male figure occupies a position through which a sadistic voyeurism or fetishistic scopophilia is satisfied. While the passive female image associates itself with spectacle and space, the female character is represented as the erotic fulfillment of male sexual desire. Thus, pleasure in looking arises when point-of-view and shot/reverse shots direct the voyeuristic gazes of the male character to the image of the female body, and the spectator identifies with that character. Gender difference functions as a central force driving the narrative forms of Hollywood cinema; the female image signifies sexual difference and the male gaze controls the representation. In the conventions of Hollywood cinema, visual pleasure is structured according to a patriarchal ideology.

Ju Dou, while raising issues familiar to Western feminist film criticism, implies the concept of the gaze with a different cultural definition. If, as in

Mulvey's scheme, the relation between man and woman is one of looking and being looked at, Ju Dou's confrontation of Tianqing represents a contradiction between an individual's sexual desire and social position. The female body, as before, is the site upon which the ambivalence of male desire and fear is mediated. Woman plays a double role: she is a signifier of male castration at the hands of society and at the same time a carrier of male desire and frustrations. In this context, one might ask: What happens when woman returns the gaze? To what extent is the active-male/passive-female dichotomy reversible? Does woman possess a masculine authority when she returns the gaze?

The protagonists in *Ju Dou* live in a world created by circles of individual desire and fear stemming from social and narrative dislocations. As placement in the cinematic narrative conflicts with location in the social system, pleasure in looking is aggravated by fear of perversion. Seer and seen form entanglements vexed by the unresolvable binaries of pleasure/pain, self/other, masculine/feminine, and subject/object. For instance, Ju Dou and Tianqing are represented in a cinematic field of vision in which seeing is associated with male sexual desire. Following Mulvey, Tianqing's voyeurism should produce scopophilia, arising "from pleasure in using another person as an object of sexual stimulation through sight" and also through identification with the image seen.[7] The protagonists' social positions, however, prevent establishment of pleasure in looking and identification with the female image.

The social structure assigns Ju Dou and Tianqing to legitimate positions of aunt and nephew while the cinematic narrative transforms their social roles into a perverse relationship. The vision of the nephew toward the aunt moves swiftly from pleasure in looking to fear of being caught. Moreover, the low social status of both mutes the possibility of an active male gaze co-opting a passive female sexuality. In terms of social placement, Ju Dou is bought by Jinshan to give birth to a male heir, while Tianqing is a poor man, adopted by Jinshan to be a worker. Both are relatively powerless, and the lineal relation of aunt to nephew bars the seer from the seen. Therefore, pleasure in looking becomes embarrassment in peeping. Desire to love is fraught with guilt.

The fourth point-of-view shot is a powerful scene in terms of explaining how looking can extinguish pleasure. The peephole finally becomes the point where a male sexual fantasy is confronted with an abused female body. Communication through the peephole from both sides creates a moment of frightened but also intense sensuality. For Ju Dou, the turning of her naked body is a gesture of gaining control of and adding meaning to the representation of her body. This is a moment of liberation for Ju Dou as she changes herself from an object into a subject seeking to possess the vision. "When Ju Dou makes contact with Tianqing," as Callahan asserts, "it alters the relations of power in the representation, shifting Ju Dou from a passive nude to a naked figure who occupies the subject position."[8] In wresting control of her body from both Jinshan and Tianqing, Ju Dou transforms herself from an animal into an individual and at the same time humanizes Tianqing by turning him from voyeur into lover. Her return of Tianqing's gaze, her silent expression, bruised body, and confrontational look raise her feelings from shame to rebellion and announce her desire to be understood and freed from abuse. For Tianqing, the reciprocation produces a tremendous psychological disturbance. The sight of the bruises on her body destroys his anxiety about looking at woman as a sexual object and strikes a sense of guilt and responsibility for what man has done to woman. Tianqing has to avert his gaze.

The representation of Tianqing presents his sexuality and masculinity as socially impotent. His restless sexual yearning and his restricted circumstances drive Tianqing to search for a ground where his desire can be restored and expressed. The female body becomes such a ground from which a male consciousness starts to search for what has been repressed and lost. Thus, Tianqing, like Jinshan, finds in woman a scapegoat upon which his subjectivity and pent-up sexuality can be vented.

In terms of the filmic point-of-view structure and psychological exploration, the film director first unfolds male sufferings by making the female body reexperience the oppressions on behalf of both sexes; secondly he searches for the lost self by imposing meanings upon the female body; and finally he restores masculinity by objectifying the female body in the field of vision. Thus, after placing woman on a stage so she is highly visible but hardly audible, male "directors" are able to locate themselves in an off-screen space, set up a subjective point of view, and direct our vision to the staged object. A relationship between man and woman as viewer and image in a Chinese context is formed.

To look at woman from a hidden space and a subjective perspective conveys gendered meanings. The subjective point of view provides the male viewer with a sense of control. Moreover, the invisible position shields him from danger and responsibility. Therefore, in order to expose the wounds of the past, express desire in the present, and hope for the future, male directors have represented woman as a mirror image that reflects the past, signifies male desire, and bears male burdens and hopes.

The representation of woman forms a medium through which male subjectivity and sexuality are sought, restored, and reaffirmed. In relation to the two men, Ju Dou is the object of multiple possessions, whether through patriarchal dominance or cinematic discourse. Her husband violates her body so as to prove his patriarchal power and to cover his sexual impotence. Her nephew possesses the vision of her body so as to fulfill sexual desire and deny his social impotence. Besides these instances of patriarchal dominance, the objectification of the female body is further reinforced by the cinematic apparatus and narrative systems. The off-screen sound effects place the drama of male violence toward the female body in an off-screen space from which only Ju Dou's screams emanate. The point-of-view structure directs vision through the peephole to her abused body. Socially and cinematically, it is the semiotic activities of a patriarchal psyche which represent woman as an object for the construction of male subjectivity and sexuality.

· The Second Order of Narrative

As the narrative switches to a second order—the triangle of aunt-nephew-husband—the thematic focus shifts from an opposition of possession/possessed to a binary of human desire/ethical confinement. While an internal restlessness motivates the love affair between aunt and nephew, prohibition takes the form of an external force which constrains desires through social standards of morality and propriety. In representing the personal crises, social and cinematic systems reinforce the clash between desire and prohibition. A closed film form is achieved through cinematic elements of tight framing and mise-en-scène. A closed social form is structured in terms of a transgressive seduction. As human desires challenge cultural values and social restraints, resultant conflicts lead the tragic love affair toward a fatal destiny. Desire for the forbidden precipitates a crisis in social relations that casts opprobrium on woman's sexuality. Cinematic representation shows the lovers crushed beneath the weight of traditional morality.

The expression of desire in *Ju Dou* unfolds in a fantasy of liberation through transgression. A strategy of using woman to initiate the illicit act and to bear the consequent punishment conceals an intent to express male desire through the representation of woman. Both male characters project their desires onto the female object: the husband physically possesses Ju Dou's body and the nephew relishes the sexual vision of her body. In the second phase of the narrative, however, it is Ju Dou who initiates a transgressive seduction and provokes another series of displacements. By seducing Tianqing, she transforms herself from one man's wife into another one's lover and reverses the relation of the two men to each other. The altered relations, which can be considered incestuous as well as adulterous in China, ironically bring satisfaction to each character's desire: Ju Dou and Tianqing produce a son the old man believes to be his. Repeated sexual bonding between the young lovers gives them much pleasure. As the protagonists pursue their desires in violation of the incest taboo, however, they are torn by internal chaos and external prohibitions.

• Closed Film Form

A closed film form sets up a confined background against which the second narrative unfolds. In a closed form, "the world of the film is the only thing that exists; everything within it has its place in the plot of the film—every object, every character, every gesture, every action."[9] An element of the closed film form in *Ju Dou* is the set design of the Yang family dye mill, where human-made structures confine desires arising from human nature. The film director introduces a self-contained world, first of all, in terms of a tight frame: the mise-en-scène is so densely arranged that people appear to have almost no freedom of movement. The sense of confinement is reinforced by alternations of long with close-up shots, or wide-angle with telephoto lenses. The long shot captures the complete setting with all the compositional weights of mise-en-scène densely arranged in deep space. Lines/shapes, machines/humans, and fabric/vat are carefully structured. The extreme low-angle shot combined with a perspective-distorting, wide-angle lens makes the already giant wooden structure even more dominant. After the whole setting is introduced, a close-up shot emphasizes and heightens each machine part in the foreground: powerful visual images of wheel/ block, pestle/mortar, and water/fire. The use of a telephoto lens compresses the dense space further. In a film space so compactly framed with compositional weights, little room is left for the characters' movements.

The confined setting dramatizes a relationship between characters and objects. A pattern of static camera position and sudden movement of objects visualizes meanings of dominance and submission. Often the ordered patterns of machine parts or the whole structure are framed in the foreground, contrasting the human figures in the background. If the heavy and looming man-made structure symbolizes the social system, the small and powerless human figures appear to be imprisoned in a cage. However, disturbance of the static patterns by sudden movement emphasizes interaction between objects and characters. Periodically, the unexpected movement of a long bolt of cloth or the collapse of a machine part will startle us, making dynamic and visual statements about human actions. Moreover, the colors of the fabrics—especially red—paint the setting with passions where the meanings of love and death commingle. High-key lighting from behind and above causes the female figure to stand out from the man-made architecture around her. Such systematic use of cinematic apparatus is a directing strategy that Zhang Yimou has consistently employed.

The closed form in *Ju Dou*'s setting serves to visually and psychologically instruct viewers' understanding of filmic meanings. Compositional patterns and suggestions of oppressive weight emphasize the power of structures over persons. As the audience of the closed form, we are vulnerably lured or willingly drawn into its world. With every object and character placed in a closed form that signifies isolation from the outside world, the film director achieves a subjective authority. The world he creates is the only space where the story takes place. The materials he organizes are the only information that tells the story. Against the background of the dye mill, and under the manipulation of the film director's arrangement, finally, the visual confinement parallels a thematic entrapment in which a forbidden love affair between aunt and nephew is represented.

In the seduction sequence, for instance, the cinematic apparatus restrains the seduction with framing and composition. Shot/reverse shots keep Ju Dou and Tianqing in separated frames. Tianqing is often set against a background of darkness. In one frame, for example, Tianqing, placed at the edge of the screen and in light, occupies one-third of the space; the other two-thirds remain empty, painted with darkness. The high contrast between dark and light and the expanse of dark space with a human figure at its edge suggests a vast and gaping mouth ready to swallow the vulnerable character. In another scene, Tianqing is set in a composition of frame within a frame. With Ju Dou upstairs and Tianqing down below, the sense of entrapment is first of all indicated by an extreme high-angle shot from Ju Dou's point of view. The tight composition of vertical columns and the diagonal stairs reinforce a sense of overpowering obstacles. The entanglement of frame within frame and the contrast between illuminated and darkened space point to Tianqing's assailability.

In contrast to the framing of Tianqing, Ju Dou appears in a position of sexual power. The sense of her seductive power and its perversion involves a carefully framed composition between the female figure and the objects around her. On the left side of the Ju Dou are bolts of pink and blue fabrics, potentially symbolizing erotic lust. On the right side of the frame is a large wooden wheel supported by a single notch, suggesting both the strength of sexual power and its immediate danger of collapse. The composed relationship between human figure and architectural objects signifies the relation between the dominant subject, Ju Dou, and dominated object, Tianqing.

Framing not only separates but also brings elements together. As Tianqing and Ju Dou are finally placed in one frame, the two human figures appear in parallel positions due to the tightly framed compositions. Characters and objects are all pushed into the foreground. In the center of the frame are the two embracing bodies. Directly behind them are symmetrical columns, pressing the characters from both sides. Across the vertical lines of columns are the horizontal lines of the structure, forming a spider's web. The upper frame is another layer of crossed lines, and the left corner is blocked by the huge wheel. The enclosure seems suffocating.

· A Restrained Social Form

In addition to the metaphorical entrapment constructed in a closed film form, moral and ethical values also restrain the characters from transgressive action. In other words, as Ju Dou and Tianqing taste the pleasure of the love affair, they are haunted by the fear of violating ritual principles—especially the principles of chastity for woman and filial piety for man. The concept of filial piety is conventionally conceived as the essential value in the Confucian tradition. Elaborated in terms of the father-son relation, the elements of filial piety emphasize the obedience of the son to the father, the suppression of the son's desire in order to anticipate the father's wishes, and the repression of the son's rebelliousness toward the father. While filial piety has constituted the core of Chinese familial and social structure for generation after generation, the idea of fidelity also occurs in the form of chastity—the highest feminine virtue in Confucian tradition. However, while the representation of the seduction seeks to place Tianqing in the position of filial son, Ju Dou remains the transgressor. The difficulty of indulging in "immoral" acts while keeping a "moral" reputation drives the protagonists only toward repression.

Mapping power relations alongside desire shows woman as the carrier of the burdens of cultural negation and physical-psychological pains, while casting man as apologist. Sexual transgression within an ethical hierarchy provides no solution for the contradiction between human desire and social institutions. Therefore, the insistence on and drive for transgression brings only social opprobrium and suffering. The inquiry into why it is woman who will bear the burdens reveals a divided male self and, secondly, a cinematic strategy for representation. After Ju Dou is realigned from her husband to her nephew, she experiences an ironic repetition in her life history. The abuse of her body at the hands of her husband for not giving birth to a male heir is paralleled by her self-abuse with chili powder as a means of preventing pregnancy. The momentary joy of sexual pleasure is paid for with prolonged pain. The desire to escape and to love ends with destruction and death. Each time, when life meets death or piety confronts sin, Ju Dou is the figure of evil. The strategy of representing gender difference and the woman character's confusion over her pain and punishment are expressed in two conversations:

1. *(Ju Dou takes out a bottle of arsenic.)*
   JU DOU   Listen to me, it's either him or me.
   TIANQING   Who?
   JU DOU   Who else should it be?
   TIANQING   How dare you? After all, he is my uncle.
   JU DOU   He is your uncle, then what am I to you?

2. *(Ju Dou and Tianqing are at the old man's deathbed.)*
   TIANQING   Killing one's husband cries out for punishment.
   JU DOU   Didn't he deserve to die? What a loyal son you are.
   (Tianqing slaps Ju Dou's face)
   JU DOU   You, too, are beating me. Revive the old man, and you can both beat me. I don't want to live anymore.

From these conversations, we recognize a divided male self—a self with internal desire but masked by an external filial identity. The transgression evokes a conflict between private psychological need and public ethical restriction, where the individual unconscious expresses personal desire in the name of ritual values. As a split self who presents alternating personalities so as to facilitate different consequences, Tianqing struggles to express male desire—a socially and politically repressed desire. The male protagonist needs an object upon which his meaning can be imposed. To represent desire, the male director requires an image through which his camera can convey meaning. In order to meet the needs of both men, the woman character is produced, standing front and center.

One should not assume that Ju Dou and Tianqing represent either heroes or rebels against the sociocultural system. Instead, they are the conflicted figures who consciously enact perverse desires while defying ethical prohibitions. Jonathan Dollimore refers to this type of situation as "transgressive reinscription," where transgression performed as inversion or perversion seeks not an escape from existing structures but rather a subversive reinscription within them and in the process a dislocation of them.[10] For instance, after Jinshan is immobilized, Ju Dou and Tianqing change their relation from aunt and nephew to that of a self-defined "couple," which violates the ethical value of filial piety. The opposition between the force of desire and the power of filial piety drives the perverse couple to search for a space where they can sustain their affair. Thus, an opposition of private/public space is constructed and alternated. On the one hand, they live like animals hiding in a private world where the wild woods, abandoned cave, and the house cellar become places for them to make love. On the other hand, they present themselves as filial son and daughter in a public sphere where they feed, bathe, and carry around the paralyzed husband. The young couple's alternating patterns of behavior imply a contradictory psychic disturbance—submission to the patriarchal authority and ethical principles while exercising individual desires.

In sum, the representation of female seduction assigns woman the role of transgressor while denying her real agency. In order to seduce man, she has to pose herself as the object of his desire by means of her sexuality. Instead of transforming herself into a desiring subject, however, Ju Dou fantasizes Tianqing to be a figure of salvation, saving her from another man's oppression. The exchange price she pays is her body, declaring, "I have saved my body for you." As a result, Ju Dou retains her object position, even though she transforms herself from the object of one man's sexual abuse into the object of another man's sexual desire. Meanings conveyed from the male representation of female seduction include the following: a seductive woman cannot consciously assert herself as a subject, but only as an object of desire for another. In the confrontation between the seducer and the seduced, she fulfills her desire through her sexual autonomy, while man can be mirrored and affirmed by being temporarily the object of female seduction. In shifting from one man's patriarchal possession into another man's sexual possession, Ju Dou's female body proves one more time the value of usefulness for her husband and the value of exchange for her nephew.

• The Third Order of Narrative

The birth of a son to the aunt and nephew proclaims the beginning of the third order of narrative: an oedipal triangle of son-fathers-mother. The narration starts from the boy's identification with Jinshan as his father and Tianqing as his "brother." It ends with an oedipal tragedy in which the boy drowns both his acknowledged and biological fathers in the dye vat. Since the narration focuses on psychological factors and cosmological elements simultaneously, both Western psychoanalytic and Chinese mythological approaches may be employed in interpreting the narrative's complexity. The film's meanings take metaphorical and literary forms when we place the father-son-mother relationship in a framework of both the Oedipus complex and yin yang mythology.

As the narrative order is transformed because of the birth of a male heir in the Yang family, a ritual of naming the baby sets an ironic tone to the relations between the child and his parents. Loud cries of the baby from off-screen proclaim the birth of the patrilineal inheritor, since he is born with "a watering spout between his legs." The camera tilts from the upper level of the house—the birthplace—down to where the village elders are gathering together to name the newborn. The composition of the mise-en-scène gives prominence to the idea of power transfer from a gerontocracy to the male heir. A group of old men sit in an ordered arrangement along the table—a social hierarchy. A soft spotlight on an old man in the center, in contrast with dark shadows on the others, highlights the symbolic position of ancestor. After the men search the family book of names and argue over the proper choice, a writing brush in close-up finally makes its circle around the character *bai* (purity). On account of its connection to his "brother's" name, Tianqing, the boy's name is rendered as Tianbai. When *qing* and *bai* join together, the phrase carries a meaning of "purity" or "innocent from any guilt." Ironically, this son of purity is actually the son of his mother and "brother." Thus the relationship between Ju Dou and Tianqing not only violates social prohibitions in the second order of the narrative but also manifests its transgression in the person of their biological son—the patrilineal heir.

· Identification with the "Father"

If we assume, according to Lacanian notions, that a child's acceptance of the Law of the Father and discovery of sexual difference occurs at about the time that he enters the symbolic order of language, Tianbai's identification with the father by his single utterance of "daddy" might be a persuasive instance. More importantly, the sudden identification with Jinshan as his father and Tianqing as his "brother" reverses the character relations (Jinshan = husband, Ju Dou and Tianqing = lovers) back to the original pattern (Jinshan = husband, Ju Dou = wife, Tianqing = nephew). In so doing, the film representation maintains the patriarchal structure by means of father-son relations, while putting Ju Dou and Tianqing in the position of being punished. This cause-effect pattern of identification and inversion makes the third narrative a realm of psychological turmoil. In Tianbai's premirror phase, he lives with his mother and two fathers—his mother's legitimate husband and nephew. As the product of an "incestuous" relationship, Tianbai has been denied by Jinshan and twice almost killed by him. Because of the child's continued dependency on the Imaginary, no real subject is constituted. After the transition to the mirror stage, however, the *absence* of his mother and the *presence* of the father initiates the child into a discovery of difference and threeness.

The absence of the mother always conveys a sense of secret incest taboo, while the presence of the father symbolizes prohibition and separation. For instance, a series of sequences reveals the maternal absence and the boy's psychological reactions toward that absence. In an external setting, the three-year-old Tianbai watches his biological but "incestuous" parents disappearing into the deep woods. He stares off-screen with an expression of pain and hate in his eyes. Again, mother leaves her bedroom to enter her nephew's room. The off-screen sound of her voice laughing or shouting resonates in the wide courtyard. As Ju Dou emerges from Tianqing's room, we see Tianbai, in a low-angle shot, standing on top of the stair and staring at his mother from a distance. The little boy's white undergarment (symbolizing his name, pure heaven) contrasts with his mother's black coat (an ironic reference to Tianqing's name, black heaven). The boy's half-naked body (the presence of his penis) alludes to his mother's sufferings from sexual abuse. The low-angle shot of the boy and the high-angle shot of the mother indicate a position and power difference. More striking is Tianbai's stare, which directly and sharply projects toward his mother, asserting a patrilineal authority over a sinful mother. The external representation reinforces a psychological contest between son and mother and thus between sexual desire and ethical prohibition.

In another sequence, an argument between Ju Dou and Tianqing on the topic of pregnancy is interrupted by the off-screen sound of something striking the window. Ju Dou comes out partially dressed and sees the child throwing stones against the house. Shot/reverse shot reveals yet another moment of psychological conflict. While the alternation between the shots brings the mother and the boy closer together, the psychological distance between the two widens. Tianbai refuses to acknowledge his mother's presence and continues to throw stones at Tianqing's window. When Ju Dou slaps the boy's face, he answers with silence and a cold expression in his eyes. The torment between a mother's love for her son and her anguish over his behavior evokes a soundless crying from a deep, inner world. The camera then pans and tilts up toward Jinshan sitting in his wooden bucket at the top of the stair singing delightedly.

The absence of the mother disturbs Tianbai's identification with the Imaginary and moves him toward an acceptance of the function and power of the Symbolic—the Name of the Father. The presence of Jinshan, the symbol of the Father, signifies a social and patriarchal law. The Law of the Father, in Terry Eagleton's account, "is in the first place the social taboo on incest. . . . The father's real or imagined prohibition of incest is symbolic of all the higher authority to be later encountered."[11] Therefore, the moment of recognition of the figure of the father brings the child into awareness of wider familial and social relations of authority and obedience. In order to become properly socialized and assume a place in the symbolic system, the child replaces his loss of desire for the Imaginary with the gain of symbolic power through his identification with the father.

Moreover, the possibility and opportunity for this identification occurs in the child's ability to code and decode messages in language. Tianbai's oedipal realization of the father and accession to language are constituted in terms of a psychological representation. Tianbai is dyeing his straws in the vat. Jinshan dozes in his wooden bucket. Mother is absent. The absence of the biological parents brings the boy disappointment but offers the old man an opportunity for revenge. Jinshan, a betrayed husband, attempts to kill the child after he finds out that Tianbai is not his son. In a silent yet tense atmosphere, a series of shot/reverse shots shortens the distance between the old man and the child with every alternation. When the old man's stick is just ready to push the child into the water, Tianbai suddenly turns around and calls him Daddy for the first time.

Thus, language is identified with mother-loss and the admission of difference. Seconds of dead silence stir up years of suppressed emotion. The sound track of the striking of the drum awakens the old man's consciousness to identify the little boy as his son. As the parents desperately search for their *lost* son in the outside world, the acknowledged father gains a son in his inner psychological world. Thereafter, a third displacement is established: Tianqing, the biological father of Tianbai becomes his "brother," and Jinshan, Tianqing's uncle, turns into the boy's father. Mother Ju Dou faces the psychological struggle between the two "fathers" and the son.

· Death of the Father

Recognition by the boy, however, does not preserve the father's ultimate power but instead brings about the father's death. Jinshan is portrayed as both a figure of social power and a sexually castrated victim. In other words, the symbolic father has his phallus removed. The Lacanian phallus signifies the necessarily absent object of desire. With the father possessing it while the mother suffers its "lacking," the phallus indicates a sexual difference. Confronting this sexual division, the male child identifies himself with the phallus, imagining that it will complete the mother and himself. An irony occurs in the representation of the father figure Jinshan, however: within the patriarchal frame lies an impotent masculinity. As Tianbai takes the place of a castrated masculine power (that of the gerontocracy), he inherits patriarchal authority through the death of the father.

The metaphor of the dead father is visualized as such: Tianbai pulls his acknowledged father (sitting in his wheeled wooden bucket) through the door and then toward a dye vat full of red water. The shot of Tianbai cuts to a reverse shot of his inverted image in the water (mirror image). The same pattern is repeated for the shots of Jinshan. Then, a freeze-frame and close-up shot of the rope that connects father and son appears on the screen for a second before it is broken. What follows immediately is a splash of red water and the old man's thrashing in the vat. Tianbai stands by and watches the scene without any sign of emotion. As the father's final struggle subsides and he floats on the water, the son starts to laugh: the first laugh in the child's life and the symbolic laugh that pronounces the power transition from patriarchal father to patrilineal son.

The establishment of Tianbai's dominance in the third order of the narrative is visualized and formalized in terms of montage editing. Thematic editing (montage) and juxtaposition of shots in the funeral scene declare Tianbai's patrilineal position and the subordination of the living to the dead. Montage editing, as pioneered by Soviet filmmakers like Knleshov, Eisenstein, and Pudovkin, stresses that meanings are constructed through the juxtaposition of shots, not by one shot alone. When each shot employs one perspective of meaning, association of the separate shots could produce a unified effect. As Louis Giannetti observes, "Only by juxtaposing close-ups of objects, texture, symbols, and other selected details can a filmmaker convey expressively the idea underlying the undifferentiated jumble of real life."[12] In *Ju Dou*'s funeral scene, for instance, the establishing shot introduces us to the funeral procession and its rituals of blocking the coffin. A close-up and extreme low-angle shot of the boy sitting on top of the coffin with the dead man's memorial plaque in his hands confirms his lineal ascension. A worm's-eye-view shot of the coffin and two figures prostrating themselves and rolling under declares the authority of the dead and the subordination of the living. The cumulative effect of the repeated shots, reinforced by slow motion, confirms the exaltation of the boy's social position and the degradation of his biological parent's social status.

· The Death of the "Brother"

Because of Tianbai's identification with the dead father and his position of true inheritor, his relation to Tianqing becomes one of "brothers" in which "there is nothing but the violent mutual exclusivity of rivalry."[13] The congruence between the psychological factors in the film and Freud's comments on the incest taboo further explains this Chinese oedipal complex in psychoanalytic terms. In the film narrative, both Tianqing and Tianbai are linked to the death of the father figure, Jinshan, the former in an aborted attempt and the latter by accident. After the death of the father, they struggle against each other in regard to the mother figure, Ju Dou. Tianbai tries to prevent his mother from violating the incest taboo, and Tianqing wishes to be Ju Dou's secret husband one more time.

The rivalry between "brothers" (actually between father and son) focuses not only on the father's death but also on the question of who rightfully possesses the woman. Tianbai's bonding with the mother and consequent hostility to the "brother" causes the final termination: Tianqing's death.

Ju Dou and Tianqing, it seems, can never be husband and wife. Years pass and still they cannot break through the social prohibitions. Throughout the film, up till Tianqing's death, they are often presented in two frames. With the heavy horizontal lines of the mill's structure blocking the characters frontally and vertical lines of cloth wrapping two sides, the closed form of the mise-en-scène produces an image of living people already entrapped in a tight coffin. Tianqing invites Ju Dou to make another reunion as husband and wife. They end up with a suicide attempt in the family's cellar. After the son finds his mother and "brother" embracing together and dying, he rescues Ju Dou but carries Tianqing to the vat. An inverted image of the two in the red water verifies one more time Tianbai's identification with Tianqing as "brothers"—not as son and father. Tianbai throws his "brother" into the vat without hesitation and kills him with a thick stick. The screaming of Ju Dou and the collapse of the bolts of red fabric announce another oedipal tragedy.

The correspondence between the concept of an Oedipus complex and the textual practice in the film *Ju Dou* uncovers a general myth about father-son relations. In an effort to reach an explanation here on the basis of a universal Oedipus complex, a number of distinctions in the Chinese cultural context must be recognized. The first distinction concerns the prohibition of incest in light of cultural convention and the concept of filial piety. For instance, Tianbai's acceptance of Jinshan as his father comes from comprehending Jinshan's symbolic patriarchal authority. Thus, backed by tradition, Tianbai attempts to prevent his mother's incestuous sexuality. For the Chinese, according to Francis L. K. Hsu, "sex, like everything else, has its place, time, and partners with whom it can be resorted to. In the wrong place, at the wrong time and with wrong partners it is absolutely forbidden."[14] Jinshan's eager acceptance of Tianbai as his son after being called "daddy" is also motivated by ethical conventions, because, as Mencius said, lack of an heir is the worst among all the unfilial acts. Bound by the concept of filial piety and a desire to revenge the sexually transgressive couple, father and son are able to repress their natural relation in recognition of social dictates.

The second distinction involves the imagined castration of woman and the symbolic castration of men. In relation to his mother, Tianbai does not present himself as the object of his mother's desire who will complete everything lacking in her. Instead, he keeps her in an imagined castrated stage by disrupting her sexual affair with Tianqing. In other words, saving his mother's reputation is worth the frustration of her sexual desires. The virtues and positions so specific to certain relationships are fixed; Ju Dou cannot meddle with her role as mother. In addition to the castration of woman, the film representation ironically presents two symbolically castrated *male* figures: one sexually impotent, another socially impotent. In confronting the two, Tianbai kills the old in order to end gerontocracy and kills the young to punish transgression. In sum, the truth or knowledge of this Chinese oedipal triangle is not simply an individual desire to reunite with the mother and to kill the father as a rival. A power struggle, set against a social and cultural context, here can be read as a search for lost male subjectivity and masculinity.

· Nüwa and Fuxi

While a triangular relationship in a Chinese film text lends itself to an interpretation from the Western legend of Oedipus, it can also find its origin in the Chinese mythology of Nüwa and Fuxi, especially since the novel from which the film is adapted is titled *Fuxi, Fuxi*. According to the version of this myth related in the T'ang collection *Du yi zhi:*

> Long ago, when the universe had first come into being, there were no people in the world, only Nuwa and her brother on Mount Kun-lun. They considered becoming man and wife, but were stricken with shame. And so (Fuxi) and his sister went up on Kun-lun and (performed a sacrifice), vowing: 'If it is Heaven's wish that my sister and I become man and wife, let this smoke be intertwined. If not, let the smoke scatter,' whereupon the smoke was intertwined, and his sister did cleave unto him.[15]

After the marriage of Fuxi and Nüwa, the goddess created human beings by patting yellow earth together; thereafter, they became the universal parents of mankind. It is a mankind where order/disorder and harmony/opposition fall under the two total categories of yin and yang. As described by Andrew Plaks, the concepts of yin and yang stress (1) complementary bipolarity—realization of one element in terms of its opposite one; (2) ceaseless alternation—a cyclical movement within a closed system; (3) presence within absence—the presence of one quality within its opposite; and (4) infinite overlapping—the perception of reality through ceaseless alternation.[16] The

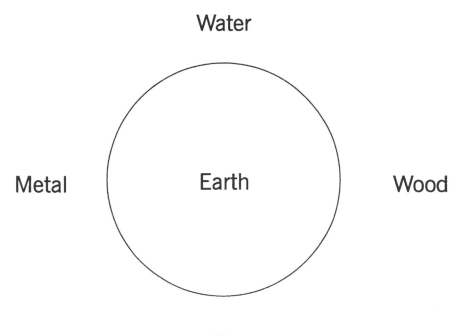

Fig. 30. The five elements in early Chinese cosmology.

archetypal form of yin and yang extends itself to the theory of five elements (*wuxing*: water, fire, metal, earth, wood). A diagram of the five elements is shown in fig. 30.

Within the circle of the five elements, each can move either clockwise or counterclockwise. The element earth, since it is centered in the middle, has the greatest possibilities to interact with its neighbors. In addition to the fact that each element can alternate both with its two neighbors and the center, there is also a vertical interaction among water, earth, and fire and a horizontal one among metal, earth, and wood.

Plaks insists that the myth of Nüwa and Fuxi can be "considered archetypal within the system of Chinese literature," that "archetypal structures are displacements of ritual relations rather than of mythical action," and that "it is the abstract formal pattern of dual interrelation that finds expression in the texts under investigation."[17] In short, the marriage of Nüwa and Fuxi functions as a metaphysical form and the terminology of yin-yang and the five elements serve as a language of literary expression.

Neither the film *Ju Dou* nor the novel from which it was adapted, *Fuxi, Fuxi,* intends to simply represent the legend of Nüwa and Fuxi. Both texts apply it as an archetypal form upon which meanings are constituted in terms of metaphysical and symbolic patterns. If we change the language system from a cinematic one into a cosmological version of yin-yang and the five elements, the triangular relationship in *Ju Dou* can be further understood according to alternations within the elements and associations with the universe. First, the narrative of the life cycle—life/death and love/betrayal—parallels the cycle of the seasons. To correspond with the story line, the four seasons are visualized through the color changes of Ju Dou's dresses and the dyed fabric. Spring, symbol of yang: the owner of the dye mill, Jinshan, purchases a young wife, Ju Dou, and abuses her for failing to produce a son. The color composition of Ju Dou's dress is white: an innocent female is being "dyed" with artificial colors. Summer, still the symbol of yang: the nephew of the mill owner, Tianqing, wins Ju Dou's love and starts an incestuous affair. The colors yellow and blue dominate the frame. Since the color yellow *(huang)* carries a meaning of pornographic sexuality and uncontrolled wild water *(yin shui)*, the film composition not only dresses Ju Dou in light yellow, but also arranges a piece of yellow fabric hanging in front of Tianqing's room, where the off-screen sound track indicates sexual lovemaking inside. Contrary to the color yellow, the color blue—which Ju Dou wears and which is being used to dye fabric—celebrates the hope of life between Tianqing and Ju Dou. Autumn and winter, symbols of yin: as the pleasure of the love affair becomes the pain of perversion and as personal desire brings the characters' death, the visual image of Ju Dou now is in black. As the color changes from pure white, sexual yellow, and hopeful blue to black, the story also completes its narrative course from the female character's suffering to the initiation of new life, the crisis of the sexual liaison, and finally death.

Second, the placement of the film characters in a framework of five-element sequences further elaborates the alternations of the triangular relations. Let's follow the simple diagram in fig. 30. The film representation places Ju Dou in the center—an earth element. Horizontally, she interrelates with the other elements of metal/*jin* (Jinshan) and wood/*mu* (Tianqing). Vertically, she is symbolized as water and has reached fire to end the cycle of life. If metal and wood form a world of yang, earth and water should be its opposite, yin. For instance, the world of the film is the world of men, signified by visual images of wooden elements. The beams of the dye mill set the film's stage. The wooden props of machines, wheels, pestle, and mortar occupy the frame. Even the surname of the Yang family has a wood component. Within the male-dominated world of yang, Ju Dou, earth, is a ground either violently ploughed by metal or endlessly depleted by wood. She has been represented as wild water (dye vat) within which sexual seduction takes place and where two men drown. The solution to end the interminable triangle of relations is the power of fire, by which Jinshan tries to kill Ju Dou and with which Ju Dou finally burns down the Yang dye mill.

From the perspective of archetypal form, it becomes clear that the narrative structure of *Ju Dou* is constructed around a series of binary oppositions. Each individual element exists and alternates with its opposite; this endless alternation of pairs motivates the film narration. Jinshan's affirmation of his *masculinity* through his abuse of Ju Dou is denied ironically by his sexual *impotence*. Tianqing's desire to live a *life* with Ju Dou as husband and wife is transformed into *death*. Tianbai's identification of Jinshan as his father displaces the real *father* to be his *brother*. Ju Dou's sexual *transgression* is seized by a web of *prohibition*. Everywhere is the implied structure of displacement: each character has a generic identity as aunt, nephew, and uncle, yet each of them pursues his or her own desire by standing in a position contrary to the socially assigned role. Displacement and inversion turn an ordered social system into chaos and an ethically valued human relation into a violation of the incest taboo.

A closed spatial system yet one with open temporal cycles further reinforces the alternation of opposite elements. In other words, the closed space oppresses characters' interrelations while the open time narrative extends the oppression endlessly. The spatial force of constriction and the continuity of time drive the narration. The narrative of *Ju Dou* takes place in a *closed* film space—the Yang dye mill. Within this space run the timeless complex relations between the characters, structured in accordance with seasonal, elemental, and generational patterns. In early spring, Jinshan purchases and abuses Ju Dou. In summer, Ju Dou seduces Tianqing and gives birth to a son. In autumn, Tianbai identifies Jinshan as his father and Tianqing as his brother. With winter come the deaths of Jinshan and Tianqing. The denouement is Ju Dou's figure and the dye mill structure aflame in the inferno. In short, only death and destruction, denying the possibility of fulfilling desire, finally halts the ceaseless alternation from one element to another.

The richness of the narrative and the multiple forms of the narration preclude exhaustive analysis. Yet what core statement does this film by Zhang Yimou make? It is true that the film we watch is a dramatic narrative about a sexual triangle. However, as the visual images of each character dissolve from our vision and the Yang dye mill burns in its final frame, we may be left with the echo of a male voice saying: "finally I have expressed what is in my conscious and unconscious mind." Consider the male characters and what they symbolize. Jinshan, the icon of patriarchal power and the figure of sexual impotence, suggests a changing world of male dominance: from an authoritarian power into a sexually castrated old man. As a result, he bequeaths the name of the father to the son who is not biologically his. Tianqing is a figure carrying a strong sexual desire which is restrained by social oppression: the sexual instinct is subordinated to social castration. As a result, he is able to produce a son yet cannot possess the name of the father. Tianbai, the patrilineal son, neither follows the old Jinshan nor accepts Tianqing but establishes a new power. The solution is to kill all of his rivals. If Jinshan represents China's past, Tianqing the present, and Tianbai the future, the film and the fiction sound a nostalgic elegy: men and power, once you had a glorious past and might have a hopeful future. But when, where, and by what have you been castrated into an impotent being? In order to utter the unspeakable, the representation of woman is created. From father figure to son and from the past to the future, all men's burdens, desires, and losses are laid on a single woman's shoulders. This is the deep structure and inner voice of the film.

· Notes

I. Jenny Kwok Wah Lau, "*Judou*—A Hermeneutical Reading of Cross-cultural Cinema," *Film Quarterly* 45, no. 2 (1991): 2–10.

2. W. A. Callahan, "Gender, Ideology, Nation: *Ju Dou* in the Cultural Politics of China," *East-West Film Journal* 7, no. 1 (1993): 52–80.

3. Rey Chow, *Primitive Passions: Visuality, Sexuality, and Ethnography in Contemporary Chinese Cinema* (New York: Columbia University Press, 1995), 170–171.

4. Daniel Percheron, "Sound in Cinema and Its Relationship to Image and Diegesis," *Yale French Studies* 60 (1980): 16–23.

5. Judith Stacey, *Patriarchy and Socialist Revolution in China* (Berkeley: University of California Press, 1983), 39.

6. Laura Mulvey, *Visual and Other Pleasures* (Bloomington: Indiana University Press, 1989).

7. Mulvey, *Visual and Other Pleasures,* 18.

8. Callahan, "Gender, Ideology, Nation," 57.

9. Leo Braudy, *The World in a Frame: What We See in Films* (New York: Anchor Press, 1976), 46.

10. Jonathan Dollimore, "Subjectivity, Sexuality, and Transgression: The Jacobean Connection," *Renaissance Drama* 17 (1986): 57.

II. Terry Eagleton, *Literary Theory: An Introduction* (Minneapolis: University of Minnesota Press, 1983), 156.

12. Louis Giannetti, *Understanding Movies* (Englewood Cliffs, N.J.: Prentice-Hall, 1990), 132.

13. Jane Gallop, *Reading Lacan* (Ithaca, N.Y.: Cornell University Press, 1985), 107.

14. Francis L. K. Hsu, "Eros, Affect and *Pao*," in *Rugged Individualism Reconsidered: Essays in Psychological Anthropology* (Knoxville: University of Tennessee Press, 1983), 272.

15. Andrew H. Plaks, *Archetype and Allegory in "The Dream of the Red Chamber"* (Princeton: Princeton University Press, 1976), 35–36.

16. Plaks, *Archetype and Allegory*, 44–47.

17. Plaks, *Archetype and Allegory*, 23, 43.

Chapter 13

The Concubine and the Figure of History
Chen Kaige's *Farewell My Concubine*
•
Wendy Larson

Yuejin Wang has pointed out an ironic cross-cultural situation: it is precisely the films of the Fifth-Generation directors, films that posit a "cultural identity that the current Chinese public are reluctant to identify, and which they keep at arm's length" that have received acclaim abroad as a "cinematic representation of Chinese culture."[1] Wang elaborates the cinematic codes that bear cultural specificity to China—understatement in emotional rhetoric, exploration of emotional subtlety, indulgence in faint sadness, a "distracted" narrative structure, and the evocation of familiar lyrical motives from traditional poetics, as well as other common characteristics such as lyricizing about departure, absence, and memory.[2] It is these codes that are broken in some Fifth-Generation films such as *Red Sorghum,* which through "the bold indulgence in violence with sound and fury" and "the shift from the quiet back alleys of townscape to the dusty and naked land" constructs a radically new cinematic code and national identity.[3] Eventually himself sliding into the position of the Fifth-Generation directors, Wang claims that while earlier films "lick the wounds" of the Cultural Revolution, *Red Sorghum* violently shatters any illusion of an innocent utopia and shows how the "indulgence in emotional delicacy for its own sake" and the traditional virtues of restraint and concealment are in fact historical restraints that limit action and fulfillment.[4]

Wang is careful to point out that the so-called Chinese cinematic codes are neither absolute nor unchanging but are really a combination of traditional Chinese theatrical consciousness, the "grammatical mold" of classical Hollywood, Chinese didacticism, and Soviet dogmatism.[5] Nonetheless, he sides with the Fifth-Generation directors in their implicit critique of the "physiology and the pathology" of the Chinese social psyche and situates this bent against the fact that now cultural identity is only meaningful when it is "posited against the Western Other"[6]—to do something else is an "indulgence" that results in complacence. As Wang implies, entry into the

Western film community occurs only through identity and specificity; Western viewers want *from* China a film *about* China.

It is along these culturally specific lines that Chen Kaige's *Farewell My Concubine* has entered the international film arena, sharing with Jane Campion's *The Piano* the Cannes Palme d'Or award in May 1993 and, like a limited number of Fifth-Generation films before it, playing widely in art theaters. In the United States, *Farewell* is mostly read as a film about Chinese civilization; commentators often interpret it as a historical epic. The twentieth-century setting, which progresses historically through the decades and recognizes the two major political and cultural events of the Japanese invasion and the Cultural Revolution, leads many reviewers to comment that this is indeed Chinese history and thus, China.

Kevin Thomas, writing in the *Los Angeles Times,* sums up this approach to *Farewell* and thus links it to Chen Kaige's *King of the Children* and *Yellow Earth:* "the films possess an epic scope much like 'Farewell My Concubine,' which spans half a century and covers a sizable portion of China itself. That's because they are subtle, understated journeys into the heart, soul and mind of their people."[7] Calling the Fifth-Generation directors the "greatest and bravest in [Chinese] history," Nigel Anderson quotes Chen Kaige's comment on the filming of *Yellow Earth* in a remote area where cameras had virtually never been before: " 'People were very quiet, very guarded, very austere. Yet reading their faces was like reading Chinese history.' "[8]

In interviews with Western writers, Chen Kaige does nothing to debunk the film's reception as a Chinese epic; over and over he links *Farewell* with his personal experience in the Cultural Revolution and a broader history outside the Cultural Revolution that he knows intimately. The entire film, he claims, is a result of his present anger at being "duped" and, like the rest of the Chinese population, falling victim to revolutionary ideology.[9] Chen places himself in the position of the characters for whom "the opera means everything" yet who have "paid a huge price to be part of the spectacle."[10] The term "spectacle" is used not only by the film's director but also by others commenting on the film's success or failure; in awarding *Farewell* the International Critics' Prize as well as the Palme d'Or, judges seemed to paraphrase Chen's words, praising the film for "its incisive analysis of the political and cultural history of China and for its brilliant combination of the spectacular and the intimate."[11]

What is the "spectacle" to which Chen, as director and critic, and other commentators refer?[12] Is it Chinese history itself, or the exhibit of history within the film, which provides a night out more pleasurable than reading an academic book and is easily accessible to those who know little? From the perspective of Yuejin Wang's incisive analysis of the Chinese cinema's entry and translation into Western film's interpretive field, *Farewell* has convinced Western viewers that it is an authentic portrayal of Chinese history.[13] Yet at the same time, the film continually turns the viewer's attention away from deep historical analysis toward an ahistorical consciousness and a gendered subjectivity-under-power.[14] In its persistent use of historical referents to panoramically parade the past before us, the film presents itself as "about" Chinese history; still, it offers no persuasive historical explanations to show why things are the way they are. The ending of the film belies such a notion and has raised the ire of officials in China, who demand that Chen explain why the main character has to kill himself in 1977, just as Deng Xiaoping comes to power and "history" is changing.

This essay investigates the way in which *Farewell* appropriates the past to reject history in favor of fantasy as the means through which Chinese national subjects who want to enter transnational culture must produce personal and cultural narratives. Contradictorily both in and out of history, Peking opera players are from the past yet are not its real actors. A character such as Cheng Dieyi exists as if drugged—and actually does fall into a drugged stupor in the story—and in a time warp, ostensibly outside the demands of contemporary global and domestic politics, purely within the realm of personal and symbolic desire.

In somewhat misleading ways, the film's category of fantasy corresponds to that used in Western psychoanalysis. Jacques Lacan constructed a formula for fantasy which "encourages us to understand that psychic formation as a mechanism for plugging the hole of symbolic castration or lack by positing a particular object as the cause of desire."[15] After his symbolic castration, Cheng Deiyi fixates on Duan Xiaolou and strives to keep intact the "particular syntax or tableau" that allows him to assume the desiring position.[16] However, the necessary tableau is the opera, a craft that, because it is uniquely Chinese, shifts the film's critique away from focus on the individual or even the acculturated subject in Chinese society and—unlike the work of Jacques Lacan, where the psychologized subject is universal—toward the specificity of (Chinese) cultural form itself.[17] The category of fantasy is an answer to this question: In an age of transnational capitalism, under what circumstances can local or national culture be staged?

In order to keep his fantasy of pure cultural form—here symbolized by the opera—alive, Cheng Dieyi lives the concubine's subservient position. This archetypical feminine position is the essence of Chen Kaige's new and compromised transcultural consciousness and is created and developed through a series of films he directs. What has been given up is precisely the historicized understanding of the communist past, which orders events into a progressive narrative and represents the story's authority through a male figure—in this case the king of Chu, Duan Xiaolou.

Western viewers see Chen's films as Chinese and, because of the historical references and their mimetic power, authentically so. At the same time, through an intense emphasis on the male characters' subjective sense of lack and disorientation, the films deviate from emphasis on Chinese social and historical issues. The films embed the narrative into a framework the Western viewer would identify as specifically Chinese at the same time as they replace a historicist presentation with a crisis of consciousness. *Farewell* is the first of Chen's films to organize the central male character's fractured being into two characters and to try to redeem the broken side of consciousness through the artistic, active, sensitive Cheng Dieyi.

In *Farewell*, the reticence and withholding characteristic of traditional cinematic codes are enveloped into the aesthetic of the opera and the appeal of the main character, with the Fifth-Generation trademark "sound and fury" all relegated to the falsely accentuated shell of history, where it functions as a domestic critique and as a hook for the Western film community. At the same time, the failure of history to act as an organizing and unifying principle brings forth a ruptured male consciousness that then molds itself into a new, if ultimately untenable, possibility. The symbolic castration and gendering of Cheng Dieyi as female and the overwhelming and ahistorical nature of his conflation of art with life, along with the resulting vulnerability of this feminine position, utilizes the opera's specularity to speak to the precarious entry of "Chinese"—national—film into the international world of prizes and transcultural interpretation. Cheng's arduous training, a lived experience that allows him access to supreme artistry and the ability to reproduce and represent the heart of Chinese culture, becomes a rarefied consciousness that turns into entertainment and exotic color when presented in film abroad and when presented within China is easily used and manipulated by political agendas. Eventually, this art even fails to maintain a viable connection to Chinese social life itself. Such, the film implies, is the fate of "local" cultures in the transnational field of film and perhaps in other cultural arenas as well.

• Femininity: A New Male Possibility

A great deal has been written about masculinity, femininity, and the post–Cultural Revolution national crisis of Chinese identity. In his *Zhongguo wenhua de shenceng jiegou* (The deep structure of Chinese culture), Sun Longji constructs the theory that Chinese men have all been turned into eunuchs, and

Kam Louie points out that in fiction and film, a number of writers and directors from the 1980s have focused on redeeming male sexuality, a strategy Louie believes is simply a concern with power and control.[18]

Chen's films generally feature a male character attempting to effect a cultural act that engages a central narrative of modern China. Such actions fall within Chen's category of *history*. In *Yellow Earth*, Gu Qing collects folk tunes from the people to be rewritten as anti-Japanese Communist Party songs, thus embodying the archetypical act of the party going to the people. Lao Gan takes over the role of teacher in *King of the Children*. In *The Big Parade*, a series of male characters in the lead roles attempt to ritualistically display the power and representational unity of the People's Liberation Army (PLA). And in *Farewell My Concubine*, the staging of Peking opera by Cheng Dieyi and, to a lesser extent, Duan Xiaolou is the quintessence of Chinese cultural form.

In all four films the male characters have an originally simple connection to a seemingly simple goal. Their initially unproblematic desire to act—a direct appropriation of the logical narrative of history into consciousness—becomes, as the films progress, complicated. In each case, the masculine, action-oriented character is *feminized*: compromised with complex knowledge, a split subjectivity, and the inability to realize his goals through planned action. Although characters are not deepened in terms of inner psychology—that is, they do not have progressively more profound understandings of their motivations or actions, and we "discover" nothing about them or their pasts—their subjective existence is made complex. This feminization process occurs only with biological males. Biological females are excluded from this process because within cultural creation, they do not occupy positions of power. Chen's films all possess profound and overarching narratives of potential unity, and each proclaims itself serious as art and as critique. And from *Yellow Earth* through *The Big Parade*, *King of the Children*, and *Farewell My Concubine*, the male character or characters are increasingly problematized and feminized.

In *Yellow Earth*, Gu Qing has the simple goal of collecting folksongs for assimilation into the anti-Japanese efforts of the Chinese Communist Party (CCP): the rewriting of the folk. The *suanqu*, or sour tunes, will be engaged on behalf of the revolutionary redefinition of the people. As Esther C. M. Yau points out, the party ban on erotic involvement—one of the rules of the party-to-people narrative—between soldiers or cadres and the people underlies Gu Qing's refusal to help Cuiqiao escape from her impending marriage.[19] The line of potential action through which the male is galvanized into national and cultural production through an erotically catalytic relation with a woman, so successfully exploited by Zhang Yimou, ends with barely a glimmer in Gu Qing's eyes.[20] The main connection in *Yellow Earth*, as in all Chen's films, is between male characters; the older male undergoes the feminizing, complicating process of consciousness and loses his ability to empower the younger. Hanhan—and the viewer—struggles in vain as Chen Kaige makes Gu Qing try three times to come over the hill in his return to the village; Cuiqiao presumably is dead. Gu Qing's mind has been made complex by his new awareness that he lacks control over even his own simple narrative (CCP to the people), and that the narrative itself may indeed be a myth; he can accomplish the single cultural act of collecting and recreating the sour tunes, but he cannot make the liberation narrative work as it should. In order to do that, he would have to construct a fantasy within which his efforts could succeed and use it to displace the history of Communist narratives.

In *The Big Parade,* many of the male characters preparing for the parade, especially the citified boys, express doubt about the meaning of their rigorous training. One criticizes from a modern viewpoint, focusing on the anachronistic nature of military ritual in contemporary life; one frames the military not as glorious battle but as sheer careerism; one flees and in this act wordlessly foregrounds the dehumanizing nature of military training. Yet all continue to prepare and ultimately perform. Through one critical stance or another, the potential soldiers profess to see through military ritual and its rationale, yet its historically sanctioned form alone propels them forward. Chen Kaige's original ending, where the sounds of the parade accompany scenes of a blank Tiananmen Square, was changed into a vision of plentitude because of PLA objections.

With the male of action and authority subsumed into the entire military structure, the female—barring the added female soldiers viewed in the altered ending—becomes a hazy moment of disembodied fantasy, an unidentifiable experience outside articulation. Women stand at the edge of the historical PLA narrative and seem to offer relief from the duplicity it demands from all participants. When the young soldier develops a fever and runs away, he seamlessly joins in with a group of peasant women working in the fields, and although their lips move, their voices are replaced with an insistent extradiegetic noise. The viewer immediately perceives that the trainee is escaping from a seemingly cruel and needlessly rigorous ritual to something more basic and good, something connected with the land. The peasant women are so divorced from military sensibility and so unaware of anything outside their own charmed, natural existence and work that they are not even surprised that a stranger has joined them. *King of the Children* takes a rather ordinary, slightly cocky novelistic character and gives him a vagueness and dislocating sensibility that borders on the insane. Time and again Lao Gan, obfuscated by his growing awareness of the impossibility of true teaching or learning, laughs at inappropriate times, loses his way in speech, or stares out into space. As in *Yellow Earth* and *The Big Parade*, the male character is shot through with a disorienting knowledge that seems to come from the land and air itself; we see many shots of barren mountains and the river in *Yellow Earth*, of the parade training ground in *The Big Parade*, and of the countryside in *King of the Children*.[21] Lao Gan's mission is one of the most overdetermined within Chinese culture: the education of children and the transmission of texts. This process becomes so fractured that the actual building block of written language, the Chinese character, breaks apart under the stress of new meaning and reforms itself in a directly mimetic representation. Lao Gan's new written form is "cow water," a nonexistent character that represents urine.

In *King of the Children* as in *The Big Parade*, the ideological critique is only too apparent. The extreme feminization of Lao Gan and the placing of a very muted (yet vociferous) erotic desire totally onto the plump Laidi and distant from the male character, however, draws our attention away from overt criticism of Chinese education and texts. The humanistic interpretation of one American critic, who claims that Lao Gan "has transformed the lives of his students," is difficult to document; in fact, Lao Gan fails to have much influence on the children, who continue their parroting (of the chant) and copying (of the dictionary).[22] Only the mute refusal of social organization and its power, as shown through the cowherd and his sullying gesture of peeing without comment, can prevent the ritualizing discourse of education from overwhelming its students and teachers.

Lao Gan's historical "meaning," both as an intellectual sent to the countryside and then as a teacher who disseminates texts, is intense and overdetermined. Because he transmits texts and creates song lyrics (against Laidi's music tunes), Lao Gan's connection to cultural form is primarily linguistic. In *Yellow Earth*, Gu Qing's political and cultural mission also is linguistic, and like Lao Gan he is stymied by a first hidden and unrecognized and then revealed meaning of the significance that comes from melody (sour tunes) and the land. While Cuiqiao's tunes have words that tell of her unhappiness, Laidi is incapable of writing the words and assigns that job to Lao Gan. In *The Big Parade*, the women are pure presence, without access to any words or sound.

Chen's films construct symbolic femininity as a means through which male subjectivity can be deepened and made aware of its own lack of belief in or control over the history that has been produced through central narratives. As Rey Chow shows, the film *King of the Children* excludes biological woman, who herself cannot be in the problematized subject position.[23]

Nonetheless, the unification of being and representation is faintly original with biological woman. Cui Qiao sings out her misery, and has the agency to act against it. Laidi can write melodies and sing songs as long as Lao Gan can provide the words. The wordless women in *The Big Parade* work in the harvest with no apparent recourse to a story about their actions. In all cases women, because they do not enact the modern unifying narratives, are not responsible for them; although they embody the more primitive and pure knowledge of lived experience, they cannot possess the deeply fractured consciousness of the central male characters. Chen's construct defines biological woman as this ahistorical, nonritualizing, existence-based understanding. As is best shown in *Farewell My Concubine,* however, when male characters are feminized, they do not imitate this woman's natural-ness, but rather become the shattered victims of what was once a unified consciousness.

• The Concubine and Cultural Position

Corresponding almost exactly to Kaja Silverman's analysis of marginalized but superaware male consciousness (such as that of gay men), Cheng Dieyi accedes to an extreme state of lack only when he can admit that he is by nature a girl, not a boy. Such a superb and delicately aware state of being is not open to the king, who plays the traditionally powerful but historically fallen male of authority, the king who should hold the mandate of the polit-ical and cultural body. After Dieyi becomes like a woman, he does not need a problematized consciousness like that of Gu Qing in *Yellow Earth* or Lao Gan in *King of the Children.* Rather, Dieyi has actually *become* the feminine itself. Looking back from *Farewell,* it becomes clear that the central male characters in Chen's earlier films are not just weakened in terms of action or complicated in terms of consciousness but are feminized in relation to the discourse of historical cultural form. Dieyi is still very young—a boy, not a man—when his digital excess is chopped off, he enters the masked art-world of opera, and he is forced to admit that he is a girl; thus he can embody the feminine position in totality. Dieyi has the best possible circumstances under which to admit his lack: he is poor, parentless, small, young, and weak, plus he is under initiation into a feminine role in the most stylized, ritualistic, and costumed art of the culture. Even so, the admission proves difficult, and Dieyi must undergo symbolic rape with a pipe before he can proclaim his femininity and begin his cultural servitude as a sexual object and cultural concubine.[24] At the end of the story Deiyi once again says the wrong words, collapsing the fantasy he has maintained for so long.[25]

Cheng Dieyi becomes a symbolic woman but, like the women in Zhang

Yimou's "red" films, pays with his life.[26] In *Farewell My Concubine,* biological woman possesses an even fainter sense of originary being and is utterly unproductive, both biologically and culturally. Juxian takes on a role—much feared by Cheng Dieyi—that is more similar to that of the domesticating woman so common in American western film and fiction, a woman who lures the man away from a creative power associated with the wild west. Juxian wants to get Duan Xiaolou away from Cheng Dieyi's contaminating influence and his tendency to drag Xiaolou into the overwhelming and obsessive practice of the opera. Although Juxian does not have the appealing naturalness of Cuiqiao, Laidi, or the women in *The Big Parade,* she is not a negative character. Many times she steps in to redeem both Xiaolou and Dieyi, to mediate between the two, and ultimately to cradle Dieyi as if he were her lost child and rescue him from a self-destructive opium addiction. Juxian's face shows pain and empathy as Xiaolou betrays Dieyi during a Cultural Revolution struggle session; she dies under Xiaolou's betrayal when Dieyi does not.

Juxian's suicide is different from that of Dieyi. She kills herself because, under terrible but historically limited pressure, Xiaolou says that he does not love her. Although Juxian is a deep and feeling character, a woman dying for the love of a man is only a common human situation. Juxian and Xiaolou have an offstage relationship that is warm and true; as they burn their clothes and destroy the wine cups they have drunk from together in preparation for a Red Guard investigation—and thus show themselves willing to cast off an illusion sustained by the past—we clearly see their strong mutual affection and physical love, developed through time and shared experience. Dieyi also views the scene from outside the door, and it throws him into despair. Dieyi and Xiaolou have a different loyalty and affection based on the bitterly shared experience of operatic discipline. Dieyi kills himself not for the excellent but common human kind of love, which is what Xiaolou and Juxian share, but because he cannot continue to be a concubine. This role is taken over by his own revolutionary son and cannot be restored after Xiaolou's betrayal, a nearly voiced proclamation that Dieyi played the concubine/lover to the corrupt official Yuan Shiqing (also called Yuan Siye).

Cheng Dieyi does become Yuan's private prostitute, but only when he can paint Yuan so that he looks like the king of Chu. In the "real-life" court of law, Dieyi refuses Yuan's life-saving patronage, which Xiaolou elicited to rescue Dieyi from the consequence of being branded a traitor for performing for Japanese officials. Japanese officials, the clearly marked imperialist presence in China, readily exchange the king of Chu for a single performance by the concubine.

The scene with the Japanese military officials brings out the implications of specificity in cultural form within a global arena. The authority of the king of Chu can be maintained only when the concubine prostitutes her art—the essentially Chinese art—before the art-loving audience, whose imperializing position corresponds to that of the international (Western) film spectator and critic. While in the West, we mark Chinese film as Chinese culturally and historically and enjoy it as such, the playing out of what was once a unified historical imperative that existed of itself through the staged, revealing, and betraying spectacle of film results in the demeaning of the concubine's art and life. The fantasy of specificity in culture cracks—the play is not the king and the concubine's to be performed for and by them but can be coerced and manipulated—until the Japanese are gone. What remains is Xiaolou's suspicion that Dieyi played the concubine not only to foreigners but also to the corrupt Chinese state represented by Yuan Shiqing.

In order to preserve Xiaolou's independence and life, Dieyi must specularize his art/self before foreigners and before the Chinese state. Thus Dieyi's attempts to maintain the powerful specificity of culture is shown to be an unsustainable fantasy. Whereas Xiaolou eventually may be able to excuse the performance for the Japanese as virtually unavoidable, Dieyi's continuing relationship with Yuan Shiqing exposes the fantasy to its spectacularly rotten core.

As Wai-yee Li describes in a study of *qing* (sentiment, love) in Chinese literary genres of *fu* (narrative poetry), *chuanqi* (tales), and *xiaoshuo* (fiction), the concubine traditionally is associated with both a moral purpose and the " 'way of concubines' (*qiefu zhi dao*), the use of devious ploys of self-abnegation to please, flatter, and seek favor."[27] Excessively adorned women are linked to culture through direct metaphors that align them with writing. Li refers to the critic Yang Xiong's (53 B.C.–A.D. 18) "oft-quoted" criticism of *fu*: " 'Or put it this way: a woman has beauty; does writing have beauty also? The answer is yes. The worst thing for a woman is to have her inner beauty clouded by cosmetics; the worst thing for a piece of writing is to have its rules and proportions confounded by excessive rhetoric.' "[28] The concubine carries not only this cultural meaning but also a political significance that arises through the role of the court poet, who represents the subservient in his relationship to the emperor and generally is assigned a feminine role in literature. Indeed, "[t]o represent the ruler-subject relationship in gendered terms (e.g., the emperor as the absent lover, the poet-minister as the abandoned woman) came to be a standard practice in Chinese literature" and is a convention that began with *Encountering Sorrow* (*Li sao;* by Qu Yuan, ca. 340–278 B.C.).[29] The theme of *Encountering Sorrow* is the quest for the divine being, a search that has secular, political, and allegorical meanings; the "deity acquires an aura of high seriousness as the 'symbolic other' in the dramatic quest for the fulfillment of political ideals." Although the deity is false, the poet possesses a "fervent and uncompromising political idealism."[30]

Li's research can help us decode the meaning of Chen's screen concubine, who is both the deceptive betrayer and the mark of idealism. *Farewell My Concubine* contains inside it the operatic performance, which itself is a quasi-historical reference to one of the earliest forms of Chinese culture in the state of Chu. Chu culture, which was magical and shamanistic, was followed by Han Confucianism and its correlative cosmology, "the most relentless order-building in Chinese cultural history." The spirit journey represented in Chu literature is a direct communication of the poet with divine powers; as Li notes, such "intense ecstatic experience cannot be easily accommodated within structures of order, where the relationship with the divine-numinous realm is regulated through officially sanctioned ritual."[31]

The film draws a clear parallel between the sociopolitical world of modern China and the opera's cultural-historical representation, and the concubine carries both the unification of bodily cultural ecstasy with political purity and loyalty and the morally suspicious posturing of the adorned female. Although in these four films directed by Chen Kaige, men construct and reconstruct historical culture, their two contemporary sides are eventually split into the two characters Duan Xiaolou and Cheng Dieyi. Duan is the historically authoritative male who has been disempowered first by foreign imperialism and its challenge to traditional values, second by Chinese revolutionary culture itself, and third by the impossibility of keeping alive a vital, nonspecular national culture in an age of transnational economic capitalism. At the film's end, in the contemporary post-Mao period, the benighted king does not really know that he just cannot reassume his throne. In fact, while not a bad sort, from the beginning Duan carries no moral presence, implying that the entire enterprise of twentieth-century cultural China has been built on illusion. In the three earlier films, Duan's character is subsumed within the historical narrative itself and its corporealization in the male character *before* he senses that the mission he is attempting to carry out is impossible or false. Cheng is the alternative consciousness based on lack that arises from the realization that history is duplicitous. Again, in the three earlier films, this alternative consciousness is also contained within the central male character *after* his ability to act on the narrative is impaired. In these films, however, this alternative consciousness does not cast itself into a discrete role with a positive goal. It remains a negative and enfeebling knowledge within the same character who once was engaged fully within the historical project.

In *Yellow Earth, King of the Children,* and *The Big Parade,* the cultural and historical missions of the male characters eventually are infected with the fantastic, concubinal lack, but in *Farewell My Concubine,* the parts are separated, with the positive values of mystery, fascination, and artistic discipline assigned to Cheng Dieyi. Only *Farewell* theorizes the meaning of the new consciousness were it to be actually performed. As long as it is staged within the trope of opera, the fantasy of a live cultural form can live on. The object of Cheng Dieyi's loyalty is not the Chinese state; in separating the state from the core of historical cultural power indicated by Duan Xiaolou as the king of Chu, a trade-off is established as one possible action. The historical Chinese political body can be split: on one side is the corrupt and unworthy state, represented by Yuan Shiqing, and on the other is the naive, weak, but still honest cultural nation, symbolized by Duan Xiaolou. This break is relatively trivial and as a political cliché around the world is easily represented: the government is bad, but the nation/people is good. We viewers, however, see from the beginning that Duan Xiaolou is not worthy of Cheng Dieyi's efforts, because Duan is too weak to protect Cheng from the ravages of political and cultural change, too clumsy and unintelligent to really comprehend the meaning of the trade-off, and too lazy to make the sacrifices necessary to sustain the fantasy. What seals the fantasy's doom, however, is that, once inserted into the situation of global film spectatorship, the concubine—whose mediation as purified cultural process is absolutely necessary if the king is to retain his throne—becomes not a unified expression and practice of the cultural nation, but only a disembodied and debased indicator of cultural and historical difference, a kind of local color parading itself before delighted viewers.

In her foreword to *Male Subjectivity at the Margins,* Kaja Silverman must defend herself for writing a book about men in order to investigate femininity. Her argument states that while women's inroads into cultural construction are significant, with most recognized culture still created by men, one of the most interesting places to look for a radically new, positive, and demasculinized consciousness is in the work (film, fiction, etc.) of men who are socially marginalized by unorthodox sexuality or historical, racial, or other social trauma. Thus Silverman analyzes classical Hollywood film to see how it first displays post–World War II male lack and then recoups it through representing feminine efforts to brace the fallen man. She then compares this approach with the work of the nonmainstream filmmaker Rainer Werner Fassbinder, who begins from a marginalized subjectivity and uses film "as an instrument for the 'ruination' of masculinity" by "returning to the male body all of the violence which it has historically directed elsewhere."[32]

In somewhat the same way, *Farewell* stages a symbolically feminized consciousness that is an attribute of a man who already "knows" of lack and is completely possessed by his marginalization. Contrasting with him is the still-deluded historical man. The strong, complex female character of Juxian tries, as do Silverman's female characters, to prop up the lacking man; she also represents a positive, a less illusionary way of life, a road possible only if Dieyi's fantasy and illusion of pure cultural form can be discarded and replaced by the intimacy Juxian shares with Xiaolou. This female road is, of course, deficient in imagination and creative reproductive power, and herein lies Chen's own misogynist vision.

In focusing on the performance and specularity of national art forms, *Farewell* goes a different direction than the films that Silverman analyzes; it presents complex issues of cultural representation that are precisely those problems foregrounded at the juncture where Chinese film enters the international market. *Farewell* succeeds not only by furthering the domestic critique of history and culture for which Fifth-Generation filmmakers and roots writers such as Ah Cheng (on whose novella *King of the Children* is based) are famous, but also for implicating the global film economy in the now impossible staging of local culture. When Chinese film is positioned within the transnational and transcultural market, any innocent notion of cultural representation immediately becomes simplistic and reductionist and reinforces the consumerist commodification of culture.

· Notes

For their enlightening discussion and comments, I would like to thank Bryna Goodman, Patricia Sieber, and Yue Gang, as well as many commentators from the audience who made valuable suggestions when I presented various versions of this paper at the University of North Carolina at Chapel Hill, University of California at Berkeley, and University of Pittsburgh.

1. Yuejin Wang, "The Cinematic Other and the Cultural Self? De-centering the Cultural Identity on Cinema," *Wide Angle* II, no. 2 (1989): 36.

2. Wang, "The Cinematic Other," 37–39.

3. Wang, "The Cinematic Other," 38.

4. Wang, "The Cinematic Other," 39.

5. Wang, "The Cinematic Other," 36.

6. Wang, "The Cinematic Other," 39.

7. *Los Angeles Times,* January 17, 1994, F10.

8. Nigel Anderson, "Film-Makers Baptized in Fire—An Interview with Chen Kaige," *Financial Times,* January 8, 1994. For other references to *Farewell* as history, see Brian D. Johnson, "The Red and the Restless," *MacLeans,* November 15, 1993,

9; David Ansen with Beirdre Nickerson and Marcus Mabry, "The Real Cultural Revolution," *Newsweek,* November 1, 1993, 74; Vicent Canby, "Top Prize at Cannes is Shared," *New York Times,* May 25, 1994, C13. Secondary themes reviewers notice are the assertion of individual rights and the triumph of art, artistic freedom, and love.

9. See the previously cited reviews plus Neil Norman, "No Hiding from the Past—Chen's Look Back in Anger and Sorrow," *Evening Standard,* January 7, 1994.

10. Adam Mars-Jones, "A Visually Stunning Portrayal of the Peking Opera: *Farewell My Concubine,*" *The Independent,* January 7, 1994. Mars-Jones is the sole reviewer I could find who specifically denied that the film was a historical epic, instead calling it "visually-magnificent, downbeat soap opera for international consumption."

11. See Canby, "Top Prize."

12. I refer to Chen Kaige as "director and critic" not only because the collaborative nature of filmmaking, with its large number of actors, technicians, and various experts, does not allow a "pure" authorship but also because in contemporary times, filmmaking demands an understanding of technology, sponsorship, and the market. As a director, Chen exercises some control over the film's production, and through mass media presentation, his interpretive comments can create or reinforce meanings he believes are in the film or those that should be directed toward a particular audience. Thus when being interviewed for an international publication, Chen may focus on the spectacle of the film; when speaking with Chinese Communist Party cadres he may take a different line. Because Chen's comments are widely quoted as authoritative statements and presented to international audiences as "expert" testimony, his words become quite significant in determining the film's "meaning." I thank Patricia Sieber for her enlightening comments on this issue.

13. Commenting on both the historical and gender-bending nature of the film, Caryn James writes that "The most stunning aspect of the film is the deft way that Dieyi's confusion—of sexual identity, art and life—becomes a metaphor for the identity crisis of China itself, as the film goes from the days of the warlords to the end of Mao's Cultural Revolution." Caryn James, "You Are What You Wear," *New York Times,* October 10, 1993, H13.

14. Mars-Jones, "A Visually Stunning Portrayal," notes that again and again "historical cataclysm coincides with personal crisis."

15. See Kaja Silverman, *Male Subjectivity at the Margins* (New York: Routledge, 1992), 4.

16. Silverman, *Male Subjectivity,* 6.

17. An example of focus on an acculturated subject would be Lu Xun's *Ah Q zhengzhuan* (The true story of Ah Q), in which Ah Q and others carry the cumulative cultural effects of thousands of years of—in Lu Xun's view—devastating cultural ideas.

18. Kam Louie, "The Macho Eunuch: The Politics of Masculinity in Jia Pingwa's 'Human Extremities,'" *Modern China* 17, no. 2 (1991): 165. Louie quotes Sun Longji's popular text on culture published by Jixianshe, Hong Kong, in 1983.

19. Esther C. M. Yau, "*Yellow Earth:* Western Analysis and a Non-Western Text," in *Perspectives on Chinese Cinema,* ed. Chris Berry (London: British Film Institute, 1991), 66.

20. See my article, "Zhang Yimou: Inter/National Aesthetics and Erotics," in *Cultural Encounters: China, Japan, and the West,* ed. Soren Clausen, Roy Starrs, and Anne Wedell-Wedellsborg (Aarhus, Denmark: Aarhus UniversityPress, 1995), 215–226, for an investigation into Zhang's use of women as erotic fulcrums to propel men into nationally significant action.

21. Zhang Jia-xuan describes the filmic technique thus: "First of all, the opening shot of the film is a low-angle extreme long shot of a huge parade ground with soldiers training. As the shot fades in, the camera begins to move slowly forward to reveal more and more of the same ground, thus underscoring its spaciousness, while the angle and distance of the shot make the figures of the soldiers appear so tiny that they form a striking contrast with the huge parade ground. Moreover, as the camera continues to move forward, it also slides up and down, seemingly creating a sense of pressure." See "The Big Parade," *Film Quarterly* 43, no.1 (1989): 57.

22. See *Los Angeles Times,* January 17, 1994, F10.

23. Rey Chow identifies biological woman as an excluded nature and reproductivity that is part of Chen Kaige's—and others'—fantasy of male symbolic cultural production. Chow also wonderfully elucidates the symbolic meaning of urine and cows through references and images that have been used by twentieth century writers and politicians. See Rey Chow, "Male Narcissism and National Culture: Subjectivity in Chen Kaige's *King of the Children,*" *Camera Obscura* 25-26 (1991): 9-41.

24. See Mars-Jones, "A Visually Stunning Portrayal."

25. There are several reasons why I believe Cheng Dieyi's difficult proclamation that he is a girl, and his subsequent behavior, should be regarded as feminization rather than homosexualization. First, following the trajectory of Chen's filmic presentation of the male character, we see that weakness and fragmentation become a symbolically feminine position through a series of characters acting in different story lines, and in some cases differing radically from the novels out of which the characters are adapted. Second, *Farewell* emphasizes the position Cheng Dieyi holds relative to the other characters and to the discourse of national cultural form, rather than any essentialized desire. Third, Cheng Dieyi's position, and that of the other fractured males in Chen's films, is one of weakness and inability to act, or symbolically that of the feminine within the social arena. However, for a well-argued discussion that focuses on homosexuality in the film, see Sang Zelan (Sang Tze-lan), "Cheng Dieyi—yige quanshi de qidian" [Cheng Dieyi—an explanatory starting point], *Dangdai* [Contemporary], April 1, 1994, 54–60.

26. The women in Zhang Yimou's three "red" films (*Red Sorghum, Ju Dou, Raise the Red Lantern*) all die or go insane.

27. Wai-yee Li, *Enchantment and Disenchantment: Love and Illusion in Chinese Literature* (Princeton: Princeton University Press, 1993), 19–20.

28. Li, *Enchantment*, 19.

29. Li, *Enchantment*, 19.

30. Li, *Enchantment*, 6.

31. Li, *Enchantment*, 6.

32. Silverman, *Male Subjectivity*, 9.

Chapter 14

•

Narrative Images of the Historical Passion
Those *Other* Women—On the Alterity in
the New Wave of Chinese Cinema

•

Yi Zheng

The self-conscious New Wave of Chinese cinema begins with a resituation of what C. T. Hsia, in his study of modern Chinese literature,[1] calls the modern Chinese "obsession with China," an obsession recurrent in modern Chinese literary, social, and political thought, which begins with that traumatic moment in "our" modernity, when, as Benedict Anderson observes: "So, as European imperialism smashed its insouciant way around the globe, other civilizations found themselves traumatically confronted by pluralisms which annihilated their sacred genealogies. The Middle Kingdom's marginalization to the Far East is emblematic of this process."[2]

It is an obsession burdened with the traumatic modern Chinese history, with a "pregazing"—"the givenness of subjectivity," which "is already part of the process of cross-cultural interpellation that is at work in the larger realm of modern history."[3] These cinematic new waves and re-presentations emerge as belated but conscious attempts at a self-recasting that is a response to and a critique of that earlier trauma and the "Chinese" own subsequent entanglement with it, including the initial moment of encounter with the imperial West and the later "Cultural Revolution" as various stages of a Chinese modernity.

These filmic practices, as self-reimaging, however, are more than what Rey Chow diagnoses via Freud as the fetishizing gaze, nor are they a belated longing *for* the lost empire. In *Primitive Passions,* which is an extended reformulation of the practice of self-gazing/display, the "autoethnography" in the Chinese New Cinema, and a critical assessment of its attendant cross-cultural inquiries, Chow looks at the formalisms of the production of the Fifth-Generation Chinese filmmakers as masculinist cultural critics. She suggests that in these new waves, the "primitive passions" of the masculinist, imperialist (in their nostalgia for a primitive Chinese empire) modern Chinese intellectuals are redeemed in their formal construction of "the primacy of to-be-looked-at–ness," in their reimaging of the countryside, the long-ago, and the woman as a Third-Worldly *modus operandi* in the increasingly "transparent" transnational market economy.[4] I agree with Chow that such "primitive passions" are "fantasies of an origin"[5] but suggest that they are evoked, first of all, as self-scrutiny, a critique of their own complicity and their endless failed attempts to redress the wound of their modern dismemberment at a moment of cultural crisis. In these self-gazings, their complicity is seen not only in their inevitable acceptance of their "othered" modernity, the irreversibility of history, and their impotence as the structured other but also in their shattered "sacred genealogies." Their critique is also a cultural critique of their very own genealogy.

Their gaze begins with the burden of a historical awareness of the non-place of modern China and its *own* undoing. In their reimaging, modern China comes to be, contrary to Kristeva's observation, with the very complexes of "our" modernity[6]—the permanent imprints of the shattering of its sacred genealogy in its first traumatic encounter with the modernizing West, and its very own "lack"—its always already lost, corrupted Chineseness. It is with a shared pregazing as such that the New Wave is hailed as a "medical discourse,"[7] a cure for or an antithesis to the shattered cultural body. As a continuation of the modern Chinese "obsession with China," this new wave marks a turning, a negation of various past attempts, and a will to shake off "the shackles of tradition" and discard "historical burdens." "Pounded and bent by strong anxiety and a clear sense of social responsibility,"[8] these self-consciously *new* filmmakers joined the search for roots that surged in China in the early and middle 1980s as a cultural meditation upon the implications and possibilities of a "national" striving for remodernization and have taken it to greater "depth." Most of the New Wave films are set in an imagined faraway, long-ago place where a naked but "Chinese" existence, that which is *outside* and *other* than the defunct traditions of the lost empire, still *is*.

The effort of these new filmmakers is described by themselves and many Chinese film critics as a cultural introspection, a gaze back/inward that reimages a primordial China, not without the shackles of tradition or the complexes of the encroaching modern history but at least with a retained native vitality to counteract them. Since it is a cultural introspection that poses itself as a critique to its own diseased modernity, traced not only in its entanglement with an outside world but *in* some essential lack in its own cultural body, it "casts its light first on peasants, women and intellectuals, the social groups in which the traditional culture has its deepest roots and the national character finds its most obstinate origins."[9] Notwithstanding the strangeness of the juxtaposition, the direction of the turn and the resonance of its cultural and epistemological reference are very telling. One witnesses the reemergence on the "new," "postmodern," "postrevolutionary" Chinese scene of the *Old Well* of the village, the *Yellow Earth* and the *Red Sorghum,* the *Hunting Ground* of Inner Mongolia and the *Horse Thief* of Tibet, *Ju Dou* in an archaic dye mill, and the wives and concubines locked up in the "museum" of the age-old courtyard of *Raise the Red Lantern.* In these films, peasants, women, exotic hunters, and wild horsemen are captured under the camera's intellectual, meditative, reverent but critical gaze as the symbolic bearers of the national character, of its deepest roots and obstinate origins, of the native vitality and its own primordial destructive force. They become bodies whose silent movement carried out the very formation and the twisting of a burdened national consciousness.

One characteristic move of these Fifth-Generation films is ritualization—those famous long shots that reveal and distance, scrutinize and caress, contemplate and perpetuate, the life and death of their (non)heroes and heroines. And by their endlessness, their repetition, their very length, these long shots recast their (non)heroes and their stories as the backdrop of the camera's contemplation, of meanings and significances that "transcend" their locality. Thus in *Yellow Earth,* Cuiqiao's life and death as a poor peasant's daughter on the yellow plateau, her sufferings, yearnings, and futile struggle, embodied in her endless, everyday movement of carrying water and singing, are solicited to "reflect" the "fate" of Chinese *people* and "elevated to a reflection upon history and culture."[10] If *Yellow Earth* is the first offering in the reconstruction of historical roots and modern consciousness in the Fifth Generation, to consecrate the offering, Cuiqiao is sacrificed four times: her love to Guo Qing, the soldier/enlightener, and his sense of discipline and moral propriety; her virginity at the arranged wedding night to a dumb middle-aged peasant; her life in a desperate attempt at self-liberation upstream against the swallowing waves of the Yellow River; and her story to the re-search of Chineseness as part of the project of remodernization, since the contemplation upon her "fate" "has produced an extraordinary train of thought in contemporary film making."[11]

If *Yellow Earth* is the beginning of the cultural, anthropological contemplation of "China" as self, it begins as a lamentation, a critique of the always already lost yellow earth that has once nurtured the "soul" of its ancestors. The critique is carried out in different directions: in its slow, static narrative and visual movement, not only is the body of the vast, barren yellow earth, with its peasants and women, under the critical gaze, but the male protagonist as a revolutionary soldier, ethnographer, and enlightener is also the object of that scrutiny. His role in the life story of Cuiqiao and his relation with the yellow earth are ambiguous. So are the rituals that display the

eruption of male energy: while the drum dance echoes a sublime revolutionary drive, the rain prayer is represented as a stupefied act of superstition. Setting out on a similar turn, *Red Sorghum,* however, casts itself as a downright
celebration of that recovered life of "primitive passions": the whole set of
the Bakhtinian "life turned itself out"—"sensuous," "carnivalesque," and
masculine. Unlike the restrained, contemplative and almost uncertain critical gaze of *Yellow Earth, Red Sorghum* erects itself as an unbridled revelry in
"carnivalistic obscenities linked with the reproductive power of the earth
and the body."[12] What is erected in that celebratory unleashing is a "cinematic milestone that proposes a powerful Chinese version of masculinity as
a means of cultural critique."[13] The film sets itself off as a "shocking
affront" to the "deep-rooted" and time "ingrained" cultural codes and tastes,
an aggression against the historical burdens and modern complexes of a
civilization with shattered and deformed genealogies—its feminization,
which is seen not only in its structured otherness by the West but in a
degenerated, in-built twist in the evolution of "a cultural priority given to
femininity."[14] It is to redress such a historical wound upon the cultural body
that a "native masculinity" is reenvisioned as a cure for historical impotence. It is in this sense that *Red Sorghum* has become the rite of adulthood
for the Fifth-Generation male filmmakers/masculinist cultural critics, whose
entry onto the (post)modern Chinese cultural scene is claimed as the critique
of "the sons"[15] and who emerge hence from Son to Man. Thus in an unmistakably Nietzschean Dionysian motif of woman, blood, and wine, "my
grandfather" is reborn as a crude but real man and a roguish hero whose
manhood is regenerated and sublimated by his ravishing "my grandmother"
and his vengeance against the invading Japanese. It is a manhood differentiated from the inhumanity of the Japanese male soldiers and the mindless
cruelty of the local bandits, a manhood recentered on the sensuous, life-
giving body of the Chinese woman and the yellow earth and perfected in
her death. In this carnival of men and their defiance against history, "my
grandmother" is offered as ravishment and life-center, young sensuous body
and regenerating mother, in the moment when she is willingly carried
away and opens herself up, pierced by the camera into a fusion with the red
sorghum field, and as a crowning gesture toward the end of the film, dies
instantaneously with the burst of the signifying universe with gushing
blood. The end of the film is a blackout, a blazing redness that fuses "my
grandmother's" gushing blood with the life-giving sun and a rebirth carried
forward by the funeral chanting of the young boy/"my father" framed in
the male narrative voice of "mine." In the redressing of the national wound
and vengeance against an imposed modern history, "my grandmother" is
offered to offer herself.

Chow defines the seizure upon "the primitive that is the subaltern, the woman, and the child" on the part of modern Chinese intellectuals as a structure of "primitive passions."[16] As she aptly categorizes it into seven essential points, the "primitive passions" emerge "at a moment of *cultural crisis*," arise as "fantasies of an origin," with "the animal, the savage, the countryside, the indigenous, the people, and so forth," and "*stand in* for that 'original' something that has been lost." The "structure of feeling" (Chow via Said) that is the "primitive passions" is a reconstruction of the primitive as the figure for an "irretrievable *common / place*," "a fabrication of a *pre* that occurs in the time of the *post*." For all this, Chow suggests, the primitive reconstructed seems to provide a way for thinking about the unthinkable— "as that which is at once basic, universal, and transparent to us all, *and* that which is outside time and language." Hence by its very definition—its destination, "the primitive is phantasmagoric and, literally, ex-otic."[17]

Chow's categorizations are extremely useful in locating the "new" cinematic seizure of the primitive in the ongoing Chinese intellectual attempt to rejuvenate itself into modernity and in its link to the high modernism of the West. However, her definition of the "fabrication of a *pre*," that "strong sense of primordial, rural rootedness" as the "paradox of *a primitivism that sees China as simultaneously victim and empire*," fails to address the implications of the very desire in the *post*-construction of the primitive not only as a *pre*, but also as an *outside*, and the tracing of such passions not in the center of a self/ culture—in this sense the shattered genealogies of the empire and its critical, intellectual traditions inherited by the masculinist (filmmaking) cultural critics, but in its "alterity," its own "other"—peasants, children, and women. The "structure of feeling" as "primitive passions" in the new cultural (cinematic) wave as yet another *post*modern intellectual attempt is not a longing for, a reevocation of, the always already lost empire, as Chow insists, but a critique, a *misplaced* critique of the shattered cultural body and its inheritors' inability to redress its modern, genealogical wound, a wound ambivalently but emphatically located on the corporeality of the category of woman (the primitive, the rural, and the savage).

These self-recastings as the cure and redress of a cultural wound inflicted by history share that "obsession with China" which is already part of a response, a complicity, and a defense. The location of that wound in the feminization of a national culture and its "men" as cultural category is to begin with the pregazing that is complicitous with the imaged self as other, to begin within one's structured otherness, and to gaze at the self as other in the reflection of the mirror that has othered it. To redress the "national" "historical" wound through the category of the feminine and translate the complexes of modern China as a collective lack into the body of the Chinese woman is to place the historical burden it tries to discard once more upon the Chinese woman by continuing to subject her as the locus of "double identification"—"the double identification with the figure of narrative movement, the mythical subject, and with the figure of narrative closure, the narrative image."[18] Chow sees such trappings as the dilemma of the "postcolonial" intellectuals in "the deadlock of the anthropological situation as created by Western imperialism and colonialism of the past few centuries."[19] And as its deconstruction, she proposes that one should move from the "narrative" to "visuality," which is the communication of the "subjective origins" of the previously ethnographized in "*visual* terms." It is a communication not in the act of looking but in the "to-be-looked-at–ness."[20] In the films of the New Wave Chinese directors, the inequality of vision, if not mitigated, is redeemed because: "the state of being looked at not only is built into the way non-Western cultures are viewed by Western ones; more significantly it is part of the *active* manner in which such cultures represent—ethnographize—themselves." What is established here is "that being-looked-at–ness, rather than the act of looking, constitutes the primary event in cross-cultural representation."[21] Chow's establishment of the primacy of to-be-looked-at–ness, which claims nothing less than "a radical deprofessionalization of anthropology and ethnography as 'intellectual disciplines,' " or at least the redemption of "autoethnography" on the part of the once colonized, depends on the singling out—taking out of the narrative sequence—of that famous frontal shot of Ju Dou in Zhang Yimou's "Oriental's orientalism," *Ju Dou.* "As she confronts Tianqing with her naked body, Judou is, we may say, taking into her own hands the 'to-be-looked-at–ness' that conventionally constitutes femininity. . . . The effect of this gesture—of quoting the most-quoted, of displaying the most fetishized—is no longer simply voyeuristic pleasure but a heightened self-consciousness."[22] The reading of Ju Dou's "turn" is extremely illuminating, for its signification does go beyond "the formalism of irony": "she turns the eroticism of the spectacle into a deliberate *demonstration* of and against the patriarchal order that crushes her. Her female body . . . becomes in this scene a literal means of confrontation."[23] But the meaning of Ju Dou's turn does not come from the "visuality" of her tired, dirty, and bruised female body. The act of self-display as deliberate defiance is staged and made meaningful only in Zhang's play of the cinematic of the look and *his* parody of the clichés of Orientalism. In this sense Ju Dou has not taken into her own hands that "to-be-looked-at–ness." The brief moment of her primacy of to-be-looked-at–ness is subsumed very soon in Zhang's filmic *narrative* of the all-consuming destructive forces of the "old" Chinese tradition: her defiance and her "fate" are both offerings in Zhang's "exhibitionist" cultural self-scrutiny; her "visuality," that "brave self-display," is displayed for the rethinking, reerection of a Chinese-ness that structures and exhibits her, including her defiance, as the primitive. Both her "turn" and her use are brutally raw ones. In the end, her visuality is literally devoured by the roaring flames she sets upon herself, beautifully, defiantly, as a final frontal gesture. After all, her "visuality" is that of a "narrative image"—the bruised, abused, and overused but essentially young and sensuous, primitively vital female figure that carries the burden of the narrative movement and whose consumption brings about the narrative closure. In Teresa de Lauretis' argument, the position occupied by "woman" on the screen is not simply a visible "image" but a "narrative image," which refers to "the join of image and story, the interlocking of visual and narrative registers effected by the cinematic of the look." In cinema as well as in traditional narrative, the female position, "produced as the end result of narrativization, is the figure of narrative closure, the narrative image in which the film . . . comes together."[24] It is this narrative identification that assures "the hold of the image," the anchoring of meaning in the flow of the film's movement. If Ju Dou is not offered as "visual pleasure," she is offered as sacrifice in the destruction and wish for resurrection of a culture, as the phoenix that regenerates in her burning. As Ju Dou's primacy of to-be-looked-at–ness is consumed in the devouring flames of tradition, Zhang's "exhibitionism," —that "basic mood of defiance" (Chow) achieved through his ingenious play of visuality, is meaningful only within the burdened historical narrative of Chinese modernity and the critical narrative of the metaphysics of otherness in a cross-cultural exchange which is the aftermath of the earlier traumatic encounter between West and East. Zhang's offering of Ju Dou's primacy of to-be-looked-at–ness in an ongoing (post)modern Chinese intellectual self-scrutiny, a cultural re-search for roots and rejuvenation, does not break "the deadlock of the anthropological situation as created by Western imperialism and colonialism of the past few centuries."[25] What Zhang is producing may very well be that "brave self-display" "that contains, in its excessive modes, a critique of the voyeurism of orientalism itself." And this new critical "autoethnography" may have accepted "the historical fact of orientalism and performs a critique (i.e., evaluation) of it by staging and parodying orientalism's politics of visuality."[26] But that critique is performed, once again, upon the defiant but "primitive" body of the Chinese woman. The visual gestures as demonstration, as "the display of a tactic," are not gestures of critical, performative self-subalternizing and self-exoticizing on the part of the "Ju Dous" as Chow suggests. They are critical, tactical gestures of the masculinist, masterly, cultural critics/

filmmakers that play themselves out on a "new" "critical" "tactical" resubal-ternization and exoticization of their primitive "alterity"—*their* woman, *their* countryside, and *their* savage.

• The "Primitive Passion" as a Transnational Cultural Monument

As a cultural movement, the cinematic New Wave of the 1980s and 1990s in China does not emerge so much as the reimaging of a self in the fashion of a "brave self-display" to the West. Rather, it is part of an intellectual, crit-ical endeavor at self-recasting that attempts to alter, to rewrite the burdened historical narrative of modern China and recenter it. It is a refabrication of "roots," of a culture's "rootedness" that is about the "post" and the "present," a new story fabricated in the entanglement of the cultural crisis of a (post)-modern China and in the "cross-cultural" exchanges of a transnationally commodified world. Chen Kaige's *Farewell My Concubine* sets itself as a step out, as a detour of the cultural anthropological new wave in recent Chinese filmmaking. It is a turning away from the contemplative aesthetic avant-gardism to a more "popular" dramatic mode, and its dramatic reflection focuses on that cultural inspection, that obsession with historical roots and modern consciousness, with irony. It is a reflection and re-presentation that betrays a similar longing but implies a critique: by a similar look backward it finds there is no elsewhere, no alternative space beyond the particular ver-sion of modern Chinese history. And as an anthropological gaze at the self as other, it finds no consolation in the far away and long ago: the lavishly set Peking opera world, with its age-old, never changing rituals of life and death, passion and intrigue, not so much alternates but rather acts out the turbulence of modern Chinese history. In the vast and sweeping movement of the film that spans fifty-two years of Chinese modernity, history and play act and index each other out in Bertoluccian spectacles.

Set as a haunting, unrequited love story between two male actors of Peking opera, Xiaolou, the "king," and his apprentice brother, Dieyi, the "concubine," interrupted and complicated by the forced entrance of a whore-turned-woman, indexed and implicated by the violence of half a century of modern Chinese history, the film purports to be a national epic, a sexual-ized national allegory without catharsis. The narrative opens in the middle of things and forces the imaged modern Chinese spectator into a frontal engagement with her own genealogy by beginning with a highlighted sense of interruption and chaotic movement, by none-too-gently reimpos-ing on her that shared sense of historical burden. It is a genealogy summa-rized by the wailing of the "perverse," feminized, man/woman "concubine"

Cheng Dieyi: "It is all our own doing! We've become what we are one step after another."

Dieyi's wailing as summary of the genealogy of the modern Chinese is twofold: it is a relentless self-gazing, a cultural introspection as critique and self-exposition of one's "own doings" in one's genealogical degeneration; it is also a translation, a translation of a "rape" into "shame," man's shame. Despite the vast span of time and the sweeping movement of history, the allegory of modern China is played out in the film on the bodies and sexuality of two Chinese men and one superfluous Chinese woman, or more specifically, on the feminization of the "concubine" Cheng Dieyi.

Dieyi's feminization is initiated by the abandonment of his whore-mother and his assignment of the female role as apprentice in the theatrical school. He is offered up by maternal abandonment and brotherly, patriarchal violence (Xiaolou's scratching of his mouth with the master's pipe) to live and act out the tragic life of the legendary concubine—to enact with perfection the fate of a woman. The process of his womanization is completed with a rape, an act that seals his fate with irreversibility. Therewith the story of the age-old play becomes the index of his life, a life that allegorizes the modern history of China, and the maxim "the concubine must die" is explicated and acted out as a historical necessity.

Turned into a half-woman and object of desire, Dieyi furthers his own "degeneration" by "enjoying" his own feminization and endangers the manhood of his brother, the "king." Instead of resisting, he accepts his "historical" fate and indulges in the "perverse" pleasures of his own otherness. In the film, Dieyi's womanization marks a national, genealogical degeneracy that is associated not only with "perverse" sexuality but also with opium addiction and willing cooperation with foreign invasion: after all, while the "king" defends his manhood and national dignity with swaggering pride, Dieyi sings to please the Japanese as a woman.

The victimization of Chinese men as national allegory is recast in the film not only on the feminized body of the "concubine" but also on the historical impotence of the "king" in his inability to act in "real" life as "real" man—that is, to control his own fate and save his brother, fend off enemies, and maintain his manly, therefore human, dignity. The extremities of history have deprived him of the possibilities of a heroic Chinese manhood except on stage and in the legendary figure of an ancient king. While the king chants and marches with martial prowess on the stage, full of pomp and forever the idol of a collectively repressed unconscious (one should not overlook the emphatic explication of the troupe master and the obsessive reference to it throughout the film), the actor off-stage barely survives by his roguishness and a sometimes defiant, sometimes sheepish acceptance of a demeaned existence. His manhood is demeaned but saved by some "native" vitality, a Chinese "adaptability," and, most important, by the bodily offering and relentless devotion of a Chinese woman.

Before her intrusion into the men's world, the woman is a whore. In fact, the Chinese women cast in the film are either (ex-)whores or communist zealots. She is a whore who offers herself all the time and nondiscriminately. In her downward path, literally a descent, she is saved by the leftover manliness of Xiaolou and in turn unwittingly saves his manhood by imposing upon him a marriage. The make-do marriage and its precarious consummation on the eve of the Japanese occupation have saved both man and woman as a suspension—a problematic, fragile redemption in their historical degeneration: the king's endangered manhood in proximity to a corrupt feminization and the woman's further whoring of herself, possibly to the conquering Japanese. But the imposition of the woman, even as a self-offering, as a consecration to the survival and preservation of a national manhood, becomes the further cause of the other man's, the brother/concubine's, deeper plunge into the darkness of degeneration. After her forced entrance, he not only indulges in "perverse," "corrupt" pleasures with another degenerate man but peddles his "sick" femininity to the Japanese—an irreversible act of ultimate betrayal. Similarly, the woman's attempt at self-redemption and regeneration by bearing the "king" a son is aborted by a miscarriage caused by their entanglement with the complexes of history and their problematic sexuality. From that point the woman and the feminized man are engaged in a deadlock of mutual loathing and hatred, daunting the artistic pursuit and historical development of the man and the "king," softened and redeemed only momentarily in their common fate as nonpersons of a shattered, othered, and self-defeating cultural and national body. In the end, of course, both the woman and the feminized man must die, carrying with them all the dark degeneracies of a corrupt femininity, and the man becomes the sole survivor. He is beaten, left with an existence without catharsis, but alive as a man, an old man. "The concubine must die" is reechoed and acted out as a historical necessity and so is the fate of the superfluous woman. The old man, alone, numb with historical burdens and the pain of loss, but rid at last of the corrupt feminization and otherness, stands still with the hope of regeneration.

As another self-gazing at one's own otherness, the film simultaneously criticizes and purveys that othering process. The camera's gaze is at once masochistic and exhibitionist: while the scenes are lavishly set and sumptuously photographed, enchanting a "Western" audience and inviting the ethnicized, feminized modern Chinese spectator "to be there," the mesmerization is undercut by its noncathartic, relentless narrative. It disturbs the visual pleasure of the Western audience, making uneasy any possibilities of identification or distance, and forces the ethnic spectator into a self-scrutiny that offers no redemption, no consolation, but reminds of and reimposes on her the historical burdens that constitute her very own "being." For her, there is no escape. And though the film consciously distances itself from the other, earlier new waves of cultural introspection, like them, it locates its object of gaze, the historical, national burdens of modern China, in its structured otherness and a "cultural priority given to femininity." As a cultural critique, it is sexualized, with a translation of the complexes of modern China into the bodies of feminized Chinese man and Chinese woman. In its effort to re-present history with its wounds, it diagnoses the complex historical problems in the feminization of a cultural body. Like Dieyi's wailing, it is translation of a rape into shame, a man's shame. And in an effort to cast it off, it unwittingly continues the metaphysics of otherness and re-places the historical burdens once again upon the Chinese woman.

Chow proposes as a conclusion of her contemplation on "visuality, sexuality, ethnography, and contemporary Chinese cinema" that cultural translation, instead of "autoethnography," should be the new site of cultural resistance in the contemporary world of "the light and transparency of commodification."[27] Such translation, properly done by "non-Western cultures," can lead to the building up of a brilliantly lit, fabulously transparent "arcade" (Chow via Benjamin) shared by anyone, "if they want a place in the contemporary world." It is an arcade "furnished with exhibits of modernity's 'primitives' such as the women in contemporary Chinese film, who stand like mannequins in the passageways between cultures."[28] It is here that Chow joins the modern masculinist Chinese intellectuals in their attempt at self-rejuvenation through the relocation of their "primitives," though hers is an attempt at the possibility of cultural translation in a "new world market." Her replacement of the Chinese primitive is with a twist: equipped with "the transparency of our media and consumer society," she is moved "not back to the 'original' but rather to the *fabulous constructedness* of the world as spoken of by Nietzsche and Vattimo."[29] But such fabulous constructedness does not bespeak the "subjective origins" of the primitive if her place in the fabulous construction is still that of the mannequin, the exhibit. In Chow's mesmerization with the modern cross-cultural "brilliance of this 'fabling of the world,' " she re-places the "primitive" Chinese woman as exhibit in the "passageways between cultures." Speaking as the new cross-cultural, (non-)Western translator-critic, she prophesies with the light and transparency of a new world economy, the future of cross-cultural work:

The fabulous, brilliant forms of these primitives are what we must go through in order to arrive—not at the new destination of the truth of an 'other' culture but at the weakened foundations of Western metaphysics as well as the disintegrated bases of Eastern traditions. In the display windows of the world market, such 'primitives' are the toys, the fabricated play forms with which the less powerful (cultures) negotiate the imposition of the agenda of the powerful.[30]

In her vision of the newly lit world, the primitive is re-placed as fabulous, brilliant forms in the hands of the cultural fabricator-critic-negotiator. In assigning her role as the toy in the display windows of the world market, as fabricated play forms in the negotiations between powers and cultures, Chow, like Kristeva, has offered the primitive/woman up and reconsigned her as the corporeality of truth. And these are the problems of the "primitive passions" in the fabulously constructed transnational world market.

· Notes

1. See C. T. Hsia, *A History of Modern Chinese Fiction, 1917–1957* (New Haven: Yale University Press, 1961).

2. Benedict Anderson, *Imagined Communities: Reflections on the Origin and Spread of Nationalism* (London: Verso, 1991), 68.

3. Rey Chow, *Woman and Chinese Modernity: The Politics of Reading between East and West* (Minneapolis: University of Minnesota Press, 1991), 25.

4. See Rey Chow, *Primitive Passions: Visuality, Sexuality, Ethnography, and Contemporary Chinese Cinema* (New York: Columbia University Press, 1995).

5. Chow, *Primitive Passions,* 22.

6. In *About Chinese Women,* Julia Kristeva writes: "[I]n China . . . [the] strangeness persists . . . through a highly developed civilization which enters without complexes into the modern world, and yet preserves a logic unique to itself that no exoticism can account for." Julia Kristeva, *About Chinese Women,* trans. Anita Barrows (London: M. Boyars, 1986), 12.

7. See Yuejin Wang, *"Red Sorghum:* Mixing Memory and Desire," in *Perspectives on Chinese Cinema,* ed. Chris Berry (London: British Film Institute, 1991), 80–103.

8. Li Suyuan, "The Cultural Film: A Noticeable Change," in *Film in Contemporary China: Critical Debates, 1979–1989,* ed. George S. Semsel, Chen Xihe, and Xia Hong (Westport, Conn.: Praeger, 1993), 57–62.

9. Li, "The Cultural Film."

10. Chen Xihe, "Historical Roots and Modern Consciousness: A New View of Chinese Film," in *Film in Contemporary China: Critical Debates, 1979–1989,* ed. George S. Semsel, Chen Xihe, and Xia Hong (Westport, Conn.: Praeger, 1993), 51–56.

11. Chen, "Historical Roots," 51.

12. Wang, "Red Sorghum," 88.

13. Wang, "Red Sorghum," 85.

14. Wang, "Red Sorghum," 81.

15. See Dai Jinhua, "Bukejian de nüxing: Dangdai Zhongguo dianying zhong de nüxing yu nüxing dianying" [The invisible female: Women and women's film in contemporary Chinese cinema], *Dangdai dianying* [Contemporary cinema] 6 (1994): 41.

16. Chow, *Primitive Passions,* 22.

17. Chow, *Primitive Passions,* 22.

18. Teresa De Lauretis, *Alice Doesn't: Feminism, Semiotics, Cinema* (Bloomington: Indiana University Press, 1984), 144.

19. Chow, *Primitive Passions,* 176.

20. Chow, *Primitive Passions,* 180.

21. Chow, *Primitive Passions,* 180.

22. Chow, *Primitive Passions,* 167.

23. Chow, *Primitive Passions,* 167.

24. See De Lauretis, *Alice Doesn't,* 140.

25. Chow, *Primitive Passions,* 176.

26. Chow, *Primitive Passions,* 171.

27. Chow, *Primitive Passions,* 201.

28. Chow, *Primitive Passions,* 201.

29. Chow, *Primitive Passions,* 201.

30. Chow, *Primitive Passions,* 201.

Chinese Glossary

•

Compiled by Sheldon H. Lu and May M. Wang

A Cheng　阿城
A Jihua　A 計劃
A Jihua xuji　A 計劃續集
A Lushi (Ah Lu-shih, Ah-luk-sai)
　阿祿師
a shan de　阿山的
A! Yaolan　啊! 搖籃
A Ying (Ah Ying)　阿瑩
Ai Xia　艾霞
Ai zai biexiang de jijie　愛在別鄉
　的季節
anlian　暗戀
Anlian taohuayuan　暗戀桃花源

ba　爸
Babai zhuangshi　八百壯士
Bai Xianyong (Pai Hsien-yung)
　白先勇
baihua　白話
Baimao nü　白毛女
baise kongbu　白色恐怖
ban　板
Banbian ren　半邊人
Baoshengong　包身工
Baowei women de tudi　保衛我們
　的土地
Baqianli lu yun he yue　八千里路
　雲和月
Bawang bieji　霸王別姬
Beijingren zai Niuyue　北京人在
　紐約
Beiqing chengshi　悲情城市
bi Qin shi luan　避秦時亂

Bianzou bianchang　邊走邊唱
Biaoyan Gongzuofang　表演工
　作坊
Bo Yang (Po Yang)　柏楊
Bu Shaotian　卜少天
Bu Wancang　卜萬蒼
budao nüxing　不倒女性

Cai Chusheng　蔡楚生
caizi jiaren　才子佳人
Cao Yu　曹禺
Chen Bailu　陳白露
Chen bao　晨報
Chen Dabei　陳大悲
Chen Kaige　陳凱歌
Chen Lifu　陳立夫
Chen Liting　陳鯉庭
"Chen lun"　沉淪
Chen Wu　塵無
Chen Yi (Ch'en Yi)　陳儀
Chen Yingzhen (Ch'en
　Yingchen)　陳映真
Cheng Dieyi　程蝶衣
Cheng Jihua　程季華
Cheng Long (Jackie Chan)
　成龍
Chongqing senlin　重慶森林
Choulou de Zhongguoren　丑陋的中
　國人
Chu　楚
chuanqi　傳奇
Chunhua　春花
Congqian congqian you ge Pudao

tailang 從前從前有個浦島太郎

Cui Wei 崔嵬

Cuiqiao 翠巧

cun tianli, mie renyu 存天理，滅人欲

Cuo ai 錯愛

Da Guangming 大光明

Da Li, Xiao Li, he Lao Li 大李，小李，和老李

Da mofang 大磨坊

Da yuebing 大閱兵

Dachun 大春

Dahong denglong gaogao gua 大紅燈籠高高掛

Dai 傣

Dai Jinhua 戴錦華

Dai Qing 戴晴

Daihao meizhoubao 代號美洲豹

Dalu 大路

Dangdai 當代

Dangdai dianying 當代電影

Daoma zei 盜馬賊

daomadan 刀馬旦

Dazhong dianying 大眾電影

Deng Xiaoping 鄧小平

Di wang jiang xiang 帝王將相

Dian sheng 電聲

dianying 電影

Dianying shibao 電影時報

Dianying wenxue 電影文學

Dianying wenyi 電影文藝

Dianying xinwen 電影新聞

Dianying yishu 電影藝術

Dianying yuebao 電影月報

Dianying zazhi 電影雜志

Dianying zhoukan 電影周刊

die 爹

Diexue jietou 喋血街頭

Diexue shuangxiong 喋血雙雄

Ding Ling 丁玲

Ding Naizheng 丁乃箏

Ding Naizhu 丁乃竺

Dingjun shan 定軍山

Dongbei 東北

Dongdong de jiaqi 冬冬的假期

Dongfang sanxia 東方三俠

Dongfang zazhi 東方雜志

Du yi zhi 獨異志

Duan Xiaolou 段小樓

Eluosi guniang zai Harbin 俄羅斯姑娘在哈爾濱

Ererba shijian 二二八事件

Erxi 二喜

fakan ci 發刊詞

fanchang 反常

Fang Yuping (Allen Fong) 方育平

Feipu 飛浦

Feixia Ada 飛俠阿達

Fenggui lai de ren 風櫃來的人

Fenghuang 鳳凰

"Fenghuang niepan" 鳳凰涅槃

Fengxia 鳳霞

Fengyue 風月

Fengyun ernü 風雲兒女

fu 賦

Fu zi qing 父子情

Fugui 福貴

funü wenti 婦女問題

Furong zhen 芙蓉鎮

Fuxi 伏曦

Gaoshan xia de huahuan 高山下的花環

Ge Jingen (Ko Ching-en) 葛敬恩

Ge Wu (Koh Wu) 戈武

Ge You　戈優
Gong Li　鞏俐
gongfu (kung-fu)　功夫
Gu Baoming　顧寶明
Gu Qing　古青
Guan Jinpeng (Stanley Kwan)
　關錦鵬
Guangyin de gushi　光陰的故事
Gujing chongbo ji　古井重波記
guofang dianying　國防電影
guojia　國家
Guomindang (Kuomintang)
　國民黨
guopian　國片
guoyouhua　國有化
guoyu　國語
Gushu yiren　鼓書藝人
"Guxiang"　故鄉

Haigang　海港
Haizi wang　孩子王
Han　漢
Hanhan　憨憨
Haonan haonü　好男好女
Hasen yu Jiamila　哈森與加米拉
heimu　黑幕
Hong Changqing　洪常青
Hong gaoliang　紅高粱
Hong Shen　洪深
Hong Tian'e　紅天鵝
Hongfan qu　紅番區
Hongse niangzi jun　紅色娘子軍
Hou Xiaoxian(Hou Hsiao-hsien)
　侯孝賢
hou xin shiqi　後新時期
Hu Die　胡蝶
Hu Shi　胡適
Hu Xueyang　胡雪陽
Huagou　花狗
huang　黃

Huang Shuqin　黃蜀芹
Huang Su　黃素
Huang tudi　黃土地
Huangpu Jiang　黃浦江
Humen　虎門
huo　火
Huozhe　活著

Ji An　際安
Jiandan renwu　簡單任務
Jiang Binliu　江濱柳
Jiang Bo　江波
Jiang Jieshi (Chiang Kai-shek)
　蔣介石
Jiang Qing　江青
jiang shi　僵尸
Jiang Wen　姜文
Jiang Wu　姜武
jianggang　醬缸
Jiangjun zu　將軍族
Jiao Yulu　焦裕祿
Jiaoyuxue yuekan　教與學月刊
Jiazhen　家珍
jidian　積澱
jiguan　籍貫
Jilong (Chilung)　基隆
jin　金
Jin Shijie　金士杰
jinbu　進步
Jincheng Daxiyuan　金城大戲院
jing　精
Jingcha gushi　警察故事
Jingcha gushi san: chaoji jingcha
　警察故事三：超級警察
jingmei　景美
Ju Dou　菊豆
Juexiang　絕響
Juxian　菊仙

kaipian　開篇

"Kong Yiji"　孔乙己
Kongbu fenzi　恐佈分子
"Kuangren riji"　狂人日記
Kuangwen Eluosi　狂吻俄羅斯
Kuanmei (K'uan-mei, Hiyomi)
　寬美
Kuanrong (K'uan-jung, Hiroe)
　寬榮
Kunlun　昆侖

Lai Shengchuan (Stan Lai)
　賴聲川
Laidi　來弟
Lan fengzheng　藍風箏
Lan Ping (Jiang Qing)　藍蘋
Lang Xiong (Sihung Lung)　郎雄
langman nüzi　浪漫女子
Lao Gan　老干
Lao jing　老井
Lao Tao　老陶
Lashou shentan　拉收神彈
Lei yu　雷雨
Li An (Ang Lee)　李安
Li Ao　李敖
Li Aying　李阿英
Li Baotian　李寶田
Li Jun　李俊
Li Liqun　李立群
Li Minwei　黎民偉
Li renxing　麗人行
"Li Sao"　離騷
Li Shaohong　李少紅
Li Shuangshuang　李雙雙
Li Taiyan　李太炎
Li Tianlu (Li T'ien-lu, Li T'en-luk)
　李天祿
Li Xiaolong (Bruce Lee)　李小龍
Lian'ai de fenmu　戀愛的墳墓
Lianhua　聯華
Lianlian fengchen　戀戀風塵

lifa　禮法
Lin (Lim)　林
Lin Lingdong (Ringo Lam)
　林嶺東
Lin Nong　林農
Lin Qingxia (Lin Ching-hsia,
　Brigitte Lin)　林青霞
Lin Yutang　林語堂
Lin Zexu　林則徐
Linjia puzi　林家鋪子
lishi fansi　歷史反思
Liu Heng　劉恆
Liu Na'ou　劉吶鷗
Liu Sanjie　劉三姐
Liu Shaoqi　劉少奇
Liumang daheng　流氓大亨
Lizhu (Li-chu)　麗珠
Long shaoye　龍少爺
Lu Ren　魯韌
Lu Xun　魯迅
Luo Gang　羅剛
Luo Mingyou　羅明佑

Mao Dun　茅盾
Mao Zedong　毛澤東
Mayi Jutuan　螞蟻劇團
Mei Lanfang　梅蘭芳
Mei Yanfang (Anita Mui)　梅艷芳
Meishan　梅山
Meiyue yingtan　每月影談
miejue renyu　減絕人欲
Minguo ribao　民國日報
Mingxing　明星
Mingxing ban yuekan　明星半月刊
Mingxing tekan　明星特刊
minzu　民族
minzu dianying　民族電影
minzu fengge　民族風格
minzu tedian　民族特點
minzu xingshi　民族形式

minzu zhuyi 民族主義
minzu zijiu 民族自救
minzuhua 民族化
modeng guniang 摩登姑娘
modeng nüxing 摩登女性
moming qimiao 莫名其妙
mo-Tai-deng-le 摩太登了
mu 木
Mu Guiying 穆桂英
Muma ren 牧馬人

na shi yige xin dalu 那是一個新
  大陸
Nala (Nora) 娜拉
Nanfu nanqi 難夫難妻
neige 那個
neishen waiwang 內聖外王
Nie Er 聶耳
Niluohe nüer 尼羅河女兒
Nongnu 農奴
nüer 女兒
Nülan wuhao 女藍五號
Nüwa 女媧

Pan Gongzhan 潘公展
Panshiwan 磐石灣
Pili huo 霹靂火
putonghua 普通話

qi 氣
qiefu zhi dao 妾婦之道
qing 情
Qing Niao 青鳥
Qing Shi 青矢
Qingchun 青春
Qingchun ji 青春祭
Qingchun zhige 青春之歌
qipao 旗袍
Qiu Jin 秋瑾
Qiuju da guansi 秋菊打官司

Qiwang 棋王
Qu Ying 瞿穎
Qu Yuan 屈原

Ren gui qing 人鬼情
Ren Jingfeng 任景豐
renyan kewei 人言可畏
renzhong 人種
Ru Ling 茹玲
Ruan Lingyu 阮玲玉
ruanxing dianying 軟性電影
Runtu 潤土

Saishang fengyun 塞上風雲
San'ge modeng nüxing 三個摩登
  女性
Sanyuanli 三元里
Shang Shuihua 商水花
Shangguan Yunzhu 上官雲珠
Shao Lizi 邵力子
shaoshu minzu 少數民族
shaoshu minzu dianying 少數民
  族電影
shen 身
Shen bao 申報
Shen Congwen 沈從文
shengui 神鬼
Shennü 神女
Shexing diaoshou 蛇形刁手
Shi bao 時報
Shi Dongshan 史東山
Shiyan Xiao Juchang 實驗小
  劇場
Shu Qi 舒琪
shui 水
Shui Hua 水華
Shuixiang de chuntian 水鄉的
  春天
shuofa 説法
Songlian 頌蓮

Su Li　蘇里
suanqu　酸曲
Sun Shiyi　孫師毅
Sun Yu　孫瑜

Taidu　台獨
taiji (t'ai chi)　太極
Taiwan jingyan　台灣經驗
Taiwan sanbuqu　台灣三部曲
Taiwan sheng　台灣省
Taiwan xin dianying　台灣新
　電影
Tan Xinpei　譚鑫培
Tang Jishan　唐季珊
Tang Na　唐納
Tang Shuisheng　唐水生
Tao Yuanming　陶淵明
Taohua Jiang　桃花江
"Taohuayuan ji"　陶花源記
Tian Zhuangzhuang　田壯壯
Tianyunshan chuanqi　天雲山傳奇
Tongnian wangshi　童年往事
tu　土
Tui shou　推手

wajin guniang　挖金姑娘
Wan Cheng　萬程
Wan'ou zhijia　玩偶之家
Wang Boshi　王博士
Wang Dulu　王度廬
Wang Jiawei (Wong Kar-wai)
　王家衛
Wang Jiayi　王家乙
Wang Xiaoshuai　王小帥
Wang Ying (Wayne Wang)　王穎
Wang Zhengfang (Peter Wang)
　王正方
Wei Ming　韋明
Weilong mengtan　威龍猛探
wen yi zaidao　文以載道

wenhua fansi　文化反思
wenhua re　文化熱
wenhua redian　文化熱點
Wenliang (Wen-liang, Bun-leong)
　文良
Wenqing (Wen-ch'ing, Bun-
　ch'ing)　文清
Wensen (Wen-sen, Bun-Hsim)
　文森
Wenxiong (Wen-hsiung, Bun-
　heung)　文雄
wo yao huo　我要活
Wohu canglong　臥虎藏龍
wu dan　武旦
Wu Qinghua　吳青華
Wu Songgao　吳頌臬
Wu Tianming　吳天明
Wu Yonggang　吳永剛
Wu Yusen (John Woo)　吳宇森
Wu Ziniu　吳子牛
Wuduo jinhua　五朵金花
Wutai jiemei　舞台姐妹
wuxing　五行

Xia Dabao　夏大寶
Xia Yan　夏衍
Xi'an　西安
Xiandai yi nüxing　現代一女性
Xianghun nü　香魂女
xiao　孝
Xiao Hong　小鴻
Xiao Jinbao　小金寶
Xiao Luo　小洛
Xiao Shuan　小栓
Xiao tianshi　小天使
Xiao wanyi　小玩意
xiaoshuo　小説
Xiaosi'er　小四兒
"Xiaoxiao"　蕭蕭
Xie Fang　謝芳

Xie Fei　謝飛
Xie Jin　謝晉
Xie Tieli　謝鐵驪
Xi'er　喜兒
Ximeng rensheng　戲夢人生
xin　心
xin funü　新婦女
Xin nüxing　新女性
xin nüxing shijian　新女性事件
Xin qingnian　新青年
xin shiqi　新時期
Xin tu　新土
xinpai de funü　新派的婦女
Xiyan　喜宴
xiyang yingxi　西洋影戲
Xu (Hsu)　許
Xu Anhua (Ann Hui)　許鞍華
Xu Feng　徐楓
Xu Ke (Tsui Hark)　徐克
Xu Suying (Hui So-ying)　許素瑩
Xu Xingzhi　許幸之
Xuese qingchen　血色清晨

Yan'an　延安
yang　陽
Yang Dechang (Edward Yang)
　楊德昌
Yang Jinshan　楊金山
Yang Tianbai　楊天白
Yang Tianqing　楊天青
Yang Xiong　楊雄
Yangguang canlan de rizi　陽光燦
　爛的日子
Yanghang li de Zhongguo xiaojie
　洋行里的中國小姐
Yangniu'er zai Beijing　洋妞兒在
　北京
"Yao"　藥
Yao a yao, yao dao waipo qiao
　搖阿搖，搖到外婆橋

Yaogun qingnian　搖滾青年
Yapian zhanzheng　鴉片戰爭
Yichang fengbo　一場風波
Yijiang chunshui xiang dongliu
　一江春水向東流
yin　淫
Yin Min　尹民
Yin shi nan nü　飲食男女
yin shui　淫水
Ying Yunwei　應雲蔚
yingxi　影戲
Yingxi chunqiu　影戲春秋
Yingxi shenghuo　影戲生活
Yingxiong bense　英雄本色
yinyang　陰陽
Youhua haohao shuo　有話好
　好説
Youqing　有慶
Yu Dafu　郁達夫
Yu guang qu　魚光曲
yuan　元
Yuan Muzhi　袁牧之
Yuan Shiqing　袁世卿
Yuan Siye　袁四爺
Yuehong　月紅
Yule pian　娛樂片
yulun　輿論

Zaochun eryue　早春二月
Zhang Damin　張達民
Zhang Daofan　張道藩
Zhang Guorong (Leslie Cheung)
　張國榮
Zhang Junxiang　張駿祥
Zhang Manyu (Maggie Cheung)
　張曼玉
Zhang Nuanxin　張暖昕
Zhang Shichuan　張石川
Zhang Songbai　張松柏
Zhang Xiuzhen　張秀貞

Zhang Yimou　張藝謀
Zhang Yuan　張元
Zhang Zeming　張澤鳴
Zhao Wenxuan (Winston Chao)
　趙文瑄
Zheng Chaoren　鄭超人
Zheng Junli　鄭君里
Zheng Zhengqiu　鄭正秋
Zhenzhen　貞貞
Zhi Song　之松
Zhong an zu　重案組
Zhongguo dianying fazhanshi
　中國電影發展史
Zhongguo shibao　中國時報
Zhongguo yinmu　中國銀幕
Zhongyang ribao　中央日報
zhongzu　種族

Zhou Enlai　周恩來
Zhou Jianyun　周劍雲
Zhou Runfa (Chow Yun-fat)
　周潤發
zhu xuanlü　主旋律
Zhuangzi shiqi　莊子試妻
"Zhufu"　祝福
zhuoshui　濁水
"Zhuyao chengfen"　主要成份
zili　自立
ziwo jiazhi　自我價值
Zongheng sihai　縱橫四海
Zuihou de guizu　最後的貴族
Zuijia paidang　最佳拍擋
Zuiquan　醉拳
zuoyi dianying　左翼電影

Filmography
•
Compiled by Anne T. Ciecko and Sheldon H. Lu

The filmography includes the films mentioned in the essays. The listings are alphabetized by English title and include director, country or region of origin, studio or production company, and year. PRC (People's Republic of China) indicates Mainland China after 1949.

Aces Go Places (Zuijia paidang). Eric Tsang and Tsui Hark (Hong Kong: Cinema City, 1982).

Ah, Cradle (A! Yaolan). Xie Jin (PRC: Shanghai Film Studio, 1979).

Ah Ying (Banbian ren). Allen Fong (Fang Yuping) (Hong Kong: Sil-Metropole, 1984).

Ancient Well (Gujing chongbo ji). Dan Tuyu (China: Shanghai Yingxi, 1923).

Armor of God (Longxiong hudi). Jackie Chan (Hong Kong: Golden Harvest, 1987).

Autumn's Tale, An (Liumang daheng). Mabel Cheung (Hong Kong: D & B Films Co., Ltd., 1987).

Battle Creek Brawl (a.k.a. *Big Brawl*). Robert Clouse (USA/Hong Kong: Golden Harvest, 1980).

Beijing'ers in New York (Beijingren zai Niuyue) [television serial]. Zheng Xiaolong, Feng Xiaogang (PRC: Central China TV and Beijing TV, 1993).

Better Tomorrow, A (Yingxiong bense). John Woo (Hong Kong: Cinema City, 1986).

Big Li, Little Li, and Old Li (Da Li, Xiao Li, he Lao Li). Xie Jin (PRC: Tianma Film Studio, 1962).

Big Mill, The (Da mofang). Wu Ziniu (PRC/Hong Kong: Xiaoxiang and Sil-Metropole, 1990).

Big Parade, The (Da yuebing). Chen Kaige (PRC: Guangxi Film Studio, 1985).

Big Road, The (Dalu). Sun Yu (China: Lianhua, 1934).

Birth of a Nation, The. D. W. Griffith (USA: Epoch, 1915).

Bitter Tea of General Yen, The. Frank Capra (USA: Columbia, 1933).

Bloody Morning (Xuese qingchen). Li Shaohong (PRC: Beijing Film Studio, 1990).

Blue Angel, The (Der Blaue Engel). Josef von Sternberg (Germany: UFA, 1930).

Blue Kite, The (Lan fengzheng). Tian Zhuangzhuang (Hong Kong: Longwick Film Studio/Beijing: Beijing Film Studio, coproduction, 1992).

Boys from Fenggui, The (Fenggui laide ren). Hou Hsiao-hsien (Taiwan, 1983).

Bridges of Madison County, The. Clint Eastwood (USA: Amblin/Malpaso Production, 1995).

Broken Arrow. John Woo (USA: Twentieth Century Fox, 1995).

Bullet in the Head (Diexue jietou). John Woo (Hong Kong: Cinema City, 1990).

Cabeza de Vaca. Nicolas Echevarria (Mexico/Spain: Iguana Productions, 1990).

Cannonball Run. Hal Needham (Hong Kong: Golden Harvest, 1980).

Cannonball Run II. Hal Needham (Warner Brothers/Golden Harvest, coproduction, 1984).

Cat's Paw. Sam Taylor (USA: Harold Lloyd Corporation, 1934).

Chan Is Missing. Wayne Wang (USA: Wayne Wang Productions, 1981).

Children of Troubled Times (Fengyun ernü). Xu Xingzhi (China: Diantong, 1935).

Chinese Girls in Foreign Companies (Yanghang li de Zhongguo xiaojie) [television serial]. (PRC: Central China TV and Shanghai Cultural Development Co., 1995).

Chungking Express (Chongqing senlin). Wong Kar-wai (Hong Kong: Jet Tone, 1994).

City of Sadness (Beiqing chengshi). Hou Hsiao-hsien (Taiwan: ERA International and 3-H Films Limited, 1989).

Code Name Puma (Daihao Meizhoubao). Zhang Yimou (PRC: Xi'an Film Studio, 1988).

Commissioner Lin (Lin Zexu). Zheng Junli and Cen Fan (PRC: Haiyan, 1959).

Cook, the Thief, His Wife, and Her Lover, The. Peter Greenaway (USA: Allarts Cook–Erato Films/Films, Inc., coproduction, 1989).

Crime Story (Zhong an zu). Kirk Wong (Hong Kong: Golden Harvest/Imperial, 1993).

Crossings (Cuo ai). Evans Chan (Hong Kong/USA: Riverdrive Productions, 1994).

Crow, The. Alex Proyas (USA: Entertainment/Jeff Most/Edward R. Pressman, 1994).

Crying Game, The. Neil Jordan (Britain: Palace and Channel Four Films in association with Eurotrustees and Nippon Film Development and Finance Inc. with the participation of British Screen, 1992).

Daisy Kenyon. Otto Preminger (USA: TCF, 1947).

Daughter of the Nile (Nilouhe nüer). Hou Hsiao-hsien (Taiwan: Chung Yi Production Co., Ltd., 1987).

Death in Shanghai (Tod über Shanghai). (Germany: Ultra-Ton Film Gesellschaft, 1933).

Defending Our Land (Baowei women de tudi). Shi Dongshan (China: China Film Studio, 1938).

Desperado. Robert Rodriguez (USA: Columbia Pictures/Los Hooligans, 1995).

Difficult Couple, The (Nanfu nanqi). Zhang Shichuan, Zheng Zhengqiu (China: Asia Film Company, 1913).

Dingjun Mountain (Dingjun shan). Ren Jingfeng (China: Fengtai Photography, 1905).

Doctor Zhivago. David Lean (USA: Metro-Goldwyn-Mayer, 1965).

Double Team. Tsui Hark (USA: Columbia Pictures/Mandala Entertainment, 1997).

Dragon: The Bruce Lee Story. Rob Cohen (USA: Universal Pictures, 1993).

Drum Singers (a.k.a. *The Street Players*; Gushu yiren). Tian Zhuangzhuang (PRC: Beijing Film Studio, 1987).

Drunken Master (Zuiquan). Yuen Woo-ping (Hong Kong: Seasonal Films, 1978).

Drunken Master 2 (Zuiquan 2). Lau Kar Leung (PRC/Hong Kong: China Film Co-Production Co./Hong Kong Martial Arts Production Co./Beijing Universal Film Service Co., 1994).

Dust in the Wind (Lianlian fengchen). Hou Hsiao-hsien (Taiwan: Central Motion Picture Corporation, 1986).

Early Spring (a.k.a. *Second Lunar Month, Threshold of Spring*; Zaochun eryue). Xie Tieli (PRC: Beijing Studio, 1964).

Eat a Bowl of Tea. Wayne Wang (USA: Columbia Pictures/American Playhouse Theatrical Film, 1989).

Eat Drink Man Woman (Yin shi nan nü). Ang Lee (Taiwan: Motion Picture Corporation Production in association with Ang Lee Productions and Good Machine, 1994).

Eight Hundred Heroic Soldiers (Babai zhangshi). Ying Yunwei (China: China Film Studio, 1938).

Eight Thousand Li of Clouds and Moon (Baqianli lu yun he yue). Shi Dongshan (China: Kunlun Studio, 1947).

Enter the Dragon. Robert Clouse (USA/Hong Kong: Warner Brothers Pictures, 1973).

Farewell China (Ai zai biexiang de jijie). Clara Law (Hong Kong: Golden Harvest, 1990).

Farewell My Concubine (Bawang bieji). Chen Kaige (Hong Kong/PRC: Tomson Films Company, Ltd. in association with China Film Co-Production Corporation and Beijing Film Studio, 1993).

Father and Son (Fu zi qing). Allen Fong (Fang Yuping [Fong yuk-ping]). (Hong Kong: Fenghuang Motion Picture Company, 1981).

First Strike (*Jiandan renwu*; a.k.a. *Police Story 4: First Strike* [Jingcha gushi 4]). Stanley Tong (Hong Kong: Golden Harvest, 1996).

Five Golden Flowers (Wuduo jinhua). Wang Jianyi (PRC: Changchun Studio, 1959).

Foreign Babes in Beijing (Yangniu'er zai Beijing) [television serial]. Wang Binglin, Li Jianxin (PRC: Beijing Film Studio, 1996).

Forrest Gump. Richard Zemekis (USA: Paramount Pictures, 1994).

Frankenstein. James Whales (USA: Universal, 1931).

Fugitive, The. Andrew Davis (USA: Warner Brothers, 1993).

Garlands at the Foot of the Mountain (Gaoshan xia de huahuan). Xie Jin (PRC: Shanghai Film Studio, 1983).

Gate of Heavenly Peace, The. Carma Hinton, Richard Gordon (USA: Long Bow Group, 1995).

Goddess, The (Shennü). Wu Yonggang (China: Lianhua Studio, 1934).

Good Earth, The. Sidney Franklin (USA: Metro-Goldwyn-Mayer, 1937).

Good Men, Good Women (Haonan haonü). Hou Hsiao-hsien (Taiwan: 3H Productions Ltd., 1995).

Hard Boiled (Lashou shentan). John Woo (USA: Milestone Pictures for Golden Princess Film Production Ltd., 1992).

Hard Target. John Woo (Hong Kong: Cinema City/USA: Universal, 1993).

Hasen and Jiamila (Hasen yu Jiamila). Wu Yonggang (PRC: Shanghai Film Studio, 1955).

Herdsman, The (Muma ren). Xie Jin (PRC: Shanghai Film Studio, 1982).

Heroic Trio (Dongfang sanxia). Johnny To (Du Qifeng) (Hong Kong: China Entertainment Films/Paka Hill Productions, 1982).

Hibiscus Town (Furong zhen). Xie Jin (PRC: Shanghai Film Studio, 1986).

Horse Thief (Daoma zei). Tian Zhuangzhuang (PRC: Xi'an Film Studio, 1985).

How to Make an American Quilt. Jocelyn Moorhouse (USA: Universal Pictures/ Amblin Entertainment, 1995).

In Our Time (Guangyin de gushi). Edward Yang (Yang Dechang) (Taiwan: Central Motion Picture Corporation, 1982).

In the Heat of the Sun (Yangguang canlan de rizi). Jiang Wen (PRC: Heat of the Sun Company, 1995).

JFK. Oliver Stone (USA: Warner/Le Studio Canal/Regency Enterprises/Alcor [A. Kitman Ho, Oliver Stone], 1991).

Jiao Yulu (Jiao Yulu). Wang Jixing (PRC: Emei Film Studio, 1991).

John Woo's Once a Thief [TV movie]. John Woo (USA: Twentieth Century Fox, 1996).

Joy Luck Club, The. Wayne Wang (USA: Buena Vista Pictures in association with Hollywood Pictures, 1993).

Ju Dou (Ju Dou). Zhang Yimou (PRC: China Film Co-Production Corporation and Xi'an Film Studio, 1990).

Jungle Book. Stephen Sommers (USA: Walt Disney Productions, 1994).

Killer, The (Diexue shuangxiong). John Woo (Hong Kong: Cinema City, 1989).

King of the Children (Haizi wang). Chen Kaige (PRC: Xi'an Film Studio, 1987).

Kitty Foyle. Sam Wood (USA: RKO, 1940).

Klondike Annie. Raoul Walsh (USA: Paramount, 1936).

Last Aristocrats, The (Zuihou de guizu). Xie Jin (PRC/Hong Kong: Shanghai Film Studio/Yindu, 1989).

Legend of Tianyun Mountain, The (Tianyunshan chuanqi). Xie Jin (PRC: Shanghai Film Studio, 1980).

Letter from an Unknown Woman. Max Orphuls (USA: Universal/Rampart, 1948).

Li Shuangshuang (Li Shuangshang). Lu Ren (PRC: Haiyan Studio, 1962).

Life on a String (Bianzou bianchang). Chen Kaige (United Kingdom/PRC/Germany/Japan/Italy/Netherlands: Serene Productions, Beijing Film Studio/China Film Co-Production Corporation/Pandora Film/Herald Ace/Film Four International/Berlin Film Forderung/Diva Film/Cinecompany, 1991).

Like Water for Chocolate. Alfonso Arau (Mexico: Electric/Cinevista/NCCA/NTDF/Alfonso Arau, 1991).

Lin Family Shop, The (Linjia puzi). Shui Hua (PRC: Beijing Studio, 1959).

Lion King, The. Roger Allers and Rob Minkoff (USA: Walt Disney Pictures, 1994).

Little Angel, The (Xiao tianshi). Wu Yonggang (China: Lianhua, 1935).

Little Buddha. Bernardo Bertolucci (USA: CIBY 200 in association with Recorded Picture Company, 1993).

Little Playthings (Xiao wanyi). Sun Yu (China: Lianhua, 1933).

Mad Max. George Miller (Australia: Warner, 1979).

Maximum Risk. Ringo Lam (USA: Sony Pictures, 1996).

Mildred Pierce. Michael Curtiz (USA: Warner, 1945).

Modern Woman, A (Xiandai yi nüxing). Li Pingqian (China: Mingxing, 1933).

New Land, The (a.k.a. *New Earth;* Xin tu). Arnold Frank (Germany/Japan, 1937).

New Woman, The (Xin nüxing). Cai Chusheng (China: Lianhua, 1934).

Old Well (Lao jing). Wu Tianming (PRC: Xi'an Film Studio, 1987).

Once a Thief (Zongheng sihai). John Woo (Hong Kong: Cinema City, 1991).

Opium War, The (Yapian zhanzheng). Xie Jin (PRC: Xie Jin–Hengtong Company, 1997).

Panshiwan (Panshiwan). Xie Jin (PRC, 1975).

Peach Blossom Land (Anlian Taohuayuan). Stan Lai (Taiwan: Performance Workshop Films, 1992).

Piano, The. Jane Campion (New Zealand: Jan Chapman Productions in association with CIBY 2000, the Australian Film Commission, and the New South Wales Film and Television Office, 1993).

Police Story (Jingcha gushi). Jackie Chan (Hong Kong: Golden Harvest/Palace, 1986).

Police Story 2 (Jingcha gushi 2). Jackie Chan (Hong Kong: Golden Harvest, 1988).

Police Story 3: Supercop (Jingcha gushi 3: Chaoji jingcha). Tong Kwei-lai (Stanley Tong) (Hong Kong: Golden Harvest/Imperial, 1992).

Port, The (a.k.a. *On the Docks;* Haigang). Xie Jin, Xie Tieli, two versions (PRC: Beijing Film Studio and Shanghai Film Studio, 1972 and 1973).

Project A (A Jihua). Jackie Chan (Hong Kong: Golden Harvest, 1984).

Project A, II (A Jihua xuji). Jackie Chan (Hong Kong: Golden Harvest, 1987).

Protector, The (Weilong mengtan). James Glickenhaus (USA: Warner Brothers, 1986).

Pulp Fiction. Quentin Tarantino (USA: Miramax Films presentation of A Band Apart/Jersey Films production, 1994).

Puppetmaster, The (Ximeng rensheng). Hou Hsiao-hsien (Taiwan: ERA International presentation of a City Films production, 1993).

Pushing Hands (Tui shou). Ang Lee (USA: Triboro Entertainment Group/ Taiwan: CFP Central Motion Picture Corporation presentation in association with Ang Lee Productions and Good Machine, 1992).

Qiu Jin (Qiu Jin). Xie Jin (PRC, 1983).

Raise the Red Lantern (Da hong denglong gaogao gua). Zhang Yimou (Hong Kong/PRC: ERA International Ltd./China Film Co-Production Corporation, 1991).

Rebecca. Alfred Hitchcock (USA: David O. Selznick, 1940).

Red Detachment of Women, The (Hongse niangzijun). Xie Jin (PRC: Tianma Studio, 1961).

Red Detachment of Women, The (Hongse niangzijun) [dance remake of Xie Jin's narrative feature]. (PRC: The China Ballet Troupe, 1970).

Red Lotus Society, The (Feixia ada). Stan Lai (Taiwan: Performance Workshop Films, 1994).

Red Sorghum (Hong gaoliang). Zhang Yimou (PRC: Xi'an Film Studio, 1988).

Red Swan (Hong tian'e). Gu Rong (PRC: Guangxi Film Studio, 1995).

Ruan Lingyu (a.k.a. *Centre Stage, Actress*). Guan Jinpeng (Stanley Kwan) (Hong Kong: Golden Harvest, 1991).

Rumble in the Bronx (Hong fanqu). Stanley Tong (Hong Kong: Golden Harvest, 1995).

Russian Girls in Harbin (Eluosi guniang zai Harbin) [television serial] (PRC: China Central Television/Heilongjiang Studio/Tian'e Film Co., 1994).

Sacrificed Youth (a.k.a. *The Rite of Youth;* Qingchun ji). Zhang Nuanxin (PRC: Youth Studio, 1985).

Scent of Green Papaya, The (L'Odeur de la papaya verte/Mui Du Du Xanh). Tran Anh Hung (France/Vietnam: Les Productions Lazennec in coproduction with La Sept Cinema in association with Canal Plus/Centre National de la Cinematographie, 1993).

Schindler's List. Steven Spielberg (USA: Universal/Amblin, 1993).

Sense and Sensibility. Ang Lee (USA: Columbia Pictures, 1995).

Serfs (Nongnu). Li Jun (PRC: August First Studio, 1963).

Shanghai Express. Josef von Sternberg (USA: Paramount, 1932).

Shanghai Triad (Yao a yao, yao dao waipoqiao). Zhang Yimou (PRC: Shanghai Film Studio/USA: Alpha Films, USG Images/France: Le Sept Cinema and Le Ministère des Affaires étrangères, coproduction, 1995).

Singin' in the Rain. Gene Kelly, Stanley Donen (USA: Metro-Goldwyn-Mayer, 1952).

Slamdance. Wayne Wang (USA: Zenith Productions/Island Pictures, 1987).

Snake in the Eagle's Shadow (Shexing diaoshou). Yuen Woo-ping (Hong Kong: Seasonal Films, 1978).

Song of the Fishermen (Yu guang qu). Cai Chusheng (China: Lianhua Studio, 1934).

Song of Youth (Qingchun zhige). Cui Wei, Chen Huaikai (PRC: Beijing Film Studio, 1959).

Speed. Jan De Bont (USA: Twentieth Century Fox, 1994).

Spring Days in Water Village (a.k.a. *Spring Over the Irrigated Land;* Shuixiang de chuntian). Xie Jin (PRC: Shanghai Film Studio, 1955).

Spring River Flows East, A (Yijiang chunshui xiang dong liu). Cai Chusheng, Zheng Junli (China: Kunlun and Lianhua Studios, 1947).

Storm on the Border (Saishang fengyun). Ying Yunwei (China: China Film Studio, 1939).

Story of Qiu Ju, The (Qiu Ju da guansi). Zhang Yimou (Hong Kong: Sil-Metropole organization/PRC: Youth Film Studio of Beijing Film Academy, coproduction, 1993).

Strawberry and Chocolate (Fresca y Chocolate). Tomás Gutiérrez Alea and Juan Carlos Tabio (Cuba: Instituto Cubano del Arte Industria Cinematograficos in association with Co./Tabasco Films, 1993).

Supercop (see *Police Story* 3).

Swan Song (Juexiang). Zhang Zeming (PRC: Pearl River Studio with Youth Production Unit, 1985).

Temptress Moon (Feng yue). Chen Kaige (Hong Kong: Tomson, 1996).

Ten Commandments, The. Cecil B. De Mille (USA: Paramount/Famous Players/ Lasky, 1923).

Terminator 2: Judgment Day. James Cameron (USA: Carolco Pictures/Pacific Western/Lightstorm Entertainment, 1991).

Terrorizer (Kongbu fenzi). Edward Yang (Yang Dechang) (Taiwan: Central Motion Picture Corporation, 1986).

Thief of Bagdad. Raoul Walsh (USA: Fox, 1924).

Third Sister Li (Liu Sanjie). Su Li (PRC: Changchun Studio, 1960).

Three Beautiful Women (Liren xing). Chen Liting (China: Kunlun, 1949).

Three Modern Women (San'ge modeng nüxing). Bu Wancang (China: Lianhua, 1933).

Through the Olive Trees (Zir-E Darakhtan-E Zeyton). Abbas Kiarostami (Iran: Abbas Kiarostami Productions, 1994).

Thunderbolt (Pili huo). Jackie Chan (Hong Kong: Golden Harvest, 1996).

Time to Live and a Time to Die, A (Tongnian wangshi). Hou Hsiao-hsien (Taiwan: Central Motion Picture Corporation, 1985).

To Live (Huozhe). Zhang Yimou (Hong Kong/PRC: ERA International Ltd. Production in association with Shanghai Film Studio for Century Communications, Ltd., 1994).

Top Hat. Mark Sandrich (USA: RKO, 1935).

True Lies. James Cameron (USA: Lightstorm Entertainment for Twentieth Century Fox, 1994).

[Two] Stage Sisters (Wutai jiemei). Xie Jin (PRC: Tianma Studio, 1965).

Visitor on Ice Mountain (Bingshan shang de laike). Zhao Xingshui (PRC: Changchun Film Studio, 1963).

Wandering Through China. (USA: Fox, 1931).

Wave of Unrest, A (a.k.a. *An Incident;* Yichang fengbo). Xie Jin, Lin Nong (PRC: Shanghai Film Studio, 1954).

Wedding Banquet, The (Xiyan). Ang Lee (Taiwan: Central Motion Pictures Corporation/USA: Good Machine, Inc., 1993).

Welcome Danger. Mal St. Clair, Clyde Bruckman (USA: Harold Lloyd Corporation, 1929).

West Side Story. Robert Wise, Jerome Robbins (USA: Mirisch Pictures, 1961).

White-Haired Girl, The (Baimao nü). Wang Bing, Shui Hua (PRC: Northeast Film Studio, 1950).

Why We Don't Sing Songs (Women weishenmo bu gechang). (Japan: Shochiku, 1995).

Wild Kiss to Russia, A (Kuangwen Eluosi). Xu Qingdong (PRC: Beijing Film Studio, 1995).

Woman Basketball Player No. 5 (Nülan wuhao). Xie Jin (PRC: Tianma Film Studio, 1957).

Woman, Demon, Human (Ren gui qing). Huang Shuqin (PRC: Shanghai Film Studio, 1988).

Women from the Lake of Scented Souls (a.k.a. *Oilmakers' Family;* Xianghu nü). Xie Fei (PRC: Tianjin Film Studio and Changchun Film Studio, 1993).

Yellow Earth (Huang tudi). Chen Kaige (PRC: Guangxi Film Studio, 1984).

Young Master, The (Long Shaoye). Jackie Chan (Hong Kong: Golden Harvest, 1979).

Youth (Qingchun). Xie Jin (PRC: Shanghai Film Studio, 1977).

Zhou Enlai (Zhou Enlai) [Parts 1 and 2]. Ding Yinnan (PRC: Guangxi Film Studio, 1991).

Zhuangzi Tests His Wife (Zhuangzi shiqi). Li Minwei (Hong Kong: Huamei, 1913).

Bibliography

•

Compiled by Sheldon H. Lu and May M. Wang

This bibliography includes the works mentioned in the essays.

Abbas, Ackbar. "The New Hong Kong Cinema and the Déjà Disparu." *Discourse* 16, no. 3 (1994): 65–77.

Accomando, Beth. "Eat My Bullet." *Giant Robot* 6 (1996): 44–48.

"Ai Xia." *Mingxing yuekan* 1, no. 2 (June 1933).

Althusser, Louis. *Lenin and Philosophy and Other Essays.* Translated by Ben Brewster. New York: Monthly Review Press, 1971.

American Historical Review. Special issue on film and history. Vol. 93, no. 5 (December 1988).

Anderson, Benedict. *Imagined Communities: Reflections on the Origin and Spread of Nationalism.* London: Verso, 1991.

Anderson, Nigel. "Film-Makers Baptized in Fire—An Interview with Chen Kaige." *Financial Times* (London), January 8, 1994.

Ang, Ien. *Living Room Wars.* London: Routledge, 1996.

Ansen, David. "The Real Cultural Revolution." *Newsweek,* November 1, 1993, 74.

———. "Chinese Takeout." *Newsweek,* February 19, 1996, 66–68.

Appadurai, Arjun. "Disjuncture and Difference in the Global Cultural Economy. *Public Culture* 2, no. 2 (1990): 1–17.

Baker, Rick, and Toby Russell. *The Essential Guide to Hong Kong Movies.* London: Eastern Heroes Publications, 1994.

Bakhtin, Mikhail M. *The Dialogic Imagination.* Edited by Michael Holquist, translated by Caryl Emerson and Michael Holquist. Austin: University of Texas Press, 1981.

———. *Problems of Dostoevsky's Poetics.* Edited and translated by Caryl Emerson. Minneapolis: University of Minnesota Press, 1984.

Bamyeh, Mohammed. "Transnationalism." *Current Sociology* 41, no. 3 (1993): 1–95.

Bao Yuheng. "The Mirror of Chinese Society." *Chinese Literature* 4 (1985): 190–201.

Barmé, Geremie. "Persistance de la tradition au 'royaume des ombres'. Quelques notes visant à contribuer à une approche nouvelle du cinéma chinois." In *Le cinéma chinois,* edited by Marie-Claire Quiquemelle and Jean-Loup Passek, 113–127. Paris: Centre Georges Pompidou, 1985.

Bassan, Raphael, "Ombres électrique sur la cite interdite: La longue marche du cinéma chinois." *La revue du cinéma* 380 (February 1983): 66–82.

Baudrillard, Jean. *Selected Writings.* Edited by Mark Poster. Stanford: Stanford University Press, 1988.

Befu, Harumi, ed. *Cultural Nationalism in East Asia: Representation and Identity.* Berkeley: Institute of East Asian Studies, University of California, 1993.

" 'Bei' haiwai xuancai yinqi zhenghan" [Overseas press materials for *City of Sadness* stir controversy]. *Minsheng bao* [Min Sheng News], August 30, 1989.

Beijing Daxue et al., ed. *Wenxue yundong shiliao xuan* [Selected readings in literary movements]. Shanghai: Shanghai Jiaoyu chubanshe, 1979.

"*Beijing chengshi* ererba" [*City of Sadness* and the February 28 incident: A symposium]. *Dangdai* [Contemporary] 43 (November 1, 1989): 111–130."

Benjamin, Walter. "Theses on the Philosophy of History." In *Illuminations,* edited by Hannah Arendt, translated by Harry Zohn, 83–109. New York: Schocken, 1969.

——. "The Work of Art in the Age of Mechanical Reproduction." In *Film and Criticism,* edited by Gerald Mast and Marshall Cohen, 665–681. New York: Oxford University Press, 1992.

Bergeron, Régis. *Le cinéma chinois: 1949–1983.* Paris: L'Harmatton, 1984.

Bernstein, Gail Lee, ed. *Recreating Japanese Women, 1600–1945.* Berkeley: University of California Press, 1991.

Berry, Chris. "Race: Chinese Film and the Politics of Nationalism." *Cinema Journal* 31, no. 2 (1992): 45–58.

——. "A Nation T(w/o)o: Chinese Cinema(s) and Nationhood(s)." *East-West Film Journal* 7, no. 1 (1993): 24–51.

——, ed. *Perspectives on Chinese Cinema,* enlarged and rev. ed. London: British Film Institute, 1991.

Bhabha, Homi K. "Introduction: Narrating the Nation." In *Nation and Narration,* edited by Homi K. Bhabha, 1–7. New York: Routledge, 1990.

——. "DissemiNation: Time, Narrative, and the Margins of the Modern Nation." In *Nation and Narration,* edited by Homi K. Bhabha, 291–322. New York: Routledge, 1990.

——. *The Location of Culture.* London: Routledge, 1994.

Braudy, Leo. *The World in a Frame: What We See in Films.* New York: Anchor Press, 1976.

Brecht, Bertolt. *Brecht on Theatre: The Development of an Aesthetic,* edited and translated by John Willett. New York: Hill and Wang, 1964.

Brent, William. "Lights! Cameras! Action!" *The China Business Review* (September-October 1994): 36–39.

Brooker, Peter. *Bertolt Brecht: Dialectics, Poetry, Politics.* London: Croom Helm, 1988.

Browne, Nick; Paul G. Pickowicz; Vivian Sobchack; and Esther Yau, eds. *New Chinese Cinemas: Forms, Identities, Politics.* Cambridge: Cambridge University Press, 1994.

Bu Shaotian. "Dianying de moluo" [The degradation of the movies], *Chen bao,* August 3, 1932.

Buck, David D. "Introduction to Dimensions of Ethnic and Cultural Nationalism in Asia—A Symposium." *Journal of Asian Studies* 53, no. 1 (1994): 3–9.

Cai Chusheng. "Zhaoguang" [Morning light]. *Xiandai dianying* 1 (1933).

——— . "Xi ru rensheng" [Art imitates life]. *Zhongguo dianying* 2 (1957).

Cai Hongshen. *Cai Chusheng de chuangzuo daolu* [Cai Chusheng's creative path]). Beijing: Wenhua yishu chubanshe, 1982.

Cai Lingling (Ts'ai Ling-ling). "Huanrao zhe 'Bei' de lunshu wu" [The critical fog surrounding *City of Sadness*]. *Tzu-li Evening News,* October 10, 1989.

Callahan, W. A. "Gender, Ideology, Nation: *Ju Dou* in the Cultural Politics of China." *East-West Film Journal* 7, no. 1 (1993): 52–80.

Canby, Vincent. "Action, History, and Love Above All." *New York Times,* October 8, 1993, B1, B8.

——— . "Top Prize at Cannes is Shared." *New York Times,* May 25, 1994, C13.

Caughie, John. *Theories of Authorship.* Boston: Routledge and Kegan Paul, 1981.

Chakravarty, Sumita. *National Identity in Indian Popular Cinema.* Austin: University of Texas Press, 1993.

Chan, Ching-kiu Stephen. "The Language of Despair: Ideological Representations of the "New Woman" by May Fourth Writers." In *Gender Politics in Modern China: Writing and Feminism,* edited by Tani Barlow, 13–33. Durham: Duke University Press, 1993.

Chen Bo, ed. *Zhongguo zuoyi dianying yundong* [The leftist film movement in China]. Beijing: Zhongguo dianying chubanshe, 1993.

Chen Dabei. "Zhongguo yingpian qiye jia de san ge e meng" [The three nightmares of Chinese film makers]. *Dongfang zazhi* 21, no. 16 (1924).

——— . "Zhongguo dianying zhi jianglai" [The future of Chinese film]. *Dianying yuebao* 7 (1928).

Chen Huangmei, ed. *Dangdai Zhongguo dianying* [Contemporary Chinese cinema], vol. 1-2. Beijing: Zhongguo shehui kexue chubanshe, 1989.

Chen Kaige and Tony Rayns. *King of the Children and New Chinese Cinema*. London: Faber and Faber, 1989.

Chen Ru-shou (Robert Chen). "Fuhao 'Zhongguo' zai dianying zhong de yiyi" [The significance of the sign 'China' in film]. *Dangdai* [Contemporary] (Taiwan) 87, no. 7 (1993): 122–143.

Chen Wu. "Guanyu *Xin nüxing* de yingpian, piping, ji qita" [On the film *The New Woman*, criticism, and beyond]. *Zhonghua ribao*, March 2, 1935.

Chen Xihe. "Historical Roots and Modern Consciousness: A New View of Chinese Film." In *Film in Contemporary China: Critical Debates, 1979–1989*, edited by George S. Semsel, Chen Xihe, and Xia Hong, 51–56. Westport, Conn.: Praeger, 1993.

Chen Ye. *Zhongguo dabaike quanshu, dianyingji* [Great Chinese encyclopaedia, film volume]. Beijing: Zhongguo dabaike quanshu chubanshe, 1991.

Chen Yingzhen. "Jiangjun zu" [A race/people of generals]. In *Chen Yingzhen xiaoshuo xuan* [Selected stories of Chen Yingzhen], 50–63. Fuzhou: Fujian remin chubanshe, 1983.

Cheng Jihua, et al. *Zhongguo dianying fazhan shi* [History of the development of Chinese cinema], 2 vols. Beijing: Zhongguo dianying chubanshe, 1963.

Chow, Rey. "Male Narcissism and National Culture: Subjectivity in Chen Kaige's *King of the Children*." *Camera Obscura* 25–26 (1991): 9–41.

——. *Woman and Chinese Modernity: The Politics of Reading between East and West*. Minneapolis: University of Minnesota Press, 1991.

——. *Writing Diaspora: Tactics of Intervention in Contemporary Cultural Studies*. Bloomington: Indiana University Press, 1993.

——. *Primitive Passions: Visuality, Sexuality, Ethnography, and Contemporary Chinese Cinema*. New York: Columbia University Press, 1995.

Chown, Jeffrey. *Hollywood Auteur*. New York: Praeger, 1988.

Clark, Paul. "Filmmaking in China: From the Cultural Revolution to 1981." *China Quarterly* 94 (June 1983): 304–322.

——. *Chinese Cinema: Culture and Politics Since 1949*. New York: Cambridge University Press, 1987.

——. "Ethnic Minorities in Chinese Films: Cinema and the Exotic." *East-West Film Journal* I, no. 2 (1987): 15–31.

——. "Reinventing China: The Fifth-Generation Filmmakers." *Modern Chinese Literature* 5 (1989): 121–136.

Clifford, James. *The Predicament of Culture*. Cambridge, Mass.: Harvard University Press, 1988.

Corliss, Richard. "The Fire in Her Eyes." *Time*, April 26, 1993, 68–69.

——. "Jackie Can!" *Time*, February 13, 1995, 82–83.

——. "Ang Lee: Persuasion." *Time International*, January 29, 1996.

——— . "Fellini Go Home!" *Time,* January 13, 1997, 68–70.

Croll, Elisabeth. *Feminism and Socialism in China.* New York: Schocken, 1978.

Crossley, Pamela Kyle. "Thinking About Ethnicity in Early Modern China." *Late Imperial China* 11, no. 1 (1990): 1–35.

Cui, Lili. "Facing the Challenge From Hollywood." *Beijing Review,* February 5–11, 1996, 13–17.

Da Huo'er. "An Interview with Xie Jin." *Jump Cut* 34 (March 1989): 107–109.

Dai Jinhua. *Dianying lilun yu piping shouce* [Handbook of film theory and criticism]. Beijing: Kexue jishu wenxian chubanshe, 1993.

——— . "Bukejian de nüxing: Dangdai Zhongguo dianying zhong de nüxing yu nüxing dianying" [The invisible female: Women and women's film in contemporary Chinese cinema]. *Dangdai dianying* [Contemporary cinema] 6 (1994): 37–45.

Dai Qing. "Raised Eyebrows for *Raise the Red Lantern.*" *Public Culture* 5, no. 2 (1993): 333–336.

Dao Yan. "Yu Hong Shen xiansheng tan Zhongguo diyi you sheng yingpian gongsi" [A reply to Mr. Hong regarding China's Number One sound film studio]. *Chen bao,* July 27, 1932.

Dauphin, Gary. "Cyber: Ready for My Website, Mr. DeMille." *Village Voice,* January 2, 1996, 15.

——— . "Chan is Missing." *Village Voice,* February 27, 1996, 72.

De Lauretis, Teresa. *Alice Doesn't: Feminism, Semiotics, Cinema.* Bloomington: Indiana University Press, 1984.

Denby, David. "Movies: *Broken Arrow* directed by John Woo." *New York* 29, no. 8 (February 26, 1996): 126.

Deocampo, Nick, and Chris Berry. "On Questions of Difference." *Cinemaya* 23 (1994): 40–43.

"Dianying wenhua xiehui jiji jinxing" [The Film Culture Association energetically moves forward]. *Chen bao,* March 26, 1933.

Diawara, Manthia. *African Cinema.* Bloomington: Indiana University Press, 1992.

Dikötter, Frank. *The Discourse of Race in Modern China.* Stanford: Stanford University Press, 1992.

——— . "Racial Identities in China: Context and Meaning." *China Quarterly* 138 (June 1994): 404–412.

Dirlik, Arif. *After the Revolution: Waking to Global Capitalism.* Hanover, N.H.: Wesleyan University Press, 1994.

——— . "The Postcolonial Aura: Third World Criticism in the Age of Global Capitalism." *Critical Inquiry* 20, no. 2 (1994): 328–356.

Dissanayake, Wimal, ed. *Melodrama and Asian Cinema*. Cambridge: Cambridge University Press, 1993.

———, ed. *Colonialism and Nationalism in Asian Cinema*. Bloomington: Indiana University Press, 1994.

Doane, Mary Ann. *The Desire to Desire*. Bloomington: Indiana University Press, 1987.

Dollimore, Jonathan. "Subjectivity, Sexuality, and Transgression: The Jacobean Connection." *Renaissance Drama* 17 (1986): 53–81.

Dong Chensheng. *Paintings of Beijing Opera Characters*. Beijing: Zhaohua Publishing House, 1981.

Doran, Lindsay, and Emma Thompson. Review of *Sense and Sensibility*. *Guoji ribao* (International News), January 22, 1996.

Duara, Prasenjit. "De-constructing the Chinese Nation." *Australian Journal of Chinese Affairs* 30 (July 1993): 1–26.

Dyer, Richard. *Light Entertainment*. London: British Film Institute, 1973.

———. *Stars*. London: British Film Institute, 1979.

———. "Entertainment and Utopia." In *Genre: The Musical,* edited by Rick Altman. London: Routledge and Kegan Paul, 1981.

———. *Heavenly Bodies*. London: British Film Institute, 1987.

———. "Action!" *Sight and Sound* 4, no. 10 (1994): 6–10.

———, ed. *Gays in Film*. 2nd ed. New York: Zoetrope, 1984.

Eagleton, Terry. *Literary Theory: An Introduction*. Minneapolis: University of Minnesota Press, 1983.

Ehrlich, Linda, and David Desser, eds. *Cinematic Landscapes: Observations on the Visual Arts and Cinema of China and Japan*. Austin: University of Texas Press, 1994.

Eliot, T. S. *The Complete Poems and Plays: 1909–1950*. New York: Harcourt, Brace and World, 1971.

Fan, Ruijuan. "An Actress' Life in Old China." In *When They Were Young,* edited by Women of China and New World Press, 156–164. Beijing: New World Press, 1983.

Fanon, Frantz. *Black Skin, White Masks*. Translated by Charles Lam Markmann. New York: Grove Press, 1967.

Feinstein, Howard. "A Chinese Actress Blossoms on the Screen." *New York Times,* April 11, 1993.

Feng, Peter. "Being Chinese American, Becoming Chinese American: *Chan is Missing*." *Cinema Journal* 35, no. 4 (1996): 88–118.

Fleming, Michael. "Snipes, Chan Say Confucius." *Daily Variety,* April 9, 1996, 1.

Flint, Kate. *The Woman Reader, 1837–1914*. Oxford: Oxford University Press, 1994.

Foerster, Grant, and Rolanda Chu. *Jackie Chan Star Profile*. San Francisco: Hong Kong Film Monthly, 1994.

Fonoroff, Paul. "Orientation." *Film Comment* 24, no. 3 (1988): 52–56.

Fore, Steve. "Golden Harvest Films and the Hong Kong Movie Industry in the Realm of Globalization." *The Velvet Light Trap* 34 (1994): 40–58.

Francke, Lizzie. "Yin Shi Nan Nu (Eat Drink Man Woman)." *Sight and Sound* 5, no. 1 (1995): 63–64.

Gaines, Jane, and Thomas Lahusen, eds. "Views from the Post-Future/Soviet & Eastern European Cinema." Special issue of *Discourse* 17, no. 3 (1995): 3–125.

Gallop, Jane. *Reading Lacan*. Ithaca, N.Y.: Cornell University Press, 1985.

Gao Miaohui and Chen Jiuhui, eds. "Beiqing zen shi" [How is the sadness explained?]. *Ying xiang* [Imagekeeper monthly] 1, no. 1 (1989): 36–42.

Gates, Henry Louis, Jr., ed. *"Race," Writing, and Difference*. Chicago: University of Chicago Press, 1986.

Gentry, Clyde III. "Mr. Nice Guy: Jackie and Sammo Reunite!" *Hong Kong Film Connection* 4, no. 2 (1996): 3.

Giannetti, Louis. *Understanding Movies*. Englewood Cliffs, N.J.: Prentice-Hall, 1990.

Gilmartin, Christina Kelley. *Engendering the Chinese Revolution: Radical Women, Communist Politics, and Mass Movements in the 1920s*. Berkeley: University of California Press, 1995.

Gladney, Dru C. "Representing Nationality in China: Refiguring Majority/Minority Identities." *Journal of Asian Studies* 53, no. 1 (1994): 92–123.

———. "Tian Zhuangzhuang, the Fifth Generation, and Minorities Film in China." *Public Culture* 8, no. 1 (1995): 161–175.

Grossmann, Atina. "The New Woman and the Rationalization of Sexuality in Weimar Germany." In *Powers of Desire: The Politics of Sexuality*, edited by Ann Snitow, Christine Stansell, and Sharon Thompson, 153–171. New York: Monthly Review Press, 1983.

Hall, Stuart. "Minimal Selves." In *ICA Document 6: Identity* (1987): 44–47.

Hammond, Stefan, and Mike Wilkins. *Sex and Zen and a Bullet in the Head: The Essential Guide to Hong Kong's Mind-Bending Films*. New York: Simon and Schuster, 1996.

Haolaiwu de qinlüe [The invasion from Hollywood]. Beijing: Shiyue chubanshe, 1951.

Harley, John E. *World-wide Influences of the Cinema: A Study of Official Censorship and the International Cultural Aspects of Motion Pictures*. Los Angeles: University of Southern California Press, 1940.

Hayward, Susan. *French National Cinema*. London: Routledge, 1993.

He Weixin. "Zhongguo dianying jie ji da de weiji" [The biggest crisis of the Chinese film industry]. *Yingxi chunqiu* 6 (April 5, 1925).

Herberer, Thomas. *China and Its Minorities: Autonomy or Assimilation?* Armonk, N.Y.: M. E. Sharpe, 1989.

Hess, John, and Patricia R. Zimmermann. "Transnational Documentaries: A Manifesto." *Afterimage* 24, no. 4 (1997): 10–14.

Higashi, Sumiko. *Cecil B. DeMille and American Culture: The Silent Era.* Berkeley: University of California Press, 1994.

Higson, Andrew. "The Concept of National Cinema." *Screen* 30, no. 4 (1989): 36–46.

——. *Waving the Flag: Constructing a National Cinema in Britain.* Oxford: Clarendon Press, 1995.

Holley, David. "Army Killed Thousands in '47 Massacre, Taiwan Admits." *Los Angeles Times,* February 24, 1992.

Hong Shen. "Meiguo ren wei shenmo yao dao Zhongguo lai ban yingpian gongsi she Zhongguo pian" [Why Americans are coming to China to set up movie studios and make 'Chinese films'?]. *Chen bao,* July 21, 1932.

hooks, bell. *Black Looks: Race and Representation.* Boston: South End Press, 1992.

Horkheimer, Max, and Theodor Adorno. "The Culture Industry: Enlightenment as Mass Deception." In *Dialectic of Enlightenment,* translated by John Cumming, 120–167. New York: Continuum, 1988.

Hsia, C. T. *A History of Modern Chinese Fiction, 1917–1957.* New Haven: Yale University Press, 1961.

Hsu, Francis L. K. "Eros, Affect and Pao." In *Rugged Individualism Reconsidered: Essays in Psychological Anthropology,* by Francis L. K. Hsu, 263–300. Knoxville: University of Tennessee Press, 1983.

Hu Shi. "Meiguo de furen" [American ladies]). *Xin qingnian* 5, no. 3 (1918): 213–224.

Huang Meiying (Huang Mei-ying). "Zaizhi de ererba" [The reproduction of 'February 28']. In *Xin dianying zhi si* [The death of New Cinema], edited by Mi Zou (Mi Tsou) and Liang Xinhua (Liang Hsin-hua), 153–157. Taipei: Tangshan Publications, 1991.

Huang Ming. "Seeing *New Woman.*" In *One Day in China: May 21, 1936,* edited by Sherman Cochran and Hsieh Cheng-kuang, with Janis Cochran, 64–66. New Haven: Yale University Press, 1983.

Huang Shixian. "Zhongguo dianying daoyan 'xingzuo' jiqi yishu puxi" [The 'galaxy' of Chinese film directors and their artistic genealogy]. *Dangdai dianying* [Contemporary Cinema] 6 (1992): 77–85.

Huang Su. "Women duiyu *Bu pa si* shijian de pinglun zhi pinglun" [Our views regarding the views on *Welcome Danger*]. *Dianying* 1 (1930).

Huang Weijun. *Ruan Lingyu zhuan* [Biography of Ruan Lingyu]. Changchun: Beifang funü ertong chubanshe, 1986.

Huang Zuolin. "Mei Lanfang, Stanislavsky, Brecht—A Study in Contrasts." In *Peking Opera and Mei Lanfang: A Guide to China's Traditional Theatre and the Art of Its Great Master*, 14–29. Beijing: New World Press, 1981.

"Humen yiri: *Yapian zhanzheng* shezhizu paishe jishi" [One day in Humen: A report of the work of the production team of *Opium War*]. *Zhongguo yinmu* [China screen] (July-August 1995): 20.

Hwang, Jim. "On Being Gay in Taipei." *Asiaweek,* December 1, 1993, 45.

———. "Cross-Cultural Resonance." *Free China Review,* February 1995, 16–17.

James, Caryn. "You Are What You Wear." *New York Times,* October 10, 1993, H13.

Jameson, Fredric. "Third-World Literature in the Era of Multinational Capitalism." *Social Text* 15 (1986): 65–88.

———. "Remapping Taipei." In *New Chinese Cinemas: Forms, Identities, Politics,* edited by Nick Browne, Paul G. Pickowicz, Vivian Sobchack, and Esther Yau, 117–150. Cambridge: Cambridge Univerisity Press, 1994.

———. *The Geopolitical Aesthetic: Cinema and Space in the World System.* Bloomington: Indiana University Press, 1992.

JanMohamed, Abdul R., and David Lloyd, ed. *The Nature and Context of Minority Discourse.* New York: Oxford University Press, 1990.

Ji An. "Fa kan ci" [The opening remarks]. *Dianying yuebao* 1, no. 1 (April 1, 1928).

Jiao Xiongping (Chiao Hsiung-p'ing). "Jingtou saoguo lishi de anxiang" [The camera-swept back alleys of history: An interview with Hou Hsiao-hsien]. *Zhongguo shibao* [China times], September 4-5, 1989.

———. Interview with Hou Hsiao-hsien. *Zhongguo shibao* [China times], June 7–13, 1993.

Johnson, Brian D. "The Red and Restless." *Macleans,* November 15, 1993, 9.

Johnson, Marshall. "Making Time: Historic Preservation and the Space of Nationality." *positions: east asia cultures critique* 2, no. 2 (1994): 177–249.

Jones, Dorothy B. *The Portrayal of China and India on the American Screen, 1896–1955: The Evolution of Chinese and Indian Themes, Locales, and Characters as Portrayed on the American Screen.* Cambridge, Mass.: Center for International Studies, MIT, 1955.

Jump Cut 31 (1986): 51–57. Special section on Chinese cinema.

Jump Cut 34 (1989): 85–121. Special section on Chinese cinema.

Kaes, Anton. "History, Fiction, Memory: Fassbinder's *The Marriage of Maria Braun* (1979)." In *German Film and Literature,* edited by Eric Rentschler, 276–288. New York: Methuen, 1986.

—— . *From Hitler to Heimat: The Return of History as Film.* Cambridge, Mass.: Harvard University Press, 1989.

Kaplan, E. Ann. *Psychoanalysis and Cinema.* New York: Routledge, 1990.

—— . "Problematising Cross-Cultural Analysis: The Case of Woman in the Recent Chinese Cinema." In *Perspectives on Chinese Cinema,* edited by Chris Berry, 141–154. London: British Film Institute, 1991.

—— . "The Couch-Affair: Gender, Race and the Hollywood Transference." *American Imago* (winter 1993): 481–514.

—— . *Looking For the Other: Feminism and the Imperial Gaze.* London: Routledge, 1997.

—— . "Who's Reading What Signs and Why." Unpublished manuscript.

Kei, Sek. "The Development of 'Martial Arts' in Hong Kong Cinema." In *A Study of the Hong Kong Martial Arts Film,* edited by Lau Shing-hon, 27–38. Hong Kong: Urban Council, 1984.

Keneally, Thomas. *Schindler's List.* New York: Simon and Schuster, 1993.

Kerr, George. *Formosa Betrayed.* Boston: Houghton Mifflin, 1965.

—— . *Formosa: Licensed Revolution and the Home Rule Movement (1895–1945).* Honolulu: University of Hawaii Press, 1974.

Kingston, Maxine Hong. *China Men.* New York: Knopf, 1980.

K.K.K. "Ping *Yi kuai qian yu Shen seng*" [A review of *Yi kuai qian* and *Shen seng*]. *Yingxi chunqiu* 9 (1925).

Klawans, Stuart. "Zhang Yimou: Local Hero." *Film Comment* 31, no. 5 (1995): 11–18.

Klifa, Thierry. "Garcon D'Honneur." *Studio Magazine* (October 1993).

Kristeva, Julia. *About Chinese Women.* Translated by Anita Barrows. London: M. Boyars, 1986.

Kui. "Guanyu aiguo junshi pian" [On patriotic war films]. *Chen bao,* October 4, 1932.

Kwok and M.-C. Quiquemelle. "Le cinéma chinois et le réalisme." In *Ombres électriques: Panorama du cinéma chinois—1925–1983.* Paris: Centre de Documentation sur le Cinéma Chinois, 1982.

Lai, Stan (Lai Shengchuan). *Anlian Taohuayuan* [Secret love: The peach-blossom spring]. Taipei: Huangguan, 1986.

—— . *The Peach Blossom Land: A Synopsis.* Taipei: Performance Workshop, 1992.

—— . *Wo anlian de Taohuayuan* [The peach-blossom spring I loved in secret]. Taipei: Yuanliu, 1992.

—— . "Specifying the Universal." *The Drama Review* 38, no. 2 (1994): 33–37.

Lai Tse-han, Ramon H. Myers, and Wei Wou, eds. *A Tragic Beginning: The Taiwan Uprising of February 28, 1947.* Stanford: Stanford University Press, 1991.

Larson, Wendy. "Zhang Yimou: Inter/National Aesthetics and Erotics." In *Cultural Encounters: China, Japan, and the West,* edited by Soren Clausen, Roy Starrs, and Anne Wedell-Wedellsborg, 215–226. Aarhus, Denmark: Aarhus University Press, 1995.

Lau, Jenny Kwok Wah. "A Culture Interpretation of the Popular Cinema of China and Hong Kong." In *Perspectives on Chinese Cinema,* edited by Chris Berry, 166–174. London: British Film Institute, 1991.

——. "*Judou*—A Hermeneutical Reading of Cross-cultural Cinema." *Film Quarterly* 45, no. 2 (1991): 2–10.

——. "*Farewell My Concubine:* History, Melodrama, and Ideology in Contemporary Pan-Chinese Cinema." *Film Quarterly* 49, no. 1 (1995): 16–27.

Lee, Leo Ou-fan, and Andrew J. Nathan. "The Beginnings of Mass Culture: Journalism and Fiction in the Late Ch'ing and Beyond." In *Popular Culture in Late Imperial China,* edited by David Johnson, Andrew Nathan, and Evelyn Rawski, 360–395. Berkeley: University of California Press, 1985.

Lee, Paul S. N. "The Absorption and Indigenization of Foreign Media Cultures—A Study on a Cultural Meeting Point of the East and West: Hong Kong." *Asian Journal of Communication* 1, no. 2 (1991): 52–72.

Lent, John A. *The Asian Film Industry.* Austin: University of Texas Press, 1990.

Lentricchia , Frank, and Thomas McLaughlin, eds. *Critical Terms for Literary Study.* Chicago: University of Chicago Press, 1990.

Leung, Ping-kwan. "Minzu dianying yu Xianggang wenhua shenfen: Cong *Bawang bieji, Qiwang, Ruan Lingyu* kan wenhua dingwei" [National cinema and the cultural identity of Hong Kong: Looking at cultural orientation from *Farewell My Concubine, Chess King,* and *Ruan Lingyu*]. *Jintian* [Today] 26 (1994): 193–204.

Lev, Peter. *The Euro-American Cinema.* Austin: University of Texas Press, 1993.

Leyda, Jay. *Dianying—Electric Shadows: An Account of Films and Film Audience in China.* Cambridge, Mass.: MIT Press, 1972.

Li Ao, ed. *Research on The February Incident (Ererba shijian yanjiu).* Taipei: Li Ao Publications, 1989.

Li, Cheuk-to. *Bashi niandai Xianggang dianying biji* [Notes on Hong Kong cinema of the 1980s], 2 vol. Hong Kong: Chuangjian, 1990.

——. "Tsui Hark and Western Interest in Hongkong Cinema." *Cinemaya* 21 (1993): 50–51.

——. *Guan niji (Xianggang dianying pian: Zhongwai dianying pian)* [Viewing against the grain: Hong Kong cinema; Chinese and foreign cinema], 2 vol. Hong Kong: Ciwenhua tang, 1993.

——. "The Return of the Father: Hong Kong's New Wave and Its Chinese Context in the 1980s." In *New Chinese Cinemas: Forms, Identities, Politics,* edited by Nick Browne, Paul G. Pickowicz, Vivian Sobchack, and Esther Yau, 160–179. Cambridge: Cambridge University Press, 1994.

Li Suyuan. "The Cultural Film: A Noticeable Change." In *Film in Contemporary China: Critical Debates,* 1979–1989, edited by George S. Semsel, Chen Xihe, and Xia Hong, 57–62. Westport, Conn.: Praeger, 1993.

Li Taipeng (Li, T'ai-p'eng) and Ge Guangyu (Ke Kuang-yu), eds. "Buduan xianying de lishi yu jiyi" [The continual reappearance of history and memory]. *Dianying xinshang* [Film appreciation] 77 (September/October 1996): 64–78.

Li Taiyan. *Li Taiyan kaipian ji* [Collected *kaipian* of Li Taiyan]. Shanghai: Li Taiyan, 1937.

Li, Wai-yee. *Enchantment and Disenchantment: Love and Illusion in Chinese Literature.* Princeton: Princeton University Press, 1993.

"Liangge kouhao" lunzheng ziliao xuanbian [Selected materials on the debate over "two slogans"], 2 vols. Beijing: Renmin wenxue chubanshe, 1982.

Liao Binghui (Liao Ping-hui). "Ji long you ya de sheyingshi" [A deaf, dumb photographer]. In *Xin dianying zhi si* [The death of New Cinema], edited by Mi Zou (Mi Tsou) and Liang Xinhua (Liang Hsin-hua), 129–34. Taipei: Tangshan Publications, 1991.

——. "Shikong yu xingbie de cuoluan: Lun *Bawang bieji*" [Temporal, spatial, and gender disorder: On *Farewell My Concubine*]. *Chung-wai Literary Monthly* 22, no. 1 (1993): 6–18.

Liao, Shiqi. " 'Disan' de hanyi: Jiemingxun de gushi he women de chujing" [The meaning of "third": Jameson's story and our condition]. *Dianying yishu* [Film art], no. 1 (1991): 39–45.

Lin Huaiming (Lin Huai-ming). "Wenren de guanzhao, shengcheng de tanxi: Niuyue kan *Beiqing chengshi*" [Warm affections, deep sighs: On watching *City of Sadness* in New York]. *Zhongguo shibao* [China times], October 18, 1989.

Lin Niantong. "A Study of the Theories of Chinese Cinema in Their Relationship to Classical Aesthetics." *Modern Chinese Literature* 1, no. 2 (1985): 186–189.

Lin, Yü-sheng. *The Crisis of Chinese Consciousness: Radical Antitraditionalism in the May Fourth Era.* Madison: University of Wisconsin Press, 1979.

Lin Yütang. *Ai yu fengci* [Love and satire]. Taibei: Jinlan wenhua chubanshe, 1984.

——. "Wajin guniang" [The gold digger girl]. In *Ai yu fengci,* 176–180. Taibei: Jinlan wenhua chubanshe, 1984.

Logan, Bey. *Hong Kong Action Cinema.* London: Titan Books, 1995.

Loh, Wai-fong. "From Romantic Love to Class Struggle: Reflections on the Film *Liu Sanjie*." In *Popular Chinese Literature and Performing Arts in the People's Republic of China, 1949–1979,* edited by Bonnie McDougall, 165–176. Berkeley: University of California Press, 1984.

Louie, Kam. "The Macho Eunch: The Politics of Masculinity in Jia Ping-wa's 'Human Extremities.' " *Modern China* 17, no. 2 (1991): 163–167.

Lovell, Alan. "Epic Theater and Counter Cinema's Principles." *Jump Cut* 27 (July 1982): 64–68.

Lu, Sheldon Hsiao-peng. "When Mimosa Blossoms: The Ideology of the Self in Modern Chinese Literature." *Journal of Chinese Language Teachers Association* 28, no. 3 (1993): 1–16.

——. "Postmodernity, Popular Culture, and the Intellectual: A Report on Post-Tiananmen China." *boundary 2* 23, no. 2 (1996): 139–169.

——. "Art, Culture, and Cultural Criticism in Post-New China." *New Literary History* 28, no. 1 (1997): 111–133.

——. "Global POSTmodernIZATION: The Intellectual, the Artist, and China's Condition." *boundary 2* 24, no. 3 (1997).

Lu Xun. "What Happens after Nora Leaves Home?" [Nala zouhou zenyang] (December 26, 1923). In *Silent China: Selected Writings of Lu Xun.* Translated by Gladys Yang. London: Oxford University Press, 1973.

——. "Lun renyan kewei" [On gossip being a fearful thing]. *Taibai banyue kan* (May 20, 1935). Reprinted in *Lu Xun quanji* [Complete works of Lu Xun], 6: 331–334.

——. *Lu Xun quanji* [Complete works of Lu Xun]. Beijing: Renmin wenxue chubanshe, 1981.

Luo Gang. "Zhongguo xiandai dianying shiye zhi niaokan" [An overview of China's film industry]. *Jiao yu xue yuekan* 1, no. 8 (1936).

Luo Xueying. "Xieren, xushi, neihan" [Characterization, narration, meaning: A symposium on *The Story of Qiu Ju*]. *Dangdai dianying* [Contemporary cinema] 51 (November 1992): 12–24.

Lyons, Donald. "Passionate Precision: *Sense and Sensibility*." *Film Comment* 32, no. 1 (1996): 36–42.

Lyotard, Jean-François. *The Postmodern Condition: A Report on Knowledge.* Translated by Geoff Bennington and Brian Massumi. Minneapolis: University of Minnesota Press, 1984.

Ma Junxiang. "Minzu zhuyi suo suzao de xiandai Zhongguo dianying" [Modern Chinese film as shaped by nationalism]. *Ershiyi shiji* [Twenty-first century] 15 (February 1993): 112–119.

Ma Ning. "Notes on the New Filmmakers." In *Chinese Film: The State of the Art in the People's Republic,* edited by George S. Semsel, 63–93. New York: Praeger, 1987.

———. "Spatiality and Subjectivity in Xie Jin's Film Melodrama of the New Period." In *New Chinese Cinemas: Forms, Identities, Politics,* edited by Nick Browne, Paul G. Pickowicz, Vivian Sobchack, and Esther Yau, 15–39. New York: Cambridge University Press, 1994.

MacDonald, Maitland. "Things I Felt Were Being Lost." *Film Comment* 29, no. 5 (1993): 50–52.

Mackerras, Colin. *The Chinese Theatre in Modern Times: From 1840 to the Present Day.* London: Thames and Hudson, 1975.

———. *China's Minorities: Integration and Modernization in the Twentieth Century.* New York: Oxford University Press, 1994.

Mao Zedong. "Talks at the Yenan Forum on Literature and Art." In *Selected Readings from the Works of Mao Zedong,* 250–286. Beijing: Foreign Languages Press, 1971.

Mao Zhenchu. "Zhongguo diyi ji lianhe liang gongsi zhi zuzhi feifa" [The illegality of China's Number One and United Pictures]. *Chen bao,* August 1, 1932.

Marchetti, Gina. *Romance and the "Yellow Peril": Race, Sex and Discursive Strategies in Hollywood Fiction.* Berkeley: University of California Press, 1993.

Mars-Jones, Adam. "A Visually Stunning Portrayal of the Peking Opera: Farewell My Concubine." *The Independent,* January 7, 1994.

Maslin, Janet. Review of *Ah Ying. New York Times,* March 30, 1984, C7.

———. Review of *The Peach Blossom Land. New York Times,* March 25, 1993, C20.

Matustik, Martin J. *Postnational Identity: Critical Theory and Existential Philosophy in Habermas, Kierkegaard, and Havel.* New York: Guilford Press, 1993.

"Mediating the National." Special issue of *Quarterly Review of Film and Video* 14, no. 3 (1993).

Memmi, Albert. *The Colonizer and the Colonized.* Translated by Howard Greenfield. Boston: Beacon Press, 1967.

Miller, Lucien. *Exiles at Home: Short Stories by Ch'en Ying-chen.* Ann Arbor: Center for Chinese Studies, University of Michigan, 1986.

Miyoshi, Masao. "A Borderless World? From Colonialism to Transnationalism and the Decline of the Nation-State." *Critical Inquiry* 19, no. 4 (1993): 726–751.

Mueller, Roswitha. *Bertolt Brecht and the Theory of Media.* Lincoln: University of Nebraska Press, 1989.

Muller, Marco. "Intervista con Xie Jin." In *Ombre Electriche: Saggi e Richerche sul Cinema Cinese.* Milan: Gruppo Editoriale Electra, 1982.

———. "Les tribulations d'un cinéaste chinois en Chine." *Cahiers du cinéma* 344 (February 1983): 16–21.

Mulvey, Laura. *Visual and Other Pleasures.* Bloomington: Indiana University Press, 1989.

Nashawaty, Chris. "Kong Kings." *Entertainment Weekly,* March 8, 1996, 28–29.

Neale, Stephen. "Prologue: Masculinity as Spectacle: Reflections on Men and Mainstream Cinema." In *Screening the Male: Exploring Masculinities in Hollywood Cinema,* edited by Steven Cohan and Ina Rae Hark, 9–20. London: Routledge, 1993.

Norman, Neil. "No Hiding from the Past—Chen's Look Back in Anger and Sorrow." *Evening Standard,* January 7, 1994.

"Nü mingxing de lian'ai zhang ye suan bu qing" [Even the stars' love accounts don't add up]. *Shi bao* (Shanghai), January 17, 1935.

O'Bryan, Joey. "A Rumble in Hollywood." *Austin Chronicle,* March 22, 1996, 34–35, 38.

Ogden, Dunbar H. *Actor Training and Audience Response.* Berkeley, Calif.: Oak House, 1984.

Ono, Kazuko. *Chinese Women in a Century of Revolution, 1850–1950 (Chuugoku joseishi, 1978).* Edited and translated by Joshua Fogel et al. Stanford: Stanford University Press, 1989.

O'Regan, Tom. *Australian National Cinema.* London: Routledge, 1996.

Oriental Cinema II (1996). Special issue on John Woo.

Pai, Hsien-yung. *Crystal Boys.* San Francisco: Gay Sunshine Press, 1990.

Patterson, Richard C. Jr. "The Cinema in China." *China Weekly Review,* March 12, 1927.

Peng, Yingming. "Guanyu woguo minzu gainian lishi de chubu kaocha" [A preliminary investigation of the history of the concepts of *minzu* in China]. *Minzu yanjiu* 2 (1985): 5–11.

Penner, Jonathan. "Wooing America." *Harper's Bazaar,* October 1993, 146.

Percheron, Daniel. "Sound in Cinema and Its Relationship to Image and Diegesis." *Yale French Studies* 60 (1980): 16–23.

Pickowicz, Paul G. "The Limits of Cultural Thaw: Chinese Cinema in the Early 1960s." In *Perspectives on Chinese Cinema,* edited by Chris Berry, 97–148. Ithaca, N.Y.: China-Japan Program, Cornell University, 1985.

——. "The Theme of Spiritual Pollution in Chinese Films of the 1930s." *Modern China* 17, no. 1 (1991): 38–75.

——. "Huang Jianxin and the Notion of Postsocialism." In *New Chinese Cinemas: Forms, Identities, Politics,* edited by Nick Browne, Paul G. Pickowicz, Vivian Sobchack, and Esther Yau, 57–87. New York: Cambridge University Press, 1994.

Plaks, Andrew H. *Archetype and Allegory in "The Dream of the Red Chamber."* Princeton: Princeton University Press, 1976.

Po Yang. "Zhuyao chengfen" [An important Ingredient] and "Qingke zhi xia, shengsi yizhu" [Life or Death at the Mercy of a Cough.] In *Si bu rencuo ji* [Stubborn to the end]. Taipei: Pingyuan chubanshe, 1967.

——. *Choulou de Zhongguo ren* [Ugly Chinese]. Changsha: Hunan Literary Publications, 1986.

Pollock, Griselda; Geoffrey Nowell-Smith, and Stephen Heath. "Dossier on Melodrama." *Screen* 18, no. 2 (1977): 105–119.

Powers, John. "Wine, Song and Right-Wing Humor." *Vogue* 184, no. 8 (1994).

Qian Jun. "Tan Sayide tan wenhua" [Said on culture]. *Dushu* [Reading] (September 1993): 10–17.

Qing Niao. "Jin yi bu de baolu" [Further exposure]. *Chen bao,* August 10, 1932.

Qing Shi. "Zi zhi yingpian de quedian" [The shortcomings of Chinese-made movies]. *Dianying zazhi* 18 (July 4, 1924): 8–10.

Rayns, Tony. Review of *The Killer. Monthly Film Bulletin* 57, no. 680 (1990): 260.

——. "Hard Boiled." *Sight and Sound* 2, no. 4 (1992): 20–23.

——. "Xiyan." *Sight and Sound* 3, no. 10 (1993): 56.

——. "Chaos and Anger." *Sight and Sound* 4, no. 10 (1994): 12–15.

——. "Hong Kong Notes." *Sight and Sound* 5, no. 6 (1995): 5.

——. "Hong Kong Notes." *Sight and Sound* 6, no. 5 (1996): 5.

Reid, Craig. "An Evening with Jackie Chan." *Bright Lights* 13 (1994): 18–25.

Renan, Ernest. "What Is a Nation" (Qu'est-ce qu'une nation? [1882]). Translated by Martin Thom. In *Nation and Narration,* edited by Homi K. Bhabha, 8–22. New York: Routledge, 1990.

Reynaud, Berenice. "Gong Li and the Glamour of the Chinese Star." *Sight and Sound* 3, no. 8 (1993): 12–15.

Roberts, Jerry. "Hollywood's New Pacific Strategy." *Face* 19 (1996): 62–68.

Rodd, Laurel Rasplica. "Yosano Akiko and the Taisho Debate over the 'New Woman.' " In *Recreating Japanese Women, 1600–1945,* edited by Gail Lee Bernstein, 175–198. Berkeley: University of California Press, 1991.

Rogers, John D. "Post-Orientalism and the Interpretation of Premodern and Modern Political Identities: The Case of Sri Lanka." *Journal of Asian Studies* 53, no. 1 (1994): 10–23.

Romney, Jonathan. "Food Glorious Food." *New Statesman and Society* 8, no. 336 (January 20, 1995): 33.

———. Review of *Jungle Book*. *Sight and Sound* 5, no. 3 (1995): 50–51.

Ru Ling. "Duiyu Meiguo ruhua yingpian de yi ci zhuangyan de shenpan" [A righteous protest against an offensive American film]. *Dazhong dianying* 5-6 (1961).

Saeki, Shoichi. "The Role of Western Literature in the Modernization of Japan." In *Thirty Years of Turmoil in Asian Literature*. Lectures delivered at the Fourth Asian Writers Conference, April 25–May 2, 1976. Taipei: Taipei Chinese Center, International P.E.N. (no date).

Said, Edward. *Orientalism*. New York: Vintage Books, 1979.

———. "Traveling Theory." In *The World, the Text, and the Critic*, 226–247. Cambridge, Mass: Harvard University Press, 1983.

" 'San ba' guoji funü laodong jie: *Xin nüxing* canjia nüjiaoguan kaimu dianli" [International Women's Labor Day, March 8: *The New Woman* takes part in the opening ceremony for a women's education centre]. *Lianhua huabao* 5, no. 6 (1935): 16.

Sang, Zelan (Sang Tze-lan). "Cheng Dieyi—yige quanshi de qidian" [Cheng Dieyi—an explanatory starting point]. *Dangdai* [Contemporary], April 1, 1994, 54–60.

"San'ge modeng nüxing" [Three modern women]. *Shi bao* (Shanghai), January 17, 1935.

Sato, Barbara Hamill. "The *Moga* Sensation: Perceptions of the *Modan Garu* in Japanese Intellectual Circles during the 1920s." *Gender and History* 5, no. 3 (1993): 363–381.

Schindler, Rick. "Woo's the Boss: Hong Kong's Celebrated Action Auteur John Woo Choreographs His First TV-Movie." *TV Guide* 44, no. 39 (1996): 5–6.

Schubert, Lawrence. "Just for Kicks." *Detour*, February 1996, 28–32.

Sedgewick, Eve Kosofsky. *The Epistemology of the Closet*. Berkeley: University of California Press, 1990.

Segers, Frank. "A Trans-Pacific Crossover: Woo at the Helm for Universal." *Variety*, August 24, 1992, 49, 52.

Semsel, George S. "Report on the Current Situation in the Chinese Film Industry." Paper presented at the Chinese Cinema Studies Conference, University of Pittsburgh, September 1994.

———, ed. *Chinese Film: The State of the Art in the People's Republic*. New York: Praeger, 1987.

Semsel, George S., Chen Xihe, and Xia Hong, eds. *Film in Contemporary China: Critical Debates, 1979–1989*. Westport, Conn.: Praeger, 1993.

Semsel, George S., Xia Hong, and Hou Jianping, eds., *Chinese Film Theory: A Guide to the New Era*. New York: Praeger, 1990.

Shohat, Ella, and Robert Stam. *Unthinking Eurocentrism: Multiculturalism and the Media.* London: Routledge, 1994.

Shui Jiang. "Meiren zai Gang chuang dongfang gongsi" [Americans set up Oriental Studio in Hong Kong]. *Dianying xinwen* 1, no. 6 (1935).

Silverman, Kaja. *Semiotics and Structure.* London: Oxford University Press, 1983.

——. *Male Subjectivity at the Margins.* New York: Routledge, 1992.

Smith, R. J. "The Coolest Actor in the World." *Los Angeles Times,* March 12, 1995.

Sollors, Werner. *Beyond Ethnicity: Consent and Descent in American Culture.* New York: Oxford University Press, 1986.

Sorlin, Pierre. *European Cinemas, European Societies, 1939–1990.* London: Routledge, 1991.

——. *Italian National Cinema, 1896–1996.* London: Routledge, 1996.

Spence, Jonathan D. *The Gate of Heavenly Peace: The Chinese and Their Revolution—1895–1980.* Middlesex, England: Penguin Books, 1981.

Spivak, Gayatri Chakravorty. "Marginality in the Teaching Machine." In *Outside in the Teaching Machine,* 53–76. New York: Routledge, 1993.

Springer, Richard. *East-West Journal* (San Francisco), April 18, 1984.

Srivastava, Aruna. " 'The Empire Writes Back': Language and History in *Shame* and *Midnight's Children.*" In *Past the Last Post: Theorizing Post-Colonialism and Post-Modernism,* edited by Ian Adam and Helen Tiffin, 65–78. Calgary: University of Calgary Press, 1990.

Stacey, Judith. *Patriarchy and Socialist Revolution in China.* Berkeley: University of California Press, 1983.

Stone, Oliver. "The Flicker of an Eye Means Nothing in Print." *Los Angeles Times,* March 26, 1992, B7.

Straubhaar, Joseph D. "Beyond Media Imperialism: Asymmetrical Interdependence and Cultural Proximity." *Critical Studies in Mass Communication* 8, no. 1 (1991): 39–59.

Studlar, Gaylyn. *In the Realm of Pleasure: Von Sternberg, Dietrich, and the Masochistic Aesthetic.* Urbana: University of Illinois Press, 1988.

Sun Longji. *Zhongguo wenhua de shengceng jiegou* [The deep structure of Chinese culture]. Hong Kong: Jixianshe, 1983.

Sun Shiyi. "Yingju zhi yishu jiazhi yu shehui jiazhi" [The artistic and social value of film drama]. *Guoguang tekan,* January 2, 1926.

Tan, Amy. *The Joy Luck Club.* New York: Ivy Books, 1989.

Tang Na. "Guanyu jixielun: Xianshi zhuyi yu *Xin nüxing*" [On mechanism: Realism and *The New Woman*]. *Zhonghua ribao,* March 1935.

Tao, Yuanming. *Jianzhu Tao Yuanming ji* [An annotated collection of Tao Yuanming's works]. Shanghai: Hanfenlou, 1922.

Tasker, Yvonne. *Spectacular Bodies: Gender, Genre, and the Action Cinema.* London: Routledge, 1993.

Tesson, Charles. "Xie Jin: Celui par qui le mélo arrive." *Cahiers du cinéma* 344 (February 1983): 12–15.

Tie Bi. "*Xin tu* yingpian shi ying hou ji" [Reflections on *The New Land*]. *Dian sheng* 6, no. 23 (1937).

Tie Xin. "Zhongguo funü wenti." [Questions concerning Chinese women]. *Xinsheng zhoukan* I, no. 20 (1934): 386–387.

Tong Zhen. "Yi jiu san er nian women de yintan" [Our film industry in 1932]. *Chen bao,* January 10, 1933.

Trinh, T. Minh-ha. "Outside In/Inside Out." In *Questions of Third Cinema,* edited by Jim Pines and Paul Willemen, 133–149. New York: Routledge: 1989.

——. *When the Moon Waxes Red: Representation, Gender, and Cultural Politics.* New York: Routledge, 1991.

Tsui, Curtis K. "Subjective Culture and History: The Ethnographic Cinema of Wong Kar-wai." *Asian Cinema* 7, no. 2 (1995): 93–124.

Tu, Wei-ming. "Cultural China: The Periphery as the Center." *Daedalus* 120, no. 2 (1991): 1–32.

Tung, Timothy. "The Work of Xie Jin: A Personal Letter To the Editor." In *Film and Politics in the Third World,* edited by John D. H. Downing. New York: Praeger, 1987.

Turovsakaia, M. I. *Na granitse iskusstv: Brekht i kino.* Moskva: Iskusstvo, 1985.

Tyler, Parker. *Screening the Sexes: Homsexuality in the Movies.* New York: Holt, Rinehart and Winston, 1972.

Tyler, Patrick E. "In China, Letting a Hundred Films Wither." *New York Times,* December 1, 1996, H1, H26.

Ukadike, Nwachukwu Frank. *Black African Cinema.* Berkeley: University of California Press, 1994.

Verdery, Katherine. "Beyond the Nation in Eastern Europe." *Social Text* 38 (1994): 1–19.

Vincent, Mal. "Pushing Hands." *The Virginian-Pilot,* August 10, 1995.

Wai Min, ed. *Taiwan de ererba shijian* [The February 28 Incident in Taiwan]. Hong Kong: The Seventies Magazine Publications, 1975.

Wan Cheng. "Chu mu jing xin de xiaoxi" [Shocking news]. *Yingxi shenghuo* I, no. 6 (1931).

Wang Jingtao. "Dianying jie muqian de xuyao" [What Chinese film industry needs?]. *Yingxi chunqiu* 9 (1925).

Wang Ning. "Lüelun Zhongguo dangdai dianying de liangnan ji chulu" [On the dilemma and solution of contemporary Chinese film]. *Dianying yishu* [Film art] 6 (1996): 4–7.

Wang Yichuan et al. "Bianyuan, zhongxin, dongfang, xifang" [Periphery, center, orient, occident]. *Dushu* [Reading] (January 1994): 146–152.

Wang, Yuejin. "The Cinematic Other and the Cultural Self?: Decentering the Cultural Identity of Cinema." *Wide Angle* 11, no. 2 (1989): 32–39.

———. "*Red Sorghum*: Mixing Memory and Desire." In *Perspectives on Chinese Cinema*, edited by Chris Berry, 80–103. London: British Film Institute, 1991.

Wasko, Janet. *Hollywood in the Information Age*. Austin: University of Texas Press, 1994.

Weiner, Rex. "China Opens Its Doors to Sundance Fest." *Variety*, October 9–15, 1995, 13, 16.

———. "Sundance Festival Takes Show on the Silk Road: Chinese Independents." *Variety*, October 16–22, 1995, 24.

Wen Gezhi (Wen Ko-chih). " 'Bei' de *Luoshengmen* benzhi" [The *Rashomon*-quality of *City of Sadness*]. *Tzu-li Morning Post*, October 10, 1989.

Whang, Paul K. "Boycotting of Harold Lloyd's *Welcome Danger*." *China Weekly Review*, March 8, 1930.

White, Hayden. "The Value of Narrativity in the Representation of Reality." *Critical Inquiry* 7, no. 1 (1980): 5–27.

———. "Historiography and Historiophoty." *American Historical Review* 93, no. 5 (1988): 1193–1199.

Wilbur, Martin. "The Nationalist Revolution: From Canton to Nanjing, 1923–1928." In *Cambridge History of China*, vol. 12, edited by John K. Fairbank. Cambridge: Cambridge University Press, 1983.

Wilkerson, Douglas. "Film and the Visual Arts in China: An Introduction." In *Cinematic Landscapes: Obervations on the Visual Arts and Cinema of China and Japan*, edited by Linda Ehrlich and David Desser, 39–44. Austin: University of Texas Press, 1994.

Wilson, Rob, and Wimal Dissanayake, eds. *Global/Local: Cultural Production and the Transnational Imaginary*. Durham, N.C.: Duke University Press, 1996.

Wolcott, James. "Blood Test." *The New Yorker*, August 23 and 30, 1993, 62–68.

Wolf, Jaime. "Jackie Chan, American Action Hero?" *New York Times Magazine*, January 21, 1996, 22–25.

Wollen, Peter. "The Auteur Theory." In *Film Theory and Criticism*, 4th ed., edited by Gerald Mast and Marshall Cohen, 589–605. New York: Oxford University Press, 1992.

Wu Qiyan (Wu Ch'i-yen). "*Beiqing chengshi* xianxiangji" [Notes on the release of *City of Sadness*]. In *Xin dianying zhi si* [The death of New

Cinema], edited by Mi Zou (Mi Tsou) and Liang Xinhua (Liang Hsin-hua). Taipei: Tangshan Publications, 1991.

Wu Songgao. "Shi nian lai de Zhongguo waijiao" [China's diplomatic achievements in the last ten years]). In *Shi nian lai zhi Zhongguo* [China in the last ten years], edited by Zhongguo Wenhua Jianshe Xiehui, 27–52. 1937; reprint, Hong Kong: Longmen shudian, 1965.

Wyatt, Justin. "*The Wedding Banquet,* Independent Cinema, and Cultural Identities." Paper presented at the Ohio University Film Conference, November 1994.

Xi. "Jin yi bu de jiantao" [A further examination]. *Chen bao,* August 1, 1932.

Xia Yan. "Baoshengong" [Indentured laborers] (1936). In *Xia Yan xuanji* [Selected works of Xia Yan]. Beijing: Renmin chubanshe, 1980.

——. *Xia Yan xuanji* [Selected works of Xia Yan]. Beijing: Renmin chuban-she, 1980.

Xiao, Zhiwei. "Constructing a New National Culture: The Problems of Cantonese Autonomy, Superstition and Sex." Paper presented to the Association for Asian Studies annual meeting, Washington, D.C., April 6–9, 1995.

Xie Renchang (Hsieh Jen-ch'ang). "Wo shengming guocheng de yige baogao" [A report on my life]. *Dianying xinshang* [Film appreciation] 64 (July/August 1993): 45–62.

Yang, Gladys, trans. *Silent China: Selected Writings of Lu Xun.* Oxford: Oxford University Press, 1973.

Yang, Mayfair. "Of Gender, State Censorship, and Overseas Capital: An Interview with Director Zhang Yimou." *Public Culture* 5, no. 2 (1993): 297–316.

Yau, Esther. "Yellow Earth: Western Analysis and a Non-Western Text." In *Perspectives on Chinese Cinema,* edited by Chris Berry, 62–79. London: British Film Institute, 1991.

——. "International Fantasy and the 'New Chinese Cinema.'" *Quarterly Review of Film and Video* 14, no. 3 (1993): 95–107.

——. "Border Crossing: Mainland China's Presence in Hong Kong Cinema." *New Chinese Cinemas: Forms, Identities, Politics,* edited by Nick Browne, Paul G. Pickowicz, Vivian Sobchack, and Esther Yau, 180–201. Cambridge: Cambridge University Press, 1994.

——. "Is China the End of Hermeneutics?; or, Political and Cultural Usage of Non-Han Women in Mainland Chinese Films." In *Multiple Voices in Feminist Film Criticism,* edited by Diane Carson, Linda Dittmar, and Janice R. Welsch, 280–292. Minneapolis: University of Minnesota Press, 1994.

Ye Yonglie. *Jiang Qing shilu* [The real Jiang Qing]. Hong Kong: Liwen, 1993.

Yin Min. "Yingpian shang zhi you se renzhong" [Colored people on the screen]. *Dianying zhoukan* 9 (May 1924).

Yoshimoto, Mitsuhira. "The Difficulty of Being Radical: The Discipline of Film Studies and the Postcolonial World Order." *boundary 2* 18, no. 3 (1991): 242–257.

Yuan Shengjun and Wang Jun. "Chen Kaige de beiju gaosu le women shenmo?" [What does Chen Kaige's tragedy tell us?]. *Zhongguo yinmu* [China screen], July/August 1996, 30–34.

Zha, Jane Ying. "Excerpts from 'Lore Segal, *Red Lantern*, and Exoticism.' " *Public Culture* 5, no. 2 (1993): 329–332.

Zhang, Jia-xuan. "The Big Parade." *Film Quarterly* 43, no. 1 (1989): 57–59.

Zhang, Jingyuan. "Disan shiji piping: Minzu, zhongzu, xingbie" [Third-World criticism: Ethnicity, race, gender]. *Dianying yishu* [Film art], no. 1 (1991): 33–38.

Zhang Kuan. "Oumei ren yanzhong de 'feiwo zulei': Cong dongfang zhuyi dao xifang zhuyi" ["Other people" in the eyes of Europeans and Americans: From "Orientalism" to "Occidentalism"]. *Dushu* [Reading] (September 1993): 3–9

Zhang, Yingjin. "Ideology of the Body in *Red Sorghum*: National Allegory, National Roots, and Third Cinema." *East-West Film Journal* 4, no. 2 (1990): 38–53.

——— . "Re-envisioning the Institution of Modern Chinese Literature Studies: Strategies of Positionality and Self-Reflexivity." *positions: east asia cultures critique* 1, no. 3 (1993): 816–832.

——— . "Engendering Chinese Filmic Discourse of the 1930's: Configurations of Modern Women in Shanghai in Three Silent Films." *positions: east asia cultures critique* 2, no. 3 (1994): 603–628.

Zhang Yiwu. "Disan shijie wenhua: Yige xin de qidian" [Third-World culture: A new point of departure]. *Dushu* [Reading] (June 1990): 28–34.

——— . "Quanqiuxing houzhimin yujing zhong de Zhang Yimou" [Zhang Yimou in the global postcolonial context]. *Dangdai dianying* [Contemporary film], no. 3 (1993): 18–25.

Zhen Chu. "Zhongguo diyi gongsi yi cheng wajie" [The collapse of China's Number One Company]. *Chen bao*, August 9, 1932.

Zhi Song. "Zhuishu *Bu pa si* shijian de jiaoshe jingguo" [A recollection of the *Welcome Danger* incident]. *Dian sheng* 5, no. 47 (1936).

Zhongguo Guomindang zhongyang weiyuanhui dangshi weiyuanhui, ed. *Geming wenxian di qishier ji: Kangzhan qian guojia jianshe shiliao-wai jiao*

fangmian [Revolutionary documents, vol. 72: The decade of recon-
    struction before the war: Foreign relations]. Taibei, 1977.
Zhou Jianyun. "Wu sa can an hou zhi Zhongguo ying xi jie" [The situation
    of Chinese cinema and theatre in the post-May Thirtieth era]. *Ming-
    xing tekan* 3 (1925).
——. "Zhongguo yingpian zhi qiantu [2]" [The future of Chinese cinema,
    part 2]. *Dianying yuebao* I, no. 2 (1928).
——. "Zhongguo yingpian zhi qiantu [3]" [The future of Chinese cinema,
    part 3]. *Dianying yuebao* I, no. 3 (1928).
——. "Dianying shencha wenti" [The question of film censorship]. *Diany-
    ing yuebao* I, no. 5 (1928).
Zhu Tianwen (Chu T'ien-wen). *"Beiqing chengshi* shisanwen" [Thirteen
    questions on *City of Sadness*]. *Tzu-li Morning Post,* July 11–13, 1989.

Notes on Contributors

Anne T. Ciecko received her Ph.D. in the Film Studies Program in the Department of English at the University of Pittsburgh. Her dissertation was on gender, genre, and the politics of representation in contemporary British cinema by women. She has published articles on film in *Spectator* and *Post Script*.

Shuqin Cui teaches Chinese language, literature, and film. She has taught at the University of Wisconsin, the University of Michigan, the University of Chicago, and Oberlin College. She holds a Ph.D. from the University of Michigan and is currently an assistant professor in the Department of Foreign Languages and Literatures at Southern Methodist University.

Wei Ming Dariotis is a Ph.D. candidate at the University of California Santa Barbara. She is currently completing her dissertation, "Gener-Asians: Transforming the Nation," which examines identity construction at the individual, familial, and national levels. Her study explores how the identity of the individual reconstructs the identities of family and nation through the transgressive sexualities of interracial and queer unions in twentieth-century Asian American and other ethnic literatures. The dissertation concludes with an examination of these issues in ethnic vampire and science fictions.

Steve Fore teaches in the Department of Radio, Television and Film at the University of North Texas. His articles on Hong Kong cinema have appeared in journals such as *The Velvet Light Trap* and *Journal of Film and Video*.

Eileen Chia-cing Fung is a Ph.D. candidate at the University of California, Santa Barbara. Her dissertation, "Dis-Orientation: The Politics of Orientalism and Sexuality in Medieval Writings between Europe and Mongolia," develops her interest in literary representation as a form of intercultural intervention and ethnic politics. She is currently a lecturer in the Asian American Studies Department at California State University, Northridge.

Kristine Harris is assistant professor of history at the State University of New York in New Paltz. Her work also appears in *Romance, Sexuality, Politics: Cinema and Urban Culture in Shanghai: 1920s–1940s* (forthcoming from Stanford University Press). She is currently completing a book, *Children of Troubled Times: Nation, Gender, Representation in Chinese Cinema, 1905–1937*.

E. Ann Kaplan is professor of English and comparative studies at the State University of New York, Stony Brook, where she founded and directs the Humanities Institute. She has written widely on topics in feminist literary and film theory, postmodernism, psychoanalysis, and cultural studies. She has a special interest in issues of cross-cultural "knowing" in relation to Asia. Her many authored and edited books include *Women and Film: Both Sides of the Camera; Rocking Around the Clock: Music Television, Postmodernism, and Consumer Culture; Motherhood and Representation: The Mother in Popular Culture and Melodrama; Psychoanalysis and Cinema* (ed.); and *Postmodernism and Its Discontents* (ed.). Her newest book is *Looking for the Other: Feminism and the Imperial Gaze*, which includes some chapters relevant to Asian cinema.

Jon Kowallis currently teaches at the University of Melbourne, Melbourne, Australia. He is the author of *Wit and Humor from Old Cathay* (Beijing: Foreign Languages Press, 1986), *The Lyrical Lu Xun* (University of Hawai'i Press, 1996), and *On the Power of Mara Poetry and Other Essays* (East Asian Institute, University of California, Berkeley, 1995).

Wendy Larson is professor in the Department of East Asian Languages and Literatures at the University of Oregon. She is the author of *Literary Authority and the Modern Chinese Writer: Ambivalence and Autobiography* (Duke University Press, 1991) and *Women and Writing in Modern China* (forthcoming from Stanford University Press), translator of *Bolshevik Salute: A Modernist Chinese Novel* (University of Washington Press, 1989), and co-editor of *Inside Out: Modernism and Postmodernism in Chinese Literary Culture* (Aarhus University Press, Denmark, 1993).

Sheldon Hsiao-peng Lu teaches Chinese, film studies, and cultural studies at the University of Pittsburgh. He is the author of *From Historicity to Fictionality: The Chinese Poetics of Narrative* (Stanford University Press,

1994). His critical essays have appeared in journals such as *boundary 2*, *New Literary History*, and *Chinese Literature: Essays, Articles, Reviews*. He is currently working on two projects: culture and cultural theory in late twentieth-century China and the poetics of visuality in modern China.

Gina Marchetti is an associate professor in the Comparative Literature Program at the University of Maryland, College Park. Her book, *Romance and the "Yellow Peril": Race, Sex and Discursive Strategies in Hollywood Fiction* (1993) is available from the University of California Press.

Zhiwei Xiao received his Ph.D. in modern East Asian history from the University of California, San Diego, in 1994 and taught at the University of Utah before joining the history faculty at California State University, San Marcos. His research interests focus on pre-1949 Chinese film and popular culture.

June Yip recently completed a doctoral dissertation, "Colonialism and Its Counter-discourses: On the Uses of 'Nation' in Modern Taiwanese Literature and Film," for the Comparative Literature Program at Princeton University. In addition, she received an M.A. in critical studies from UCLA's School of Film, Television, and Theater in 1992. Yip currently resides in Los Angeles with her husband and two young sons.

Yingjin Zhang (Ph.D., Stanford University) is assistant professor of Chinese, comparative literature, and film studies at Indiana University, Bloomington, Indiana. He is the author of *The City in Modern Chinese Literature and Film: Configurations of Space, Time, and Gender* (Stanford University Press, 1996), co-author of *Encyclopedia of Chinese Film* (under contract with Routledge), and editor of *Engaging Texts: Essays in Chinese Comparative Literature and Cultural Studies* and of *Romance, Sexuality, Politics: Cinema and Urban Culture in Shanghai, 1920s–1940s* (both accepted by Stanford University Press). His critical essays and book reviews have appeared in many English and Chinese journals. He is currently working on a book-length study of contemporary Chinese cinema.

Yi Zheng received her Ph.D. in English from the University of Pittsburgh. Her research interests include Asian American literature, women's studies, Chinese literature and film, and romanticism and modernism in the English and American literary tradition.